# Aquarian Wisdom

Order this book online at www.trafford.com
or email orders@trafford.com

Most Trafford titles are also available at major online book retailers.

Print information available on the last page.

ISBN: 978-1-4907-7040-6 (sc)
ISBN: 978-1-4907-7039-0 (e)

*Trafford rev. 06/17/2016*

www.trafford.com
North America & international
toll-free: 1 888 232 4444 (USA & Canada)
fax: 812 355 4082

# Aquarian Wisdom

By Rev. Ellen Wallace Douglas

Also by author:

The Laughing Christ
El's Rae: A Memoir
Homeward Bound
Be Still and Know
The Peaceful Silence
Divination Through the Ages
The Beckoning Light
Home to the Light
The High Road Home
Concordance of The Aquarian Gospel of
    Jesus the Christ

The lessons of Archangel Gabriel and
Jesus the Christ used with permission

Holy Bible, Authorized Version

Cover design by Evie Ann Douglas

# Contents

# Preface

The reason for writing this book is to bring to light topics taught by Archangel Gabriel (1987-1999) and Jesus the Christ (1995-1999) which may not have been dealt with in my earlier books. Gabriel is the Announcer of the Ages. As with all my writing, this manuscript was inspired. Years after sitting at Gabriel's feet I can still consciously recall some of his teachings, but surely there are many which do not come readily to mind. The hundreds of hours of Gabriel's lessons are recorded and available, in print or sound. The reader is strongly encouraged to hear/read these lessons in truth. See sacredgardenfellowship.com. Jesus' teachings are also available. Jesus came concurrently with Gabriel for four years (1995-1999) to clarify errors in scripture, due to carelessness or intent.

It would be impossible to impart fully to the reader the depth of my gratitude or the height of my joy at having been Gabriel's student for those twelve wondrous years. When Gabriel gave his Farewell Message on December 2, 1999, there were about two hundred people present. All Gabriel's students desired to show our appreciation to Reverend Penny for her willingness and spiritual devotion to channel Gabriel and Jesus. It was my privilege to hand a check to beloved Reverend Penny. After all, what earthly token of gratitude would be possible for a heavenly visitor such as an archangel?

Perhaps these brief essays will be more willingly read by seekers of truth in this busy age we live in. They are not dated nor numbered for a reason. The reader is encouraged to open the book at random, for as surely as the sun rises, the needed essay will be there. The guidance of spirit is available to all. Artists maintain their works were inspired. All great works come from Heaven. The ancient adage is immutable: 'As above; so below'. Gabriel came not to teach but to "Remind you of what you already know." All wisdom is ours because we are all children of the Living God. Thank God that this is so.

The essays herein are not divided by topic. They were merely alphabetized as I received them. When it was time to divide them into sections the answer came: use the same section titles provided in *The Aquarian Gospel of Jesus the Christ*, Levi. In referring to *The Aquarian Gospel*, references are AGJC with section and chapter number. MBD stands for *Metaphysical Bible Dictionary*, with page number. ACIM stands for *A Course in Miracles* (1975). *ACIM Orig.* refers to the 2012 copyrighted material of Helen Schucman's original notes. *The Voice Celestial* is designated as TVC. Another indicator of *A Course in Miracles* is *The Course.*

Regarding the book's title, this is the beginning of the Age of Aquarius as one segment of the greater zodiac, described in the *AGJC, Introduction.* The wisdom of the ages is the truth brought to us by Gabriel and Jesus the Christ. At one time Jesus said to us, "Listen to Gabriel; he is a good teacher."

Once, at a Gabriel seminar, he was asked about quoting him. He said, in effect, "You do not have to say, 'Gabriel said thus and so. . .'. I give you the truth. Teach the truth I bring; live it." There are many ways in which spirit can bring us truth. Gabriel came to Mary and Joseph foretelling Jesus' coming birth. Gabriel came to Elizabeth and Zacharias announcing the coming of John, who became the Baptist. They all saw and heard Gabriel. This is an example of clairvoyance and clairaudience. This author was blessed to hear *and see* Jesus one time in my life; in 1984. It is described in my memoirs. (We exchanged many conversations when he channeled through Rev. Penny (1995-1999).

Another example of clairaudience is the dictation given by Jesus to Helen Schucman, in the 1960s and 1970s. The product was *A Course in Miracles,* given to Helen. The Voice dictated to her for seven years. Direct revelation was the means of communication from spirit to John for the Book of Revelation in the New Testament. Revelation is a 'knowing' that is received directly from spirit. The Bible gives an example in Matthew 16:17:

*"And Jesus answered and said unto him, Blessed art thou, Simon Bar-Jona,: for flesh and blood hath not revealed it unto thee, but my Father which is in Heaven."*

Gabriel explained that there are many entities in the spirit world who long to bring truth to earth, but there are few humans who are willing and able to receive this wisdom. Very few acknowledge the possibility of such communication. Eventually humankind will become aware of the possibility, and will communicate - not only with spirit entities, but also with animals, plants and even rocks. *Messages from Water* describes the power of human thought when directed to a stagnant pond, and restore it to purity.

# Section I
## Aleph

## Chapter 1 A Beautiful Analogy

We are approaching Christmas, the holiday season when we celebrate one of the holiest days of the calendar. Archangel Gabriel told us that the two days of our earthly years in which angels come closest to Earth are Christmas and Easter. Of course! The first was the birth of the prince of peace and the second was the day when he rose from the 'dead'. By the first he came forth in a miraculous birth. It was miraculous because the Holy Father begot him, from the power that was in Him. There are two eyewitness accounts of the holy birth which are found in the Infancy chapters of *The Apocrypha*. The second day of joyous celebration is the day when Jesus appeared to his followers three days after 'dying'.

The infant Jesus came forth in a manger, the lowliest of places. Yet kings came from many miles to celebrate the occasion because, as astronomers, they knew a significant event was imminent. The birth was heralded by the spectacular appearance of a star in the heavens. The kings believed it was worth the trip to respond to the heavenly sight. They also must have known that the brilliant star signified the birth of a child who would change the world forever.

The calendar which most of the world now uses designates the current era based on Jesus' birth; the Christian Era. Much more than the calendar changed with his coming. He was born into a world of fear, where Rome's cruel rulers reigned. Palestine was the center of commerce, though, and he could reach many people with his message. His message was incredibly different from any of the other roving preachers of the time, whose teachings were limited to the Old Testament writings.

Jesus chose twelve men as his apostles in whom he saw the potential of spiritual growth. He taught them in private lessons as well as teaching the public when he walked the countryside. He loved children. Many people chose to follow him, including women. Gabriel said all references to Jesus' women followers were purged from early transcripts of the Bible.

Mary Magdalene, who Gabriel told us was never a whore, was wealthy by inheritance, and Jesus asked her to find lodgings in advance for his company. In exchange she requested to be among his followers, and he agreed.

The beautiful analogy; the irrefutable analogy, is the comparison of Jesus' birth and life to our own. Jesus says to us now, *Holy child of God, when will you learn that only holiness can content you and give you peace?"* (ACIM 15: III: 9:1). In *A Course in Miracles,* Jesus tells us to remember him not in a manger. Instead, we must give up our shabby littleness that binds us to guilt and weakness. We are children of God, and Jesus came to awaken us - all humanity - to our holiness. The kingdom of God *is within us.* We were told by Gabriel that every cell of our physical body has a nucleus of *spirit!*

Our journeying away from Home is coming to an end. This is the age of awakening for the human family. We are on the cusp of the Age of Aquarius. 'The Age of Truth', Gabriel said. That is why Gabriel came (1987-1999); to announce it. That is why Jesus came (1995-1999); to remind us of our divinity. That is why eleven Master Teachers came to earth concurrently with Gabriel and Jesus. They all came to various locations on earth, and all with the same message: 'Wake up, children of God and live from the Lord God of your Being.'

For two thousand years we have failed to get it right. Jesus' teachings and commandments were all about love and forgiveness. How and why have we gotten it so wrong? God is persistent and will call us Home until we listen and return. This is the beautiful analogy: *"My birth in you is your awakening to grandeur."* (ACIM T 15: III: 9:5)

## Chapter II  A Glimpse of Heaven

Many individuals proclaim they believe in Heaven, based on the Bible, Bible study groups, or parents' belief, but some still privately wonder if it really exists. The commonly accepted phrase is, 'No one ever came back to tell us'. This reveals a person who disbelieves unless he sees, like Doubting Thomas. The apostle Thomas would not believe that Jesus had come back to life until he saw the wounds in the resurrected body of Jesus.

Many people refuse to allow themselves to read, hear or see anything contrary to their old beliefs. For those who are willing to open their minds to the possibility, they read what writers tell us about Heaven. Mediums and psychics have spoken to and received information from entities in the spirit world. Loved ones are comforted when they hear from their relatives on the other side of the veil. In recent years many individuals have described their near-death experiences. Angels, holy residents of that spirit realm, are coming to earth more frequently than ever before because more people are ready to accept them. There are several ways in which we can learn about Heaven. Three of them are offered here:

First, writers of recent decades have informed us about their experiences of communicating with those in the spirit world. Communicating with those in the spirit world should convince us that there is a spirit world of God which not only exists but with which we can communicate. Some individuals who have communicated with spirits: Joan of Arc, Emanuel Swedenborg, Johannes Greber, Edgar Cayce, Levi, and Reverend Penny Donovan.

Joan of arc, a 15th century French peasant, was guided by a spirit voice to lead a victorious French army against the English. She was burned at the stake for witchcraft, but five centuries later she was canonized by the Roman Catholic Church. Emanuel Swedenborg wrote several books about his conversations with various entities in the spirit world, including Socrates. Johannes Greber was an early 20th century catholic priest in Germany who was introduced reluctantly to the spirit world of God. His book is entitled *Communication with the Spirit World of God*. His book was translated into English and published in 1974.

Edgar Cayce, The sleeping profit, healed thousands of people on earth by reciting treatment methods he received from entities in the spirit realm. In 1907 Levi received *The Aquarian Gospel of Jesus the Christ* from spirit. Gabriel confirmed its validity. More recently Ernest and Charles Holmes wrote *The Voice Celestial* (1960). Although the book was not described as channeled information by the publishers, this author perceives the content departs greatly from all other writings of Ernest Holmes.

Secondly, many books have been recently channeled to earthlings. Judy Boss wrote *In Silence They Return*, 1972; *Emmanuel's Book,* 1985 was received from spirit. Several lessons were channeled through Rev. Penny Donovan from Archangel Gabriel, 19877-1999. Lessons from Jesus the Christ also were received by Rev. Donovan, 1995-1999. (see Bibliography). *Love and Life are Eternal,* by Nancy B. Elliot, 2008. *The Universal Consciousness,* by Bristow, 2009.

Gabriel came to tell us who we are: sacred children of God; made in His Image. He told us we must begin to live from the Lord God of our Being. The beloved archangel came to give us a glimpse of what we are, why we are here and how we shall return. Only those who accept communication from God's holy messenger will hear and read his lessons in truth. Everyone will, eventually, because all God's children - all humanity - will return Home to Him. It is only a matter of time.

"The freedom to leave behind everything that hurts you and humbles you and frightens you cannot be thrust upon you, but it can be offered you through the grace of God. And you can accept it by His Grace, for God is gracious to His Son, accepting him without question as His Own." ACIM Text 11: VI: 6: 3-4

The third example of communication with the spirit world is by direct revelation, as when a person has a near-death experience. These stories all mention a bright light at the end of a tunnel. Those who 'came back' were those who have not as yet done what they came to do on earth. Direct revelation also refers to a sudden answer to a long sought for question. Some call it an 'Ah-ha' moment.

## Chapter 3  A Human Holiness

The title of this essay is from a film directed by Ingmar Bergman, as seen in a TV documentary (Sep. 2015) about his life. This is the scene: A young woman asks her uncle if he believes that God has hands and feet and eyes. His response is something like this, 'do not say God, but say there is a human holiness in each of us'.

Suddenly, upon watching this, I recalled a comment Archangel Gabriel made about the human body. He said every cell of the human body has a spirit nucleus! No wonder Jesus told us *The kingdom of God is within you* (Luke 17:21). These are words, and words are merely symbols. Only in *feeling* the holiness within can we profess to know it. Some may call this blasphemy, but given these words by Gabriel and Jesus is it not blasphemous to *deny* them?

We study biology in high school and learn about the miracle of the human body. So much of its activity is self-governed. We do not have to think about breathing. It is unnecessary to tell our heart to beat. Our digestive system operates in perfect harmony if we do not stress it with too much food or drugs. The elimination system also works automatically without our interference. The human body is truly a miraculous machine. With all these bodily processes being done for us, what is left for us to do? Move the body, of course. At every age physical exercise is required for good physical health.

Feelings are part of our physical existence. We are sentient beings. Feelings need to be expressed because if they are not, many problems may occur. If feelings are expressed immediately they cannot fester and become resentments or cause depression. Emotions are out-of-control feelings. We all get excited at times; we all feel blue at times. Some people get bored. Gabriel once said, 'if you are bored then you are probably boring.' Life is full of opportunity, variety, and options. If and when emotions (out of control feelings) become common it helps to seek counseling. Gabriel provided us with an excellent way of dealing with a personal problem: place two chairs facing each other. Sit in one and speak about your problem, honestly. Then sit in the other chair and respond as if the problem belonged to your best friend. Your response would be objective because you want to help your friend.

Our body does not have a mind of its own; we direct it from our minds. The brain does not think; it processes thought, Gabriel said. The brain is an organ which is still being analyzed and researched by scientists. The mind is part of the divine Mind of God. That is why 'as above, so below' is true. All ideas come from the ethers; 'up there'; or spirit. All inventions manifest first in spirit; all art. Creation is its name. When we have 'a mind of our own' we are listening to the ego self. We change our minds constantly through our day. At times it takes great effort to focus on one activity. The Mind of God is unalterable, eternal truth, and its Source is love.

The choices we made during our last lifetime we are now living out. God granted us free choice. We should treasure it. But we should also consider carefully what choices we make. We must understand that everyone chooses their situations and experiences for a reason. The reason is there is a lesson therein. We need not join in the pain a person has chosen; we have the choice to listen and empathize. We are responsible for our choices. This is the hardest lesson for us to learn.

We have a spiritual essence. Usually it is not acknowledged until maturity; some never acknowledge it. We sleep to our own divinity because we have convinced ourselves we are 'only human'. If we are only human form it is difficult to explain compassion, our capacity for love, our poignant regrets. Guilt does not come from our legs or torso. Passion is not a product of our digestive system. Our spirit, the true Self of us, beckons us to become more; to return to an awareness of God; to acknowledge our Creator as our Creator. That is all we are asked to do;

that is all that is necessary to become, in consciousness, what we always have been in truth.


## Chapter 4   A World of Love

If someone told us there is a world of love some of us would quickly book passage. Whether by an ethereal train or a space ship or a supernal boat, we would buy a ticket and go there.  Or perhaps we would immediately begin to question, to doubt, to wonder, to deny the possibility.  Some of us would question the credentials of the messenger, the 'plausibility' of such a world. Some would call it fantasy and relegate it to science fiction. 'Dreamers' might be assigned as the bringers of the message. In truth we already live in a world of love, but we are usually unaware of it.

This world of form in which we find ourselves is a world of form *in which* we must find ourselves - our true Selves. Archangel Gabriel came to announce the new age - The Age of Aquarius. It is the age of truth. We can only 'find' ourselves when we realize who we are; what we are. In his lessons in truth Gabriel explained that we are direct offspring of God, whether we believe it or not. We have free choice in what we do on earth, but what we are is not alterable. God created us in His Image, which is love. The spirit world of God is love; unconditional, eternal love.  It is the world of creativity. We could call it Heaven.

Heaven is where we all will transition to upon our 'death'. No longer will we have need of our physical form. Communication will be direct thought. The beauty of the landscape will entrance us.  The peaceful silence will take some getting used to, because it will offer a comfort and security that we have not known here on the earth plane. There we will behold countryside, a city, a lake upon which we may sail. There are books available which describe Heaven. Borgia's *Life in the World Unseen* is one of them. Springer's *Into the Light* is another.

There is no darkness there; no time; no work; no status; no money. There is only light, peace, and love. There is only joy and harmony. The interesting truth is that the deniers may deny they could ever deserve such a place, but angels attend us to heal and teach us. Angels comfort us and assure us we are exactly where we belong: in that bright and light place of love. For the little ones who transition there is a nursery for those who pass over at birth or a very young age. In that place the buildings are small and appropriately arranged to suit their needs. Angelic caretakers are present for them. As they grow - and they will grow up there - teachers will instruct them in positive ways. Instructors will guide them in lessons of love. For those who pass over in a sudden accident they will awaken to attending angels who explain they are in Heaven, and safe.

We can wait for our demise, when we leave our body behind and rise to Heaven. Or we can begin here to create Heaven on earth; a world of love on earth. We have the power to do so, as children of God. The problem is we have turned our power over to our own self-created ego. We have turned our thoughts away from God and His love. We focus on the material world that we have made. We focus on the negative behavior that we and others have made. And we wonder why we live in a world of chaos. The chaos began with us, as we allowed the ego to rule us.

This is the age to awaken to our Source and the love instilled in us by our Creator. This is the era when we take back our power from the ego of us. Fear is the ego's favorite weapon. We have come to fear many things; many people. Faith can dispel the fears; faith in our Maker, faith in love and its power. It is not an easy task, but it is our destiny.

Only a few people seem to be so optimistic that they live a life of love and peace; joy and harmony. Native Americans had faith in Mother Earth and respected all of her creatures. Today, humanity has turned away from peace, and lives by judgment, anger, and violence. Life appears complex, yet Gabriel said we have only two choices; love or fear. We all have the choice to turn one way or the other. We can focus on God and positive or we can focus on not-good and negative. We can focus on judgment and hatred or we can focus on love and peace. Small groups gather all over the world and pray for peace, but the majority chooses to focus on the not-good.

This planet we live on, this Earth, is a world of love because the love of God, being everywhere, is in the very air we breathe. But in the darkness of our ignorance we turn away from what we cannot see. We deny our spirit self because our eyes cannot see it. We turn instead to negative thoughts and behaviors. It has become a tragic habit of the ages. We have become too comfortable in the rut of negative attitudes and behaviors. It has become such a habit that to climb out of the rut seems an arduous, if not impossible, task. It is an arduous task only when we focus on the negative behind us. Living today based on the past is a tragic error in judgment.

In the Bible (Gen. 19:26) there is a story about Lot and his wife. As the inhabitants fled from Sodom and Gomorrah they were instructed by angels not to look back. Most of them did not, but Lot's wife could not resist temptation and she looked back and turned to a pillar of salt. Salt is a preservative; our memory preserves our past. (MBD 405-6). Clinging to the past keeps us stuck in it. 'Now' is the only time in eternity. Now is the only time we should pay attention to. People have the habit of 'remembering' the past; reminisce about it; hold to 'nostalgia' to hang onto what no longer exists. We re-enact wars on the fields once bloody with soldiers' dead bodies.

As we individually and as groups turn to the Now and decide to change our perspective a new world can come about. That ancient book - the Bible- tells us of a new earth and a new Heaven. This conversion from a world of chaos to a world of love will come about; not because it is written somewhere, but because it is inevitable. It is inevitable because we once did reside in Heaven, that place of love and peace. We think we left, but we did not. As the prodigal son returned to his loving father we shall return to our loving Father. This is true because heaven is our natural habitat. The reader is encouraged to hear/read the lessons in truth which Archangel Gabriel brought to earth at sacredgardenfellowship.org

## Chapter 5  All is Forgiven

When another wounds us emotionally or physically and then apologizes, we may say 'all is forgiven'. When it is said there is a peacefulness that comes over us. We may say it because an explanation has been given to clarify the action's reason. Or we may learn more about the perpetrator and realize the wounding was not intentional. Forgiveness does not require a reason. It comes from the heart. When there is acceptance and understanding, the heart is calm. Jesus told us, when asked how many times we should forgive, *I say not unto thee, Until seven times: but, Until seventy times seven.* (Matt. 18:22).

It is hard to believe that Jesus meant we should keep a log of every time we forgave. We can safely assume he meant times without number; countless times; all the time and in every circumstance. With this in mind we are motivated to review the times we refused to forgive another, then explain to ourselves the 'justified reason'. There is an inherent sense of power in the unforgiving person. It is the power of judgment. We assign ourselves this power from our ego. The ego of us reminds us constantly that we are the ruler of our own lives; the dictator of our feelings; we do not need anyone else to tell us how to live; no one knows us like we do.

Daily and often throughout the day we hear this commanding voice of the ego. When Jesus walked the earth and taught the multitudes, he spoke with a gentle voice of compassion. Can we read his words and imagine him yelling them at his listeners? When he spoke to the multitudes his words were heard, even though the crowds were large. He spoke with the power of truth and the conviction of faith. He knew he was a son of God. He called his followers 'children' because he knew they had much to learn from him. One of the greatest lessons he taught was forgiveness.

*Those you do not forgive you fear.* (ACIM19: IV: 11:6). Fear comes from judgment, and we constantly judge our peers. We judge because our ego establishes a baseline of behavior and then we compare everyone to it. Our baseline comes from our own experiences. This is an unstable foundation, for everyone has different experiences. This explains why judgment is so common - and so acceptable in society. Judgment is contagious. Mass consciousness is evoked to condemn the perpetrator, to find and punish him. Someone must be blamed and punished.

This is not to say that justice ought not prevail. We simply must give some thought to 'justified judgment'. Archangel Gabriel made it clear to us that because God granted us with free choice we decide our lifetime experiences every incarnation. *All wounds are self-inflicted.* (Gabriel). This being so, how do we now justify judgment? The trend now is to believe we 'blame the victim'. We are saturated with the idea of blame. Who can we blame for our belief in separation from God? - as if we could be separate from God! But we always look up when we pray, as though God is 'up there', and we are 'down here'.

Religionists raised us to fear God. God is love and because He is a God of love, He would never give us anything but blessings. We, as children of God, are truly made in His Image of love. Love is all there is. Love is the greatest power there is. Judgment has no place in our true hearts. Forgiveness includes forgiving ourselves. We must forgive ourselves for choosing wounds which we do not deserve. We need to forgive ourselves for disbelieving we are children of God.

Blaming ourselves is not productive or reasonable. It was from our ignorance of our origin that we chose wounds of pain and sorrow. Are we to blame for ignorance? To stop judging we must forgo fear of others; fear of God. Forgiveness is a very freeing attitude. We release the heavy burden of judgment in favor of the freedom of acceptance and love. Instead of cherishing the labels we put on others we can cherish the peace of mind that naturally follows the forgiving heart. It is a matter of choice; a change of mind; the unconditional love of God.

# Chapter 6   All the Angels

Archangel Gabriel described the angel world on July 27, 1991, in his seminar entitled *Angels, Aliens and Earthlings* (See Bibliography). God gave all the angels free choice, but only in the realm of good. Angels do not comprehend anything that is not good. I happily provide an example. One day at another seminar, during a brief break, Tinkerbell (Gabriel's primary helper) asked Gabriel what it was - pointing to a dark spot in the heart area of an attending student. Gabriel said, "That is sadness." When Tinkerbell asked what sadness was, Gabriel said, "It is the opposite of love." But knowing only love, Tinkerbell could not comprehend sadness.

With joyous surprise we heard Gabriel say that every human being, without exception, has many angels - 144,000 to be exact. They are with us awaiting our every request, from finding a parking spot to deciding on a career. It is important to thank them for every helping act. There are so many angels that our finite brain cannot comprehend the number. Gabriel described the archangels, but only a brief description is given here:

Ariel - Water; baptism. He is the light below the surface of the water which the old mariners called mermaids.

Gabriel - Announcer of the Ages; spirit of truth. The Annunciation - to Mary and Elizabeth. He announced the Age of Aquarius; this truth age, in his lessons (1987-1999).

Metatron - Devoted to helping humankind. He was the pillar of light which led the Israelites on the desert.

Raphael - Healer. Source of all healings.

Uriel - Repentance. He went to Noah to remind him of the pending deluge.

Michael - Protector. Comes to disperse our thought forms of war, pestilence, death.

Zadkiel - Mercy. He stopped Abraham from sacrificing his son Isaac.

Lucifer - When humankind descended in consciousness to earth, losing awareness of its divinity, we chose many negative behaviors. After many centuries of living with hatred, prejudice and wars, five archangels approached the Throne of God to save humankind from the error thoughts it was living by. One archangel would be chosen to mirror our perceived evil in others that we may wake up to our Higher Self. Lucifer agreed, knowing he would be called a devil for a very long time. Michael told Lucifer he would help him. In truth, there is no devil or hell.

There are layers of angels, and some of them are found in the Bible:

*Seraphim*
Angels of the First Cause. Unaware of earth; see humans only as holy, as children of God.

*Cherubim*
Recorders of all things said or done; everywhere.

*Thrones*
Do not come to earth. Give archangels authority to come to earth.

Principalities
Concerned with the spiritual path of all life: human, animal, plant. Work with governments and world leaders.

*Powers*
Come to earth as devas, gnomes, and fairies. Concerned with evolution of all earth life except humans. Send forth thunderstorms, flowers, snow, trees.

*Virtues*
Bestow their purity upon humans. That purity filters down and is seen as miracles by us.

*Angels of destruction*

Angels of destruction do not engage in negative behavior. They will wipe out only our negative thoughts, habits, behaviors, attitudes without question; never humans. They destroyed Lemuria and Atlantis; Sodom and Gomorrah. We must be very careful what we ask of them, and be willing to let go of our blockages and accept the love of God.

There are two of Gabriel's comments presented here which will hopefully encourage the reader to read and/or listen to all the lessons he taught us in his twelve years of teaching. One is his reason for coming when he did - at the end of the twentieth century, and the other is part of his farewell message. All excerpts from *Gabriel's Farewell Message* 12/3/99. Pages only supplied. Speaking of the cycle of his coming:

"I was here two thousand years ago. I come every two thousand years because it takes you that long to really take in and live the lessons that are brought to the earth - not only by myself but by other teachers as well - who come and teach truth to you. Then you have to take it in and sow the seeds of truth." p. 13

Regarding his departure Gabriel said,

"It is the night that I leave the earth for 2,000 years . . . My influence will remain and angels who work with me will remain . . . I loved teaching. I loved being with you. I loved bringing you truth and watching you grow, seeing your lights get brighter, seeing your fears dispel, watching you come into your own, as it were. It gave me great joy." p.14

The influence of his teachings:

"Long after I leave this earth, the words that I have given to you . . . will travel throughout the world. In generations to come that which was done through her by me will still be alive and well upon the planet earth. Why? Because that is how we bring the consciousness of humankind up. That is the reason we taught you how to read and write." p.4

Refer to Gabriel's teachings at sacred gardenfellowship.org

# Chapter 7   An Accident-free World

We read the paper, see the news, talk with neighbors and hear constantly of accidents maiming and killing people. It is often said that we can have an accident whenever we leave our homes. Accidents involving cars, trucks, trains, boats and planes, make headlines so often that we are convinced we live in a world where chance rules, and accidents ae unavoidable. Lightning strikes, floods and hurricanes take many lives. We wonder too how God could let all this happen.

Belief in all this chaos engenders fear in us, on a regular basis. When the truth is revealed to us, we shrink back from it because we are so grounded in fear; so determined to believe we live in a world where safety comes only at a high cost. New cars have warnings about the 'blind spot', pending accidents, and lane-drifting. There are alarm systems to secure homes, and multiple locks on city apartments.

What if someone said, 'There are no accidents.'? It is likely we would think him insane. Only when heavenly teachers come to awaken us can we study the lessons and learn from them. "*If you will accept yourself as God created you, you will be incapable of suffering. Yet to do this you must acknowledge Him as your Creator.*" (ACIM 10: V: 9:5-6). Some people disbelieve in 'a god who could allow such chaos'; others were taught to fear God and so cannot believe that God is Love. Others accept the philosopher's idea that 'God is dead'. Death is impossible for One Who was never born.

When Archangel Gabriel visited Earth (1987-1999) he said he came to teach nothing new; only to remind us of what we already know, but have forgotten. He reminded us that God gave all humanity - His beloved children - free choice. We choose every experience, every relationship, and every situation in our lives. We even choose when, where, how and with whom we shall end our earthly experience. Nothing, Gabriel said, can harm us without our permission - and then this profound statement - "*because God wouldn't allow it*". Only by our free choice do we suffer anything. God granted us free choice when He created us from spirit; as spirit.

The rational mind poses questions like 'why do we freely choose pain, suffering, tragedy?' Only God and our Higher Self know why. The answer lies in reincarnation. In a real sense, there is no such thing as reincarnation, because the truth of us is that we are spirit, and spirit is eternal. As children of the eternal God, we must also be eternal. This is the truth of us, the origin of us, which we have forgotten, and which Gabriel came to remind us of. Archangel Gabriel informed us that all references to reincarnation were purged from early Bible manuscripts. Reincarnation continues on the wheel of karma until we realize it is not necessary. Until we desire not to return again, having learned the lessons of love and forgiveness.

The Bible makes at least one reference to reincarnation. See Mark 6:14-16. More recently, books have been written about this topic, such as *Lives of the Master,* by Sanderfur; *The Search for a Soul* by Stearn. A number of experiences come to mind to suggest we have past lives: Visiting another country and knowing the local geography; bringing to the current lifetime a musical talent which others name 'child prodigy'. There are no prodigies. (AGJC 37:12) The talents one learns in one lifetime are recalled in later incarnations. This is the age when we must recognize that our lives are self-created and we must take responsibility for that truth. It is a universal lesson.

When we accept the truth as Gabriel taught, and decide on a different road to travel, calmness will prevail in each of us, and eventually peace will prevail on the Earth. Most people pray for peace on Earth. Peace on Earth begins with you and me, and every human being. Other species on Earth already know peace. We do not need 'accidents' in our lives. We must learn to stop them. As we turn to truth, live it, and stay focused on *now* with love and forgiveness, 'accidents' will become a thing of the past. Our lessons are all around us: plants, and trees do not vie for space; creatures do not compare their fur with each other. Call it instinct or love, but do not deny its truth.

# Chapter 8   Angel by Night

*"But the angel of the Lord by night opened the prison doors, and brought them forth, and said,*
*Go, stand and speak in the temple to the people all the words of this life."*
Acts 5:19-20

The Sadducees had the apostles imprisoned for healing the sick. The Sadducees were a sect of priests who did not believe in immortality of the soul, or the miracle of healing. Disbelieving in healing, they feared it. This freeing of the apostles from prison is just one of the many miracles that were performed by angels for Jesus and the apostles.

Miracles of healing are still known - by the people and also the medical community. There are stories of doctors commenting on a miraculous healing they could not explain. Recently I was told about a man who was scheduled for heart surgery, but the final pre-op x-ray revealed a healthy heart. The doctors could not explain it. Today angels are the subjects of many books. Angels have been around as long as humans, because God created them to 'watch over us.' Archangel Gabriel made this very clear. When God endowed us with free choice, He knew we would make some negative choices, including decisions to suffer pain.

Anyone who has had a miraculous healing, a speedy recovery, a near death experience or a miraculous turn of events in their lives, believes in angels. Nor will they ever be dissuaded.   As a blessed student of Gabriel's teachings, I accept the truth of angels forever.  The truth is beyond 'believing.' We want so much to 'believe' another will change their ways. But they often do not. We know, without a doubt, that we have free choice. We need to come to know that anything that happens to us is planned *by* us. No one can hurt us without our permission. *God would not allow it.* This makes perfect sense; human parents do not *allow* their offspring to suffer.

We habitually blame God for 'natural' disasters, storms, illness, etc. The blame lies not with God, but with ourselves. The prisons in which we find ourselves are of our own making.  One of the most confining prisons is that of addiction.  Gripped by an impulsive, compulsive, excessive use of a destructive substance or behavior we spiral down a terrible road of misery. We take others with us as we go, for many are personally affected.

It is a prison from which escape is possible, with help.  Humans can help, angels can help, but we must have a little willingness to be helped. An addict writes her own script, choreographs her own days and excludes others more and more. We try to write the script for others, too. We become the center of attention in the home as alcohol becomes the center of our attention.  Many addicts struggle with the unanswerable question of 'why?'  It merely provides us with a terminal distraction.

When one finds sweet recovery, it becomes clear that somehow, sometime, a miracle has occurred.  Perhaps angels came in the night to whisper in our sleeping ears, 'There is a better way.' Perhaps God put words in another's mouth so we could hear from a friend or a counselor the words we needed to turn our lives around. Perhaps relatives and friends prayed for us.  Perhaps all of the above.

But beyond doubt, a miracle has happened in our lives. The monkey is off our backs, at last. But we must never forget that although the monkey is off our backs, the circus is still in town.  At every turn there is temptation. The one legal drug is our nemesis.  Vigilance is essential to maintain sobriety. Others, with the same problem, demonstrate to us that we are not alone.

When an angel opens the prison doors for us, we can fly out into a new life of caring and responsibility; of love and acceptance; of peace and joy; of forgiveness and sharing.  God works in wondrous ways His miracles to perform, and we can be the joyous recipients of His love. The body is the temple of the Living God. From that temple we can and should speak to anyone who seeks relief from the monkey. This life, then, is our blessed life; this life gives us the opportunity to help others leave their prison.

# Section II
## Beth

## Chapter 9   Archangel Center Stage

When Archangel Gabriel visited Earth to teach us the wisdom of the ages, there had been a great deal of planning; he did not just 'drop in'. The time was right (1987-1999) for us to hear these lessons in truth, Archangel Gabriel explained. He said it takes humanity about 2,000 years to accept a new idea. This is the beginning of a new age: the Age of Aquarius, or the Truth Age. Reverend Penny, by choice, had been taught over a period of five hundred years 'of earth time' how to channel an archangel.

The first time he visited no one expected him, including Rev. Penny, his beloved channel. She knew at her spirit level but not consciously. Gabriel had to remind her of her training and her acceptance of the task. She said to him, who will believe I am channeling an archangel? So he said, 'then call me Lucas'. For four years we did. But when he gave the lesson *Angels, Earthlings and Aliens* (7/27/91), he announced his true identity. Then he said, "Henceforth you shall call me Gabriel." Gabriel pronounced his name with a short 'a', and the accent on 'el'. We readily accepted his holy title.

Gabriel's lessons were announced by a printed flyer sent to all who had attended his previous seminar. When asked for the title of his next talk, he said that his angels had to first watch us to see if we had learned the previous lesson. Those of us who planned to attend paid a deposit for the very reasonable total cost - sixty dollars! Everyone was invited. Some came once but did not return, disbelieving in Gabriel's authenticity. As Gabriel told us, they simply were not ready for his teachings.

Prior to the day of Gabriel's presentation, Rev. Penny was instructed by angels regarding her diet and her need to sequester from others for a time to focus on prayer and meditation. On the day of the seminar, we gathered for refreshments as we paid for the session and socialized. About twenty to thirty of us were 'regulars' and it was a wonderful fellowship to be part of. Newcomers were welcomed with open arms. As the starting hour approached, we took our seats, and became quiet. Reverend Penny came on stage and sat with hands in her lap, palms up. Her eyes were closed. The sound man (Rev. Penny's brother, Joe) started a CD of instrumental meditation music. For many seminars the CD *River of Life* was played. In a few minutes the signal was given, and it was time for Archangel Gabriel to arrive.

Please do not think of this event as 'possession'. Rev. Penny gave her full consent to the channeling experience because of her deep faith in God and her constant love of Jesus. When the music stopped, Gabriel stood up and approached the microphone. He always began with, "And how be you this day in your time?" We would chorus, "Fine; welcome." At first he spoke sans blackboard, but one day a blackboard was put on the stage. He asked why it was called black when it was a green board. When he wanted a diagram put on the board he asked someone to write ("I never learned how to write," he said), it was usually Rev. Penny's daughter, Linda, who drew at his direction. One day he himself printed a word on the black board and we all cheered. Several of us took notes of his lessons in truth; others listened only. Virgil, the scribe, as Gabriel called him, sat at a table in the back of the room and assiduously took notes for Penny to read later. I sat at another back table and took notes for later reference. Then I was totally unaware that Gabriel's teachings would lead me to authorship of several books.

Gabriel always took questions at the end of the seminars. One day a woman approached the microphone and Gabriel gave her an answer. She said, "I didn't ask the question yet." He knew our thoughts and we became accustomed to this. Many angels assisted Gabriel during these talks; primarily an angel we dubbed 'Tinkerbell'. Her real name was Belle Leah (spelling mine; it never was shown us). She was familiar with the English we spoke and the social life of humans. Gabriel told us that before he came to teach us he learned English in the UK, and then came here and found out we don't speak English! He had grand sense of humor.

After all the questions were answered Gabriel said, "I will see you all again." He sat down and remained quiet for a few moments as the meditation music was played. Rev. Penny was unaware of the lesson, for she was in full trance. We had to relate to her his message of the day. Such dedication on her part was astounding. To sit for an hour or two at a time, not knowing what is said through your mouth, takes incredible faith and trust.

Gabriel told us that angels monitored her body constantly to be sure it was in a healthy balance. The first time he ate was when he asked for a banana. Another time he was given a glass of water with ice cubes. He took a drink and said, "There's a glacier in my glass!" Everything is relative; a hunk of ice is a hunk of ice. The seminars went like this: a short break in the morning, lunch for an hour on premises, an afternoon break, closing about 4:00PM

Gabriel remained during the breaks; for lunch he would withdraw from Rev. Penny, but remain present in the room to hear our comments about the lesson. At one of these lunch times an angel asked Gabriel, "What is that?" pointing to a dark spot in the chest of an attendee. Gabriel said, "That is sadness." The angel said, "What is sadness?" To which Gabriel replied, "It is the opposite of love." But knowing only love she could not comprehend Gabriel's words. At another time Gabriel explained that the opposite of love is apathy, but love is everywhere, and what is everywhere can have no opposite. Gabriel said when God created angels he gave them free choice *only in the realm of good,* and anything not-good is beyond their understanding. To the human species God gave free choice across the board.

Gabriel did not answer personal questions because 'you have psychics and mediums to do that'. When Gabriel explained that reincarnation is factual, it set us all to wondering about our past lives. Gabriel said this is the one that counts. He said that we have experienced so many lifetimes on Earth that *we have met every other person now living!*

Those twelve wondrous years of listening to Gabriel were not only the highlight of my life but I believe were the primary reason I came to Earth this time. Hearing an archangel speak of timeless wisdom, taking notes and writing books for posterity was the most lovely and powerful experience imaginable. He taught lessons that were easy to hear, like we are all children of God; holy offspring of the Father. Some lessons were tough to hear, like the fact we plan our entire lifetimes. The reader is strongly encouraged to hear and/or read the many lessons Archangel Gabriel taught. See the website sacredgardenfellowship.org

## Chapter 10   Arrival in Heaven

Thank you, angels, for welcoming me! Oh, my, it is far more bright and beautiful than I expected! Your lights, too, are much brighter than I ever imagined! When I was fifty my father came to me from spirit; he had passed when I was five. He told me he was waiting for me, to show me around Heaven. He said the colors and lights 'are different here'.

I read so much about this place while on earth, but being here is a spectacular event, indeed. I would like to rest awhile before I acclimate myself to Heaven again. Yes, I understand that this circular journey called karma has been my history. But now I am on the return trip Home, at last. I had hoped that this time I would ascend and remain here, but I guess I need at least one more earthly experience. I used to tell my friends on earth that I desired greatly to ascend but Plan B was cremation. I also told them that when I made partial payments for my pending cremation I recorded same in my computer under 'air travel'.

How I would love to see the Master Jesus and Archangel Gabriel. I will? Then I can thank them in person for their visitations on earth! I so enjoyed their lessons in truth! Oh, how grand that I will be able to see them sometime soon - oh, that's right - there is no time here. I look forward to seeing the temple on the hill, the lake, the museum, the library. And - okay, I am rambling.  But I am so excited to resume this great adventure. I will rest and adjust to my surroundings as I have done every time I arrived here from an earthly experience.

As you know, I was blessed to hear Archangel Gabriel and Yeshua at the end of the last century while I resided on the earth plane. How joyous we were to hear from them the wisdom of the ages, the corrections of scripture and the missing elements of Yeshua's life. So many people turned away from Gabriel's teachings, but Gabriel said they just were not ready for his lessons in truth. Then the truth dawned on me that I would write the lessons taught by these magnificent spirit entities! Thus began my writing career. You know all this? Of course!

I first wrote about Jesus the Christ and explained the difference between the man Jesus and the Christ Light in him. Then I wrote my memoirs so my grandchildren would know about my life. I knew somehow that I had another book to write but did not have a clue as to its contents. Then one magnificent day Jesus came to me, expressing through Rev. Penny, my mentor. He told me my first two books were okay and would help others. "Your next book will be --" (and I was all ears to hear what he was about to say!) ". . . a book of meditations based on Scripture, the *Course,* and your own experiences. It will be translated into many languages and inspire generations to come. I will help you. Be open to guidance. Do you have any questions?" Through tears I said, "No, no, no. Thank you!"

Little did I know that the book would be the first of a trilogy of meditation books, or that I would continue to be inspired to write several more books. But through the years I was wonderfully inspired, and words and ideas flowed through me to the keyboard, the printed page and finally publication. What a wondrous legacy I left behind.

Pardon me - you know all this already? You angels are so aware of everything! I should have known. Of course, my thousands of angels updated you on my earthly life so you would know just how to welcome and comfort me on my arrival here. What day is it? Oh, there I go again, thinking there is time here. But I read once that occasionally there is a 'softening of the glory' here. It is upon us now? Alright then I will go with my angels for acclimation and a little rest. Thank you for welcoming me here. I look forward to all the adventures that Heaven offers.

Yes, I understand it is quite different here - no time, no gravity, no competition, no status -- wow, such adventures await. Did you say, "Be still?" Oh, gee, I used to talk too much on earth, too. It's a problem of clergy, I think. Goodbye for now, dear angels.

## Chapter 11  Atlantis' Lessons

When we resided in Atlantis eons ago, we had very large heads and small bodies. We focused our attention on technology, as we turned our backs on our spirituality. Who could describe this history of humans but Archangel Gabriel? He said the scientists performed atrocious experiments on their peers. When asked if Atlantis would rise again, he said, "Hopefully no, thank God." But there are some entities on earth now who were Atlantians, and they are a vicious lot. The remnants of Atlantis are off the southeast coast of America, where numerous craft have disappeared.

We were the Atlantians, and now we are the earthlings. One may deny reincarnation, but denial does not negate the truth. The key problem with our experience on Atlantis was turning our backs on the spirit Self of us. Then, as now, we were spirit in essence. Denial of our truth does not, cannot, change our truth. And the truth of us is we are spirit, brought forth eons ago by the Author of life. God, first and only Cause, created us and gave us free choice. We used that free choice on Atlantis; we have that free choice now.

The Old Testament mentions Atlantian giants (Gen. 6:4; Numbers 13:33; Deuteronomy 2:11 & 20, 3:11 & 13; and Joshua 12:4, 13:12, 15:8, 17:15 and 18:16). When we destroyed Atlantis by the misuse of energy, we began living on this planet. We now seem to be traveling the same road of destruction through technology. It is essential this time to turn our thoughts, our beliefs, and our knowingness to the very essence of our being, spirit. Our task of awakening begins with focusing on our spirit Selves, the Christ Light within. Perhaps our hesitation to do so is based on the fact we cannot see spirit.

In John 8:58 we find Jesus saying, 'Before Abraham was, I am.' How easy for us to believe this when we proclaim Jesus as the *only* son of God. Gabriel told us the entire human race is the only begotten of the Father. As such, we must take responsibility for ourselves and turn within to His Kingdom. In so doing we will not turn our backs on technology; we will only shift our focus. Technology, like art and all life on earth, originates in Heaven. Heaven now holds wonderful inventions which have yet to be 'discovered' by humans.

Focusing on Heaven within will enable us to create what today we imagine, with emphasis on the good and constructive. As Atlantians we focused on horrible experiments, had no respect for life, and the result was self-destruction of our home planet.

We have another chance at life on earth. Journeying down the same old roads will not save us. Looking back will never save us. Many of our activities focus on the past. Genealogy and archeology are only examples. The story of Lot's wife (Luke 17:32) is a lesson for today. If the past is positive and worth repeating, why is today's society permeated with destruction and violence? Violence and destruction are now considered *entertainment!*

It is time to turn our attention to Jesus the Christ, and live as he lived. He said, 'follow me' for a reason. The reason is that he came to show us the way. Jesus told us we can do everything he did (John 14:12). Gabriel reminded us of Adam sleeping in Eden, then said that nowhere in the Bible does it say Adam woke up. Adam represents humanity, and we are still asleep to our Creator and our own divinity. Our sleeping state is over. Now we must wake up to our inborn divinity.

Spiritual brothers and sisters are we all. At this time on earth we are finally beginning to care for each other. The exclusion of tribes was followed by exclusion of religious beliefs. Ecumenism has found a home. More and more people are able to see spirit; we have believed in angels all along. We are spirit; we are eternal; Heaven is our natural habitat. There is no fear of death, because there is no death. Jesus overcame the world with love (John 16:33). We are the generation to commence a return journey Home, at last. Jesus lived on the cusp of a new age, that of Pisces; we live on the cusp of Aquarius, the Age of Spirituality.


## Chapter 12   Attributes of Love
*This chapter expounds on Chapter 13 of I Cor. Paul wrote to the people of Corinth.*


*Love is kind*

Kindness is one of Love's features, according to Paul's first letter to the Corinthians. When we are raised in an atmosphere of kindness, as we mature we choose to either remain  kind to others or we turn away from being kind because  others perceive us as being 'too soft' as a kind person, or they make us feel vulnerable to criticism. Kindness costs nothing. We always appreciate it when expressed to us, although we may turn it away - especially in grief - because then is when we feel the most vulnerable.

It is a strange perception that when we are kind to a stranger that person thinks we have a hidden agenda - our kindness being a 'price to pay' for an expected payback. That is *their* lack of trust, but we have a tendency to pull back and opt out of the kindness because of their misinterpretation. It takes courage to continue to be kind in that situation. Continued kindness will prove itself to be offered for its own sake.

If a kind attitude expresses softness maybe that is why we reserve it for loved ones. Everyone appreciates kindness. The person raised in that atmosphere expects it, and the person not so raised by a loving family is surprised but glad for it. There once was a saying 'be kind to animals', as though kindness to other humans was a given. We ought to be kind to animals because they are living entities. Domestic creatures comfort us, and wild beasts can be tamed with kindness and training.

Our current way of being kind is to 'pay forward' in a restaurant or other store. It is a kindness of anonymity, but still a kindness. There are times when a person may shun kindness openly, because s/he chooses to be independent. We rush to help another because we think they want it. Seldom does it occur to us to ask if our help is desired. At one time nurses, seeing a patient slumped in a hospital bed, would rush to hike them up and puff the pillows behind. Then nursing became more patient-focused, and patients were asked if they wanted help.

When proffered, kindness brings a good feeling to both, as a rule. Kindness makes both giver and receiver feel good inside. Maybe that is because a connection is made between two people as they honor the God within each other.

*Love envys not*
Is there a person who has never envied someone something? It is a quirk of human nature that we believe 'the grass is always greener on the other side of the fence'. This constant outlook means that we are never satisfied with what we have. The rare individual who is perfectly content with her/his possessions is seen as complacent, lazy, or anti-social. But this lack of envy gives the person a good feeling about life, self and others. Those brave souls have a peace of mind which envy denies. God is love, and as His children we are too. Envy does not belong with love. Love is content with what it has, what it *is*.

*Love vaunts not itself*
Bragging has no place in the character of the person who expresses love. It is true that we are all children of God and therefore we are much loved by our Creator, but that love is a given. We are love in essence - that is a given. But love does not call inordinate attention to how we look, what we possess, or what our accomplishments are.

*Love is not puffed up*
The person who draws attention to himself desires greatly to be noticed by others. He longs to be considered special; to be considered better than others. This behavior is unbecoming of love. In truth, the individual who seems egotistical is inwardly longing for attention because he is unaware that he is loved grandly by God; may not even believe in God.

*Love does not behave itself unseemly*
Behaving unseemly would include pushing, shoving, elbowing others; shouting and cussing. Another example is the drunken person who is noisy, vulgar, and boisterous, uses profanity and insults others. This behavior offends others in various ways and many people choose to leave that person's presence. Extreme examples are the murderer, the rapist.

*Love seeks not her own*
This describes the person who is greedy or one who hoards. Love shares.

*Love is not easily provoked*
The provoked person is one who has certain expectations of others and when the others' responses do not comply with those expectations, she is provoked; angered at what is seen as a failure to comply. Love accepts without expectations. Love has no hidden agenda to be met.

*Love thinks no evil*
The person of love focuses always on good, positive, caring thoughts. We can look at the word 'evil' and backwards it spells 'live'. Love is optimistic; sees good in others; makes lemonade out of a lemon, whether the lemon is a situation or a problem. Love does not criticize or judge. Love does not see negative behavior but sees beyond it to the child of God within.

*Love rejoices not in iniquity*
There are people who are very happy with injustice, wrongs, and wickedness. They love to see the misfortune of others. They may be game-players; they may even try to trap another person into making mistakes, and then watch for the fun of it. Love seeks and finds only people of good intentions; good motives; positive acts.

*Love rejoices in truth*
To rejoice in truth means to celebrate justice, to celebrate the righting of a wrong. It means learning the truth and rejoicing in it - even if it does not square with one's predetermined opinion. We know the truth when we hear it, but if our minds are already made up we fail to embrace the truth.

*Love bears all things*
It has been said that God does not give us more than we can handle. We have all wondered at the courage, strength and tolerance of others when they endure physical, mental or emotional stress. Perhaps we have surprised ourselves at our own fortitude. Love is the sustaining power of our forbearance.

*Love believes all things*
We are coming to understand that our five senses betray the truth. We are beginning to believe in a mighty power which created us, abides in us,

and can be demonstrated by us. Believing truth then knowing truth is our goal. We believe we can do all things, as we are guided by the still, small Voice for God.

*Love hopes all things*
*If in this life only we have hope in Christ, we are of all men most miserable.*
*But now is Christ risen from the dead, and become the firstfruits of them that slept.*
*I Cor 15:19-20*
To hope is to desire with an expectation of obtainment. We hope for what we do not have, and yet we have every expectation that we will receive it in the future. We still hope that life is eternal, even though Jesus the Christ demonstrated it. Yes, he was and still is a child of God. He reminded us that everything he did we can do also. He came to show us the way. When we follow him, our hope will turn to expression. We will wake up to the Kingdom of God within us, as told by Jesus himself. Then we will know our true, eternal Self.

*Love endures all things*
All human generations have endured much. History reveals that hundreds of previous generations endured much. Humankind will endure until we awaken and express the love that we are. We will walk the Earth as Jesus did. We will exhibit love and forgiveness as he did. It will be a New Earth and a New Heaven.

*Love never fails*
God is Love, and God never fails. He created us, he sent angels to watch over us and we know that anything is possible with God. When we are inspired to act in a certain way, God shows us the way and brings us those who can help us succeed. Love, like God, is eternal.

Paul provides us with words of wisdom to live by. The further we seem to be from love, the more difficult spiritual growth becomes. When we apply the love we feel toward 'special ones' in our lives to all others, our growth spirals upward. As we treat all others as spiritual siblings, they will begin to see themselves as such, also. Everyone becomes; everyone wins.

## Chapter 13   Beams of Light

One day at a seminar, Archangel Gabriel was asked a question about race by an African-American lady. There was an unusual silence. Then Gabriel said he had to look closely to see the color of her skin. He explained that when he looked at us he saw us only as beams of light. In that one comment we understood that we are indeed spirit and the angel realm sees us only as spirit entities. Perhaps in meditation this is how we need to picture ourselves as we go within. In James 1:17 we find, *"every good gift and every perfect gift is from above, and cometh down from the Father of lights, with whom is no variableness, neither shadow of turning."* Also in Ephesians 5:8 we find, *"for ye were sometimes darkness, but now are ye light in the Lord: walk as children of light"*.

Sometimes in a psychic circle we see a spirit as a beam of light, and sometimes it is the hazy form of a human not materialized in physical form. After his resurrection Jesus materialized in physical form to many people in several different places. He chose to materialize to prove that life survives after what we know as death. Yet we still fear death. We tell ghost stories because we believe in ghosts when there is no such thing. What we think are ghosts are in truth earthbound individuals who did not accept their transition to another realm at the time of their demise. They are known as 'earth-bound' souls, and remain so until they accept the transition to the spirit world. They can be encouraged to do so.

If on a daily basis we could see others as beams of light we would accept them as spiritual siblings. If we could know that in our heart of hearts we are truly beams of light, children of the Father of lights, we would accept ourselves as divine creatures, as offspring of the living God. Everyone is our spiritual sibling, regardless of their race, religion, color, or culture. Everyone came forth upon the planet earth with the blessing of our Creator. It matters not what we choose to call our Creator. There is one God; one life; one light.

Now humans care if people in other countries are afflicted by disease or flood or fire or hurricanes or earthquakes. We rush to help the 'others', or donate to their relief. When a child in Texas falls into a well this whole country, and even the world, prays for his rescue. Perhaps it is because we know *at some level* that we are all connected. We habitually perceive ourselves as separate from God, but the natural man cannot perceive spiritual things (I Cor. 2:14)

This New Age is the Age of Truth. It is the age for us to awaken to our light self, to our divinity. We pray to God as though He were out there somewhere. Now is the time to become aware of God within. The light of our spirit is eternal, therefore we are eternal. God, like the father of the Prodigal Son, awaits our return. *"Take heed, therefore that the light which is in thee be not darkness. If thy whole body therefore be full of light, as when the bright shining of a candle doth give thee light."* (Luke 11:35-36)  If the light from one candle can fill a room, how much more could we enlighten others when we let our light shine forth - having no dark part!  The 'dark part' is fear, anger, judgment, etc. But we already know our own 'dark part'. When we identify it we are reluctant to give it up, because we have become so comfortable with it. Archangel Gabriel said our worst fear is that we *are* children of God!

Now, momentarily, we can touch into Heaven as we go within and picture ourselves as children of light, beams of light, eternal beams. The New Age will see a wondrous awakening, as the coming centuries bring more and more believers - then *knowers* - of the holy light within.  It will be a New Earth and a New Heaven! It will be the Will of God finally expressed on earth.

## Chapter 14   "Beloveds of God . . ."

When Archangel Gabriel came to a small church in upstate New York, on October 25, 1987, his first three words were "Beloveds of God . . ." Everyone paid attention to this 'new voice'. It was not a masculine voice, for Reverend Penny's voice is definitely a higher octave and easily recognized as feminine. But the voice came as one in authority. It almost sounded like a command. Gabriel then proceeded to give a twenty minute talk on how important we humans are to God, and how much

God loves us. He said we must awaken to the totality of ourselves; to know we are much more than a body; to live from the Lord God of our Being.

After that Sunday evening service Gabriel came many times to present us with lessons from the spirit world of God. Weekend retreats, day-long seminars and frequent Sunday evenings. He taught everyone who cared to attend. Some walked away, either in disbelief or a lack of interest. Some, who did not know Rev. Penny's innate integrity, honesty, and natural psychic ability, denied his authenticity.

Several of us took advantage of the opportunity to learn the wisdom of the ages and went wherever he taught. Everyone was welcome, but Rev. Penny asked that we not advertise Archangel Gabriel. The media would likely have ridiculed and criticized the teachings because the source could not be interviewed. Or because his teachings were based on the premise that the real world is one we cannot see. Gabriel knew - and he told us - that everyone was not ready for his teachings. Rev. Penny told us one time that she lamented to Gabriel that so few people attended the seminars, but Gabriel said he would prefer ten devoted students to a hundred when most are not getting the lesson.

The reader must understand that we did not know that evening the channeled voice was Archangel Gabriel. When Rev. Penny arrived home after church she was told by Gabriel who he was. She said, "Who is going to believe I am channeling an archangel?" Gabriel responded, "Then call me Lucas." And so we did, until 1991 when he gave a lesson *Angels, Aliens and Earthlings.* In that seminar he described the seven archangels and the vast array of angels in Heaven. After describing the archangels, he was asked if he was an archangel. He said he was, and then asked if we knew which one. No one answered. Then he said, "Henceforth you will call me Gabriel. I am the Announcer of the Ages."

I cannot speak for the other students, but in retrospect I am astounded at the holiness of this teacher to whom I have become so devoted. Here I was, sitting at the feet of the very same archangel who spoke to Mary:

*Hail, thou that art highly favored, the Lord is with thee: blessed art thou among women.*

*And when she saw him, she was troubled at his saying, and cast in her mind what manner of salutation this should be.*

*And the angel said unto her, Fear not, Mary: for thou hast found favor with God.*

*And, behold, thou shalt conceive in thy womb, and bring forth a son, and shalt call his name JESUS.*

*He shall be great, and shall be called Son of the Highest: and the Lord God shall give unto him the throne of his father David:*

*And he shall reign over the house of Jacob forever; and of his kingdom there shall be no end.* Luke 1:28-33

In that hallowed time two thousand years ago Gabriel also came to Zacharias, whose aged wife, Elisabeth, was pregnant with John the Baptist. Gabriel said:

*Fear not, Zacharias: for thy prayer is heard; and thy wife Elisabeth shall bear thee a son, and thou shalt call his name John.*

*And thou shalt have joy and gladness; and many shall rejoice at his birth.*

*For he shall be great in the sight of the Lord, and shall drink neither wine nor strong drink; and he shall be filled with the Holy Ghost, even from his mother's womb.*

*And many of the children of Israel shall he turn to the Lord their God.*

*And he shall go before him in the spirit and power of Elias, to turn the hearts of the fathers to the children, and the disobedient to the wisdom of the just; to make ready a people prepared for the Lord.* Luke 1:13-17

The archangel's words this century were spoken in modern English. But once in a while he greeted us before his lesson: "How be thou this day in your time?" During the years Gabriel visited he told us eleven Ascended Masters also came to earth - to several countries - to teach all humanity the same lesson, for he said he brought only one lesson, presented in different ways so all would understand: we are children of God, part of Him, and we must awaken to our holiness and learn to express it.

Here, in the twenty-first century, I wonder at the manner of salutation Gabriel used when he said, "Beloveds of God." In that short phrase he told us explicitly that we are beloved by God and worthy to hear his instructions. He commanded our attention then. We listened intently. Many of us still study the lessons in truth which he taught.

Gabriel, this sacred entity, ageless and eternal, came to Earth at the inception of a New Age; to awaken us all to our true selves - children of God, beloved by the Father in Heaven. And there was I, so wonderfully blessed, to sit at the feet of an archangel to learn of our holiness, too. Thank God for that sweet, sacred hour when Beloved Gabriel first came to our small group of ordinary people, worshipping in a small church. Thank God for the holy messenger and his blessed lessons in truth presented those twelve wondrous years. The Announcer of the Ages, right here in America, to announce to all humanity the Age of Aquarius; the Age of Truth.

## Chapter 15  Beyond White Noise

Webster defines white noise: meaningless commotion, hubbub or chatter. White noise can help a person sleep when there is a lot of family noise in the background. From a metaphysical standpoint we live in a world of white noise. The sounds of voices, cars, buses, trains and planes fill our daily world with noise; meaningless commotion.

In the scheme of eternity, the world sounds and even the activities in it are without meaning. That is so because what we have convinced ourselves of is that life on the planet Earth is our only life, and the Earth itself is our home. When Jesus brought to us (1995-1999), through a dedicated channel, the truth of ourselves, he explained that we do not belong here on earth. Heaven is our natural habitat. We left the spirit world of God - in consciousness only - and came to live on Earth. We must ask why we left that holy realm of eternal perfection. It is a fair question and one that must be asked, when we are ready for the answer.

Archangel Gabriel provided the answer when he came to Earth from 1987 to 1999 and, also through a dedicated channel, gave us the reason for our current predicament on this earth plane. Solid form seems to be the proof of earthly life. What we perceive with our senses validates us and our surroundings. Gabriel did not bring us any new information, nor did he seek a 'following'. Nor did he come to gather followers of his beloved channel. Individuals who channel spirit entities are trained to do so. All mediums do not use their talent wisely. That is why the Bible says, *Beloved, believe not every spirit, but try the spirits whether they are of God: because many false prophets are gone out into the world.* I John 4:1

In the creation of the human race, God breathed us into a spiritual existence. In that spirit world we were all one with God and knew it. We loved God and each other. It was Heaven. It was joyful, peaceful and safe. God created us with free choice. Angels have free choice but only in the realm of good. Angels do not understand anything but good. God gave humankind free will across the board, without exceptions. The spirit energy of all creation is a high, very fine, rapid vibration. With our free will we decided to manipulate the energy of spirit. Since spirit energy is the highest vibration in all creation, any manipulation slowed down its vibration. To make a very long story short, we have continued to manipulate the energy until we reached a nadir point. Matter is of the lowest possible energy rate. We simply cannot reduce the vibration more. We 'discovered' white noise to cover background sounds, enabling us to sleep.

Beyond the hubbub - the white noise - of the everyday world there is a spirit world which remains full of peace, harmony and joy. When we learn and accept our journey from that supernal place we will desire greatly to return to our Source. Many people think that without action and a busy life our existence would be boring. That is because we live in an action oriented society on earth. There are peaceful places on the planet which we visit for solace and comfort. We do this in times of mourning or stress. Mountains, deserts, rivers and lakes all give a feeling of serenity and calm, enabling us to return to life's activities.

It is almost as if God created them for us so we would have a place of respite from the hectic world. In those silent times we are refreshed. We get centered and healed there so we can return to the busy life. Some people seem to have peace all the time. Some clergy do. It is not a collar or a robe which brings peace. It is not theology or ritual; it is a state of mind. It is faith in a higher power. It is acceptance of life as experiences come to us. It is focusing on *now*, knowing everything is just the way it is supposed to be *because God gave us free choice.*

If we are not joyous and happy we can change our life simply by making other choices. Creatures can teach us how to focus our attention, keep in the now, and accept our circumstances. They do these things so well. The pets we cherish express their freedom constantly. Leashes limit them; rules we lay down limit them. Wild beasts are beautiful to behold in their natural habitat. They are free and respond only to instinct. We are free, and can choose to live only by spirit guidance.


## Chapter 16   Bits and Pieces of truth

When Archangel Gabriel first came he said that he would come for twelve years, as long as Rev. Penny was willing to channel his lessons. He would not; could not come unless she was a willing instrument of truth. We all have free will and not even angels can abrogate it.

At the time I did not know why taking notes was necessary. It would be years later that my reason for being at Gabriel's feet was clear to me. Gabriel visited us for twelve glorious years to bring one lesson: We are children of God and should wake up to our divinity and learn to live from the Lord God of our Being. He noted, after a few years, that he brought the same lesson every time, but used different words to help us all understand the message. Here are some of his bits and pieces of truth.

Probably if I lived to be a hundred I would still be writing Gabriel's message of truth, brought to us in an atmosphere of love, peace and joy. His patience, humor and understanding were so consistent and powerful we sat entranced with his words. An example of his humor: One day he was given a glass of water (at angelic instruction, for angels constantly monitored Rev. Penny's body), and in the glass was an ice cube. When he took a sip he said, "There's a glacier in my glass." We all laughed, and I smile at it still. It proves everything is relative!

In twelve years Gabriel taught us so much about our lives, our error perceptions, humanity's past and future, the reason why we came to Earth in the first place, the way to go back Home to God. There is so much information to pass on. The reader is strongly urged to read or hear the lessons in truth that he brought to our awareness. See sacredgardenfellowship.org

I have been greatly blessed with the task of passing on Gabriel's lessons in truth. By the Grace of God He has made me an inspired writer, and angels constantly help me to recall his teachings so I can pass them on unaltered by my ego self. Thank God for His wisdom and His angels. In one of Gabriel's seminars, titled *"Angels, Aliens and Earthlings"* (7/27/91), he described the world of angels. When he spoke to us he had many angels with him. His primary assistant was an angel we named Tinkerbell. At first Belle Leah (author not sure of spelling; Gabriel spoke; rarely wrote on the blackboard) did not like the nickname, but later on she said she did. At another seminar Gabriel was asked why we each have 144,000 angels; "Why not just one?" was the question from a man in the audience. I never heard Gabriel laugh so robustly! He said, "One? You would drive one crazy!" When a friend of mine planned to drive from Upstate New York to Florida, destination unknown, I told her that probably half of her angels were in Florida preparing a place for her. It turned out that she bought a winter residence and loves it.

I moved many times due to my employment, and sometimes asked for angelic help. Other times I foolishly did not. I listened to my ego and went ahead to find a house or an apartment. One house I found had squirrels in the bedroom. Another house had floors so uneven I could place a marble on the kitchen floor and it rolled thirty feet down to the living room! I found them. But when I asked angels to find me a home - and I gave some basic requirements - they always found the perfect place! Why are we always surprised when angels help us? We need to begin relying on them.

At the microphone one day I began to ask Gabriel a question (he always took questions) when he said to me, "An angel named your car." I was startled, and said, "What did they name it?" And he said "Joymobile!" It would be three cars later before I had decals placed on the two front doors of my current Joymoble. Regarding cars, I once was seeking a new vehicle to replace the old one which had many miles on it. Three times I found a new car, paid a deposit and went home thinking that the bank would probably not approve it. Three times the bank did not, and my deposit was reimbursed. Then at a Gabriel seminar, he told me that my very thoughts cancelled my purchase. He told me to picture the car of my desire; picture washing it and putting gas in it, and give no thought to the bank. A few days later I found the car I envisioned and the bank approved it! *Then* I kept thinking that I did not deserve a new car - and it was stolen! Gabriel said, 'You couldn't leave well enough alone.' He told me to pray for the thief and thank God for return of my vehicle. What a lesson! Our very thoughts influence our lives so much.

Many times angels came to my assistance and they still do. They always seem to be one step ahead of me. If I keep my mind open, they remind me of every task I planned for the day. Even now, as I read or hear Gabriel's lessons, I recall bits and pieces of his lessons and his stories. I am looking forward to thanking him in person when I reach the other side.

# Section III

## Gimel

## Chapter 17  By Faith We Live

In the New Testament, Paul's letter to the Hebrews includes an entire chapter (11) in which he explains the faith by which biblical people lived. He notes the faith of Abel, Enoch, Noah, Abraham, Isaac, Joseph, and Moses. These names are all familiar to anyone who reads the Bible regularly, clergy, religious student, or casual reader. Without thinking of our faith we do rely on Something to watch over us. We may call it a Higher Power, Jesus, God, Lord, Allah, Yahweh, Great Spirit, or another Name. Whenever danger is imminent we all cry out for help. Whenever we get to the end of our rope, so to speak, we ask for divine assistance. It seems to be human nature. It is our innate spiritual nature which makes us mentally desire help, and then verbally ask for help.

Unfortunately, for some reason, there are individuals who either do not think God will help, or they call too late. Archangel Gabriel told us that when a person takes their own life, they immediately change their mind. But jumping off bridge is usually fatal. Gabriel also said "We never stopped a speeding train." We live by the laws of the world, and not even angels can interfere with our free choice. Sadly, some of us have faith in money because we think it will provide everything we need. We cannot use money when we are starving to death; when we are thirsting for water; when we are bleeding to death or have no air to breathe. Money is simply a medium of exchange. Many see money as power; sometimes worship those who have a plethora of money. Monetary wealth guarantees nothing. The wealthy are numbered also in the suicide rates.

Nevertheless, our daily lives consist of more faith than we realize. We drive through a green light without giving it a thought, but is it not faith in the green light that gives us such confidence? Dwellers of large cities take elevators and subways regularly, with full expectations of a safe arrival. It might be called confidence, but what is confidence but faith in an outcome? The person who embarks on a new venture surely has faith in success. Complete self-confidence will bring success. Gabriel said that Bill Gates (computer inventor) never had a thought of failure. Faith in a certain and sure outcome is the primary ingredient of success - in business and in life.

Faith in a Creator - the Entity Who put us on earth - brings us every good thing and every good experience we desire. What we plan is what we get. There are no accidents. Nothing happens to us without our permission; God would not allow it. A seeming tragedy can be seen as a blessing. Do we really believe that God would give us anything but a blessing? Forest fires draw people together in cooperation; new growth of trees and other flora come up through the new soil. Floods bring neighbors in touch with each other. That is quite a phenomenon, in a world where we choose to live an anonymous life. How many of us know our neighbors? Anyone who is new to New York City is told, 'Don't look anyone in the eye,' and 'Don't look up at the tall buildings.' We seem to have a persistent fear that the 'other' will harm us. We have no faith in any 'other' person.

The 'other' passengers on the airplane when we fly are all unknown to us, and will ever be so. Yet, if the plane should crash we all enter Heaven together, as planned. What a special moment to share! Gabriel explained that, in addition to planning our lives, we also plan where, when, how and with whom we shall transition (die). Only the angelic world and our Higher Self would be privy to such knowledge. Gabriel came not to scare us, but tell us there is absolutely nothing to fear. Fear and love cannot sleep in the same bed. Our fears include many things. We could draw up a long list of our fears. Gabriel said all our fears, in truth, go back to the one original fear: belief that we left God and He will never take us back.

He will take us back, because He created us and He loves all His children, as human parents love all their own or adopted children. We don't like everything our kids do, but we love what they are - ours. Their human bodies we brought forth. Their spirit essence God brought forth. God does not like everything we do on earth, but He loves us for what we are - His. Human offspring do not always 'come home' again, but inevitably we will all go back Home to Heaven, our natural habitat. It is an immutable law. By this faith, with this knowingness, we must live.

## Chapter 18  Bygone Days

We read the history of our old beliefs and wonder how we could have believed what we did. The earth was flat; so we thought. The sun revolves around the earth; so we thought. There were many gods; so we thought. Now we know the truth: the earth is a round planet which revolves around the sun; humanity has come to believe in one God, though we call Him/Her/It many different names. The reason our beliefs change is mostly due to science. Astronomy, in its use of powerful telescopes, has proven what we now accept: all planets revolve around our sun. Moses, thousands of years ago, believed in one God. That idea continued to be accepted until it became a universal truth.

Astrology preceded astronomy; paganism preceded modern religious belief systems; anatomy came before modern medicine. We grow and develop as we learn new truths. It is called change. We learn arithmetic, then math, then calculus, etc. Each division is followed by another. It is called growth. We have come to value science as it reveals more and more to us. There is one topic we will not study except to memorize it. It is called religion. The only way to have change and growth in the field of religion is to accept what we cannot perceive with our senses. It is called metaphysical, or 'beyond what is perceptible to the five senses'. All our hours are filled with what we see, hear, smell, taste and feel. Seeing ourselves as only a physical body we deny our spiritual aspect. It matters not what it is called, but 'supernatural' comes to mind.

Some people believe that what we cannot discern with our five senses is unworthy of study. Magic, miracles, ghosts, etc. fit within this realm of denial.  Magic is making someone see what is not true. Miracles are the method by which we learn about love. (ACIM 1: I: 3). There is no such thing as a ghost; the nebulous form we see is an earth-bound soul which stubbornly clings to form instead of moving on into the next sphere of existence. When we gently remind this form to move on, it does. One of the spiritual gifts noted by Paul is discerning of spirits (I Cor. 12:10)

Metaphysics is the study of supernatural things. 'Supernatural': an order of existence beyond the visible observable universe. If nature is the expression of God on earth, what can be 'beyond' it? 'Metaphysical': beyond what is perceptible to the five senses. (Webster's Collegiate).The Creator is not something we can view, but we can perceive the manifestations of His creations in flora and fauna. Gabriel said there are other universes.

For those who need 'proof' that metaphysics is true, and supernatural things exist, see the series of books entitled *The Supernatural,* published by The Danbury Press in 1975, the series *Mysteries of the Unknown,* published by Time-Life Books, 1986, and *Findhorn,* 1974. Spiritualism is the religious denomination begun in England and America in the nineteenth century, which believes in communication between the spirit world and earthlings. Mediums and psychics bring messages from spirit to assure us they are in very much alive in a lovely place of light and love. In such messages we understand there is no 'death', only an absence on earth of our loved ones.

We attend religious ceremonies, pray, and meditate from a standpoint of faith. *"Now faith is the substance of things hoped for, the evidence of things not seen."* (Heb. 11:1). Faith has substance; evidence! Are these not real things; true things? One area of faith is belief in God, another is a belief in the spirit world of God; another is a belief in fairies, devas and sprites. another is a belief in angels; God's messengers. When life is good and we are prospering, we do not always think about God; some never do. When tragedy strikes we fall on our knees, literally or figuratively, and ask a Higher Power for deliverance.

Jesus the Christ came to earth to reveal what we can do. We immediately placed him on a pedestal for worship and decided we would be the best we can but could never emulate Jesus. The Bible tells us that Jesus said (many times) 'follow me'. He came as a pattern (1 Tim. 1:16), an example (John 13:15) to show us the way Home. He was and remains forever our elder brother. Our error is that we forgot his message of love and forgiveness, focusing instead on the miracles he performed. He said we can do everything he did, when we follow him. (John 14:12). Jesus then provided us with a book for spiritual growth. Its title is *A Course in Miracles,* published in 1975. Can we read this book and not believe that the spirit world communicates with us?

Then, late in the twentieth century (1995-1999), Jesus came to channel information about the Bible. He explained the parts which were purged from the original writings, like all references to reincarnation and words about the many women disciples who followed Jesus in his travels. He said some changes were deliberate; others were errors in translation. The most astounding error in translation: the phrase, Jesus Christ, only begotten son of God, was originally written, Jesus Christ, begotten son of the only God.

Archangel Gabriel came (1987-1999) to teach a small number of us who sought truth. Gabriel brought only truth. Some truth was joyous to hear; some difficult to accept. He came because he knew we were ready to know truth. Eleven Master Teachers came to earth simultaneously - to various centers of light - where communication with the spirit world of God is accepted. These twelve centers of light will grow and expand outward until the whole world hears and accepts the truth. The truth is we do not belong on earth. Heaven is our natural habitat. We are all prodigals and will one day, each in our own time, return unto God, mighty Creator of our spirit Selves.

Bygone days are no more than preludes to today. What we are now is the culmination of all our past incarnations. If we dwell on the past nothing can change. Learning is change. If we open our minds to truth and open our hearts to unconditional love, our angels will point us to all things from which we can learn. We can choose to follow the intuitive thoughts or ignore them. The choice is ours. Love and truth are eternal. Yesterday is forever past; tomorrow is what we design today. Building blocks are love, truth, peace and harmony. Tomorrow we can sing; today we write the music.

## Chapter 19   Changing Times

We need only read history books to see how times have changed. Time itself is distinguished by our clocks and calendars, which only change as we change them with minutes and hours; months and years.

Tennyson wrote:

Ring out old shapes of foul disease;
  Ring out the narrowing lust of gold;
  Ring out the thousand wars of old,
Ring in the thousand years of peace.

Upon reading this I am reminded that Gabriel said we are now beginning a thousand years of peace. It does not seem that way in 2016, but we do not know what the future holds. Time was invented by humans and by it we live. Someone suggested that there is no history, only biography. We change our minds, our employments, our homes, our relationships, our careers, etc. We are people of change. We change our thinking, our habits, our behaviors, and our opinions. Small wonder that we are so confused. Science reveals new truths and our thinking changes. Scientists discover answers to medical problems and we expect longer life; we alter our habits to improve our health. Writers of fiction present new ideas to the world and some of us embrace the possibility of their 'inventions'. It is now known that a fiction writer published a book describing a luxury liner hitting an iceberg and sinking. Strangely enough, he was on the Titanic and was one of the first to drown!

Does this give credence to the idea we can receive the truth before events, or that we are living out a planned lifetime, or other options? It is human nature to resist anything new. For example, there is still a 'Flat Earth Society' which denies the roundness of our planet! But there is always a segment of society - be it ever so small - which seeks to know the truth about Earth, the universe and we the people in it. It is these individuals who are working in laboratories, excavating the Earth's surface, or taking time to meditate, as the prophets of old. These are ways that new ideas, new discoveries, come to be known by us. It is almost as if we are constantly searching for something we want to know, or something we want to experience. When a person conquers an addiction, or overcomes an affliction, they often say they felt like something was missing; like an emptiness was in them. Recovery brings a sense of wholeness. We all can start 'living' anew.

So much is happening on our planet Earth at this time. Communication has changed so we can talk to *and see each other* while we are thousands of miles apart. Perhaps this amazing progress in communications is ours so that we can more readily see we are all connected. Regardless of race, color, language or religion, we have some basic things in common. We all have feelings and emotions. We all bleed red blood. We all desire peace on Earth. Once a year, at holiday time, we speak of peace on Earth, but we do little to bring peace into our own lives. Each person can create peace in one's life. We can make amends, forgive others, and begin to think in terms of togetherness and cooperation; of unity.

Change is our right, our choice, our power. Time can be used creatively, yet we waste much time in anger, fear, resentment etc. This is a good time to begin to change to a positive-focused life; why not now? Why not this generation? Archangel Gabriel said it takes humanity two thousand years to learn something new. Now is the time to fully accept what Jesus the Christ said so long ago - at the beginning of a new age (the Age of Pisces) -

*Neither shall they say, Lo here! or, Lo, there! for, behold, the kingdom of God is within you.* Luke 17:21

For two thousand years we have been struggling to understand these words. Now is the time to accept the profound truth of them. Now is the time to accept the holy kingdom within each of us; to acknowledge divinity as our birthright, and to thus become what God intended for all His children. The kingdom of God has always been within us, as when God breathed us forth. We have simply forgotten. This is the time of remembrance. Gabriel came to remind us. Listening to him - and all reader are advised to do so - we will be about our Father's business and awaken to our divinity. We need not wait another two thousand years.

## Chapter 20   Cheer Up!

*These things have I spoken unto you, that in me ye might have peace. In the world ye shall have tribulation: but be of good cheer; I have overcome the world.* John 16:33

Some of the lessons taught by Archangel Gabriel were joyful to hear, like: We are children of God. Life is eternal. We each have 144,000 angels to watch over us. Other lessons Gabriel (1987-1999), and Jesus the Christ (1995-1999), taught were difficult to hear and more difficult to accept, such as: We plan our entire lives. Humanity has been asleep for centuries. The original Bible contains many errors.

When Jesus the Christ walked the earth he taught forgiveness and love. We have remembered his miracles more than his teachings. Believing only in the miracles we placed him above us as the only Son of God, and accepted a God who would have His only son beaten and crucified. Jesus always knew he was God's son; he also knew we are all children of God. That is why he came: to show us the way Home.  The great Master teacher, Jesus, explained several erroneous passages in the Bible. Two stand out in my memory: The Bible states that Jesus is the only begotten son of God. Originally it was written that Jesus is the begotten son of the only God. This has a completely different meaning.

 And the other:  Jesus did not suffer on the cross. He had the ability (as many humans do now) to have an 'out of body' experience. We have since glorified sacrifice and suffering.  Gabriel clarified for us the story of the Garden of Eden. He reminded us of Adam's deep sleep, and then added, "Nowhere in scripture does it say he woke up!" We remain asleep to the divinity in us. We plan our lives simply because God gave us free choice, which neither He nor the angels can abrogate. Jesus himself chose to come to earth and save us all. (John 10:17-18). Gabriel told us the outcome: only on the cross did Jesus realize he only saved himself; it is up to each person to save him/herself by choosing to return to the Father.

We have tribulation in the world because we have caused the tribulation by free choice. Jesus could foresee future humanity, as a prophet. He also knew that if and when we adopted the lessons he taught we too could ascend to the Father. And we all will. At one of Gabriel's seminars there was a pregnant woman in attendance. Gabriel said to her, "The child you are carrying will ascend." It is one of Gabriel's statements that are burned in my memory.

When Gabriel told us we each have 144,000 angels we were amazed, and wondered why our lives were not perfect. But Gabriel said angels can only watch over us and protect us until we do what we came to do. But angels can never go against our free choice. "We have never stopped a speeding train," said Gabriel. At another seminar Gabriel asked the audience 'How many of you believe in the hereafter?" All hands went up. Then he said, "If you don't believe in the hereafter, what are you here after?" He told us that we have only one life, and the gasp of the group was palpable. Then he explained the one life is the life of our spirit, and it is eternal as God. We live out a chosen lifetime, an earthly experience, and then return to the Astral Plane. We have done this repeatedly. It is called the wheel of karma. Reincarnation is a fact. *By choice* we can get off the karmic wheel, and return to the Father. Each person must choose.

We are children of God and at some level of our being we know it is true. But we have turned our power over to the ego and it controls our lives. It tells us we are not worthy, not able, not qualified, not talented, not holy, not anything but a physical body with a short span of life and then we 'die' to be no more. We listen to the ego constantly. Gabriel came when he did because now is the time for us to awaken to our own divinity as children of God. We are at the beginning of the Age of Aquarius - the Age of Truth, Gabriel said. At the same time Gabriel and Jesus came, eleven Master Teachers visited Earth in several countries. Gabriel's message was for the world, as was Jesus' message. It is time to exercise our free choice, to tell the ego to sit in the wings as God takes center stage in our lives. *These things have I spoken unto you, that my joy might remain in you, and that your joy might be full.* John 15:11

# Chapter 21  Citizens of Heaven

Wester's dictionary describes a citizen as 'an inhabitant of a city or town entitled to the rights and privileges of a freeman. A member of a state. A native or naturalized person who owes allegiance to a government and is entitled to protection from it'. The word is from the French for city. The commonly accepted usage today does not mean a city or state inhabitant but rather an inhabitant of a nation or country.

We accept our citizenship of this country as a right, but rarely as a privilege. Archangel Gabriel reminded us that we have more freedoms than any other nation in the world. We pay allegiance to our native land, salute its flag and sing its anthem. We enjoy the land, the food it produces and the scenery it offers everywhere. We have rivers and lakes, mountains and plains, forests and deserts.

The terrible Second World War brought citizens from various countries together. Soldiers and sailors married women from other lands. Inter-marriage has now become common. Communication methods have drawn us even closer. I watch live tennis matches from Australia, Germany, France, and England, and take it all for granted. We are beginning to see the human family as one great tribe, with a variety of colors, languages, and cultures. The United Nations was formed in 1945. The term 'united nations' was first used by President Roosevelt in 1942. Today 193 nations sit in its General Assembly.

From this idea of a united family of nations perhaps we can more readily comprehend the unity of all humankind as children of the Living God - whatever we choose to call the Author of life; our glorious Creator. What a vast imagination must be in the Mind of God. In this variety of people there is a common goal - it is peace on this planet. We can enjoy personal freedom, family groups, national pride, and international cohesiveness only when peace is the reigning factor.

When God created us He gave us free choice. History as written reveals a very slow progression from barbarianism, brutal monarchies and vicious wars to a desire for personal space, for universal respect and expression.

Science has opened to our awareness the functions and needs of our bodies. Plagues and epidemics are of the past. All this progress is by our efforts to learn and apply our findings. We could not do it without the help of a Higher Power, whether we acknowledge It or not. Much credit is given to our geniuses, but all discoveries originate in spirit. 'As above so below' is an axiom for all time. All inventions come from a holy place called Heaven; the same place from which we all come.

Heaven is our natural habitat. When we finally return Home, we shall find a peaceful place. Only in that heavenly realm is peace an eternal constant. There is no night there, no physical requirements of eating and drinking, no money, no status, and no 'jobs'. We can participate in any activity that appeals to us. Reading, studying, enjoying libraries and museums are just a few options. Scientists make discoveries there, but only when a human on earth is open to the new idea is that discovery 'found' on earth. River, lake, stream and mountain are there. Communication is mental. Transportation is unnecessary. Thinking of a different place takes us there instantly.

Many books have been written about the other side, Summerland, or beyond the veil. Heaven has many names such as these. A weather-free atmosphere awaits us. There is an absence of clocks! No time constrictions. It will be, in effect, a brand new way of 'life'. It is the spirit life, and everyone we knew on earth will be there. Family, friends, acquaintances, and pets await our joyous return. Previous 'enemies' will have forgiven us and themselves.

We will remember the place when we arrive; when God calls us Home again; where we belong, as His beloved children. There is nothing to fear, not even death. Especially not death, for Heaven affords a sanctuary where defense is unnecessary, allegiance simple, and citizenship a given for God's family - humans here; light beings there. Citizens of Heaven.

# Chapter 22   Commandments of Men

When Jesus the Christ visited the earth (1995-1999) and presented lessons in truth, one of his comments was, "I broke every rule. I listened only to my Father's Voice for direction." We need only read Exodus, in the Old Testament to know he broke the rules laid down by his predecessors: on the Sabbath day burn no fires, do no work, heal not, only rest and pray. He also knew that he would leave a New Testament to live by. The Jewish tradition and scripture is for Jews; the New Testament was left by Jesus as a new way to live, in a new age of humanity. Jesus came at the beginning of the Age of Pisces. The fish remains a symbol for Jesus' followers. Archangel Gabriel came to announce the New Age - the Age of Aquarius.

We still note our calendars based on the beginning of the Christian era. Jesus also said, in John 14:12, that everything he did we can do - and more, if we believe in him and follow righteousness. Perhaps he meant that we, too, should break every manmade rule and accomplish miracles and good works in our lives. This is not to say we should break the laws of men - for we cannot. The laws break us, if we let them. We are in charge of our lives. God gave us free choice to be in charge.

Paul advised the Colossians: *"If ye then be risen with Christ, seek those things which are above, where Christ sitteth on the right hand of God."* (3:1). What are the things that are above? Perhaps he meant the fruit of the spirit. Turning to Galatians 5:22 we find: *The fruit of the spirit is love, joy, peace, longsuffering, gentleness, goodness, faith, meekness, temperance: against such there is no law.* These are God's laws and there is no law against them.

We need not break a manmade law to enjoy the fruit of the spirit. They are available to all, without cost or permission. All these fruits were expressed by the great teacher, Jesus. Every one of them. When he said he broke every rule, he meant the Old Testament rules, written by men. Jesus healed on the Sabbath, taught on the Sabbath, told the people to rescue an animal from a pit on the Sabbath. He reminded us that the Sabbath was made for man; not man for the Sabbath. The children of God are greater than the Sabbath; it is a day of rest to reflect on life.

The prophets of old stemmed from the pagan beliefs in many gods. Moses believed in One God; Creator of us all. The Ten Commandments were 'cast in stone'. Jesus told us, at the end of the twentieth century, that such rigidity is contrary to the changing, growing, becoming stages of humankind; of all life. The doctrines of men must be replaced with the laws of God; the higher laws of spirit. Jesus knew what the people believed, and said, *But in vain do they worship me, teaching for doctrines the commandments of men.* (Matt.15:9)

Free choice allows us free thinking, free action. Psychologists tell us we use only ten percent of our brain's capacity. We have the capacity to seek and obtain all the fruit of the spirit. We lack the desire to achieve them. We choose instead the easier, softer way. Instead of love, we judge and hate; instead of joy we focus on tragedy; instead of peace we wage war; instead of patience we seek instant gratification. We turn from gentleness' option and choose instead violent action; instead of goodness we choose and brag about doing things that are not good. We know the difference. Instead of faith we listen to those who believe God is dead, or at least uncaring. Instead of meekness (humility) we are arrogant braggarts. Instead of temperance we eat and drink in excess.

We make these choices because we have freedom to do so! Where can we go to make a change for better - if we so desire? There is no 'place' we need go to. The location of decision making is within. Jesus gave us *A Course in Miracles* so that we might understand our true Self and learn how to attain the fruit of the spirit for self and others. The guidance for receiving the fruit of the spirit is within us all. Our Source, God, will provide every means and every person necessary for us to achieve the fruit of the spirit. The only choice required of us is to ask God, in private, in our heart of hearts. The answer is certain as the sunrise. *We ought to obey God rather than men.* (Acts 5:29)

# Chapter 23  Communication of Life

It was with great wonderment that I learned all life forms can communicate - not only each species with its own kind, but all species with other species! Recently we have heard about the 'horse whisperer' and the 'dog whisperer'. There are talented individuals who can understand what these animals are 'saying' to them. Many years ago a garden in Scotland was planted in sand - a type of soil unconducive to plant growth. But some talented persons could listen to the plant devas who gave instructions about planting times, kinds of fertilizer, and harvesting data. The garden was called Findhorn and the book describing it is available by that name. The astounding thing to me in reading *Findhorn* was the scope of knowledge and the worldly wisdom that the plant devas exhibited.

What difference does this make to humankind, when we have not as yet learned how to communicate with each other! If our communication skills were honed, would we have need of psychologists, psychiatrists or the plethora of prescription drugs flooding the commercial market? Is it possible that this one thing would 'lighten our load'; comfort our days and free us up to be more creative?

An ability to listen to our pets would negate a need for experts (veterinarians) to treat and medicate them. A couple years ago my cat, Kitters, stopped eating and drinking and using her litter box. I was very concerned. Believing as I do in spirit communication I called an animal communicator and asked her to tell me what was wrong with Kitters. Because I called in the evening, the medium said she would find out and call me the next day. In the morning she called and said this is what she got from my cat: "I have a blockage in my intestines, but I will get through this." And she did.  A day later she began her usual schedule of eating and drinking. Five years later I put 17 year old Kitters down. No, I sent her up, for one day on the other side we will re-unite.

At this writing I called the animal communicator again, since Emily was pooping outside the box and had diarrhea. The psychic said, "Emily's body is deteriorating and she knows it; no diet change will reverse it".

Emily was appreciative of my love, and said to the psychic: "tell her I appreciate all the love she gave me."

If we accept the idea of communication from the beasts of the field we might also accept them as having intelligence. As intelligent beings, they could convey to us that they dislike being caged, trained, abused, bred, slaughtered and eaten. I cry whenever I see young calves caged and chained to hinder movement more than six feet, so humans can have the 'delicacy' of veal. Laws are in place to deny photography in slaughter houses. A friend once told me she could not eat meat for a month after passing by an abattoir.

Archangel Gabriel did not tell us to refrain from eating flesh. He said if our bodies crave protein, we will eat flesh. He also told us that when animals are slaughtered they scream and their peers hear it. Death then comes in a state of terror and the vibration of terror remains in the flesh we ingest. He told us that when we first came to earth we were vegetarians. He said we were not meant to eat flesh. Then he said something which struck me profoundly: Humans do not have tearing teeth. Perhaps with this in mind we can understand the reasoning of vegetarians and vegans. When the Master Jesus walked the earth he did not eat meat; only fish. And toward the end of his life he refrained from eating fish, also.

In acceptance of communication from creatures to humans we can learn more about how animals can help us, willingly. The fish of the sea could impart secrets of the deep we cannot as yet access. The whale's song would be comprehensible to us. What, I wonder, could they tell us? Flying creatures could impart to us their information. This reminds me of what Gabriel said about birds. When they sing in the early morning it is for three reasons: to praise God's sunrise, to alert their neighbors that they are awake, and to aerate their feathers so they can fly.

How wonderful it would be if we understood the messages of birds, fish, frogs, snakes and other species. How magnificent would be our walk in the woods then.  What possible advantage would there be to inter-species communication? Birds could inform us of traffic jams on the road ahead and prevent us from sitting long hours on the highway, unable to move. Flying friends could inform us of pending tornado and hurricane directions. Actually, we can learn much now from them. Each kind of bird has its characteristic (see *Animalspeak by* Ted Andrews), and we can observe their flight pattern, direction of flight, etc., and glean guidance for our daily lives. Direct communication would increase that assistance.

My favorite example of birds' communication is their migratory behavior. Clouds of migrating birds swoop to and fro without any visible (to us) guidance. They never collide. That is communication at its finest. It is innate instinct that directs them. It would be grand indeed if we could learn their secrets from them. If whales and other sea creatures could tell us about impending storms as we cruise or sail the oceans many disasters could be avoided. With that kind of help, the Titanic would have averted destruction by avoiding the iceberg which caused its demise. The destruction by tsunamis could not be prevented because of their power, but many lives could be saved by evacuation. Some day we will make a scientific effort to decipher the messages creatures send each other. Then we will learn to communicate with them.

All Life breathes and has a consciousness and intelligence. Why then would communication not be possible? When will we allow our imagination to soar into the concept that *all life* is capable of 'speaking'? If the Findhorn devas can give us information about planting and harvesting times, then we can certainly accept that beasts can communicate with us, also. We know that gorillas can teach us, that our pets can save us from disasters, that dogs can learn to locate rubble-covered bodies and drugs. Dogs are carefully trained to guide the blind and be companions to those in need of help in daily living.

Exploring more possibilities is our responsibility. When we reach out to 'other' life we will increase the excitement and beauty of our own. Gabriel told us that all creatures become very still just prior to an earthquake. Unless we listen to them and become aware of the stillness we cannot receive the message. Gabriel explained to us that Jericho's walls collapsed because Joshua walked barefoot around the fortress; asked the angels to tell him when the earthquake would hit. He knew the ancient walls were beginning to weaken. The vibration of shouting and horns blowing brought down the walls. Mother Earth communicates in her own way. Mother Earth never surprises us. We must listen to her.


## Chapter 24   Communication: its pain and power

Communication is our method of exchanging information, educating, explaining, and learning. It can be verbal, visual or electronic. We exchange information, by sign language or even silently, by our body language. Here we discuss only verbal communication.

Most of us have engaged in fiery exchanges when angry. Even the most phlegmatic person can have such outbursts. The over-bearing person, the high-pressure salesperson, the domineering parent all use the power of the spoken word to intimidate, convince, or control another. It is assumed the other person will respond as planned, and often they do. The reasons why some people use verbal angry expressions are beyond this essay. It is the anger itself that we address here. Archangel Gabriel told us that if we could see our aura when we are angry we would never be angry again, for it is (my words) like daggers of fire bursting from us. We can use or misuse the power of the spoken word. Misusing the power always affects the angry person; often the target individual.

The point we miss is the fact that it is the person expressing in angry outbursts is hurting the self, more than the other individual. Regret often follows the angry spurts. 'If only we could take it back'; 'If only I had not said it'. But of course we cannot undo it. All we can do is apologize; make amends. This we should do or the guilt will smolder in us and provide the groundwork for the next outburst. When we 'justify' our anger we delude ourselves. Anger is never justified.

The reasons we need to review an angry 'habit' are few but serious. In the first place everyone on earth is our spiritual sibling. We are all children of the Living God. Secondly, we are responsible for our own God-given power, and the guilt that follows misuse of it. Regret will eat us up. We must forgive ourselves, forgive the one whom we perceived injured us, and decide to become more accepting of others. All this can be done when we honor ourselves and seek guidance from the Holy Spirit. We must consciously seek it. Thirdly, we probably get angry because we recognize an old habit we once exhibited but have since given up; now we are intolerant of that habit in others instead of understanding. The perceived injustice may be from our earlier years or even from a past incarnation.

The power of the spoken word has also been used for beneficial purposes, of course. The patient professor, the charismatic leader, the understanding teacher all use communication as a supportive expression as well as a guiding force for good. Most people can recall at least one person who acknowledged us as valid human beings. Perhaps there have been several such role models who inspired us.

The path to patience, when we quietly accept others instead of engaging in angry disputes, is a path of emotional maturation. We must take the first step - the step of decision. If we are in earnest, our angels will guide us by nudging our memory before we explode. They are always around, waiting our instruction - all 144,000 of them. We ought to use them, listen to them, and thank them. In doing so, we can find a life of acceptance, negotiation, resolution. These qualities then provide us with peace of mind and peace of soul.

Acceptance begins with forgiveness. Judging others is not an internal secret. Often our judgment is visible to the one we are judging or a third party who we know will join us in the judgment. A raised eyebrow, a rolling of the eyes and looks of disgust are visible. We want them to be seen. Is it to let others know we see ourselves as superior? The target of judgment feels the sting - from words, looks, or attitudes. The sting is often exacerbated by the target's acceptance of the idea they are truly 'less than'. No one is less than anyone else.

Good communication is a skill worth attaining. It requires honesty, sincerity, and a belief in equality of all people. Poor communication hurts. An unwillingness to communicate at all (the silent treatment) hurts the most, because the door to communication is slammed shut and makes any kind of understanding is impossible.

As counselors have taught us, the best method of communicating is for us, the listeners, to re-state the speaker's words *as we understand them*. This is the point of mutual comprehension. This is the point of mutual understanding. This is the point of good and powerful communication.

# Section IV
## Daleth

## Chapter 25   Cost of a Secret

*"Then assembled together the chief priests, and the scribes, and the elders of the people, unto the palace of the high priest, who was called Caiaphas. And consulted that they might take Jesus by subtilty, and kill him. " Matt.* 26:3-4

The chief priests of Jesus' time were jealous of Jesus because he could perform miracles and they could not. So they decided to get rid of him. The scribes and elders concurred. Judas was offered thirty pieces of silver to tell the priests where they could find Jesus. In today's market the value of thirty American Eagles are worth approximately $630.00.

We are blessed to now know the truth about Judas Iscariot. Archangel Gabriel explained that Judas was what we call today a 'hitman', hired to kill someone. People of Jesus' time never travelled without protection since the countryside was full of men waiting for passing travelers to rob them; there were no laws then. So Jesus hired Judas to protect him and his followers - his apostles, friends, and the many spiritual women (not disclosed in the Bible). As Jesus preached, Judas was nearby for protection and could not help overhearing Jesus' lessons. Over time Judas came to love the man Jesus. He also accepted his teachings.

Before Judas betrayed Jesus, Jesus went to Judas and told him that he would betray him. Judas protested loudly and said he could not; would not do it. Jesus reminded Judas that before birth he had agreed to do it. Still Judas protested. Jesus explained the importance of Judas' betrayal. It was planned in order for Jesus to complete his life plan. Jesus said to Judas, "If you love me, you will do this." And Judas relented.

What Judas thought he was doing was inform the priests where Jesus was so they could talk to him, but when they seized Jesus he realized he had been used by them.  In his fury, he returned to the palace and threw down the thirty pieces of silver. Scripture tells us that Judas hung himself. He did not. Because he had been a hitman in the past he had many enemies. When he was in a state of grieving for his friend Jesus and feeling guilty for the betrayal, he was not vigilant for his safety. In that vulnerable state of mind he was found by an old an enemy who killed him and threw him off a cliff. When Judas passed into spirit he saw Jesus and ran from him, in his continuing guilt. But Jesus reached out with his magnificent aura and pulled Judas back to him. He held him close in brotherly love until Judas understood, and his guilt melted away.

From a metaphysical viewpoint, Judas represents the unredeemed life forces (MBD, 375). As custodian of the money for Jesus' band, Judas signifies the material, and Judas was greedy to add to the coffer. To redeem the Judas faculty we must become fearless in affirming our unity with the spirit of purity. We have a higher vision of life but still do underhanded things. We call it 'human nature'. Now we must go within, to our spiritual nature, and listen to the Holy Spirit direct us.

We must ask for help from the Holy Spirit. God is a triune God: Father, Son, and Holy Spirit. The Father is the Creator. Today we hear clergy say 'Mother-Father God.' This is not disrespectful. The two energies of all creation are the active and sustaining energies. Humans choose to call them male and female. To create, the two energies work together to produce planets, rabbits, roses, etc. The Son is Christ Love; agape love. The Holy Spirit is the transforming energy of God. In order for us to turn our lives around and follow a spiritual path we need the Holy Spirit's guidance. Keeping our divine nature a secret - to self and others - costs us only awareness of our truth. We have to consciously seek and ask the Holy Spirit for guidance. He does not come to our aid until asked.

All we need to do is ask, then listen, then do. *"Settle it therefore in your hearts, not to meditate before what ye shall answer: For I will give you a mouth and wisdom, which all of your adversaries shall not be able to gainsay nor resist."* Luke 21: 14-15

# Chapter 26   Creation and Existence

Creation: "the act of bringing the world into ordered existence. . . WORLD." (Webster's Collegiate 11ᵗʰ ed.).  When Archangel Gabriel came to Earth to visit and to teach us the wisdom of the ages, from 1987 to 1999, he told us that as children of God and co-creators with Him we created the Earth on which to reside while in physical form.

Existence means reality as presented by experience. We all have experiences. Life itself consists of experiences. Many people live their entire lives reacting to experiences which seem to come at them from nowhere. Such a reactive life reveals a belief in a world of chaos - driven by 'fate'.  Because we see 'accidents' every day we find it easy to believe in life on Earth as a chaotic existence. Far above this world of chaos we perceive there is a world of spirit. Into space we have sped and beheld our planet Earth from afar. 'Earth-rise' came into our vocabulary. There is ordered existence in the world of outer space, where millions of stars and planets exist in harmony.

Astronomers through the ages have been able to see, with powerful telescopes, more and more of the heaven's structures. We wonder if there is life there. Now we know there is. Space travelers have been seen here numerous times. Gabriel explained that they come and watch us bury the dead and wonder why we are so wasteful. They wonder why we don't ascend, like they do. They cannot understand we have not learned how, as yet. It was discomfiting to hear Gabriel say that this is the only planet which still practices disease and death.

Many people exist, and many others ask questions about life. It was a dedicated channel and a group of truth seekers which drew Gabriel to upstate New York, and he found us eager to learn. He always took questions about the vast range of topics he taught. Simultaneously eleven Master Teachers came to light centers around the world. Gabriel and the eleven all brought the same message, which in effect was: 'Wake up, children of God. Acknowledge and live life as your sacred selves. You are holy and powerful; you never left God; He loves you eternally. You are strangers here on Earth. Come Home to God, your Source'.

As this Age of Truth - Aquarius - dawns on humankind, it is fitting that God send His messenger of truth, the Announcer of the Ages, to inform us of our true essence. This blessed generation is on the cusp of the New Age. *The Revelation of John,* in the New Testament, describes a New Heaven and a New Earth. The book must be read as symbolic of humankind's journey back home to God. It is not a description of Armageddon. Read or hear Gabriel's explanation of *Revelation.* See Discography.

Some of us cannot look at the heavens on a starry night and deny the existence of a power great enough to create what we behold. The scientists explain the rotation of the Earth on its axis and its revolution around the sun. We live in the suburbs of the Milky Way, one of the many galaxies in the universe we know. Gabriel said there are many other universes, also. Creation is what we are part of. God knows that we think we left Him, and He knows we cannot. The clay cannot leave the ceramic pot without destroying it. We cannot exist without God's imprint.

We are co-creators with God, but through the centuries we have convinced ourselves that we are 'mere mortals', victims of fate, political rulers, our neighbors, and strangers. Inside each of us, unseen by surgeons, is a spark of divinity. It is the sacred space of our spirit Self, seen only by God. He beckons us to return. He does this by urging us to pray, to meditate, to attend a house of worship, to help a neighbor in need, to help a stranger in distress. He speaks to us constantly- His is the inner urge to walk a chosen path of love, peace, harmony, and joy.

Choices are our constant option. But consciously stepping on a path of spiritual growth, we find there is no choice. Only good beckons us; only love expresses through us; only peace finds a place within us.


## Chapter 27   Defenselessness

We are accustomed to the word defense because it is used in many ways in our society. Sports teams have positions called defense. The martial arts are all about defense. Nations believe they need to defend themselves, so they establish armies and armaments to do so. Homeowners believe they need to defend their property and their lives against potential intruders. Automobiles have alarm systems that sound if a person comes too close. Where does this idea of the need to defend ourselves come from? It surely is not new. We established the U.S. as an independent republic of the people, for the people and by the people. President FDR said, "We have nothing to fear but fear itself." Fear itself engenders wounds, pain and suffering.

We have established a strong military defense system to protect these freedoms. All countries have established their own military defense. How then, can one accept the idea of being defenseless? On a personal level we need to consider this concept. We need not protect ourselves, because we are children of God and we ought to realize that God protects us throughout our lives. We feel especially vulnerable when we are small, when we are young, when we are unarmed, when we are wounded, when we are old. We think that all danger is from outside of us.

Because we are unaware of our divinity as children of God, we see ourselves as a body. This body seems vulnerable indeed. The truth of us is that we are holy and need no defense. This truth from Gabriel staggers our imagination. We cannot conceive of such a life as that. Certainly a new freedom would be ours. We could walk anywhere, anytime, knowing that God is with us protecting us in His love, His eternal love for us. This kind of freedom is beyond our imagination, because we have been fearful for so long. Fear and love cannot sleep in the same bed. There is no magic wand that we can wave to dispel all this fear. There is only one antidote to fear, and that is love.

Some people believe that we should fear God. Others believe that God is love. It is one thing to believe that God is love, but it is another to *know* that God is love. To know that God is love takes practice. It takes practice to undo all the centuries of belief that we are separate from God. When we pray our eyes always look up even if they are closed because we believe that that is where God is. We see ourselves as a frail small limited body. We do not see ourselves as a spirit which is love, which is eternal, which is how God created us.

Now is the time we need to begin to practice. If not now when; if not us what generation? We can begin to practice now, and begin to raise our children as children of God. We can say to them (when they are beleaguered), 'Go within and ask your Guardian Angel to help you'. We can teach them to be fearless, faith-filled and unneedfull of defenses. This sounds like a huge, impossible task. It is huge, but it is possible. Listening to the Master Jesus.; listening to Archangel Gabriel will show us the way, the truth, and the life.

 Gabriel came for 12 years (1987-1999) to teach us; Jesus the Christ came for four years (1995-1999) to teach us. What better teachers are there than these? Also, Gabriel told us that eleven Master Teachers came to various places on Earth at the same time that he did. The message was the same for all humanity: for all countries, all cultures, all races, all languages, everywhere on the planet. Everything Gabriel said and everything the Master Jesus said in those years is available in print and/or recordings. Kindly refer to sacredgardenfellowship.org. Jesus himself said, listen to Gabriel; he's a good teacher. The one message brought by these spiritual entities, to all earthlings, in effect, was: Wake up, children of God, and learn to live from the Lord God of your Being.

 If we begin now it may take several generations for everyone to believe in defenselessness. But it will come because it is the truth, we know truth now, for Gabriel taught us truth - or, as he said, he would not have come to earth. Asking angels to protect us, expecting and accepting their protection, we are all protected.


## Chapter 28  Discarding Hell

Archangel Gabriel explained that originally the word 'hell' meant a shallow grave. A grave that beasts could dig up and devour was considered the worst possible event after death. Various mythologies refer to hel, hades, Duat, underworld, and 'lowest of three worlds'. (*Mythology*)

Since the earliest known civilization humanity has believed in, named, and described a place where the 'dead' reside and 'bad' people enter when they 'die'. It is appropriate to use quotation marks because there is no death as we perceive it (life is eternal, as demonstrated by Jesus the Christ). We who consider ourselves 'living' are the dead ones. This is true because we are dead to our Origin and our Essence. Our Origin is God (we are made in His Image). God is Love. A creator imbues in the created a part of himself; therefore we are love, also. Love is our essence.

For those of us who believe in a God of love, we also believe that He is everywhere present and all-powerful. What is omnipresent can have no opposite. The realm of God is the realm of spirit. The spirit world was created by God first. We are His spirit offspring. The spirit world of God is eternal, is love, and is perfect. We all resided in that beautiful spirit world until one day we thought we could create something else. We created form and happily reside in human form, unaware of our original aspect, spirit and unaware of our Originator, God. The problem is that we cannot see the spirit of us with our physical eyes. *But the natural man receiveth not the things of the Spirit of God: for they are foolishness unto him: neither can he know them, because they are spiritually discerned.* I Cor. 2:14

The finite world experiences life and death and we have come to accept these two experiences as the whole of our existence. Paul. In 2 Cor. 4:11 provides us with clarification: *For we which live are always delivered unto death for Jesus' sake, that the life also of Jesus might be made manifest in our mortal flesh.* The mortal man Jesus could not be made manifest in our mortal flesh, but the spirit of Christ within Jesus could be made manifest in our mortal flesh. There is a difference between Jesus the man and the Christ light within him. In all God's beloved children there is this same Christ light, which we cannot see with mortal eyes. Jesus reminded us that the Kingdom of God is within us. Gabriel told us that every cell of our body contains a nucleus of spirit!

In addition to this structural definition, we have a persistent wish to relegate someone we hate to a place of eternal suffering. This wish also contradicts the Will of a loving God. Jesus told us to forgive seventy times seven. Are we to keep a tally on the times we forgive, or did he mean without limit? Forgiveness does not come easily to us. The more heinous the crime the quicker we are to condemn and even pray the perpetrator will 'go to hell'.

Gabriel reminded us he has been around forever and he never has seen a place called 'hell' or an entity named 'the devil'. Humans made them up to punish those we judge and condemn. Condemnation follows judgement; the Bible exhorts 'Judge not' (Matt. 7:1; also found in Luke and John). When it comes to our children we see them as the lovely ones we birthed. We do not always like the things they do, but we never wish them to go to 'hell'.

God loves us as His created children. It is unlikely that He condones all our negative behavior, from lying to murdering. He loves us because He knows us and knows what we are: made in His Image; love; eternal; perfect. To surrender our belief in a hell may take several more centuries. The first step in our surrender will be when we first hear or read the concept which sounds so incredibly impossible. Our ego will call to mind all the wounds we perceive have been inflicted on us in this lifetime. Our ego has all the power we once had but we gave it over. The ego's favorite weapon is fear. It will tell us we should condemn our 'enemies' to hell lest they hurt us again.

The spirit Self of us knows better. We know, at our spirit level, that we are God's Own. We, like the Prodigal Son, think we left God and He will never take us back. There is no 'never'; we cannot leave God; and *in us* is the option to return Home.

# Chapter 29   Earth's Last Day

Archangel Gabriel explained that the end of the planet Earth will come someday. It will not end in violence and destruction. It will end in peace. We will love it until it becomes the peaceful planet it once was. In its beginning it was verdant and lovely, unoccupied by beast or human. It was created in love and shall end in love. It will end when we no longer have a need of it for our temporary lives; for our physical forms. Heaven is our natural habitat and to It we shall return. As co-creators with God we created this lovely planet which has revolved on its axis for millennia. It has circled the sun for century upon century. And all the while, aware of its rotation and circling or not, we have been busy on it. Millions of years we have evolved - not from plants and creatures - but from a rudimentary body we created. We created the forms (bodies) to house our spirit, and we knew it.

Over time we forgot our spirit, our origin, our God-created Selves and believed our physical form and this physical place was all that was. How wrong we have been. Throughout all time here we have employed our God-given imagination. We have used our imagination to create lovely works of art and terrible works of war. We received from our Creator inspiring words of wisdom which have comforted us through pain and suffering. How real the pain and suffering was. Now we understand how unnecessary it was.

Forgetful of our origin, we lost awareness of our ability to rise above the pain and suffering. Then, after millions of years, one day a man named Jesus came to remind us of our divinity. He saw us as his brothers and sisters. We *are* his brothers and sisters. He came to save humanity from its dark and false belief it was only human. Because he performed miracles - to demonstrate what we too can do - we placed him on a pedestal and proclaimed an untruth: that he was the only son of God.

Gabriel clarified the Bible phrase that says Jesus was the only begotten son of God. The original words were: Jesus was the begotten son of the only God. And we are, too. Jesus came to save humanity because he knew we had come to believe in form as our only 'life'. He knew he was divine and did not understand why we failed to accept our divinity. His intent was to save humanity; all humanity, not just his countrymen. Only hanging on the cross at Calvary did he realize he had only saved himself. He was a brilliant light as he looked over the crowd there. The light surrounding him could not be seen by the human family on the hill. Only spiritual eyes see spirit. Some of the spectators were full of hate; some joyous at this suffering; some crushed with grief that this man of peace was dying.

The Prince of Peace did not suffer on the cross. He had the capacity to focus his consciousness on his Higher Self, and rise above the pain. We have the same ability but have *forgotten how to use it*. He knew that the portal we call death was one that he would walk through and then come out the other side as a living, thriving, holy child of God. He knew it would take three days in the tomb for him to de-moleculareize his body and appear in form to his followers.

He said many times that we should follow him. He came as a way-shower; an example. He even told us that his every act we too could perform. (John 14:12) He said he would not leave us comfortless; that he would send a Comforter. The name of the Comforter is The Holy Spirit, or Holy Ghost. We have all felt the Comforter in times of distress. It was the Comforter's assistance that beckons us to a better life; an honest life; a loving life. Some of us have seen the Master Jesus himself in form. Others have received messages from him through a blessed channel.

For five sweet years Jesus the Christ came to Earth (1995-1999) to remind us of who we truly are; to clarify some Bible passages; to tell us of the words that were purged from original manuscripts; to assure us that we are all on our way Home to God. This story of the Earth's end is a paraphrased version of the truth Gabriel told us. When we no longer need this planet for a temporary residence we shall go Home to stay.

# Chapter 30 Easter

*This essay is based on "The Easter Story" presented by Archangel Gabriel on April 11, 1993. See Bibliography.*

Some call Easter Resurrection Day, for Jesus, in rising from the 'dead' demonstrated that life is eternal. Why did Jesus do this? What are we resurrected *from?* When God first breathed us forth into life we - humankind - were and are forever Divine Essence. We dwelt in perfect love and loved each other. God commanded the angels of Heaven to protect and serve humankind. Then we began to create wonderful adventures, and in so doing we decided we did not need each other or any angels to help us. We perceived our spiritual siblings as 'enemies' and believed our survival required us to slay or be slain. Wars ensued; and it was also a war of the self of us against our own divinity. Some spirit entities that knew and remembered their Source, came to teach us. We listened for a short time but did not fully grasp their message. We eventually killed all the prophets who came to help us. And so it was necessary for one to come to show us the way home. We also slew him. His name was Jesus; his Light was the Christ Light.

We understood new beginnings, and Earth demonstrated newness with the season called spring. We celebrated spring with pagan rituals. So a man named Jesus came to Earth to show us the light. He had to live among us, and see all our error perceptions of limitation and fear so he could know the depth of our plight, and then reveal to us how we can return to the light by using his example.

He took it upon himself this short but difficult lifetime, for he knew that he was a child of God. He knew that we too are children of God, but we had forgotten that truth. So he came to show us that what he did, we could also do. Jesus did not come to start a new religion, and he did not die for our sins; early church fathers imposed these ideas on us. We messed up his true intent, but truth will out. In order to get peoples' attention he had to die a remarkable death, for passing quietly would have gone unnoticed by the multitude.

Our scriptures do not include the many countries Jesus visited, including India, Tibet, and even North America. Indigenous people here wrote of him. He traveled to teach and learn. He learned how to change the molecular structure of his physical body, which he used later. He learned how to lift his body into the light - the light which is also in our physical form. He learned how to bring back light into its fullness, so the body could be brought up away from its heaviness and into light and truth. We are spirit, dwelling in a physical form, trapped in a three-dimensional world. We lay down our bodies in what we perceive as death, and return again and again to Earth. There had to be something to teach us that we could return home at any time, with our bodies. Thus Jesus planned the crucifixion and the resurrection.

Jesus practiced changing the molecular structure of his body. It was in these practice sessions that he walked on water, and appeared to those many miles away from where his physical body was. He practiced because he knew at Calvary he would have to overcome a great deal of stress as well as overcome the ethers around him, which were full of hate and fear. He also had to overcome the limitations of the physical form. In the Garden of Gethsemane he knew he had sufficient Christ Light in him no matter what they did, so he could not be pulled into the physical form and be trapped there - or his life would have been for nothing. He had only a short period of time to rise above the physical entrapment. He knew he would leave the garden at Gethsemane as a prisoner.

He went to the apostles and asked them to join him in prayer, but failing to understand, they fell asleep. A great fear came to Jesus, knowing what lay ahead for him. Contrary to Scripture, he went back to the disciples to tell them he wanted to leave the garden, but he found them asleep. As he looked at his sleeping, dedicated followers, he was reminded that all of humankind was asleep to the Christ, to the God, to the life, that was within them. He was reminded why he came, so he went back into the garden. He lifted himself up out of the consciousness of Jesus the man, into the consciousness of the Christ, the son of God. He said, "Thy will, not mine, be done!" He then had the power and strength to go forth and do what he had to. He knew that in a little while he would be free forever from the Earth.

He was centered in the light; the Christ within him, from 9a.m. until 3p.m. At that time he knew the body could no longer bear the stress, and he said, *"It is finished."* (John 19:30) He then entered into the Astral Plane, which consists of a strange mixture of light and darkness, truth and error, reality and shadow. He taught those residents how to free themselves from their entrapment on the Astral Pane. Meanwhile his body was put into the borrowed tomb. It was 'borrowed', but it had been supplied with all the necessary things for him to lift his body into the light, transform its molecular structure and bring it forth resurrected.

From birth Jesus was an Essene, as was his family. His mother, Mary was taught by the Essenes how to treat one who was to ascend (resurrect). During the three days of entombment Jesus' body was treated by angels and helpers. His etheric body, his astral body, and his mental body were all treated by helpers from each of those planes. Thus all the layers of life - what we term God - could be made manifest in the physical form. The tomb was sealed on authority of Pilate, who was also an Essene, unbeknownst to the Romans. He knew the part he was to play. The soldiers chosen were the most fearful; cowards even. Spirit soldiers of the White Brotherhood [do not take this as a racial title] marched up and down, scaring the soldiers. Someone had to break the seal, but the person would be killed. So Archangel Michael offered, "I shall be glad to break the seal!" And he did. The frightened soldiers agreed on what story to tell, unwilling to admit cowardice and sure death by Rome.

The first to greet Jesus was his mother. They had a strong bond; she always knew his mission. She told Mary Magdalene and Judith, who were with her. Mary Magdalene ran back to tell Peter and John. When they ran back to the tomb, Peter went in to see, but John knew what Jesus had done. What Jesus did in resurrecting was to show humanity what we can and must do, to free ourselves from this shadow existence on earth. We have poured our limitless Self into human form and accepted a victim role.

God is love, and it would be impossible for God to ever inflict pain on any living thing. The God in us is pure love, unspeakable joy! Forever! Jesus never sought worship; he came as an example. He came to demonstrate that we can lift ourselves out of the limitations we have created, and into the freedom that we already are. That was his mission. That was the whole purpose behind it and nothing more. He came to love us past our mistakes. He turned around, and he walked back, and he said, "Here, let me take your hand. Let me show you how. This is what you do." And he literally did it. That is the meaning of Easter.

## Chapter 31   Emissaries of Light

At one of Archangel Gabriel's visitations (1987-1999) he was asked if Jesus would be coming again. And his answer was that Jesus would not come again because if he did he would only be killed again. This was a puzzling comment. Thinking about why he was crucified it became clear to me that he was teaching the opposite of what people then believed: fear, judgment, prejudice, hatred, and revenge. Is our present world all that different? If Jesus came in flesh he would teach the same lessons he taught then: love, forgiveness, peace and joy. Who would believe him this time?

He would say this is the beginning of a New Age, and the Christian religionists would quickly rage against him because they think the term New Age is anathema. Many Christians today disbelieve that it is possible for humans to communicate with the spirit world of God. Jesus came teaching and living his gentle precepts at the beginning of a new age then; the Age of Pisces. A fish sign still denotes Jesus.

Jesus also performed many miracles. He did this not to astonish us, but to demonstrate to us that everything he did we also can do (John 14:12). We turned our back on his teachings and focused on the miracles, placing him on a pedestal to worship, but never emulate. This action exonerated us because of course the *only* Son of God cannot be emulated. Unfortunately the Bible erroneously states Jesus was the only son of God. Gabriel explained that the original wording was 'Jesus Christ, begotten son of the only God.' Gabriel also told us that *all humanity* is 'the only begotten Son of God.'

In truth Jesus has come to Earth (1995-1999) to teach us the same lessons he taught then - to love and forgive; seek peace and know joy. He spoke to us through a dedicated, spiritually evolved woman of the cloth. He said all references to reincarnation were purged from early scripture, as were all references to the many women who followed Jesus. Gabriel told us that Jesus was married secretly because he knew his destiny and did not want Mary killed too. The custom then was to have a wedding feast and weeks or months later the wedding ceremony took place. The wedding feast in Cana when he turned water into wine (his first miracle) was for his own wedding. What do we do with all this truth imparted to us by Gabriel and Jesus? Do we fashion it into something else and renounce it, as we did the ancient prophets? Gabriel said that God sent us prophets and we killed them all. Then, the greatest one, Jesus, we killed also.

Because this ageless wisdom comes from spirit entities we cannot kill them, even if we wanted to. Many will deny and argue that this is not truth; that Gabriel came only 2,000 years ago; that spirit entities do not come to Earth any more, etc. Archangel Gabriel is the Announcer of the Ages. This is the beginning of the Age of Aquarius - the Truth Age, Gabriel said.

When our small, blessed group sat at Gabriel's feet we knew in our hearts that he was telling the truth. He exuded a loving atmosphere; expressed compassion; answered all our questions. Permeating peace prevailed. Gabriel closed every lesson with an exquisite prayer to the Father. He told us he would come for twelve years and he did. On December 2, 1999 he gave his farewell message. But all his lessons were about waking us up to our own divinity. He told us nothing new, he said. He only reminded us of what we have forgotten: that we are God's children.

We have brought our consciousness down away from God so far that we believe He will never take us back. Adam fell asleep in Eden and Gabriel reminded us that nowhere in the Bible does it say that Adam woke up. We are the sleeping ones and it is way past time to awaken and live from the Lord God of our Being, as Gabriel put it. When we accept the truth of us, the truth of God's love for us, the possibility of communication between earthlings and spirit, then we will be on our way to a world of peace. We will make it happen, as children of God. We will understand we need no middle-man between us and God. Direct communication from God is possible. If we think it is not, how many times have we received a telephone call from a friend we had just been thinking of? How many times did we have a close-call driving? How many times did we review our life and realize our heart said one thing and our head another? We were conflicted because we did not listen only to God's Voice. We are light beings; we are God's offspring; we are eternal.

Soon we will raise our children to know they are children of God and they should always listen to the Voice for God which directs them constantly if It is sought. Prayer and meditation will become an essential part of daily life. Acceptance of all people everywhere will prevail. Acknowledging the brotherhood of humankind will be a given, and a loving God will direct our every path because He loves us, and because He wants us to return Home to Heaven, our natural habitat. Then we will no longer be in need of emissaries of light.

## Chapter 32   Fear of Love

It is often said that if we are hurt when a romantic love relationship ends we tend to be fearful of another love experience lest we will be hurt again. Perhaps the memory extends much further back. Possibly our soul still contains old memories of failed loves. Is there something else that we fear? Are we afraid that if we reveal our affections we are vulnerable? To reveal our affections means that we show a 'soft side' of us, and in that softness we do not have our defenses up, against possible hurt by others. What are we so fearful of? Interestingly enough in our youth we continue to have that innocence of babyhood, and babies are always loving; never defensive. That explains the plunge we take as we 'fall in love' the first time. It is called 'puppy love' - maybe because puppies are not defensive, either.

The fear of being hurt again is indicative of basing our current behavior on past experience. Humanity seems to be convinced of this criterion. What is so glorious about the past that we choose to base our decisions on it? How wonderful it would be if subsequent times we 'fell in love' were as thrilling as the first time! All feelings of love are not romantic. We love our parents; our children; our friends. The great misfortune of our lives is that we experience different 'kinds' of love. Our love of immediate family is not the same as our love of 'extended' family. We love friends one way and family another. If we belong to a group of like-minded people, such as a writers' group, a knitting group or a book club, we come to love those folk in a different way from family.

When the Master Jesus walked the Earth his life was a constant expression of love. He loved children; he loved women - not as potential lovers, but as humans equal to men. Archangel Gabriel told us that all references to the many women who followed Jesus were purged from early scripture texts. He also said that Jesus would, before speaking to a group, invite the women to move from their 'accepted' place in the back to sit in front of him. Of course that disturbed the men in the crowd. But Jesus did not follow the 'acceptable' mores of his society.

Jesus the Christ came to show us a better way to live. He was not understood because he was different. The rabbis did not like him because, unlike him, they could not perform miracles. The Romans in power did not like him because he spoke of another 'kingdom' which they feared would displace them. The Pharisees did not like him, for they believed that only the Pharisees could do the work of the Lord. The Sadducees did not like him because they did not believe in the immortality of the soul (implied by Jesus' phrase "the Kingdom of God is within."), or the resurrection. The Bible tells us of Lazarus' resurrection. Even some of those Jesus healed did not like him. Not because they were healed but because they did not all *remain* healed.

A healing is forever unless the healed person insists on recalling the ailment prior to the healing. This was true in Jesus' time and is true now. When a person constantly tells others of 'how sick they were' the malady returns. At one time Gabriel said that love and healing are the same. In *A Course in Miracles* we find this remarkable statement: *"All healing is essentially the release from fear."* T - 2: IV: 1:7 surely love releases us from fear, also.

Can we then extrapolate that all love is essentially the release from fear? Only when we recall Gabriel's words that love and healing are the same. Only when we can accept unconditional love, for agape love has no conditions. For all our believing in many emotions, Gabriel told us there are basically only two: love and fear, and all our fears go back to the first fear - that we left God and he will never take us back. Of course we cannot and did not 'leave' God. So our fears can be dealt with. They must be dealt with if we are to experience unconditional love. Since God is our Creator, and God is Love, we are imbued with His Essence. We are love, loved and loveable. Connecting to our Source we can; must learn and live a life of unconditional love.

The way to accomplish such a life lies in our ability to accept others just the way they are, without judging them. The way to accomplish a life of unconditional love is to know that everything is just the way it is supposed to be. We may not like the way things are, so we can act in such a way as to change them. Everyone has free choice. The world today is the result of everyone making their personal choices, through history. We often say 'why does God allow such things on Earth?' We might rather ask ourselves why we chose the options we did to bring into existence such a world. After giving us free choice, God held to His decision and therefore cannot abrogate our choices.

# Section V
## He

## Chapter 33   Finding Common Ground

War will become obsolete when we have perfected the art of negotiation. Until then we will continue to see each other as different; agreement as impossible. We humans distinguish each other by language, nation, and religion. On a smaller scale we huddle in groups defined as clubs, neighborhood, organizations and villages. In ancient times tribes sought to keep their heritage pure by marrying within the tribe. We know now that such inter-marriage led to mental and physical abnormalities.

In modern times, WWII engulfed humanity in an incredibly destructive war. Death, mutilation and wounded veterans were the result - not to mention thousands more with lingering mental issues. But wars did not end. Recently sanctions became an option to warfare, but still some factions of humanity pursue the wasteful, destructive option of violent confrontation. WWII also resulted in military personnel meeting and marrying those of other nations; other languages. The world became smaller. Communication technology has shrunk the world even more.

Negotiation of differences is possible; reconciliation of differences can be accomplished. Perhaps negotiation will become possible only when we see ourselves as sharing the same characteristics of humanity. We are one race of humans. We are either children of a Creator, with innate compassion, or simply physical forms living out a brief existence without purpose or reason. Faith alone will allow us to accept humanity as having some basic traits across all physical boundaries and language barriers.

For instance, is there a French smile, a German laugh? Do salt-water tears flow only from American eyes? Love extends beyond national borders, overcomes language differences, for it is universal. So is laughter, music, joy. We all bleed red blood. Royalty is becoming a thing of the past. 'Common' people now become leaders. In the United States a haberdasher and a peanut farmer became presidents. 'Common' people are inventing uncommon things. Abraham Lincoln said, "God must have loved common people because he made so many of them." He apparently saw himself as a leader of men. There will always be leaders and followers, but that does not negate the oneness of humanity.

If we take the word 'common' to be ordinary, routine, lacking privilege or status, then we would deny our holiness. 'Ground' as a synonym for dirt is common indeed, yet without soil we would not survive on this planet Earth. One commonality we share is compassion. When someone is lost at sea our hearts go out to the loved ones in their grief. When floods and forest fires rage, we run to help, or send money, or gather in prayer. We would mot care unless we felt a relationship.

Humanity is growing, slowly but surely. We do not keel-haul or rack our enemies any longer. As a human family we disbelieve in slavery now. More people disdain execution of prisoners. One by one, nations are allowing freedom for their people. NATO and other allegiances are being formed; treaties signed. Although the League of Nations did not survive, the United Nations is alive and well. It exists because leaders realize governments can cooperate. If the national governments can unite and individual members can form relationships, how long can it be before we acknowledge that we all are one family of God? Ecumenical councils are making an effort to cross religious boundaries and find common ground. Some churches are losing members - not because we are becoming less spiritual - but because the churches are choosing to remain exclusive. The oneness of humanity is demanding inclusiveness.

Racial barriers have begun to fall; people who fall in love with those of the same sex are seen by some as deserving of recognition, marriage, and parenting. Judging others as 'different' denies our common human features. It also denies us peace of mind. Hands folded in prayer signify universally a posture of holy worship. It does not matter what name a person uses for God. The major religions of the world share the same basic principles: The Golden Rule, Honor thy father and mother, Love thy neighbor. We are one; we are sacred children of One God. *Oneness,* by Moses, reflects more shared principles.

In Exodus 3:5 (GNT) God said to Moses, at the burning bush, *"Do not come any closer. Take off your sandals, because you are standing on holy ground."* Our feet represent understanding, so when we 'take off our shoes' (stop denying truth) we can understand the truth, and the truth will make us free. And the truth is we are one human family which has its Source in God.

## Chapter 34   Flesh and Spirit

*"For the flesh lusteth against the spirit, and the spirit against the flesh: and these are contrary the one to the other; so ye cannot do the things that ye would."* Gal. 5:17

There is a tendency to believe that flesh and spirit are separate in every way; that it is impossible to accept them together for any reason. God is a Spirit and the Author of all life. We perceive ourselves as physical beings only. Without spirit we would not exist; we could not exist. We are not human beings becoming spiritual; we are spiritual beings living out a brief life, temporarily, in a physical body. Most people cannot see spirit, but we perceive the expression of spirit in love, joy, peace harmony; all sourced in spirit.

Paul's persistent and unsolvable problem is accepting himself as he is. He perceives no kind of cooperation between flesh and spirit.  He mentions his problem obliquely in II Cor. 12:7-8: *"And lest I should be exalted  above measure through the abundance of the revelations, there was given to me a thorn in the flesh, the messenger of Satan to buffet me, lest I should be exalted  above measure. For this thing I besought the Lord thrice, that it might depart from me."*

Paul could not understand his problem, nor could he understand why God did not take away the affliction satan gave him. Gabriel has now told us satan does not exist, but Paul and his peers believed he did. Apparently Paul believed that he could/would be 'exalted above measure' if only he did not have the 'thorn in his flesh'.  He clearly saw an eternal schism between the flesh and the spirit. At one time when Archangel Gabriel was answering questions about scripture, I went to the microphone and asked Gabriel what the thorn was in Paul's side. To our utter amazement he answered that Paul was ". . . what you call gay; but I don't know why you use the term, because they usually are not happy."

St. Paul's name was originally Saul, but after he was struck blind his vision was restored and his name became Paul. He had been converted to Christianity. Metaphysically Saul means will, and Saul's strong personal will turned into Paul ('little') as subservient to God's Will, and a convert to Christianity. We could argue day and night about why Paul chose to come to earth as a gay man. Only God and Paul's Higher Self know. Gabriel was asked one time why some people are gay. He explained there are two reasons. One reason: when a person has several lifetimes as one sex and then decides to experience life on earth as the opposite sex, it is essential to take the required time to align their energy to the energy of the new sex. If they impatiently birth without taking time, there is a conflict about their sex that lasts a lifetime.

The other reason: When a person lives a life of hating homosexual people (homophobia) they realize, upon reaching Heaven and reviewing their life, that in order to learn a lesson of acceptance and love, they should return to earth as a homosexual individual. The Ten Commandments of Moses do not mention homosexuality. Humankind has consisted of straight and gay people since time began. Gabriel said everyone living has already been saint, murderer, and homosexual through our many incarnations. At the time Paul was preaching and writing about Christianity, it was punishable by death to be gay. For two thousand more years homosexuals would be ridiculed, laughed at or put to death because of their inborn sexual orientation. Efforts to 'convert' gay people have failed. Finally laws are being passed to give them freedom of expression.

Parenting is an act of love, as is homosexual marriage. Children care about those who raise and care for them - universally. Love is what we are; love is what we do; love is what we share. There are some heterosexual parents who abuse their children, unfortunately. We all came to learn; we all choose the lessons and we all decide whether to

79

learn or not. No one can explain why an individual would choose a lifestyle (homosexuality) that would incur such prejudice and hatred. Paul then - and all homophobic humanity - has the same lesson to learn: accept everyone as our spiritual sibling because of who they are, not by what they do or how they express their love.

## Chapter 35   Forerunner of Peace

John the Baptist, born to Elizabeth when she was 'stricken in years,' came *to guide our feet into the way of peace'*. (Luke 1:79)  Archangel Gabriel announced to Zacharias that his wife would bear a child even though she was an old woman. (This miracle somehow gets lost as we focus on the miracle of Jesus' birth. It is no less a miracle than Jesus' birth). The only way such guidance was possible was for us to repent. Repent means basically the same thing it meant then: 'to turn from sin and dedicate oneself to the amendment of one's life.' (Webster's Dictionary)

In Dan.7:13-14 we find part of Daniel's dream described:

*I saw in the night visions, and, behold, one like the Son of man came with the clouds of heaven, and came to the Ancient of days, and they brought him near before him.*

*And there was given him dominion, and glory, and a kingdom, that all people, nations, and languages, should serve him: his dominion is an everlasting dominion, which shall not pass away, and his kingdom that which shall not be destroyed.*

Now David dreamed of the Son of man coming to earth with the clouds of heaven, but only when John the Baptist preached did we hear the portent of the kingdom of Heaven coming to Earth. *Repent ye, for the kingdom of heaven is at hand.* Matt 3:2

To the people of Israel this must have sounded impossible. People followed this man of the wilderness because of the news he brought and the promise it contained. *Repent ye, for the kingdom of Heaven is at hand.* This is the first time we find the word 'heaven' in the New Testament. It is the first time that any humans heard of the possibility that Heaven could actually come to Earth. John was a hermit who lived in the desert, wore animal skins and ate locusts and honey. By all accounts he was an outsider and a curiosity. But his words of promise came with great conviction. So his peers listened to him and came forward to be baptized, as they confessed their sins. Then John said that one came mightier than he, who would baptize not with water, but with the Holy Ghost. And when John saw Jesus approach, John said, "*Behold the Lamb of God, which taketh away the sins of the world*". John 1:29

Only when we repent are we able to know peace. Repentance must precede peace, because we cannot reconcile guilt and peace. Sins - or faults - trouble us. Sometimes we are a little uncomfortable when we hurt another, judge another, discount another. Sometimes we are greatly distressed. Guilt ensues. By merely a change of mind we can turn away from guilt or any degree of discomfort and move forward in a different, more positive, direction.

Regret is another story. 'Regret' means 'sorrow aroused by circumstances beyond one's control or power to repair' (Webster). There is no emotional sting like that of regret. We cannot re-write, re-do, or correct our words/actions. The guilt will, with the ego's help, crush us and keep us imprisoned. Forgiveness must release us from the pain. "*Forgive and ye shall be forgiven.*" Luke 6:37

When we dedicate ourselves to changing our ways, only good comes to us. Only good *can* come to us. It is God's immutable law. "*But seek ye first the kingdom of God, and his righteousness; and all things shall be added unto you*". Matt 6:33. Peace can be ours. It is attainable. It merely takes a little willingness on our part to seek it. Repentance opens the door to forgiving ourselves and others; of knowing we are worthy to enjoy peace: peace of mind; peace of soul. In that peaceful place we have the confidence that we are are safe, secure, protected and most importantly, loved - by God. This peace may still be beyond our understanding yet we shall feel it and know it.

# Chapter 36   Fourth and Last

There are many phrases from Archangel Gabriel's teachings which stick in my mind. One of them is, 'This is your fourth and last planet'. Much fiction has been written about Atlantis. Gabriel confirmed that its remnant is located deep in the waters off the northeast coast of the United States. He told us that the Atlantians developed their technology but not their hearts. They had huge heads, but very small hearts. They had no compassion or caring for one another. They used their fellow countrymen for terrible experimentation. The Bible refers to them in Genesis, Chapters 4 and 5. The end of Atlantis came with excess, uncontrolled experimentation and misuse of energy. Some of the people now on earth were Atlantians, accounting for some of the violent individuals and groups. When asked if Atlantis would rise again, Gabriel said 'No, thank God.'

Prior to Atlantis we lived on Lemuria, which followed Mu. Like all our planet-homes it was originally green and lush and beautiful. Over time we destroyed the other planets. Now we are in the process of destroying the Earth. That is why Archangel Gabriel and eleven Master Teachers came to earth at this turning of the ages. Aquarius is the truth age, the Age of Spirituality. We must begin valuing Mother Earth and nurture her, as she has nurtured us for millions of years.

There are no written 'histories' of Lemuria or her forerunner, Mu. This is not surprising, considering we do not have any writings on earth before cuneiform writing and cave drawings. It does not matter, for now is the only time worth our consideration. For longer than our minds can comprehend we have resided on a planet 'far from home'. As children of God our home is Heaven. That is our natural habitat. Planets we have created are all as temporary as our physical bodies.

Angelic intervention has come to guide us. If we do not pay attention to these spirit entities now we shall have to begin again. On each planet we occupied we had to start as we started on Earth - rudimentary bodies, no language or social structure. Gabriel said, 'This cannot be'. So this is our moment of truth. God has sent Archangel Gabriel and eleven others to come to various centers of light on earth with the same message: 'Wake up, children of God, and live from the Lord God of your Being'. Is this any different from Jesus' messages 2,000 years ago:

*The Kingdom of God is within.*
*Follow me.*
*I came to show you the way.*
*I am the way, the truth and the life.*
*Everything I do you can do.*

Is this any different from Jesus' message in the 20<sup>th</sup> century (ACIM):

Ask for light and you will know you are light.
There is nothing about me that you cannot attain.
O my child, if you knew what God wills for you, your joy would be complete!
Because I am always with you, you are the way, the truth and the life.
When your body and your ego and your dreams are gone, you will know that you will last forever.


We can learn these lessons now, and live them. That is why angelic beings come to awaken us now. No longer believing in magic, but in ourselves as children of God, we can teach what we learn and become residents of a peaceful earth, before we return to our Creator Who knows only peace. We have been far from God (in consciousness) too long. Like the Prodigal Son, we can return to our Creator. There we can live a heavenly life of positive ideas and manifestations.

We are truly blessed to be on this planet at this time - the beginning of the New Age - the cusp of the Age of Truth, the commencement of a lasting peace on earth. Let us join with each other to make only peace and joy a reality on earth, before joining the Father of all creation in our natural habitat, Heaven. Heavenly days await us when we return to God's Home and our natural habitat. We celebrate that truth!

# Chapter 37  Freedom of Forgiveness

There is a heavy burden we carry, sometimes for many years. It weighs us down, it slows us down, and it becomes even heavier with time. We become accustomed to its burden. We choose to carry it; we choose to hold it and we choose nurture it as we go. It is called resentment. We are the only ones who can put the load down and refuse to carry it further. The word 'resentment' means re-feeling. We feel a hurt over and over again, refuse to let it go; and this is resentment.

We nourish our resentment by sharing it with others who are burdened with their own resentments. We nourish it also by constantly justifying it to ourselves. We sometimes even add other resentments to the original one. We come to love our resentments as though they are a part of our very nature. Sometimes we say, 'That's the way I am', or 'You would, too, if it were you.' We hold resentments to us like dear friends.

There is a key to unloading our resentments, but it is not a universal key. For some of us the key is a sudden and painful reminder that we ourselves are guilty of the same behavior that caused our 'enemy' to wound us. For others the key might be someone telling us, 'I forgive you'. Still others might consider forgiveness because they constantly hear the very word 'forgiveness'. Some of us may lie on our deathbed and pray the Father to forgive us our trespasses.

To not forgive is a power play. In effect we are saying, 'I have the power to *not* forgive you', and the resentment seems cozy and justifiably comfortable. We all seek power of some kind, even if only over own lives. Controlling others is an unfortunate passion of some individuals. The unforgiving person usually becomes ill, disliked or a hateful of all others. But all become uncomfortable with self. This is so because innately we are loving children of God, whether we acknowledge that truth or not.

Only by letting go of resentments can we know freedom. We can know the freedom of 'traveling light' through life. We can enjoy the freedom to be who we are without the distraction of old angers. It is an interesting awareness that the person we resent is often totally unaware of our original anger and continuing resentment. We are not hurting them by it. We are the only ones carrying the burden, and the lonely burden is the heaviest one.

Only in retrospect do we see the benefits of forgiveness. We are free to live unburdened by them. We show others the benefits of forgiveness by the changes in our behavior. The changes can't be missed by those who love us. Our Father in Heaven does not see us as 'sinners' but as His children who have made mistakes and He knows that all mistakes can be rectified, just as easily erasing with a pencil or a key on the keyboard. *All sins shall be forgiven unto the sons of men.* (Mark 3:28)

When we list those we intend to forgive it is essential to list God, for we have all, at one time or another, become angry at God for a problem or a circumstance. We must also list self, for we know now that we have become angry with self for a myriad of reasons. A list is a good idea for it causes us to think about everyone in our lives whom we resented. Sometimes it takes a friend or a counselor to ask us questions that make the resentments surface in our mind.

This is an undeniable truth: Forgiveness gives us freedoms we have not known in a very long time. It usually takes a person at least thirty years before he is willing to consider forgiving others. It can be sooner given the right circumstance. Manmade laws give freedoms at eighteen or twenty-one. Jesus would not have been listened to before the age of thirty, because society at that time considered thirty years to be the age of maturity.

One need never have to forgive if s/he never has held a grudge; never allowed anger to fester and become resentment. There are few such fortunate ones. They are blessed to have freedoms we all aspire to with forgiveness.

# Chapter 38  From Ambiguity to Unity

Whenever we need to make a decision - and every day we must make several in this hectic world of ours - we analyze the situation and make a choice based on personal history and experiences. This process is fraught with problems.

For one thing, analysis leads to paralysis, it is said, and rightly so. We swing between the pros and cons of a decision, weighing all arguments. This is time consuming and unnecessary. It is time consuming because we come up with a vast number of options; unnecessary because there is a better way. Our personal experiences, in retrospect, did not always bring a positive outcome. So why do we rely on it so heavily? Too many times we have looked back over our choices and wondered why we chose what we did.

One problem is that we listen to our head which tells us one thing, and then our heart, which tells us another. Immediately we have a conflict and analysis seems to the only way to arrive at a 'well thought out' answer. We recognize the conflict and sometimes even verbalize it: 'My heart tells me one thing, but my head tells me another' is often our lamentation. Perhaps we need to understand where these two sources get their information. Our heart, besides a physical pump for our blood, represents the source of our caring nature. We speak of someone being 'big hearted', or 'all heart'.

We care for others because we are feeling humans and we love others. We may love them in different ways, or in varying degrees, but we love them. This caring nature is not part of the physical structure of the heart, but history has assigned our caring, loving nature to its non-physical function. Love is the Essence of God, and we are loving entities because God created us from Himself, Which is Love. We could not exist without God, and we seek others to love because it is our *nature* to do so.

Analysis comes from our belief in the ability to think. We believe the source of our thoughts is our brain. The brain does not think; it processes thought. The true Source of our thoughts is the Mind of God.

We also have 'a mind of our own', which is our ego-voice. The ego's self-will run riot is what brings us most or all of our error thoughts. Depending as we do on them means we are relying on the ego for answers. We know now that the ego lies to us. It uses fear to control us, to convince us that death is a reality, that pain is our birthright, and that we are tiny, insignificant people without it.

We have settled for this ambiguity in our lives and consider it as the real living experience. Perhaps it is this ambiguity which leads us to believe that life is challenging at best and tormenting at worst. We accept that conflict as normal. We believe it is what life is really all about. Then someone came along who tells us we are loved by God and He would never let anything happen to us *unless we requested it*. The 'someone' was Archangel Gabriel, the Announcer of the Ages. He, Jesus the Christ, and eleven Master Teachers all came to Earth in the late 20th century to awaken us. See SacredGardenFellowship.org

The Bible contains the story of the Garden of Eden, in which Adam fell asleep, and from him God created woman. Nowhere in the Good Book does it say that Adam woke up. Symbolically, Adam represents the human race. We fell asleep to our divine nature, and came to believe in separated selves. In that separation period we made up the ego. Since then we have given it all our power.

When we acknowledge our unity with God and all humanity as the Son ship of God, we will abandon the concept of separateness. We will leave ambiguity behind. We will listen wholeheartedly to the Voice of God. As a human father guides his children, God guides us when we know He exists and when we ask Him to. It is not difficult to hear God's guidance. *Be still and know that I am God* (Ps. 46:10) will suffice. Leaving behind the raucous ego we can and must someday listen to the still, small voice of holy guidance. It, like love, never fails.

# Chapter 39  Games of Life

All games of life are not held on a playing field with pigskins and other animal hides. I am reminded of the day that Archangel Gabriel, sitting for a moment in the anteroom of the church sanctuary, saw a football on the floor. He asked what it was and the explanation was given. Then he said, did anyone ask the pig if he was willing to give his life? Laughter followed. Then we realized he was referring to the sanctity of life; all life.

 If we consider games as entertainment, temporary escapes from life's chores, or fantasy, we must admit they represent something that is an aside to life itself. Players who don uniforms have an occupation. That is a given. But what role do the spectators play? We are not participants but viewers. We are in the bleachers to watch others and have fun. In that role we are spectators and not players; we are finding relief from life's challenges and chores.

The purpose of all ballgames is competition. Competition results in winners and losers. We praise the winners and downplay the losers. Some games, based on time, can end in a draw; no winners or losers declared. In others, like baseball, the game is played until there is a declared winner. We envy the winners their fame. Sometimes a final score arouses spectators to physical revolt. Competition and envy are not limited to games.  In our working lives we compete for higher wages, titles, recognition. In our personal lives we compete for 'better' neighborhoods in which to live; larger houses. We even impose competition on our children, by asking who gets the better grades; is most popular; attends the 'best' college. The extreme of competition is war and we have engaged in many.

Competition permeates our lives. Who really is 'better than'? Only recently have we come to replace competition with an attitude of helping others. Now we recognize and assist those who cannot do for themselves, instead of seeing them as 'losers'. Non-profit organizations have been established for that purpose. About a hundred years ago the Red Cross was established to rush in and help those suffering from the ravages of war. Now we have 'first responders' who rush to help and comfort those afflicted by floods, fires, hurricanes and earthquakes. We do not see them as losers but brothers and sisters in need. Perhaps we are growing spiritually. Perhaps we are finally learning to abide by the rules of love, as spelled out in the thirteenth chapter of John's first letter to the people of Corinth. We still have a long way to go.

We become impatient with others when they do not see things as we do. When we become impatient we often lash out verbally. This is not being patient of others. Love expressed is patient and kind. There are many individuals who thrive on being rude, inconsiderate and sometimes hurtful and sadistic. Perhaps they do not know how to do loving things because they never were taught, or never received love from a parent or guardian. In truth they fail to acknowledge, as we all do at times, that God is love and God created us from Him. We contain love as children of God.

We all know the braggart who boasts of any 'success' demonstrated by excess wealth, strength, recognition, or title. Love does not brag nor engage in battle; does not engage in competition. Love simply *is*. When we doubt ourselves or God we are not choosing a good life. With God all things are possible. I recall a story Archangel Gabriel told about a man in England who heard that his brother he left behind in America was very sick. He had no money but longed to see his brother. He went to the dock where ships sailed for America and he sat on the dock for three days and three nights. On the fourth day a man approached him and said he had an extra ticket because his friend was unable to sail; did he want to go?

When we see ourselves in a victim role, we own the role and make it ours. When we know that God put us here for a reason and we accept God in our lives, seeking for self and others only good, we cannot fail. In our heart of hearts do we really believe that God would give us anything but a blessing? He has blessed us with life and provided us with a legion of angels for support. Turning away from good and seeking to be 'better, richer, or stronger' does not exemplify the characteristics of God's love - for us, for others, for seeming 'losers'. When we express patience, kindness, gentleness, hope and tolerance we can travel a spiritual road. Our choices today will determine experiences in our next lifetime. All our choices will eventually determine when we will ascend to the Father for good, and not return to the Earth with its seeming 'victories'.

## Chapter 40 "*Go, And do Thou Likewise*"

There is a significant meaning to the word 'do' in this command of Jesus. He did not say 'teach', for some reason. Could the reason be that teaching only goes so far? Someone once said 'there is no such thing as teaching; only learning.' A teacher or professor can speak to a hundred students, but if only twenty understand the lesson, what did the teacher do for them? Archangel Gabriel told us that of the multitudes that Jesus taught only a handful understood his message.

These were the words of Jesus after he told the story of the Good Samaritan (Luke 10:30-36). This parable describes a 'certain man' who, while traveling from Jerusalem to Jericho, was robbed, beaten and left for dead. A priest (Levite) came upon him and passed by. A Levite (natural religious tendency; not necessarily spiritual, MBD, 402) came along and also passed by. A man from Samaria had compassion and helped the man and took him to an inn. The Samaritan also paid the innkeeper.

'Jerusalem' means *habitation of peace* (MBD, 342). The word 'Jericho' expresses the . . . reflected breath and mind, the outer, intellectual - in contrast to the inner spirit.' (MBD, 339). When we, as a human race, decided to leave our natural habitat, Heaven, we came to this lovely planet and exhibited robbery, abuse, and abandonment. Perhaps Jesus himself represents the Good Samaritan to humanity. Jesus came late in the twentieth century to 1. Write *A Course in Miracles* (1965-1972), a book for spiritual awakening, and 2. To 'Straighten out the crooked places' in the Bible (1995-1999). He did so in order to correct some of the many errors in translation - accidental or purposeful - and to explain the truth that was purged.

One of the men who passed by the wounded, forsaken traveler was a priest - now defined as 'a mediatory agent between humans and God'. The other man was a Levite; the descendants of Levi, and were the generation which served in the temple as priests and lower places in religious worship. In their time such men would probably have been seen as compassionate individuals, but perhaps they both were aware that, on this lonely road, no one would see them ignore a fellow traveler, and so they passed him by. People from Samaria were seen by Jews as outside the Jewish religion. 'Metaphysically, Samaria represents a state of consciousness in which Truth and error are mixed'. This particular Samaritan listened to, and obeyed, the voice of truth which overcame the voice of error in his mind.

There are stories which describe some members of this generation who ignore or stand by and watch as others are abused and beaten. Even worse, today many people gape at one or more people ganging up on a helpless victim. Some say they do not want to get 'involved'. Whether we like it or not, we are all involved with each other. We all need each other. Perhaps the observers feel helpless to assist - or fear injury to themselves. Or maybe they reserve help for only loved ones. God is no respecter of persons (Romans 2:11), and we can learn to be equally accepting of everyone. God loves His entire human family, and we ought to love each other because He is the Author and Creator of us all.

We have become very good at learning to pass a test. Our education system demands it. There is a higher 'test' which elevates us to a higher road. It is the test of learning Jesus' teachings - then *doing* them. In James 2:20 we find, *But wilt thou know, O vain man, that faith without works is dead?* We talk more than we listen, even though we have one mouth and two ears. In the morning when we leave our homes, hopefully a place of peace, we hasten out to a world of activity which is governed by competition, a drive for success, an economy that demands worship of money and stuff. Stock brokers, merchants and employers hold power over us. We join the game willingly. When the games cease, and we are no longer active in the world of business, we are no less than the worker we once stood beside; nor more.

There is a common thread which binds humanity together, regardless of color, culture or language. We are human physically. We are spirit in truth. God respects us all as spirit; as His offspring. He loves us for what we are, not what we do. We love ourselves for what we do, not what we are. We have forgotten our divinity over eons of time. In doing the Will of God we find peace in and out of our homes. In doing anything else, guilt and low self-esteem overcome us. Self-love - love of our God-created spirit Self - is our goal, not the narcistic self-love of our ego.

# Section VI
Vau

## Chapter 41   God's Gift of Free Choice

When God created us from Himself he gave us total free choice. To His countless number of angels he gave free choice *only in the realm of good*. Maybe that is why, when a stranger helps we say, 'You're an angel.'

We leave it to the mathematicians to calculate the total number of angels which God assigns to humans, given to us by Archangel Gabriel that we each have 144,000 angels and the Earth is populated with about eight billion souls. Like everything else created by God our minds cannot comprehend such a vast amount. We blessed students listened to Gabriel for twelve years (1987-1999), and in his lesson titled *Angels, Earthlings and Aliens* he described the angel world. The number given above relates only to the countless angels which come to Earth. Another countless population of angels never comes to Earth, and has its own 'job description'.

We can wonder if God knew the extent of negative choices we would make in our freedom of choice, but believing God is omniscient we must assume that He did have foreknowledge of it. We know, in our limited human wisdom, that a sunny day cannot be appreciated until we have experienced a rainy day. Days of contentment are only appreciated after days of struggle. We can blame God or another human for our painful experiences, but if we do we are discounting our free choice options.

Every person and every situation in our earthly life is chosen by our free choice. Denying this truth does not change anything. In denying its truth we deny that God gave us free choice. There are many ways we can demonstrate free choice. In fact we choose a hundred things every day - what to wear, what to say to those we live with or meet along the way, what job to work at, the route to it, how we perceive ourselves, where to live, who to make friends with, who to trust, and so forth.

What keeps us from using free choice? Others' opinions, imprisonment, employers, parents, professors, etc. seem to interfere; yet these very experiences came to us by choice, also. Our problem is that we exercise our free choice *with limits*. These are self-imposed limits. The ones we describe as having a 'free spirit' do not care about others' opinions. With a sense of self, even a person behind bars can make choices of exercising, schooling, library use, practicing behavior that is acceptable in and out of prison. Creative ideas in the workplace benefit the creator and others. Creativity is the paramount choice we enjoy. Before we reach the age of responsibility we are limited in our choices because our parents choose to keep us safe and alive until we are on our own.

Our sense of responsibility can stunts our free choice. We assume that we are responsible for others when freedom of expression beckons us to walk the creative road. Gabriel informed us that we are only responsible for ourselves. We can be responsible *to* others. One choice we often balk at is sacrificing our freedom to 'be there' for others. Some people willingly and joyfully care for others. It is a given task for some occupations, such as the nursing profession. That free choice can be accommodated with other choices, such as parenting. Men have always had free choice of occupations without consideration of fathering a family. Only in the past century have women had free choice of employment outside the home. Now free choice has opened the entire spectrum of employment options to half the human population!

Our abuse of free choice is evident in every sign that says, 'no swimming' because the water is polluted - by the free choice of others. Our abuse of free choice is also evident in the smog which covers cities and sometimes nations with air polluted by others' free choice. By free choice we have relentlessly pursued energy sources for power. Coal mining killed thousands with 'black lung' disease. Oil spills have contaminated our oceans and destroyed vast numbers of sea life and bird life. By free choice we make war on others, and by free choice we die for our country. The conscription of WWII denied us free choice. Having lived in that time I can assure you that there was a national passion to join in a common effort to overcome our enemies. Some few chose not to join the armed forces. They were called 'conscientious objectors'.

Now war is losing its appeal. We are seeing it for what it is: shameful, wasteful, and preventable. We can use our free choice now to choose peace. When enough of us choose peace, nations will resolve all issues at the table of negotiation. War is no longer an option, for the energy now available to humans can destroy the planet. By our free choice humanity will survive; a new energy will be discovered; peace will prevail. Finally we will use our free choice only for positive expression. That is God's Will for us. As we choose to listen to the Voice of God more and more, we, the human family will awaken to the truth of us. In doing so we will become aware of only one road back Home. Choice will lose its meaning. We will be truly free.

## Chapter 42   God's One Son

God's one Son is us - all of humanity. Archangel Gabriel explained this to those of us ready to hear it. Many are still not willing to hear this truth. It seems so difficult to accept. We believe that God created all life, with its myriad of variety in the mineral world, the plant world and the animal world, so we can also accept the vast diversity of humans on earth. Of eight billion people now on this planet, only *one* qualifies to be holy? And if God would create such a singular entity, to be His *only* Son, what would the purpose be, if we already believed in a God of Creation, unreachable, unseen, and all-powerful?  He is seen as the only embodiment of God Himself. Why should mankind require a *representative* of God? In His all-encompassing, all-powerful, all knowing existence, God created all of us with a mind which thinks. We pursue ideas, invent, and create with our minds yet ought never to question our true origin. Have we not all asked these ancient questions?

'Why am I here?'
'Where did I come from?
'Where am I going, and how?

95

'What is the meaning of life?'

Archangel Gabriel explained that we ask questions because we *can know* the answers. Otherwise the questioning becomes a futile game played by God - go question but you will never find the answer. This generation is questioning rather than accepting, all things because 'that's the way it has always been', or 'history has shown us this to be so'. What has history shown us but conflict, dissention and war? Why, indeed, are we *numbering* our wars?

The Christ in Jesus had/has/is the power of God, and the man Jesus came to show us that the light of Christ is also in us. When we accept Jesus the man, who came to show us The Way, the Truth, and the Life (John 14:6) as Christ we will know the truth of us. Jesus made his brief journey to Earth to show us the way, to be a pattern (I Tim. 1:16) for us to follow. He lived an example life (John 13:15). He did so that we may emulate him. He tells us in scripture that everything he did we can do. (John 14:12).

As we read the Bible we can see that Jesus' life was an example of love and forgiveness. He loved people, and preached constantly to them. He loved children - 'and a little child shall lead them'(Is. 11:6) - because they demonstrated acceptance, curiosity, gentleness, and trust. Children do not come to us to demonstrate hatred and bigotry. There is nothing in God's green Earth like the feeling we derive from seeing a new-born baby; nothing. But perhaps I say this as a mother.

Forgiveness was expressed by the Master Teacher, Jesus. How many of us could find it in our hearts to forgive the one who flogged, spit upon, stripped, and then crucified us? How did he survive such horrible abuse and intolerable pain? He did not. As the Son of God he could rise above the pain, by staying focused on the Christ within. To believe he endured no pain on the way to the cross, the nailing and the crucifixion, stuns the mind. The explanation is simple. He had an 'out of body' experience. Some ordinary individuals today have also experienced this.

When Jesus said 'follow me' - and he said it many times in scripture - he did not mean that we all must be crucified. That mode of persecution has long passed. He came as a man Jesus, and as the embodiment of what God created him to be - love incarnate. He taught and lived unconditional love. He expressed forgiveness even on the cross. These are the characteristics of his that we can emulate.

Love is defined quite well by Paul in his first letter to the Corinthians, in Chapter thirteen. It is a guidepost for our lesson in love. Forgiveness of everyone for everything is also a challenge. We must turn again to Gabriel's teachings. He made it clear to us that no one ever 'hurt' us without our permission, and we never 'hurt' anyone without theirs. What a concept! It is based on the truth that we have free choice, and a loving God would never hurt His Own. Prior to our embodiment on Earth, we choose carefully all our experiences to learn the lessons we have chosen to learn. God and the angels know our plan. God told the angels to watch over us, and they do. But they cannot interfere with the choices we make. Our Higher Self knows our life plan. But it is not consciously remembered.

When we keep Jesus on the Cross and perceive him to be the only begotten Son of God we cannot possibly emulate him. But we are encouraged by religious leaders to *try*. A loving God would not set us on such a frustrating journey as this. The God of Love loves us, and when we ask, He guides us. We must learn to unlearn the past, for it is no more. When we decide with conviction that we will not make any more decisions based on our personal past or the past of Earth history, then we can know all things we desire to learn, simply by listening to God. Meditation is the way to listen to God; prayer is talking to God.

Instead of 'wanting' and 'needing' - both of which imply lack - we must be aware that God supplies all our needs. Our 'wants' are what other people have and tell us we should have. Desire means 'de' from and 'sire' father - desiring only God's Will for us brings us only blessings. Do you believe that God would bring you anything but blessings? All humanity is the only begotten Son of God. This is what the Bible was originally written to say, but translators changed it to say Jesus was the only begotten Son of God.

Now is the time to follow the life of the Christ, demonstrated by the man Jesus. He is the example for us, the way-shower for our lives; a specific pattern which we can imitate. Because all humankind is the only begotten Son of God, within each of us is the Living Christ. We are all asleep to our own divinity, just as Adam was asleep to his.

## Chapter 43   He Must Increase

*He must increase, but I must decrease."* John 3:30

This biblical phrase suggests an analogy - that John the Baptist represents humanity, with its inclination to judge, criticize and condemn. This attitude and behavior must decrease. Jesus the Christ, the Love of God made manifest, must increase in the hearts and minds of us all. The love of God must increase; the ways of men must decrease. This is going to come about by choice, yet it must eventually come about for the human family. It is a must because we are all children of God, children of love, and only in human form do we see ourselves less than this.

John the Baptist was speaking of Jesus to his own disciples. He wisely knew, and told them, that a man can receive nothing except what is given from heaven. The words of Archangel Gabriel come to mind. He said that we   all plan our lives and everyone in them (with their permission, of course).

If we plan negative behavior, we well may ask, 'how can this come from Heaven?' The answer is: because God gave us all free choice. What we plan prior to a lifetime on Earth is a lesson we want to learn. Then we decide how we shall learn the lesson. If it entails a negative act by or toward us, it will be so. Our every desire is ours. Every request we make to God is answered. Another will agree to wound or even kill us by our request. They have their own reasons for the action, also.

They may refuse because there (on the Astral Plane) we know only love. But we say - and you have heard this before - 'if you love me you will do it.' These were Jesus' words to Judas who loved Jesus and refused to betray him. Love prevails in Heaven, where we plan our earthly lives. We are sons and daughters of the Living God; the Creator of all life. God loves us forever and unconditionally.

The idea of planning our lives causes us to wonder how we have the power to do it and why God gave us the power. God birthed us from Himself and thus His attributes are ours. We are love, peace and joy. When we come to Earth we become absorbed into a society which practices disease, death and all manner of negative behavior. Our Higher Self knows better, which is why our soul longs to return Home to our natural habitat, Heaven.

So many questions arise about why are we sick, why do the young die, what makes someone kill another, why is there war? We may choose sickness to avoid responsibility or escape a situation or to help another learn patience with a patient. A person may choose a short life just to help the survivors accept the eternality of life. This happens when the deceased sends back a message from the other side that they are joyful and alive. A person must hate themselves in order to kill another. A strong sense of national patriotism will take some off to war. It used to be said that old men choose war and young men die in it. Gabriel told us that powerful men make a lot of money in war and those who so desire can do dastardly deeds under the cover of war.

At one time I asked Gabriel why, in Ireland (then engulfed in religious war), did dissension perpetuate. He said that some people there died with so much hatred and vengefulness they did not stay on the Astral Plane long enough to learn about love and acceptance. They chose to return immediately to 'get even' with others.

We are holy offspring of a loving God. We have simply forgotten our origin. On the Astral Plane we touch once again a realm of love. But there is so much more to life than the Earth and the Heaven we can conceive. There is, indeed, a seventh Heaven, but we have a long way to go to truly join again with the Father forever. We have been away a very long time from God - only in our consciousness - and all energy realms must be redeemed. It will take time, but we can hasten the time with a little willingness to do so. The Laws of God must increase; the laws we make must decrease. The Love of God must increase; the judgments we impose must decrease.


## Chapter 44   Heavenly Helpers

When Archangel Gabriel first came it was like a magical moment. Then, as he continued to visit and teach us, I realized that he came to give us heavenly instruction, even as he had come to Mary, the Blessed Mother, and Joseph, the human father, 2,000 years ago. What inexpressible joy to be there, sitting at his feet, and learning the truth; the wisdom of the ages. And what joy it gave us to hear that all humanity is the 'only begotten son of God'.

Thoughts of criminals came to mind; thoughts of those who had hurt us in one way or another - physically, emotionally, mentally. But as time went on, Gabriel explained that we all had been saints; all murderers; all homosexuals in our past lifetimes. We have had so many past lifetimes, Gabriel said, that we have *met every other person now living on Earth*!

Gabriel's lessons have affected my life in more ways than I can tell; more ways I believe, than I can even identify. He became my teacher early on, and one day I went to the microphone (he always took questions) and I told him so. He looked at me and said, 'And you are my student'. It was a magnificent moment in time.

Gabriel told us that each and every human being has 144,000 angel helpers. He spent one seminar (see Bibliography) explaining all the archangels, and all the layers of angels in the Heaven world; more than our minds can comprehend. Our angels do not discuss our requests, or argue about who is going to answer our call - they simply get busy to help us. They help us in a vast variety of ways - simple things, like finding a parking spot or choosing our daily clothing. They help us locate the car of our choice, or choose a college to attend, or who to marry. Gabriel said we should always thank our angels, for they appreciate being acknowledged. Our angels guide us and laugh with us.

There are Master Teachers, or Ascended Masters, who help us from the Heaven world. They are humans who have studied, learned, and grown into masters and now reach out to help us on our path to become Master Teachers, also. This should not surprise us, for all learning is a progression of lessons. No one can teach better than those who have walked the path before us.

For those who seek answers from the spirit world of God through a psychic, or a medium, it is important to understand their function. Most answers sought are about life on Earth - a relationship, a house, a car, a situation. Anyone and everyone can learn to become a psychic because we all have that latent ability. Some few are 'natural' psychics; knew from birth that they were prophetic, clairvoyant, clairaudient, or clairsentient. On a conscious spiritual path we need to seek the aid of a person who can help us along the way; one from whom we learn to become aware that we are in fact children of God. And how to live daily that sacred person we are.

Guides on high are those who help us tread our way on the spiritual path by nudging us along when we seem to falter. It is like a voice - unheard but known - asking if we really want to go down the path of temptation. The tempter is our ego, for there is no devil nor a place called 'hell'. Gabriel explained that humans made up those ideas. In the wilderness, Jesus was dealing with his own ego. Our ego is more powerful than it ought to be, but we have given it its power, and now we must harness it. The ego has its place, but we must relegate it to the sidelines and give the Holy Spirit our full attention. Spirit must be our only guide as we live out our time on Earth. Loved ones who have passed over can help us, such as in dreams when they visit. We can ask them to visit with us. They may choose not to, for their own reasons. No one - no medium, no psychic, no channel, can tell an entity in spirit what to do. Free choice prevails there, also.

If the number 144,000 personal angels seem inconceivable, think of having a Guardian Angel who will, for God, answer all your prayers. Let that entity deal with the 144,000. Our job is merely to listen and do.

## Chapter 45   Heavenly Peace

Silent night. Holy night. Sacred night. Every time we lie down for the night we seek a rest from the day's busy-ness. Our desire is to relax, rejuvenate, and replenish ourselves. In that sleeping time we visit the astral plane. Dreams reflect the pre-sleep state of mind. Nightmares may follow viewing a 'horror' movie. A cup of tea and a comforting poem may lead to pleasant dreams. The body requires periodic rest. Our mind requires occasional retreat from worldly activities. Our spirit is always at peace. Created by the Author of life, we are spirit in essence and eternal in existence.

Upon rising we feel rested and prepared for another day. We may recall a dream that was lucid; we may interpret it. Or we may awaken feeling that, although there is no clear recollection, we have been some special place and learned some profound lesson. Spirit always has lessons for us when we ask. In sleep may be the only time we listen. A restful sleep means we have had a heavenly peace. A restless sleep may be the result of a worried mind, or an over-worked body.

Our spirit (Higher Self) remains unaffected by physical exercise and impairment. Our spirit Self is and ever shall be at peace in God, Creator of us all. We are His Image and Likeness. Mortal eyes are not equipped to behold spirit. Few humans have the gift to see our spirit essence. It may be described by us as a kind of conscience, because it nudges us when temptation beckons in any direction that is not upward, honest and true.

When we lay down our mortal body and transition to spirit, people sometimes place a monument atop the remains which reads, 'Rest in peace.' The inscription suggests that we will sleep eternally. Do we still believe that? Would a loving God want us to sleep forever and miss the continuing creation of life? Adam, son of God, fell asleep in the Garden of Eden; nowhere in scripture does it say he woke up. Our long sleep has not been a restful one. It is full of activity. It is permeated with the notion we must always be busy doing something. It is small wonder we seek nighttime sleep and sometimes daytime naps, or siestas. Family, work, travel, hobbies all combine to keep us so busy we cannot 'fit everything in'. It is an insane way to live. Its charm lies in the fact we have no time to look within. Heaven forbid we should peak within and find the Kingdom of God there!

Archangel Gabriel told us that every cell of our body has a spirit nucleus. Combine this with Jesus' words 'the kingdom of Heaven is within', and the truth of us is clear. We are holy children of God. That fact can convince us that there is a peaceful silence worthy to be sought while we are *awake*. In our waking moments we can hear the Voice of God, if we so choose. Every positive gut hunch, sudden idea, inner urge is an indicator that we can. Gabriel said God speaks to us constantly.

Creation is not an historical event; it is an on-going becomingness. Scientists tell us the universe is expanding (*The Universe in a Nutshell*, Stephen Hawking). Perhaps we must expand our thinking to encompass the glorious growth. We, as the Creator's children, are co-creators with Him, of this expanding universe. Halted as we are in this persistent sleep state, we can choose to awaken and co-create with God again. We busy ourselves making things, but we do not create. We make war; God creates peace. We judge, fight, destroy. God accepts, remains calm, builds in constructive ways. This planet Earth is an example of God's creation. We stand in awe of its beauty; enjoy the varied terrain of mountains, deserts and valleys. The hand of God has created this place we call home.

We came to visit and we fell asleep. In our awakening we shall see the truth of us, leave this beautiful home and go Home again. We will be with God in our consciousness and again co-create with Him. Creation's Source is love. We are love. Our soul longs to return Home. Gabriel, Jesus the Christ and eleven Master Teachers all came, as the Age of Aquarius (2,000-3,000) approached, to show us how to return Home. It is a heavenly place; with heavenly peace.

## Chapter 46   Heaven's Mansions

*"In my Father's house are many mansions: if it were not so, I would have told you. I go to prepare a place for you."* John 14:2

Jesus was very specific about the contents of Heaven. He clearly states that his intent is to make a place ready for our arrival there. He also firmly states that he would not tell us so unless it was true. We need hear no more to be certain that Heaven awaits us all. Jesus does not say that only readers of scripture will ascend to Heaven; or only those who repent, although he suggests we should do so.

In the 18th century Swedenborg wrote a book, *Heaven and Hell,* in which he describes both as seen by him in a trance or dream. We know, from Archangel Gabriel, that there is no hell. What, therefore, Swedenborg was describing was the lower Astral Plane. The ones who go to the lower Astral Plane are those who *expect* a barren, lonely place. Those who live a life of justice and mercy; of love and peace, will go to the higher Astral Plane. On earth we always receive what we expect. This pertains beyond earthly life, also. If we expect some kind of punishment on the other side, we will surely not get forty lashes in Heaven. But we will find ourselves in a dry and desolate place, living in a small hut, with no friends. Even here and now, we see this as a hellish existence.

Angels attend those in the lower astral and assure them that they are worthy of the light, and should go into the light, because God loves them just as they are. Gabriel carefully explained that although we plan our lives down to the detail, the spirit of us is forever and is unaffected by what we think and say and do. Just as we love our children for what they are and not for what they do, so God loves us for what we are - His children - and not for what we do. God knows that when we err, we do it out of ignorance. We are ignorant of our Essence, which is Love. Love never errs, and when we remember our innate divinity we will choose only to do good, think good, and know good. In this knowingness we can reach down to those who still are unaware of the love within them, and offer a hand up.

The origin of the word 'hell', Gabriel explained, meant a shallow grave. A shallow grave meant that wild animals could scent the buried bodies, dig them up and eat them. This was a greatly feared event. Even now, we would not choose such a circumstance. So we bury the dead bodies six feet under the surface so the scent is not found.

Some have written about Heaven's various mansions, having learned through dreams, trance, or channel from the spirit world. This is the time we must learn ourselves - learn as they learned or better yet, to know through revelation. Jesus said, *And ye shall know the truth, and the truth shall make you free.* John 8:32 The truth will set us free from all our error perceptions. Our greatest error perception is the belief that we are only a body; a physical form; separate from each other. We are so much more. If we were only a physical body, we cannot explain our conscience. We cannot understand why we desire to pray, to meditate, and to do good works. A body does not have a caring attitude. Our body has no compassion for another who is wounded. Our body does not know guilt; it is a magnificent machine which houses our spirit.

We think the body has a mind of its own. We often say 'my body is telling me . . .' Does this make sense? The truth of the matter is we think that we deserve punishment (for a perceived bad action) and so our body responds with a headache, and we 'listen' to our body! We are in total control of our body simply because we are spirit in essence. Spirit knows no pain. It is eternal. We are eternal. Jesus demonstrated the action of spirit his entire life. Nowhere in scripture do we read that Jesus could not teach because he had a headache, or a bad cold. He was never ill. He was never ill because he lived in the knowingness of his Christ Self.

One of the many mansions of Heaven which I loved reading about is the nursery, where babies 'born dead' or who passed into spirit at a very early age reside. The environment is totally equipped with small things - trees, houses, etc. Angels attend them, and teach them of divine truths. Angels attend us all when we pass over into the spirit world. We need not fear the transition, but only focus on the light ahead and behold our guardian angel.

When a person passes suddenly, as in a car accident, much care is needed to explain they are in Heaven. I once had a co-worker who was killed in an auto accident. This woman loved life; was a joy to know, had a loving husband and a young daughter. Weeks later I asked a medium how she was doing on the other side. The medium said that when she was told she was in Heaven she got hysterical because she loved her life and family on earth so much. Angels comforted her until she was calm. Then they explained to her that she planned it, and why.

How can we plan an 'accident'? Because we are, in truth, spirit. Our spirit is in control of our lives. God gave us all free choice. When we say 'I am my own worst enemy', it is true. It is true because we *believe it.* What we have forgotten is that we are our own best friend and can plan anything we choose. We can accept responsibility for ourselves, or we can believe in a Creator who makes some suffer with cancer, others with heart problems, etc. All illnesses can be healed because illness is not our birthright; health is.

The many mansions in Heaven are in truth states of consciousness. On earth we experience many different states of consciousness. Heaven affords us wondrous other states of consciousness. Perhaps these were alluded to by Shakespeare: "There are more things in heaven and earth, Horatio, than are dreamt of in your philosophy." (Hamlet, 1.v.166). The other side offers adventure without stress, existence without worry, peace without interruption. Heaven's mansions await us. As we return to Heaven, loved ones and pets greet us there; vast reunions take place. Jesus has prepared a place for us, just as he said he would.

# Chapter 47   Holiday Observance

The word holiday is derived from the words holy day, and days of religious observance were so called. Over time special national days, such as July 4th in America, became holidays. Perhaps it is time to think of *all* days as holy days. For twenty centuries we have been speaking, and even memorizing, *The Lord's Prayer.* "*Our Father Who art in Heaven . . .*" We readily acknowledge the fatherhood of God. We must either see God is childless, or call Him Father because we know ourselves to be His children.  As His children we must inherit some aspect of Him.

From our biological parents we inherit certain traits, like behaviors or eye and hair color. Fathers imbue us with these character traits. That is a given.  From this perspective we can assume that as God's children we inherit certain traits from God; traits like peace, love, joy, harmony. We do not usually *act* peacefully, lovingly, joyously or harmoniously. That does not mean we do not know how. Our actions are chosen by us. Holy traits are God-given.

As children of God we constantly refer to God as our Father in prayer. We seldom apply that paternity to our daily living. We fail to see that what we are is separate from what we do. We love our own offspring for what we know them to be, and see their actions as separate. The spark of divinity which we inherit from God never dies. It is within us, though unseen. Never do we hear a surgeon leave the operating room saying, 'I saw a great light inside that man. It must be the Kingdom of God the Bible refers to.' Spiritual things cannot be discerned by mortal eyes (I Cor. 2:14)

Because we cannot see spiritual traits, we can choose to either deny them or simply to have faith in their existence. To understand faith in what we cannot see does not require complex formulas or theological argument. Take, for example, the wind. We cannot see it. We can readily see its effects, when the wind blows a flag on a pole; tree leaves flutter on branches, waves ruffle the ocean's surface, and the sails of a boat billow.

Love is another example. We cannot order a cup of love at the diner, nor purchase a quart of love at the market. Without a doubt we can see/feel the effects of love - in a hug, a kiss, a holding of hands, and a pat on the back. And, of course, in making love with a partner. The holy aspects of us are not seen, either. We are unable to measure or purchase a cup of joy, a gallon of peace, a sheet of harmony. But we know in our hearts that joy, peace and harmony exist. They do exist - at least in brief moments of time, if not in the majority of our days. We have a deep desire to seek and experience these spiritual attributes because they are deep within us. When we have found and owned spiritual traits we find surrounding us a glorious population of joyous, loving people living in harmony. Like begets like.

Earth is a school where we learn about ourselves. John had a wonderful revelation about the future: *And I saw a new heaven and a new earth: for the first heaven and the first earth were passed away; and there was no more sea.* (Rev. 21:1) The only way a new earth and Heaven can manifest is by abandoning the old earth and Heaven. That does not mean destroying the earth with explosives, but rather to love it until we do not need it anymore.

Transformation is the required method of bringing a new earth to this old earth; a new Heaven to the Heaven of old. The Heaven of old is the belief that God only can live there, but not us. Yet, being omnipresent, God is everywhere, and Heaven is therefore everywhere. We just cannot see it with mortal eyes. In transforming our thinking we can and will bring about a new Heaven and a new earth. It is not only possible; it is inevitable. It is the promise of God. That is why it was revealed to John.

Our daily task is our holy task of seeking peace, love, joy, and harmony. For those who enjoy these traits, it is necessary to reach down and help others attain them. We are not here to live separated lives and die, but to live a cooperative life of sharing; a real life of unity. We cannot die; our body simply transforms. We cannot choose to transform ourselves, except in a change of thinking and acting. Transformation to our holy Selves is not about changing us; it is about awakening to our innate divinity. God's Will for us is to become all we are capable of becoming. He could not will any less for His Own. Becoming more than we are is not possible, but becoming aware of what we are is possible. The time is upon us now to bring about a new earth and a new Heaven. The method is to become aware of our innate attributes, express them without fear, and help others on that fearless and wondrous journey.

## Chapter 48  Home of Unity

When we enter an earthly residence and feel the love and peace of the place, we unconsciously acknowledge a certain comfort there. We want to stay awhile and enjoy the peaceful presence and the loving company of the people living there. It is a home of unified acceptance and love. It is a home of unity that we are occasionally blessed to find here on earth.

The human race - 'the only begotten son of God' we are told by Archangel Gabriel - is on a grand adventure to find life in a heavenly home of unity. A God of love would not desire anything less. We can still believe that 'the fear of God' will make us good people. Or can we come to understand that God loves all people everywhere.

It is our habit to focus on the differences in the human family. We see different colors of skin, we hear different languages, and we read about different cultures. Our focus is on differences. Sometimes our focus leads us to judgment, prejudice, hatred and wars. Then we justify all these negative attitudes. Our human judgment is never justified. How could we possibly know what justice is to all concerned. God is just.

Prejudice is the offspring of ignorance and hatred. It has no place in God's world. God's realm is Heaven. From Heaven the Earth was created: a lovely, verdant expression of loveliness. Then humans came to occupy it.  Our diversity was an example of the vast scope of God's imagination.  Early on we saw differences, even in the tribes of our neighbors. Conflict was 'justified', and has been ever since.

As rulers sought control of land and people, wars increased in violence, cruelty, and numbers afflicted. Wars of old meant wounds and fatalities to only warriors. Current conflicts include wounds and fatalities of peaceful citizens. Somewhere on earth there is a conflict and we accept that fact. Our error perceptions have overtaken our faith. Peace seems to elude us at every turn. From domestic violence to border wars conflict is reported and we rail against them.

We all desire peace and prosperity. The United Nations was formed to bring into being a peaceful world shared by all countries. Small nations welcome the effort; large ones balk at conceding any power to another government. Peace on Earth will probably not come about from nations down to individuals but rather from individuals up to governments. When peace-seeking groups increase in number and popularity, the possibility of world peace will dawn on our war-ridden consciousness. Many people still believe that peace is for weaklings, that war is inevitable, and that humans were made to fight. Competition permeates society. From sports to finances to international trade, to military force we are steeped in the idea of competition. We do so because we focus on differences; and everyone becomes a winner or a loser. Our Creator sees us as neither.

Now we are guided from this seeming competitive nature to a world family of unity. Archangel Gabriel, Jesus the Christ, and eleven Ascended Masters have come to Earth to guide us: to awaken us to our truth and to provide a road map. Each person has a responsibility to take a tiny step toward unity. The beginning is not in the home; it is in the human heart. We each have a human heart and we all have a connection to God, whether we see it; feel it; believe it or not. Unseen but known by wisdom or revelation, some are blessed to know our truth.

Our truth is that we are beloved children of God. We must re-read the Christian Bible and all other bibles of the world, with an open mind and heart. We must read between the printed lines and know what we are and why. Then we can accept others - all others - as varying notes on the musical scale that produce all holy teachings of the world's concert.

Together in cooperation unity is possible. God sees us as one with Him. We see us as separate. In spirit we are already one; in form we accept separation. We can adjust the lens of our spiritual view and see all our human brothers and sisters as one with us, and one with God.

# Section VII
## Zain

## Chapter 49   Hostage to the Ego

"Would you be hostage to the ego or host to God?" This question was asked by Jesus in *A Course in Miracles* T -15: III: 8:1.

This may seem presumptuous to some, but 'host to God' is tantamount to saying, as in Luke 17:21 . . . *the kingdom of God is within you."* The ego, whose greatest tool is fear, was created by us. Archangel Gabriel told us that in our earliest days on earth we made up this helper to warn us of pending danger. Over time we have turned more and more of our innate power over to it. The ego has become our false guide. It constantly tells us that we should be afraid, that we are tiny, insignificant creatures struggling to survive on earth.

Looking at the Milky Way, our neighborhood in space, our ego reminds us of our littleness. Viewing natural wonders on earth we are reminded of our littleness by the ego self. Looking at the huge corporations in the business world we see an impossible road to success in it. Employed by businesses which are controlled by powerful Boards of Directors, we feel insecure and helpless. Sometimes a life partner tries to control our every move. Other examples could be given. All our experiences of feeling less than are instigated, shored up and supported by, the ego.

Efforts to succeed over any hardship or challenge are met with the ego's favorite warnings, like 'What makes you think you can?' 'You are too old, sick, stupid, poor, to accomplish anything.' Too often we listen to the ego which is pretending to be in control. It has no power over us *unless we give it.* We see many individuals who have succeeded and wonder how they did it. They have chosen to listen to the God within instead of the ego self. We all have the same choice. In this seemingly complex world there are only two choices to make: Taking the road guided by the ego self or the Christ Self of us. Ego is always negative; our Higher Self is always positive. One tears down; the other builds up.

Paying constant attention to the ego's shouts we remain fearful, doubtful, and unsure of ourselves. We take whatever comes to us in life without complaint or question, or railing constantly against it. Oftentimes we settle for servitude, obedience to another and accept it as 'our lot in life.' The ego has been victorious! What life brings us is what we have requested. God's Will for us is peace, joy, and prosperity. Because He is love and loves us unconditionally, He would not have it any other way. But when we ask God to let us come to earth and learn a lesson in patience, acceptance, or understanding, He tells us that He will not forsake us or interfere with the free choice He gave us in the beginning.

In effect, the ego holds us hostage every time we listen to its dire, unwarranted warnings, its fear-based threats - its negative response to every instance when we desire to grow, to experience life in different ways, to embark on a new venture. Because it has a loud voice it gets our attention. Because it has a loud voice we believe it has authority. It has no authority over us without our permission. Because so many people around us listen to the ego every day we tend to do the same - whether to be 'accepted' by others, or whether it is easier to give up without a fight. It takes fight, with courage, to overcome the ego.

The ego has its place as a warning device, to keep us safe in traffic, at home and work, or walking. It is not necessary to eliminate it, Gabriel told us. We need only to thank it for its services and tell it that we are going to live from the spirit within us. Living from that voice - the still, small Voice of God - we will venture forth with self-confidence, self-assurance that we will never go astray. Temptations may still come, but they will no longer overwhelm us. The ego, fearing for its life, will present temptations, but listening to God within we will quickly recognize the ego at work and ignore it. We brought our ego into being and we can therefore decide on how much power to give it or take away from it.

We seem confronted with a hundred decisions a day. It was with great relief that we heard Gabriel say we actually have only two choices: listen to the still, small Voice of God within, or listen to the ego's shout of negativity. Listening to the ego we have become hostage to it. Listening to the Father we cannot fail. All our needs are met by Our Father when we accept Him and listen to Him. Nothing is more powerful than His still, small Voice.

## Chapter 50   Humble Beginnings

*And when she could not longer hide him, she took for him an ark of bulrushes, and daubed it with slime and with pitch, and put the child therein, and she laid it in the flags by the river's brink.* Ex. 2:3

Then the Pharaoh's daughter found the baby, and she named him Moses, and she raised him as her own. The name Moses means 'drawing out from the water'. Esoterically it 'represents man's development in consciousness . . . from the negative side'. (MBD, 460). Moses gave us the Ten Commandments. They are cast in stone, which indicates rigidity impossible to attain. But it was the beginning of a new stage of growth for humanity. Moses envisioned a land of plenty for his people and with Joshua's help he reached the Promised Land.

Terah gave birth to Abram. God later changed his name to Abraham: *Neither shall thy name any more be called Abram, but thy name shall be Abraham; for a father of many nations have I made thee.* (Gen. 17:5) Metaphysically, Moses means 'the quality through which man has faith in the forces invisible'. (MBD, 18). The Arian Age began approximately when Abram was born.  The ages are the 2,100 year divisions of our universe circling around a Central Sun. (AGJC, 3-4). Because of the 'precession of the Equinoxes', the next age upon Earth was the Piscean age. Jesus the Christ was born at its beginning. *And she brought forth her firstborn son, and wrapped him in swaddling clothes, and laid him in a manger; because there was no room for them in the inn.* (Luke 2:7). At this lowly place angels sang praises to God at his birth and the manger was alight with a holy Presence. They proclaimed *on earth peace, good will toward men.* (Luke 2:14) Archangel Gabriel (visiting Earth 1987-1999) told us there is not a human being on

Earth who has not heard the name Jesus; *a name which is above every name.* (Phil. 2:9).

All have heard the name; all do not worship him. Some discount him because they have faith in another religion. Some worship him, place him on a pedestal and proclaim he died for our sins. Others see Jesus the man as an elder brother who came to show us the way, the truth and the life. As our brother he brought the Christ Light in him and said we have the same light in us. Gabriel explained that Jesus came not to be worshipped but to be followed. Jesus told us that he would send a Comforter, and he did. The Holy Spirit is ever available for guidance; *we must ask for it.*

Fast forward 2,100 years and we are at the inception of the Age of Aquarius. Gabriel said it is the Age of Truth. As Gabriel is the Announcer of the Ages, he told Mother Mary an age ago that she would give birth to Jesus and as such she became the Blessed Mother. To announce the New Age, Aquarius, he came to a small church in upstate New York. It was another humble beginning of another age.

The difference was that instead of a brief moment in time, for the Annunciation to Mary and Elizabeth to announce the coming of Jesus and John the Baptist, Gabriel visited Earth many times over a period of twelve years. His audience was usually small, but his messages are for all humanity. He came to awaken us to our true origin in the Creator, clearly stating that we are holy children of God and must wake up to our Higher Self - our God-given divinity. We are not the victims we perceive ourselves to be. We are the lights of the world. All humanity is 'the only begotten son of God'. It is time to begin our journey back home to Heaven, our natural habitat. We 'left' God only in our consciousness.

Jesus the Christ also visited our small group on earth, concurrently with Gabriel, from 1995 to 1999. He desired to 'straighten out the crooked places' in scripture. Some errors were intentional; others the result of poor scribing. Gabriel's and Jesus' teachings of the late twentieth century are all available in print and/or audio recordings. See Discography. All these great Lights have come to Earth to show humankind a new way; a way to grow and become. And their beginnings were all humble. When a person is ready to step consciously upon a spiritual path, it begins in a humble setting or attitude. This may occur from a traumatic experience, loss of ability, loss of a loved one, or a revelation. We do not always identify a humble beginning except in retrospect. Humbleness is a rare human quality; humble beginnings introduce us to Heaven's expression.

## Chapter 51 Inspiration and Usurpation

The current definition of inspiration in Webster's dictionary: 'a divine influence or action on a person believed to qualify him or her to receive and communicate sacred revelation.' Usurpation is defined as 'to take possession of without legal claim.'

The root word of inspiration is 'inspire', which means inhale. We accept that inhaling means life. When breathing stops we are physically lifeless. God, the mighty Creator, breathed us forth and gave us life in *spirit form*. That spirit form is eternal. The physical body must have the breath of life to support our physical form; our spirit is forever, as part of God.

When we go within to our spirit self - in quiet moments of reflection - we are then most likely to be inspired by divine influence. The artist often tells us that the drawing, the painting, the sculpting, the writing, came from a source other than her own mind. The communication comes in silence, is received and communicated as sacred revelation. It is that revelation, received by the viewer/reader as sacred revelation. The sacred revelation often makes us gasp in wonderment.

Many individuals who are not considered 'artists' have inspired thoughts, also. They are the inventors, the problem solvers, the housewives, the counselors, the soldiers, the engineers, the laborers, who suddenly receive an inspired thought which they cannot explain. The inspired thought comes when we are open to receiving it. What interferes with inspiration is usurpation. Inspiration comes from the spirit realm of God. In contrast, usurpation comes from the ego.

We all have been told, 'You are your own worst enemy'. The name of the 'enemy' is the 'ego', and it is our own worst enemy. It is our own because we have created it, and it is our enemy because it blocks inspiration. The ego's favorite tool is fear, and at every turn it will discourage us, delay us, postpone good, and eventually harm us, with its fear-based power. We have given this part of us all the power it has. We have the ability to retake the power.

The person with the biggest ego is easy to identify. Her way is the only way; her ideas the only good ones, her life the best, etc. We all have seen or known such people. Their grandiose attitude is a cover for a feeling of inferiority. No one is inferior to another, but when a person feels that way, a compensating behavior becomes habit. Unfortunately we often engage in battle with them. The battle of egos ensues. It can happen in the workplace, the home, on the street.

The reason the ego usurps the inspired thought is because it wants to be in charge of us. It wants us to believe we need it to survive. It wants us to believe our body is the reality and totality of our being. It constantly reminds us we must value the body because it wants us to accept the body as our only life. The ego fears that if we begin living by inspiration it will die, and it is afraid to die, because it is fear-based. It has become a mighty power in our lives.

The greatest challenge for us is to recognize when the ego is ruling our attitude and behavior. We can and must ask our angels to assist us in this recognition. Recognizing is the first step, then having a conversation with the ego. We can tell it to take a walk, stand in the wings of our theater of life, or any instruction that will allow us freedom to choose. We do not need to try destroying the ego; it can continue to protect us in small ways. We created it to do so.

Over time we have handed over our power to the ego until now it rules our lives. Everyone is capable and qualified to receive intuitive, inspiring thoughts. Poverty holds us back. Poverty can mean impoverished purses, self-confidence, emotional control, physical weakness. None of these can usurp the inspired thought *unless we let it.* We are children of God; we are here to live, learn, and awaken to our spiritual selves. Only the ego-based life will fail to participate in living. The ego says we live only a short time, we are unable to learn, and we cannot become more than a body. We are so much more. We are inspired when we seek inspiration.


## Chapter 52   Interpretation and Truth

Interpretation is an ongoing process in our daily lives. We interpret behaviors, attitudes, body language, even meanings of what people say. Communication is a problem because what one person says is often interpreted differently by the listener(s). The Tower of Babel (Gen 11:9) is not only an ancient example of this confusion; it is a modern example of our inability to communicate effectively with each other.

Our interpretations are based on individual belief, judgment or circumstance. Belief usually comes from parents; judgment may emanate from parents, teachers, or past life experiences. Circumstances are the result of all our life experiences. Billions of humans inhabit this lovely planet Earth, and each person has a variety of interpretations, which change with circumstance and relationships. It is no wonder that the world seems to be a place of such confusion. "He said; she said" is just a tiny example of the problems we experience in our lack of communication.

Interpretations, or perceptions, vary by person, nationality, language, and social mores. Additionally, our interpretations vary over time as we experience a variety of situations in life. We can conclude, then, that interpretations are variable at best and infinite in variety at worst. In this world of such variability, there is little that we can count on that is constant, and constantly dependable. Truth is the only constant. Truth is dependable. Truth is what is real, actual, factual, and beyond question. I was amazed to find in Webster's New Collegiate the following definition 2a: 'transcendent fundamental or spiritual reality.' Spiritual reality is truth! Gabriel brought us truth and told us we are spirit and spirit is the only reality. When Jesus the Christ was asked by Pilate: "*What is truth?*" Jesus did not answer. The Bible mentions truth often:

*"For the law was given by Moses, but grace and truth came by Jesus Christ"* (John 1:17)

*"And ye shall know the truth, and the truth shall make you free."* (John 8:32)

*"And because I tell you the truth, ye believe me not."* (John 8:45)

Jesus' prayer to God (John 17:17) included this: *"Sanctify them through thy truth: thy word is truth."*

There are many other references to truth in the Bible. For those of us who cherish scripture, we take these words seriously. Given that truth is spiritual reality, we must ask ourselves what is spiritual reality? God is a spirit and will give us truth *if we seek it*. God speaks to us constantly. He does so by words spoken to us by friends, by writings we are guided to read, by creative thoughts and by direct revelation. The only way we can know the truth is to seek it, accept it when it comes, thank God for it, and incorporate it into our lives. It is our habit to interpret, analyze, criticize, and discount anything we see/hear that does not fit our pre-conceived ideas. That is our fundamental problem. Open-mindedness is essential if we are to find the truth we seek. Listening to others with our heart instead of our mind can reveal to us another person than the one we judge based on our ego self.

There is a freedom which truth brings. It is the freedom to listen to truth, and respond to it, as the spiritual persons we are. In His wondrous creations, God created us from Himself. Therefore we too are spirit and truth. But God also gave us free choice. We have historically made choices which range from small errors to tragic results. War is not about truth; it is about judgment, hatred and revenge. We profess to desire peace but rarely create peace in our personal lives.

To be free in this biblical sense is to live a life directed by our Creator, not determined by what our neighbors think, own, wear, or say. It takes courage, open-mindedness, and a willingness to change. Foregoing judgment and labeling we can open our hearts and minds to the Will of God and come to know truth. And come to be free.

## Chapter 53  It Came to Pass

The Bible is replete with the phrase 'it came to pass' and 'it shall come to pass.' This can easily be verified by the *Exhaustive Concordance of the Bible*. When we contemplate this fact we wonder why the words are so often stated. Today we have a phrase that 'the only thing that stays the same is change.' Life seems to present challenges that require us to change. Yet, as Archangel Gabriel explained, our entire lifetime is planned by us just so we can learn from our experiences. Experience brings change if we are to learn from it.

How we did laugh when Gabriel reminded us that nowhere in the Bible does it say, 'It came to stay.' Basic, simple comments like this came from Gabriel often. Another I now recall, 'feet represent understanding.' How logical it is! Gabriel also commented on the fact that we 'tell time' "You don't tell time anything - time tells you to do everything!" Recently people are reminding friends going through a stressful time, 'This too shall pass'. Every painful experience, every stressful event, every tragic moment does pass. Gabriel said time heals nothing. Perhaps he meant that only our willingness to overcome heals.

One wonders what life would be like if there was no change. There are groups who never change their religious beliefs. There are those who never accept new inventions. There are people who cling tenaciously to the 'old ways'. Most of us change because we are forced to, by circumstances. We may protest, and dig in our heels before we make the change, but when we do it becomes clear that change brought about a positive result. It does not make change the next time any easier. We balk at change because we expect only the worst. Disraeli said, "What we anticipate seldom occurs; what we least expect generally happens." Today we say 'Life is what happens when we are making other plans.' Whenever we are confronted with a new situation, instead of raging about it, we should first ask ourselves, 'what is the lesson for me in this?' This takes a great deal of practice, for we judge self or others harshly for a painful event.

Everything comes to pass. Everything brings us a lesson. When we learn the lesson we move on to other lessons. If an event seems to repeat itself it is because we have not as yet learned the lesson. We exist on the earth to learn and grow. Earth is a giant school of learning. When we learn a lesson well we can pass it on to others. It is said that experience is the best teacher. It is true, but only if we learn from the teaching experience. When we seek, we find. When we seek truth, it comes to us. This truth-seeking is not always a conscious endeavor. But when the truth comes at us suddenly, we recognize it immediately. When Gabriel first came I knew somehow that he spoke words of truth. One day Gabriel described the crucifixion. Some of us in the audience wept. When asked why, Gabriel said those who wept were at the scene of the crucifixion. I have no idea what role I played in that long ago time, but perhaps then is when I began to seek the truth about life itself, so that when I heard Gabriel I knew that here was the answer to my inner quest.

Our seeking will always bring us answers. Our secret yearnings to be free will find solace. Prayers and meditations are exercises in which we engage when we seek to become more than we are. Striving to learn what we cannot find in books, we ask the God of our understanding to help us understand the road ahead. Never looking back with nostalgia or guilt, we focus on a happy now, knowing it will bring a joyous tomorrow. This is promised in The Book of Common Prayer:

*"Give thanks unto him for a remembrance of his holiness,*
*For his wrath endureth but the twinkling of an eye, and in his pleasure is life:*
*heaviness may endure for a night, but joy cometh in the morning,"* Ps. xxx.4 (also Bible, Ps. 30:5)

All misery, pain and distress endure for a brief moment of time in the scheme of eternity, but joy endures forever because it is the joy that comes with unconditional love. Unconditional love comes from God to us. All misery shall come to pass, but joy - as love and peace, endures forever.

# Chapter 54   "It's Her Time!"

When a woman has waited nine months to bring forth a new human being, this phrase announces the pending birth. Excitement permeates the minds of all relatives and friends who know the mother-to-be. This is the time to ask if the woman is in a safe place; has a helper at hand; is as comfortable as possible. Whether a nurse, a doctor, a midwife or a relative will attend, everyone is concerned that someone is there with her. Preparations have all been made and now all the waiting is over. Everyone anticipates the news about hour and minute of birth, the weight, length, the amount and color of hair. The new mother counts toes and fingers; nurses her infant if she desires to, and soaks up all the joy inherent in that exquisite moment of welcome.

Until recently no one knew the sex of the baby coming. Somehow this heightened the excitement. According to Archangel Gabriel the people of pre-recorded history did not even connect the sex act with the birth of a baby! Now, of course, we can know the sex in utero. How wonderful is modern science that we can see the embryo moving inside its mother!

Gabriel told us that the day will come when women will decide they do not want to be limited for nine months and embryos will mature outside the body. It is up to others to determine what, if any, effect this will have on the baby's nurturance. Birth itself is a miracle of life. No one can look at a newborn without a feeling of spiritual warmth. Wordsworth nailed it when he said of human birth, "Trailing clouds of glory do we come . . ." Yes, fresh from Heaven to this planet Earth, do we come forth to live out our lives here.

Gabriel was once asked why some women have a short labor and others struggle for many long hours to bring forth the infant. He explained that the infant knows what it planned for life's experiences and just prior to birth reviews the plan, then has some indecision about fulfilling it. Of course the birth will occur; that cannot be denied, but in reviewing one's plan sometimes it seems insurmountable, and the fetus balks. Finally, the decision must be made to come forth and live out the plan. For some reason this author compared the birthing of an infant (which I experienced four times) with the re-birth of the planet Earth. Gabriel made an astounding statement about our ecological efforts. Gabriel told us that if some people had not begun caring about Mother Earth thirty years sooner, it would have been too late to rejuvenate her! *Thirty years* - of the millions of years she has been in existence! In a few decades we have done so much damage to her that we have nearly destroyed her. She spent millions of years in developing and in only a few decades humankind has inflicted such damaging abuse! It reminds one of a human being which requires more time to physically mature than any other animal species. In one quick decision we can destroy or begin to damage the body and brain, with various kinds of negative behavior, such as drug abuse.

Many people still deny that the planet is in danger. Warming glaciers will inevitably raise the sea level which will swallow miles of shoreline. Ocean liners have dumped human waste in the vast and seeming self-cleaning seas. Lakes and rivers have been polluted. The very air we breathe is polluted by emissions of vehicles, factories, and mines. The health of many millions has been compromised in the name of greedy wealth and power. There seems to be no responsibility, no moral compass, no spiritual motive in us.

Simply put, we have replaced our belief in a Creator with other gods. The gods of money, fame, political power, personal power have superseded faith in the God of our beginning. The ego is winning us over to believe we have all the power. Without God, we can do nothing. That is an immutable truth. With faith in God and reliance on His guidance, there is nothing we cannot do. Church attendance is not the answer. Kneeling quietly in prayer and turning our lives over to the care of God *as we understand Him* will bring us every sincere desire. Angels attend us when we do not turn our backs on them. We must ask, then listen, then live, from *the Lord God of our Being.* When we do, we will restore Mother Earth. We must do so if we desire to remain living here. It's her time!

## Chapter 55  Jesus' Guidance

*"The truly helpful are God's miracle workers whom I direct until we are all united in the joy of the Kingdom. I will direct you to wherever you can be truly helpful and to whoever can follow my guidance through you."* ACIM Orig. T 4: VIII: 102

Jesus came to live a life of love and forgiveness as an example (John 13:15) for us all. He gave his peace to us by his very presence. He often told us to follow him. The word 'us' is appropriate for two reasons. First, his message was intended for all who read the New Testament. Second, some of us were on the earth at the same time Jesus was. Now we know - from Archangel Gabriel - that we do live many lives on earth at our own choosing, with our free choice.

The sixth Principle of Miracles (ACIM Intro) states, "Miracles are natural. When they do *not* occur, something has gone wrong." In this context, Jesus performed miracles because they came through him naturally. He told us to follow him, and said, *"Do as I do"*. Everything he did we can do (John 14:12). We, like Jesus, can become miracle workers. There are specific lessons for us to learn in order to become miracle workers. We can name them at will, but we are unwilling most of the time to look at ourselves. The fear of what we will find *inside us* keeps some of us from ever meditating - sitting in silence and listening for the Voice of God. That Voice will direct us unerringly on our spiritual path to our fulfillment as miracle workers.

The greatest distraction from stepping upon a conscious spiritual path is our focus on our bodies. The body is a temporal thing. We all believe in death because we see it constantly. Many people fear death because they perceive it as a state of non-existence. The spirit of us, created by the Father, is eternal as God Who brought us forth. Gabriel astounded us with the fact that Earth is the only planet that still practices disease and death. *"Death is swallowed up in victory. O death, where is thy sting?* (I Cor. 15:55). Jesus proved to us, by his resurrection, that he overcame death. He proved to us, by his resurrection and ascension, that it can be done. Gabriel assured us we all will ascend and be raised up to heaven.

There have been so many interpretations of the Christian Bible that Christianity has become a vast variety of denominations. What a great and glorious religion it could be if all these groups could find common ground in Jesus' teachings. Exclusion creates the denominations; revolt and analysis have brought about much dissention. All these interpretations fail to understand the all-inclusiveness; the love and forgiveness that Jesus taught. 'Judge not' has been completely ignored. Jesus the Christ chose to return late in the twentieth century (1995-1999). He came to clarify some of the many errors in scripture. Some words were put in his mouth by scribes or their masters who wanted to print 'what was acceptable' to people then. The lack of literary accuracy resulted in errors of translation undetected by any proofreader or editor.

The worst such error was pointed out by Gabriel, when he told us that 'Jesus, only begotten son of God' was originally written, 'Jesus, begotten son of the one God.' This one error has distorted the meaning of Jesus' life and our perceived destiny. Instead of putting Jesus on a pedestal to worship but never emulate, we need to see him as the man Jesus and the Christ Light that was, and remains, inside him. That Light is also inside us, and we must learn to acknowledge and live by it. Now is the time to go back (meaning of 'religion') and begin our journey Home to God as Jesus intended.

*"Do not make the pathetic human error of 'clinging to the old rugged cross'."* (ACIM Orig. 4: In.:4). We can overcome the cross by learning the message of the crucifixion. Only frustration can result from worshipping Jesus and then being as good as we can be, knowing we can never do what he did, or be what he was. Jesus was a man who ate, drank, laughed, and cried. He had within him - *and knew it* - the Christ. We all have that light within. We all have the choice to seek it. As he promised, Jesus will be with us always. His guidance is sure. We must *choose* to listen to the Voice of God, for it was that Voice that Jesus obeyed.

Before he raised Lazarus, Jesus said, *"Father I thank thee that thou hast heard me. And I know that thou hearest me always: but because of the people which stand by I said it, that they may believe that thou hast sent me,"* (John 11: 41-42). When

125

Jesus came (1995-1999) he told us that when he walked the earth he broke every rule, and listened only to the Voice within him. That is our goal. It can be achieved. It does not take work but only acceptance, a little willingness, a decision to meditate and hear God's guidance. That is what Jesus did; that is what he continues to do; that is our mission on earth. Then we will be united in the joy of the Kingdom.

## Chapter 56  Jesus' Plan

*The following essay is based on the truth teachings of Archangel Gabriel, who visited Earth many times from 1987 to 1999. The reader is encouraged to hear them/read them.*

Jesus had experienced many incarnations on Earth prior to his birth as Jesus. He was Hermes, Melchizedek, Joshua, Joseph, and Buddha. After his transition from Buddha, he surrendered himself to the Will of God for five hundred years of earth time. Then he desired to come to earth to save everyone. Jesus knew, through all his lifetimes, that he was the son of God. He was perplexed that everyone else did not see the truth of themselves - all children of the Living God. So he went to Archangel Gabriel and said, 'I am going to Earth to save the people'. And Gabriel said, in so many words, 'Go for it'.

Jesus went to all the men he chose to be his disciples, and they agreed. As described in the apocryphal book *Infancy*, eye witnesses said Mary, Mother of Jesus, was a virgin before the birth and a virgin after the birth of Jesus. His mother, Mary, often chided Joseph that he was not Jesus' real father. Jesus loved his parents dearly. As a child he practiced his skills, raising a playmate after his friend died. He would tell the teachers what their lesson would be before they taught it, and they wondered how he knew. When his father erred in his woodworking shop, and a piece of wood came out too short, Jesus would stretch the wood to its proper size. The apocryphal books tell of the miracles Jesus performed as an infant. In his crib he told his mother that he was the son of God, as promised her by Gabriel. These 'hidden books' of the Bible also tell of the healings imparted to babies by the very clothes Jesus wore as an infant, as well as the water in which he was bathed.

It is widely believed that Jesus worked in his father's carpenter shop until he was baptized by John. From a young age he traveled far and wide. He went to Egypt, the Himalayas, even North America, as Native Americans report in their 'myths'. Only by virtue of his spiritual abilities could this be so. He was always a teacher, and in every land he also learned lessons for his journey. In the Himalayas, in the Himis monastery, he was known as Issa. It was in Egypt that he became christed, as described in *The Aquarian Gospel of Jesus the Christ.* In the time of Jesus, teachers had to be thirty years of age to be recognized. Thus it was that Jesus went to the Jordan to be baptized by John at that time and commence his holy mission.

The forty days in the wilderness were days of temptation - not by the devil (who does not exist) - but by his ego. Jesus knew that he had in him all power, all knowledge, from God. But when his ego tempted him he remembered his plan to save the world and did not succumb to his ego's pull. While in the wilderness, he built a fire one night and sat in its warmth. A lion approached, felt the love emanating from Jesus, and lay down beside him. In those days, lions had no reason to fear man. And Jesus was fearless. In his early years he walked everywhere or rode a beast. He used boats to traverse the waters. Then came the night when the disciples traveled across the sea and Master Jesus walked on the water to assure them they were alright. Another time, as he sailed with his disciples, he calmed the raging sea. The Bible relates these moments.

During his entire life he knew what he planned to do - be crucified and then resurrect, to show humanity that there is no death. Pilate was an Essene, as was Jesus and his family. When Jesus was taken before Pilate, he winked at Pilate and gained a private session with the governor of Judea. Pilate offered Jesus a safe escape, but Jesus told him it was his time. It may disturb some readers that Jesus did *not suffer* on the cross, or during all the abuse inflicted on him. The reason is that he raised his consciousness into his Higher Self; his God Self; the Christ Light within him. This elevated consciousness occurred in the Garden of Gethsemane, when he prayed, *Not as I will but as thou wilt.* (Matt. 26:39, Mark 14:36)   Before that moment, when he went to the disciples, his intention was to tell them to flee with him. But when he looked at his sleeping followers he remembered that all humanity was asleep to its own divinity, and he returned to his prayers and made that fateful decision.

As Jesus carried the cross, on the way to the crucifixion, he saw a man whom he had helped long before on a country road. He knew the man had not seen his family in many years.  Jesus looked at him and said, 'Turn around', and when the man did, he saw his family. Jesus also healed some of the members of the jeering crowd. As a Roman soldier nailed Jesus' feet, Jesus became aware that the soldier had twin sons at home with epilepsy. He said to the soldier 'Today your sons are healed'. When the soldier returned home he learned that his sons were healed the same hour in which Jesus was crucified.

On the cross the Master was hung with two men. One of them cried out in anger and pain. The other looked at Jesus and asked why he, a great teacher, was being crucified. Jesus told the man that he (the man) was a son of God. The man protested, and said only Jesus was. But Jesus stated 'And look where I am'. Then Jesus mentally showed the man a view of Paradise, and the man looked again at Jesus and said, 'We are the sons of God'.

The three days in the tomb were spent by Jesus the Christ in changing the molecular structure of his body so he could appear in form to his disciples and thus prove there is no death.  He appeared to about fifty people, in various places, to show them that he still lived. When it came time to break the seal on the tomb, no person could be found to do it, for fear of death in defiance of the Roman rulers. Archangel Michael said he would gladly break the seal, and he did.

Jesus' plan for his final incarnation had been carried out. But something happened he had not planned. As he hung on the cross, and looked out over the assembled crowd, full of fear and anger, he realized that he had not saved the world; he had only saved himself. Only Jesus, God and

Gabriel could know this. In a seminar by Jesus he was asked what his greatest regret was in his lifetime as Jesus. He answered it was the crucifixion; because it was unnecessary.

# Section VIII
## Cheth

## Chapter 57   John's Four Chapters

If I had to choose one section of the Bible for inspiration, it would be in the 14th through the 17th chapter of the Book of John, in the New Testament. The Old Testament of the Patriarchs is the Jewish Bible. The New Testament of Jesus the Christ came, of course, after he died and resurrected. These chapters contain the words of Jesus the Christ at the Last Supper, prior to his arrest and crucifixion.

It was the Last Supper, in an upper room. Jesus had already washed the feet of his twelve disciples. Now we know that feet represent understanding. Jesus desired greatly to have his followers understand his message of love and forgiveness. He knew that soon he would go to Gethsemane and there be arrested. He knew what lay ahead, and these verses were his last instructions to his devoted followers. The words of the Master Jesus were given the disciples, but were intended for us all. In Chapter 14 he tells us to be calm; to remember that in Heaven there are many mansions (states of consciousness); that he was going to prepare a place for us. He boldly stated, *"I am the way, the truth and the life."* Then he said that seeing him, we also saw God. No one, he said, could come to the Father except through him, which meant that to know the way (his path of love and peace, joy and forgiveness), accepting only truth, and living as he lived would one be *aware* of their eternal life.

Verse 10: he channeled the words given him by the Father in Whom he lived.  Jesus said we ought to believe in him and if not, we ought to believe in his works. Everything he did - and more - we can do because he went Home to God. Anything we ask in his name he would see it done in order to glorify God in His son (us - the human family). He told us he would ask the Father to send *another* Comforter in his name to remain with us forever. In this statement he was promising us eternal guidance of the Holy Spirit.

We cannot see the Spirit of Truth, even though it lives *in us*. Jesus said he would come back even though he was leaving for a little while. Thus he was saying he knew he would be absent from his body (crucifixion) for a while but would return. Because he lived we all shall live - in spirit. And some day we all will understand that the Light of the Christ dwells in us all.

Verse 26: The Comforter (Holy Spirit/Ghost) will remind us of all things he said. This reminds me of Archangel Gabriel's words that he taught us nothing new, only reminded us of what we have forgotten.

Verse 29:  He predicted his crucifixion to prove that he could predict the future.

In Chapter 15 Jesus makes clear that he represents the beginning of our growth in awareness of our divinity, which produces positive benefits. Without the Christ Light - the Love of God - we are nothing. But with it in our consciousness we can do anything. It was a powerful promise; a true one. He intended his words to bring us abundant joy. As he loved us, we should love each other. This love is the unconditional love of the Christ, not love as we perceive it - divided into 'kinds' of love.

He reminded us that when we engaged in negative behavior it was clandestine and covert. But being aware of the negative, in contrast to goodness and holiness of God, we *'have no cloke for our sin'*.  He clearly states that he was hated without a cause, because his life consisted only of unconditional love and its expression. We have been with him from the beginning because God created us all as one great human family.

Chapter 16: Jesus said it was 'expedient' for him to leave because only by his asking would the Comforter come to us. Upon coming, the Comforter would reprove the world 'of sin' because we did not believe him; would reprove the world 'of righteousness' because Jesus ascended to Heaven, to be seen no more in flesh; would reprove the world 'of judgment' because we mistakenly judged the 'prince of this world'. He told us the Spirit of Truth will give us words to speak and tell us of the future. The world, he said, would rejoice at his going and coming back to show life is eternal and full of joy. Proverbs would give way to plain speaking. He said, "*I have overcome the world.*" Jesus overcame the world because he was the expression and embodiment of God's love. Love will someday completely overcome the world when we all recognize God's love in ourselves and each other.

Chapter 17 contains Jesus' final earthly prayer with his disciples. It should be read. In it he thanks the Father for his life's mission and apostles. He prays for them on their journeys. As a devout prayer from the son to the Father, it defies paraphrase. Cross-referenced books include I Corinthians, Colossians, 1 John, Romans, I Peter, Hebrews, Galatians, and Ephesians.

## Chapter 58  Judas' Conversion
*This essay is based the truth about Judas' life as give us by Archangel Gabriel; date unknown.*

Traveling today is not what it was centuries ago. Mostly people remained in their home area. Communication was limited to word of mouth. Commerce increasingly required men to travel in order to sell and deliver goods between communities and between countries. Two thousand years ago traveling was treacherous. Robbers and murderers attacked unarmed groups, and rarely did anyone travel alone. The groups, upon planning a necessary trip, hired protectors - what today might be called 'hitmen'. In the pioneer days of the westward movement in the U.S. wagons usually carried a man with a rifle to ward off attackers.

When Jesus traveled with his disciple they were not armed. They did not carry weapons. Their leader, Jesus, was a man of peace; Prince of Peace as foretold by Isaiah 9:6. So to ensure that their journey of faith would be uninterrupted, a protector was hired. His name was Judas. He was well known as a protector and had killed others in his trade. He traveled with Jesus and his disciples on all their journeys.

As the group traveled, Jesus taught his lessons to anyone who gathered to hear him. There were other traveling preachers, and so he was not always seen as the Son of God. But when he began performing miracles - turning water to wine, healing, walking on water, etc., people took more notice of him and he gained followers. Judas became part of the group, and as such he was always in the audience when Jesus preached. Jesus' teachings were new and sometimes difficult to comprehend, but the love he expressed and the patience he exhibited reflected a man of truth, which Jesus was.

As Judas listened to Master Jesus, he became fascinated with the new teachings and developed a bond with the man he was to guard. Over time Judas came to love Jesus as a brother, instead of as an employer. Jesus was aware of the change in Judas' perception. Jesus also knew the part Judas was to play in Jesus' final days - just as Jesus himself knew, birth, his own destiny.

After all the traveling, Judas continued to follow Jesus, now as a disciple himself. Then came the day when the priests, who hated Jesus because he performed miracles (which they could not) planned to have Jesus arrested by the Roman soldiers. The chief priests and elders knew that Judas was a follower, and secretly told him they wanted to merely talk to Jesus. They would pay Judas thirty pieces of silver in exchange for knowledge of Jesus' whereabouts. Judas saw no harm in the deal, maybe hoping that the priests were finally ready to accept the presence and teachings of this man of peace.

As the time approached for the Last Supper, Jesus said to Judas, privately, that the time was nearing for Judas to betray him. Judas protested, saying he could not do so. But Jesus reminded him that he had agreed to his part before coming to Earth. Still Judas protested, saying, "I cannot." Then Jesus said, "If you love me, you will do this." And, as Gabriel put it, "Judas went to betray the man he loved."

When, at the Garden of Gethsemane, the Roman soldiers seized Jesus and arrested him. Judas realized he had been used and saw the impact his betrayal had on the Master. He was wild with anger, and went to the priests in the temple, and he threw down the thirty pieces of silver and departed. (Matt. 27:5). Contrary to scripture, Judas did not commit suicide. As a 'hitman' in his earlier years he had garnered many enemies. Now, in his guilt and grieving state he was vulnerable. He was not protecting himself from danger. One of his enemies took advantage of Judas' situation and murdered him. When Jesus ascended to Heaven, he encountered Judas. Judas fled from him, stinging with guilt over his betrayal of Jesus. But Jesus reached out with his aura, and pulled Judas to him. He held Judas in his arms until he had calmed him; released him from his feelings of guilt.

## Chapter 59  Knowing God

*"Love not the world, neither the things that are in the world. If any man love the world, the love of the Father is not in him."* I John: 2:3

With our patriotism we proclaim that we love our native land. We love our families, neighbors and co-workers. We may love our jobs. When we realize, at some point in life, that there must be something more, we seek an understanding of a power we cannot see. It is a higher power. Our soul is longing to return Home to our true native place, Heaven. We are being reminded that our Father in heaven loves us no matter what we have done in life. Sometimes guilt takes us to our knees and we seek forgiveness. Fear may incite us to ask the unseen God for rescue.

Someone once said, "The unexamined life is not worth living." What we need to examine is the life of our unseen Self; our spirit Self. When Jesus said that the kingdom of God is within, no one then really understood it. It was too esoteric for the pragmatic thinking of the time. In this day of industrial and electronic knowledge, it still is. If we truly believed that the kingdom of God is within us all, we would know God. We would know God as our true Creator, Father, instructor, and guide in our entire life.

The starting point to know God is to know that *God is*. The book of Job relates some of the wonders we cannot control, like rain, earthquakes, tsunamis. There must surely be a power greater than we. The greatest power is love, and God is love. Humans have tendency to believe only in destructive power. We see earthquakes as destructive, but Archangel Gabriel explained that in order for new ideas to flourish, old ideas must be abandoned. We all become compassionate after an earthquake. It is a reflective response to help each other in the aftermath of a tragedy. In such moments we come closer to God, by seeing Him in our neighbors.

The ancient axiom *Know Thyself* is forever true. When we know ourselves as created children of God we understand the familyhood of humanity.

In the special, quiet moments of life when we are inspired, there comes a knowingness that all is well and we are safe in God. The Psalmist reports: *"Be still and know that I am God."* (Ps. 46:10). In that stillness we do know God is; we do know God loves us unconditionally. We know ourselves and we know God. This has nothing to do with grandiosity, pride, power, or specialness. Grandiosity is a cover up for low self-esteem. Pride, some say, stands for 'please remember I direct everything.' Power is a sense of control, and we have all known - or been -- controlling people. Specialness is a sign that others are seen as separate from us. Since we are one family of God, separateness is impossible.

To know ourselves as His children is to know Him. Gabriel reminded us, 'You are in the world, but not *of* the world." This planet Earth is noted in the Bible: *He . . . hangeth the earth upon nothing.* (Job 26:7). It is our temporary residence. It is as finite as our bodies. The world (earth) will end some day; when we stop loving it as our only home. We will all have come to love God and His world more than all the distractions of earthly life: stuff we own, things we do, places we travel, 'special' relationships.

A new freedom will be ours: the freedom to know God; to know God *in us*. The peace on earth promised by the Prince of Peace will become a reality. We can imagine a total freedom; we can bring to us a world of peace. When we finally have a peaceful world our next step is to depart this world forever; to be with God in His realm of Heaven. It is then we shall know God in His fullness, and know that we are part of that fullness.

We may think this is a far-off time, but let us remember what Gabriel said to a pregnant woman at one of his seminars: "The child you are carrying will ascend." In the coming generations we will see ascension as a way to depart earth forever, and forego the karmic wheel which has bound us so long. Knowing God in us, as us, we will seek to *live* the God in us and live from that spark of power. It is in us now; we sometimes suspect it now; we will *know* it then.

## Chapter 60   Laws of Chaos

We cannot live by the laws of chaos and still believe in God, because they are antithecal. Perhaps the writer had it right when he said, "God made man in His own image, and man returned the compliment." God is love and love is God's image, yet we continue to consider ourselves as mere bodies. In returning the compliment we see God in our own image - a physical form with power in His hand, sitting on a cloud and imparting punishment to wrong-doers.

We all believe we deserve some kind of punishment - a small thing, like a headache or a backache; or a large punishment, like life in prison. And we 'justify' the punishment by identifying some wrong we did another - or some wrong another did to us. We seem to accept the idea that some people are meant to suffer while others have a trouble-free or pain-free life. This implies a capricious god. "*Then Peter opened his mouth, and said, Of a truth I perceive that God is no respecter of persons.*" (Acts 10:34) We are all the same in God's sight.

We see ourselves as separate. In that separateness we feel a need to find someone we can love, trust, form a family with. In finding that 'other' we find security. We determine that blood is thicker than water. We are as safe as a cradled baby while on earth because God cares for us. "*And the tree of the field shall yield her fruit, and the earth shall yield her increase, and they shall be safe in their land, and shall know that I am the Lord*" (Ezek. 34:27)

In our belief that everyone has her own truth, we have lost sight of the fact that truth is truth. Our reality once was that the Earth was flat; that the Sun revolved around the Earth. Now we know the truth - which is that the Earth is an orb and it revolves around the Sun. When one is beleaguered with tragedy her reality is that life is difficult. To the one who does not experience many bumps in the road of life her reality is that life is comfortable. The truth is that what we expect is what we get. If we do not like our lives we can change them with our free choice, or we can change our personal perspective of the situation. Truth needs no defense. It simply is.

The truth of life on Earth is that it is illusion. It is illusion because it is so temporary, we feel so vulnerable and prone to suffering. God is eternal; love is eternal; life in God's realm is eternal. Since we are made in God's image, we too are love, and eternal. We have come to accept the phrase 'going home' when a person dies. Finally, after two thousand years, we accept the truth brought to us by our elder brother, Jesus. The Christ in him is the Christ in us. This earthly life is merely a school of learning.

We have chosen to make this earth life also a place of punishment. Pain and suffering seem inevitable. That is part of the chaotic life we choose. Some individuals live a very long life in good health while others suffer debilitation and terrible illnesses. We can blame this on a God of love, or we can become aware that perhaps, with our God-given free choice, we decided we deserve our pain. If we have free choice from God, we need to ask when he bestowed it upon us. His birthing us into spirit was the moment He granted free choice. Our children, upon maturation, know they have free choice.

Being God's children we are love, as is our Creator. Love does not suffer or cause suffering. The idea of punishment is ours. The idea of suffering is ours. Pain and misery are of our own creation. We are, in truth, our own worst enemy. We judge ourselves severely. We invite pain to learn what it is like, for we have inflicted pain on others in past years or past lifetimes. Our pain now is the payback *we have chosen*. We design and live out the punishment we think we deserve. Forgiveness of self will dispel the pain. Forgiveness is necessary only as a cure for judgment. That is why it so very important to remember the scriptural injunction 'Judge not'. Matthew, Luke and John all make this statement.

There is no judgment to be made. We have never harmed another without their consent, and no one ever harmed us without ours. *God would not allow it.* In His all-encompassing love we exist. Now is the time to dispense with the laws of chaos (ACIM T 23:2: *h*), and begin living from our God Self. Now is the time for living by the Laws of God. (ACIM, T 15:VI: 5: 10-12)


## Chapter 61   Let Him Save Himself

*"And the people stood beholding. And the rulers also with them derided him, saying, He saved others; let him save himself, if he be Christ, the chosen of God.* Luke 23:35

Golgotha, or Calvary, was the name of the hill on which Jesus was crucified. This method of punishment was common then. There is a symbolism of Golgotha (place of the skull). "The skull is the place where intellect is crossed out, that Spirit may win an eternal ascendancy." (MBD, 240)

The mocking crowd, as they beheld Jesus on the cross, urged him to save himself to prove he was the chosen Son of God. They thought that if he was the Son of God he claimed to be, he could come down off the cross and appear in perfect physical form. They did not know that in fact he would save himself, when he resurrected on the third day. Nor did they know he would appear to many people in form before ascending.

All humanity, when breathed forth by God, was given free choice. In his God-given free choice, Jesus decided to come to earth and save humanity. He knew he was a Son of God. He could not understand why the rest of us did not know we also are. Through all his lifetimes on earth he knew he was a Son of God. As Hermes, Melchizedek, Joshua, Joseph, Buddha, and Jesus, he *always knew* that he was a Son of God. He had many other lives besides these. These are the ones Archangel Gabriel described for us because they were the ones in which the man who became Jesus had a shift in his consciousness.

When Jesus decided to come to earth to save humanity, he told Gabriel about his plan. In effect, Gabriel responded with, 'go for it'. Jesus' plan included all his disciples who agreed beforehand they would serve him. We all plan our lives prior to physical birth. Everyone agrees to participate with us, by their free choice. Jesus planned the resurrection because it would call the world's attention to his life, death and resurrection. If he died quietly with no one present, he would not have been noticed.

Gabriel explained the stunning truth of Jesus' awareness on the cross: As Jesus looked out over the crowd at Calvary; he saw only the fear, anger, distrust, doubt and vengefulness of them all. He alone was a shining light in that dark setting. No one else could behold his light, for mortal eyes cannot see spirit. (I Cor. 2:14) In that murky air he realized that he had only saved himself. No one can save another. Gabriel asked his audience how we would feel if someone asked us to suffer for all the wrong-doings of our neighbor.

When Jesus came in the 1990s he was asked if he would have changed anything if he could live his life over. He said 'the crucifixion; it was unnecessary.' Of course he cannot do it over, any more than we can re-write our lives. When Gabriel was asked if there would be a Second Coming, he said, 'No, he (Jesus) would only be killed again.' What Jesus taught so long ago is what we must read, and learn, and live by. Some of his words were altered errantly or intentionally. Much of what was originally written in the New Testament has been purged.

Jesus visited us (1995-1999) to 'straighten out the crooked places' in scripture. His lessons of those years are available in print and/or disk. See Discography. Also, he brought forth, through Helen Schucman, a book entitled *A Course in Miracles*. Unfortunately there are many Christians who will not accept channeling in any form. Because of this rigid obstinacy, the truth will take a long time to be accepted. Gabriel said it takes humanity about two thousand years to learn something new.

Gabriel shall return in two thousand years to announce a new age, the Age of Capricorn. Mark your calendar! Meanwhile, read the Bible with a new perspective, one of symbolism. The Bible is a book of symbolism. The Book of Revelation, for instance, is not about an apocalypse. It is about my life and yours. It describes our journey (without distance) from God and back to God. Gabriel spent two days explaining the symbolism. See sacredgardenfellowship.org

## Chapter 62   Levels of Accomplishment

Public education affords us all the opportunity to learn the basic subjects of reading, writing and arithmetic. We swell with pride upon receiving a high school graduation certificate, whether we earn it timely or later in life. Relatives share our joy.  Commencement is a fitting word because our life of worldly learning now begins. Some of us enter an apprentice program to qualify us for the title of 'journeyman' in a trade. Others enter a higher education institution to study the discipline of their choice, leading to a degree which indicates preparedness to enter a chosen field of work. Some continue on to 'graduate degrees' to enter a field at a higher level of accomplishment.

We achieve other accomplishments, like marriage and family. Carrying a child for nine months and delivering it is a blessed accomplishment. A newborn comes ". . . trailing clouds of Glory" as Wordsworth says in his *Ode on Immortality*. Learning to live with others peacefully is a social accomplishment which carries no 'degree'. Life presents to us a variety of experiences and a variety of individuals with whom to interact. Some become friends; some 'enemies', some acquaintances. Some people remain in our lives for many years; some we know for a few months; some we spend one minute with in an elevator.  In-laws become part of our birth family.

Every day of our working life can provide us with an opportunity to meet new friends or even a potential mate. Learning to live cooperatively is essential to our very health and well-being. Social accomplishments include acceptance, understanding, tolerance, compassion, forgiveness. These attributes are all free. Sometimes our egos rebel at such generous attitudes. It is our ego, actually, which rejoices in all our accomplished tasks and lessons. Our egos glory in the separated self - the self which sees 'others' as 'different' people. The ego insists that whatever we accomplish is the result of a solitary experience; a special, individual mind.

Creators and inventors of the past have not always had advanced degrees. Jesus the Christ did not. Moses and the prophets of old did not. They were inspired by spirit. This inspiration is available to us all. From an earthly viewpoint tapping into it could save time and money. From a spiritual standpoint it is an awakening to our Christ Self.

Of course we need basic information like how to read and how to write. But now we can read from a computer screen in lieu of a book - or 'listen' to a book. Now we can type on a keyboard and leave pen and paper behind. Cursive writing, to the dismay of some, is becoming a lost art. Now we can make instant calculations instead of dividing and multiplying 'by hand'. Technology has exploded in the past hundred years. Technology has grown apace while our spiritual growth has been largely ignored.

It is our spiritual nature that accomplishes cooperation with others. It is our spiritual nature that accomplishes a family and forms a sense of unity in the family. As we move from childhood into adulthood and expand the scope of our friends, we find it necessary to expand our horizon of understanding to include the world. WWII took many lives, maimed others, and ended in the worst destructive force ever invented by humankind. It also gave us new medical information as war wounded were treated. Most importantly it expanded our awareness of other cultures, and intermarriage between them has resulted.

The concept of unity of all religions surfaced in the mind of Jeffrey Moses and in 1989 he published *Oneness: Great Principles Shared by all religions*. All religions agree on The Golden Rule, Love Thy Neighbor,

141

There is One God, and twenty-six other principles noted by Moses. In this unity of religion we can see a unity of all people, everywhere on Earth. We are, in effect, one people; one family of God. A human family is sourced in two parents; the family of God is sourced in our One Creator. Our spiritual birth imbues us with love and wisdom. God is omniscient and as His own, we too are omniscient. All wisdom is ours when we seek it. First comes acknowledgement of this truth; then application. We will not learn quantum physics without some background in science, but invention comes from above.

The artist who paints on his easel will often tell you that he mentally 'sees' his work before he manifests it with paint. Some writers, including this one, are guided by intuition. The ideas come from 'above' (spirit), as I recall lessons taught by Archangel Gabriel (1987-1999). "As above; so below" is an eternal truth. Faith in the One God as the Source of all wisdom enables us to seek the answers we desire. Our greatest accomplishment will be when we realize that we are already accomplished, as explained in *A Course of Love* by Mari Perron, first receiver, 2014

## Chapter 63   Life as We Know It

Life as we know it is limited to the planet Earth. We read about Atlantis and wonder what it was like. Archangel Gabriel presented a lesson on Atlantis and what it was like. (*Atlantis Rising*, 8/24/97). Several books of the Bible mention giants. They were the remnants of Atlantis. They were considered giants because they had huge heads. Archangel Gabriel explained they had very small hearts, and cared not for each other. Some of the population thereof performed atrocious experiments on their peers. The remnant of Atlantis is in the vicinity of the 'Bermuda Triangle'. This, Gabriel said, is the fourth planet we have called home. Before Atlantis we lived on Lemuria, and prior to Lemuria we lived on Mu.

Originally they were all lush, beautiful planets on which to exist. But we polluted and destroyed them, and we are in the process of destroying Earth. We humans love to think we are the most intelligent of all the residents of the universe - if indeed the other planets are occupied at all. Many planets in the Solar System have a population. Yet Gabriel said that we are the least developed. He said Earth is the only planet which still practices disease and death. Occupants of other planets come and observe us bury the dead, and wonder why we are so wasteful. They wonder why we do not ascend as they do. They do not understand that we have not as yet learned how!

We seem obsessed with the idea that any extra-terrestrials must be 'out to get us', instead of seeing them as curious about us and having intentions of helping us; teaching us. Star Wars is a household name. We are so war-oriented that cooperation between planets seems impossible. Objects in the sky cannot be identified so we expect them to have negative connotations. We fear them, and if possible we capture and hold them hostage. There are stories of this behavior. There are also stories of earthlings being taken by them. This strikes us with terror, but I wonder if those captives are taken to another planet far lovelier than Earth, where peace and cooperation prevail.

Perhaps now we are sending out invitations to other planets to seek a mutual communication and an inter-stellar conference. We may flee in terror if they look *different* from us. Now is the time to consider communication with other planets in order that we may learn from them. Perhaps, in observing Earth they do not want to land and become friendly because we are constantly at war with each other.

As I write this I learned that several spottings of space ships have occurred over Native American Reservations. I also learned that one of the clauses of Indian- US Government treaties prohibits military presence on Indian lands. It is interesting to note that researchers are constantly reaching to outer space, digging in ancient ruins and diving deeply into the seas. Applying all this curiosity and seeking, what might we learn if we pursued a working relationship with our spirit selves?

First we would need to accept the idea that we have a spirit self. What else could Jesus have meant, when he said, "The kingdom of God is within"? The only way we could access information from it is through meditation (listening to God). Only a few humans are engaging in that practice. Are afraid of what we will find? Archangel Gabriel said our worst fear is we will find out that we *are* children of God! To go within and access our spirit self (our innate beingness) would enable us to know *anything* we desire, provided we possess the background information required to comprehend it.

Will fascination with the past we do not know be any different from the past we do know? Would we find even more wars, greater cruelty, or more consuming plagues? The past reaches back all the way to our origin, as a Thought of God. Do we remember it? Or do we choose to deny it, fearing that if we are children of God and left Him, He would surely never take us back. Nonsense. The human father of the Prodigal Son welcomed his wayward offspring with open arm. an embrace and a banquet in his honor. So too will our Creator respond when - not if - we finally return Home. Life as we know it can become life as we love it. It is a choice for us to make.

The world and life as we know it therein are of our own making. Life as we known it is full of distressful events - accidents, sickness, pain and sorrow. We assume that is life and we deal with it. We are in truth so much more. We remain in that slumber state Adam experienced, and since the Bible does not tell us Adam woke up, maybe we assume that we never will, either. But our souls long to return Home, knowing their origin. Our original Home is Heaven. It is our *natural habitat.*


## Chapter 64   Life in All Forms

In Chapter One of the book of Genesis, God created the earth and seas, followed by grass, herbs and fruit. Then He created the sun and the moon. Then He brought forth fish and fowl. Next came the beasts and creeping things. And *'God saw that it was good'*. Then God made man in His own Image and gave him dominion over the fish, the fowl, the beasts, the cattle and the creeping things. Many Christians have come to believe in a Creator far greater and more powerful than a human being could ever be; others still believe in an anthropomorphic God. The real misinterpretation was with the word 'dominion'. Webster tells us it means 'supreme authority: sovereignty'. Archangel Gabriel said the words meant to cooperate with.

Humans have used this authority to slaughter creatures of every kind. From fly swatters to whaling boats we have chosen to interpret God's supreme authority as 'power to destroy, use and abuse'. Most of the killing has been to feed ourselves. Archangel Gabriel said we were not made to eat animal flesh, and pointed out the fact that humans do not have tearing teeth. We even boast of our killings by stuffing and displaying the dead creatures and fowl we have conquered. Early frontiersmen slaughtered thousands of Bison and left them to rot; all in the name of 'fun'.

Gabriel explained that when we first occupied the earth we were vegetarians. Then entities came from other planets and told it was good to eat the flesh of creatures. The truth of the matter was that they had eaten all the beasts on their planet and had begun to eat each other. Because these visitors from outer space came from the heavens we thought they were gods who came to help us.

Ecologists, vegetarians and vegans are now awakening to the idea of giving up flesh-eating ways. There are nutrients in all plants, fruits and vegetables to feed us in a healthy way. Gabriel even gave us insight into our diet. Raw is best, he said, then steamed and boiled. Fried food is worst. Frozen food is alright; canned food has too many chemicals. Processed food is worst.

We have also used beasts to hunt, guide and comfort humans in need. We own millions of pets for fun and companionship. Domestic animals have been known to save lives. We have used horses in battle, ox for plowing, mules for carrying loads and towing canal boats. We leash dogs and cage birds for our pleasure. Now we are manipulating dogs' copulating behavior to produce designer dogs.

Seeing-eye dogs do us a service and we carefully train them to do so. Adoption centers are becoming common as they take in strays, neuter them and find adopters. When ants invade our homes we grab a powerful chemical to destroy them. Ants were a problem at home for an attendee at a Gabriel seminar, and Gabriel asked if the person had talked to the ants. When the laughter subsided, we heard the archangel say we could easily speak to the ants, and tell them lovingly to kindly leave our home.

The Native Americans, when hunting, would ask the bison or the deer if they were ready to give their lives for human use. If the answer was negative, the Indian knew it, and he did not take it. This probably sounds as incredible to the reader as it did to the writer. Then I read about Findhorn (a garden in Scotland that flourished in sand), and now I understand. Plant devas exist and they communicate to humans who are willing to listen and gifted to hear.

We understand that life is expressed by animate creatures, but there exist books which tell that even rocks can communicate. All species communicate within their species. One example of this is the flight of huge flocks of Canada Geese and other migratory species. These talented flyers fly and swoop in vast numbers without ever touching each other. Surely they keep in touch by a kind of communication.

Humans communicate with each other but someone once said that our greatest problem is communication. The reason might be that one person speaks and twenty listeners hear the words in twenty different ways. Interpretation is the problem. It is one reason why, in a counseling setting, a listener rephrases the speaker's words to confirm the intent. We can learn to communicate with each other, when feelings do not interfere. Creatures do not interpret messages; they know the meaning. They listen and do by animal instinct.

In recent years we have seen the horse whisperer and the dog whisperer. We are accepting these communication options. More and more we need to explore the possibilities open to all of us. Re-interpreting 'dominion' we can have grand adventures in inter-species communication. Someday we will hear the tree scream when chopped down, as Gabriel told us happens. The language of the whales has never been understood, so they plan to leave the planet. A brook will tell us its secrets; a Canada goose will explain its unerring flight pattern over thousands of miles.

An adventure in communicating is ours to enjoy. We can all communicate with our pet cat or dog with motive and practice. The last time I had a sick cat I called a medium and she 'tuned in' to Kitters. The message the medium received from Kitters: 'I've got a blockage in my intestines, but I will get through this." And she did!

This is the time when we need to open our minds to the possibility of communicating with all other species. Maybe we can start by learning from mediums and psychics. Everyone is psychic; we just discount it or fear it. Now is the time to *use* it. Perhaps we can learn simply by a desire to learn; our personal angels will aid us. We each have 144,000 of them to help us in all our desires. They await our request. They know our journey. When we ask them for assistance they are always there. When we thank them for their assistance they hear our appreciation. Gabriel said that when our angels help us we should 'always thank them.'

# Section IX
## Teth

## Chapter 65   Life in Dinkyville

Have we not all felt diminutive in the presence of someone else at times? Perhaps we found ourselves in the company of a more educated person, or a so-called 'celebrity', or a very wealthy person, or a prominent politician. We feel tiny, or dinky in their presence. Sometimes, if they notice us at all, they speak to us and suddenly make us feel comfortable with them. Their willingness to acknowledge us is the sign of a person who remembers where she came from.

Unless one is born into a prominent family of wealth and fame, there is a universal tendency to see ourselves as 'smaller than'. Usually a grandiose attitude is a fine mask for an inner feeling of inadequacy, but a famous person can also feel humble when in front of a huge, appreciative audience. The person who feels small may desire to simply be near another who has acquired fame, as though it could be contagious. Young children, although small, are not inclined to feel small. They have a sense of self that demands recognition - and they receive it. Only when a parent reminds a child to be still unless asked to speak, or repeats 'a child should be seen, but not heard' is the child inclined to feel diminutive, unimportant or unworthy of attention.

As one becomes educated and socializes with others, there is a realization that one can make her own way in the world. The new 'social media' explosion has helped to make some people 'successful'. But there are those who, in their personal life, feel diminutive even if successful in their field of expertize. Some people seem determined to make others feel unimportant. Perhaps it makes them feel 'better than'. One wonders what the criteria are for better or smaller than. No one has written a book on that.

Perhaps it is written in the Good Book. Yes, the first criterion for living as a 'good' person was set forth in the Ten Commandments of The Old Testament. Moses received them, and then broke them in wrath at his followers' behavior, then returned to the mount for another stone containing the commands. (Exodus, Ch. 32-34) This is indicative of our behaviors still: we know what is 'good' but behave in opposite ways. St. Paul had such a problem: *For that which I do I allow not: for what I would, that do I not; but what I hate, that do I.* Rom. 7:15

We are all prone to 'not good' behavior. We tend to see ourselves as bodies, and what we think and do is the way we see ourselves. In truth we are so much more. The Essence of us - that eternal being of us - is spirit. Spirit is breath, and we all have the breath of life. When we expire we no longer have the breath of life (physical form), but we are still living because we are spirit. In the spirit world of God breath is not required for life.

While on Earth we see each other as separate and different. What we fail to see is the eternal spirit Self that we are. Some day we will acknowledge that spirit in each other, even though we still will not be able to see it. It is in the acknowledgement that we will come to understand that we are all - all - children of the Living God. In this new understanding of ourselves and each other there will come a realization that what we value on Earth - fame, wealth, accomplishments - have no meaning.

Spirit is perfect and eternal. It is Love, for it was created by God, and God is love. As we see others as equals in the eyes of God, a new awareness dawns on us: we all are children of God, but what we do and say does not reflect that perfection. Our only task, spiritually, is to treat all others with love, acceptance and forgiveness. We are not 'bad' people. We are simply unaware of our own spiritual perfection. Our task is to reach out to each other as children of love and lift each other up in prayer for an awakening to our spirit Selves.

In the new time of awakening we all will have a wondrous sense of Self-esteem. We will esteem ourselves as God esteems us. We will know we are worthy as God's own. We will realize earthly endeavors do not define us. God defines us as perfect and eternal just as we are. Then the doing will reflect that perfection, for choice will be irrelevant. The only choice for perfection is good. When we choose only good we can stop living in

149

Dinkyville. Not because we have moved away, but because we have become aware of our true Selves.

## Chapter 66   Life's Horizons

The ant rushing along the sidewalk does not see the horizon we see. Its horizon is quite different; perhaps unaware of the sky at all. Perhaps if you could ask him about the sky he would not understand the word. My dog can see the sky. Being several inches higher than the ant he can see much more of the world around him. His horizon is larger than the ant's but smaller than that of humans.  If we told him that he was going to fly to Europe, he would not understand. Similarly, the giraffe, although very tall, can only see a horizon which includes trees, land, and thus a horizon within his reach, on that vast African plain.

Humans have the benefit of creating beyond self, and taking up residence in a high-rise affords one a far distant horizon. A trip by airplane gives an incredibly large vista; a horizon in all directions, revealing the land masses of mountains far away. There is always a place where land and sky meet, albeit the horizon moves as the aircraft moves. The passenger in a hot air balloon sees a distant horizon which moves slower. The mountain climber sees a distant horizon which remains still, allowing for contemplation of the scene. When space travel became possible, the astronauts could see the planet Earth, floating in space. I wonder if any of them recalled Job's reference to God's placement of our planet: "*He stretcheth out the north over the empty place, and hangeth the earth upon nothing.*" (Job 26:7)

All these visible horizons relate to physical eyesight. As far as we know, only mature humans contemplate such things. Infants have limited horizons - the edge of the cradle and a body standing near; a mother's face and hair while it is nursing; a face below when it is held high. The art of walking opens new vistas which the toddler cannot help racing toward; new horizons for exploration. Then the trips outdoors and an entirely new world opens to this young, inquiring mind. School extends their world even more, as the growing child meets others - others who speak a little differently, have another color skin, and do things in different ways. What a grand opportunity parents have to teach acceptance of others.

When and if higher education becomes possible, an even vaster array of different 'others' is met. The time to learn responsibility is here, if not learned sooner. For those who do not have access to higher learning, the workplace will surely put the maturing person in daily contact with different 'others'. It is a wonderful opportunity to learn about diverse cultures, languages and social mores. When a person reaches the third decade of life, or soon thereafter, if one is not caught up in the mass consciousness, philosophic thoughts begin to enter the mind. Mass consciousness, or herd mentality, is for those who need to do what the neighbor is doing; wear the same clothes, hear the same music, enjoy the same sports. Fortunately, some colleges encourage students to think creatively. The herd mentality says only 'gifted' people can create - artists, musicians, writers.

The horizons of creativity possible to humans are limitless when we accept the premise that it is true. As children of God we all have creativity within us. Too many times we get a wonderful, creative idea, and then our ego shouts, 'what makes you think you can do that?' or 'You are too old, too ignorant, too poor, too sick, to do that'. Our responsibility is to *not listen* to the ego, but rather to listen to the still, small Voice of God which says, 'You can do anything you think you can do - or you would not think it. Express yourself, my child.'

The limits we perceive ourselves to have are established by our five senses, which convince us that we are 'only human'. Our opinions of ourselves are based on the fearful ego which denies our spiritual origin. The daily routine of 'work and play' takes up so much of our time that a creative urge is usually ignored or minimized. This is the time; this Age of Aquarius, when we are beckoned more strongly to embark upon a creative venture. An inspired thought comes to our attention so that we can allow creativity to flourish through us.

Only when we listen to our Father, and ask for His guidance, do we receive the inspired thought. Responding to the inspired thought we are fulfilled and fully expressed; fully living life. And only then can we be fully joyous, as God intended. Expressing our innate talents is why we are here. God will not let us down - ever. He patiently awaits our awakening; our expressing; our creativity. Everyone in the world will

151

eventually wake up and express themselves. Then only joy will prevail, for there will be no horizons of accomplishment. Joy can be ours. It is our birthright.

## Chapter 67   Lot's Wife in Today's world

We gathered as usual to hear the seminar *Master Jesus III*. It was January 17, 1998. In the seminar *Master Jesus* (1/18/97) Archangel Gabriel gave us a description of Jesus' life, and in *Master Jesus II* (5/17/97) Gabriel described the life of the twelve disciples. We expected another glorious seminar by Gabriel about Jesus, but Yeshua himself came to speak to us! Yeshua is his Jewish name and it will be used throughout this essay. The following quotations are Yeshua's words that day.

He began by saying, "Peace be unto you my brothers and sisters in the light. My heart is full of joy to see your faces, to be in your presence, to feel your love; to feel the bonding in fellowship one with another in the presence of God." Yeshua then told us why he came: . . . "To straighten the crooked places, that the truth of what I brought might be fully understood and lived, and not bound by the old ways." There is a Law of Vibration. He said that when we first came to earth we came in at a very low frequency - we were not fully conscious of the form and the earth, because our attention was still in spirit, ". . . because it was from the spirit that you came forth."

Yeshua then explained that our connectedness to God within us to the Father/Mother God was transferred to the family, clan, and tribe. We believed our spirit was contained in our blood, therefore inter-marriage was required. Complete sacrifice thus became blood sacrifice. We never reached for anything new, but focused always on the past. In the Old Testament a man was 'son of' someone else because we clung so rigidly to the past.

Then came Moses, "who did not understand God, but knew there was one God. He knew how people thought. He knew he had to bring them out of the worship of idols, and into the recognition of one loving, all-pervasive Presence." Moses went up the mountain ("the highest place of spiritual contact that one can attain to within the unit of their present understanding"). All of the Ten Commandments contain particles of truth, "but the totality of them is lost, and symbolically [of] the out-picturing of Moses' own consciousness, these were cast in stone."

Coming down from the mountain Moses saw his people had reverted back to their old ways and in his anger he smashed the tablets. Symbolically it was "what was going on within Moses: to smash his rigid, unyielding, unmoving, unallowing attitude." He went up the mountain again. Each time he went up it symbolized that he grasped a higher truth. Few of Moses' followers wanted to grow; most remained focused on the past. Nothing is more limiting than 'Thou shalt not', because it disallows any growth; any forward movement.

The Roman rule of the Hebrews symbolizes the consciousness of the times. The people were, in truth, in bondage to themselves; to their thinking of always looking back. Many stories and symbols were presented that they did not comprehend. One example is Lot's wife. She is never named in the Bible, but symbolizes our stagnation when we live in the past. "Salt is a preservative corresponding to memory. When we remember the pleasures of the senses, and long for their return, we preserve the sense desire. This desire will manifest somewhere, sometime, unless the memory is dissolved through renunciation." (MBD, 406)

Yeshua came in the late twentieth century to clarify the message of love he had brought us in the beginning of the Age of Pisces. "And even when I came I was not accepted. Why? - Because I broke every rule. I loved. I loved openly. I loved freely. I cared about people. I didn't care if it was the Sabbath. If someone needed healing, so be it; be healed. I didn't follow the rules of the synagogue; I didn't follow the rules of Moses. I didn't follow any rule except the internal rule of my Father within me. And because I came, inviting the unenviable into my home, into my presence, to my table to eat, that was unheard of - that was not acceptable."

Old ways must give way to new ways. Looking back - never a good idea for growth - we see a world scarred and beaten by our negative attitudes of hatred and war. We remain so afraid to grow and become something *else*. God will show us the way into the loving and caring people He created us to be. We must become willing to trust Him implicitly. We must let go of the past and turn our faces forward and upward. It is then we will know a better way; a newer way. The past is gone; the future unknown. The present is the only time we have. The future is the only time we can affect. What we think, what we say, and what we do *today* are the foundation blocks for all of our wonderful tomorrows.

## Chapter 68  Love and Fear

We like to think that love and fear are opposites, yet we are now learning that love can have no opposite. God is Love, and God is omnipresent. What is everywhere can have no opposite. We, as children of God, are love in essence. It is the core of our being. God did not create love; God *is love* (I John 4:8). All creation has its genesis in love. Humans made up the idea of fear when we first considered ourselves as separate from God. It is impossible to be separate from God. If God were not our core, we could not exist. When the belief in separation began we feared that because we thought ourselves separate from God he would never take us back. Then we began our fear of God.

Archangel Gabriel assured us that we never left God and why it would be impossible. He said every fear that we have now stems from that first fear. We have certainly thought up many varieties of fear. 'Spooky' stories, ghosts, hauntings, dangerous places and fearful sounds and sights are all things we have learned to fear. In our efforts to survive or overcome we have learned that dangerous places can be conquered, fearful sounds and ghost stories are brief. There is no such thing as 'ghosts', but rather earth-bound spirits who refuse to leave a cherished earthly residence. They sometimes frighten us with their antics. They can and will move on when we gently speak to them.

Any one fear is short-lived, but we continue to find things to be fearful of, such as earthquakes, epidemics, floods, and sometimes other people. Fear is contagious. It spreads quickly and unabated when fed by those who readily join a small group of fearful individuals or a charismatic leader. Street gangs are joined out of fear. Those who break the law fear being caught. Once tried and sentenced, other prisoners are feared. Fear feeds on itself. Some leaders use fear to attract followers.

Love is constant, dependable, and ever present. We cannot photograph it but we know it exists. No artist has drawn a picture of love, but we know it exists. The proof of love's existence is in its expression. We recognize a hug, a caress, a kiss as expressions of love. Yet unconditional love does not require touching. We can empathize with strangers who are experiencing a personal tragedy. We willingly donate time and money to those in distant countries when disaster strikes them. Love has no limits. Parents can love one child or many children.

We are more familiar with fear than with love. The news is full of 'bad' behaviors, actions and people. How seldom we hear 'good' news! When we do, it is because it is seen as *special*. It seems that more time is spent in worry, fear, doubt, and apprehension than is spent enjoying love and its various expressions. We speak of 'loved ones' as being close family and friends. This leaves everyone else outside our loving nature, and thus to be feared. We recognize fear quicker than love. Fear seems to face us head-on. Love is often recognized only in retrospect. We seem to be more comfortable with fear than with love. Our rut of fear has become more comfortable than our outreach of love. We identify our own fears readily. We easily recognize others' fears. We may join them in fear or we may make an effort to comfort them. The desire to comfort is an expression of love. The desire to heal or help is an expression of love. Love's expressions are always appreciated; fear's expressions never are.

We must come to understand that love is all-encompassing because it is of God. Accepting our responsibility for making fear real to us, we can also accept the responsibility to eliminate fear in our lives. There is nothing to fear when God is watching over us. Faith in a mighty Creator and Protector allows us to live a life of freedom from fears. Nothing happens to us without our consent *because God wouldn't allow it*. God created love; we made fear. Love is the great overcomer. Fear need not overwhelm us. We have the means and the power to overcome fear, for we are love; image and likeness of God.

We can eradicate our fears. The innate power of love is ours. It is time to identify and evaporate our fears. They are baseless and without substance. Accepting God's love as permeating the universe, we can ask the Father to show us the way to clear away the debris that fear brings into our lives.

## Chapter 69   Love in the World

In this world of ordinary people and extraordinary events, we have learned through the centuries (thanks to science) that the Earth is not flat, that the Sun does not revolve around the Earth, and the moon can be reached by us. All this learning took time. First we discover the truth, then we accept it, and finally it is taught and passed on to other truth seekers. These human discoveries about our physical universe are, once known, easily described. What is difficult, if not impossible, is to describe our emotions.

The difficulty stems from the fact that everyone is different in experiencing emotions. Everyone is also different in willingness and/or ability to describe the emotion. Let us take love as an example. So many books have been written about love. So many love songs have been composed. Why does it defy our description? No one book nails it; no one song provides us with a definition accepted by all. But all the books and all the songs are understood by some of us. Personal experiences that we have had are tweaked by words, or a melody. We associate personal events with music we heard at the time, and we respond with a smile or tears. We recall the person we were with and the place we were.

It seems the basic problem is that we see love in so many different ways. We love our partner in one way. We love our parents in another way. We love our friends in still another way. We even love strangers thousands of miles away, when we hear they have been affected by fire, earthquake or other disasters. We respond with prayers, donations or, in some cases, even our time and energy, to assist the afflicted. All this compartmentalizing of love does not scatter its power. There seems to be no limit on our capacity to love. Parents of large families love all the offspring equally. Extended families gather at reunions which sometimes number in the hundreds. An effective leader loves his followers.

Jesus the Christ taught love, and more than this, he lived a life expressing love and forgiveness. He did not rail at Herod but instead called him a fox; *Go ye, and tell that fox, Behold, I cast out devils, and I do cures today and tomorrow, and the third day I shall be perfected.* (Luke 13:32)

It has been taught that we should 'love thy neighbor'. Our neighbor is not just the person next door. It is everyone sharing Mother Earth with us. We are capable of *that much* love because God created us from Himself, and *God is love.* (I John 4:8). We may profess to believe this but when we hear of the many people in the news who have committed a crime, we Judge them harshly. We judge them to be less than us, and we decide to hate them instead of love them. My mother used to say "They are more to be pitied than censured." Today we know from Archangel Gabriel that they need our prayers more than our condemnation.

What we truly hate is the behavior of another, not the person. Psychologists are helping us to understand this. It is an essential lesson we have learned in dealing with partners and children. We can identify with this distinction in our own lives. Mistakes we have made, people we have hurt, decisions we have made that had a negative impact on others, are all things we desire to be forgiven for. The actions are not us; they are our behaviors. Behaviors can be changed. Criminals can be rehabilitated, attitudes can be softened, and different decisions can be made.

Perhaps it all begins with us. To acknowledge the hurts we have caused, and the pain we have inflicted, is a start. The next step is self-forgiveness.

Some of us need to ask God's forgiveness for blaming so much on Him. Then we can approach the injured party and ask forgiveness. It is not necessary that the other person forgive us - that is their own issue. Forgiving ourselves and making amends are the most freeing things we can ever do. The backpack full of weighted guilt and shame falls off our back and gives us a new freedom. When this occurs we move fearlessly ahead with our lives. And in living a life of love and forgiveness we draw other loving people into our lives.

## Chapter 70   Love's expression

*Love is patient and kind; it is not jealous or conceited or proud; love is not ill-mannered or selfish or irritable; love does not keep a record of wrongs; love is not happy with evil, but is happy with the truth. Love never gives up; and its faith, hope, and patience never fail. Love is eternal. . . . I Cor. 13:4-7 GNT*

My mother used to say, 'patience is a virtue; have it if you can. It's often found in women, but never in a man.' But my mother did not know my husband very well. In truth, I think my husband's patience is why we were able to stay married for twenty-two years. And remembering my mother, I think my dad must have been a very patient person.

Patience is accepting all situations as they occur; accepting all people just as they are. Very few people have such a quality. Any situation that is not in our self-created schedule irritates us; sometimes to the point of fury. People who do not fit our criteria of behavior can also annoy us. We judge them as though our mode of behavior is the best one - or the only one. Judgment slams the door in love's face, preventing us from reaching out to another. Kindness is an attribute of gentleness. A kind person is affectionate, loving, forbearing, empathetic. To be sympathetic means to cry with another;  to join another in their sorrow. This reaction does not help either. Empathy says 'I know you are in pain and I am here to help you if you want me to'. We can assist another by listening and caring, but joining in the pain itself is counter-productive.

When we are jealous of another, we believe the material ownership, title or personal relationship makes him better than ourselves; that if we had the same possession/title/relationship we would replace him on that pedestal. No one is better than another, for God created us equal, and in His eyes we are forever so. No possession, position, title or relationship increases our value in God's view.

Being conceited is having - or showing - an excessively high opinion of oneself. Although we are all children of God, and therefore are eternal, it is inappropriate to think of oneself as superior to another. To be proud means to be arrogant and act in a superior way. This attribute is the antithesis of feeling/acting as equal to others. 'Ill-mannered' means rude; insensitive to others' feelings; uncaring. A selfish individual constantly puts self first and foremost; then may or may not consider others. When one is irritable, s/he is easily angered, judgmental, critical and generally uncomfortable to be around.

Keeping track of 'wrongs' means gathering resentments. Resentment means to re-feel. It is wasteful because it is unproductive. It is harmful for it hurts only the person who holds resentment. The target of resentment probably is unaware s/he is the target - or if s/he knows, cares. The only people who are 'happy with evil' are those who find joy in hurting another, or many others. It is an indicator of one's very low opinion of one's self. Gabriel told us that one who kills another must hate himself. Killing another may feel like one has power over another. This is never the case, because whatever happens to us is by our own design. This is true because in His love for us, God would not allow us *ever* to be harmed. By our free choice, given by God, we create our experiences; all of them. We rejoice in truth. We know truth when we hear it, but sometimes we deny it. If the truth does not 'fit' our pre-determined opinion, we will deny it. Friends are always truthful. That is why friendship is so precious. Never giving up means having an infinite amount of determination, self-confidence and endurance, in order to reach a goal. It includes a deep and abiding faith that the outcome will be achieved. Faith means to be loyal to, to be steadfast in allegiance to. Alexander Pope wrote: "Hope springs eternal in the human breast."

In Romans 8:24 we find that hope requires infinite patience: *For we are saved by hope: but hope that is seen is not hope: for what a man seeth, why does he yet hope for? But if we hope for that we see not, then do we with patience wait for it.*

Love is eternal. Gabriel explained that when we love a person, even if we later break up or divorce, the love continues forever. It is true because God is love and God is eternal.

## Chapter 71   Measuring Love

We depend on scales for weighing products that we use and eat. The weight determines the value. Physicians weigh us; veterinarians weigh our pets. These weights determine our health and the health of our household members requiring vets. Products in the manufacturing process are weighed for value and application. It would be impossible to imagine a world without such measuring devices. This material planet on which we live contains a plethora of measurable substances and measuring devises. Physical things require physical measurement. But there is no scale with which we can measure love and its expression. The reason is that love is of God; God is love. Love is eternal and everywhere present. Love cannot be measured.

All physical scales have a limit, beyond which they will break. Love has no limit. A parent can love twenty children or one child. We can have dozens of friends and love all equally. Love has no defined limits or capacity. The error perception we have come to accept is the 'kinds' of love we experience. We love our parents with a devotion and affection unparalleled. There is also no love like that which we feel toward our children. We would, and sometimes do, lay down our lives for these beloved offspring. We have a 'platonic' love for friends which is differentiated from conjugal love. Homosexuals love their own sex, and we are amiss if we deny them true love. Sometimes we love our co-workers who share a common goal of service or production. The Master Teacher Jesus did not teach us *kinds of* love. He taught us agape love; unconditional love.

Jesus the Christ lived a short but powerful life in which he loved everyone. He accepted everyone with gentleness, compassion, and tenderness. His character was one of strength, courage, and endurance. A God of Love does not express Himself in kinds of love. We have compartmentalized love and we choose who we should love and who we should not love. As His children we have chosen to separate the love in us into segments, just as we have chosen to separate ourselves from Him, Who created us from love. This separation does not exist; it is only our consciousness which denies our oneness with God. We take the love from which we were created, and distort it; assign it various degrees. To say that the Love of God is sectioned off is the epitome of self-aggrandizement. It is our mammoth egos. It is the blasphemy resulting from our worldly judgment. Turning to the Bible we find Daniel deciphering the writing on the wall of Belshazzar's palace. A hand was seen writing on the wall, by everyone present but none knew what the words meant, until the captive Daniel was summoned. One of the phrases was

*TEKEL; Thou art weighed in the balances, and art found wanting. (Da. 5:27)*

Like all of scripture, these words were intended for modern man. Our bodies can be weighed, but when our character is at stake, what scale applies? Daniel spoke of our character, not the body. God probably wonders why we break up love into segments, choosing to exclude some spiritual siblings on earth and hating others. This skewed is sourced in our error thoughts. It is the ego at work in us. We went astray from our very essence, love. Our straying was the result of our belief in the separation - separation from each other and separation from God Himself. Separating from God is as impossible as separating the clay from the ceramic bowl.

A terrible separation took place in our perception when we decided we could create outside of God - an impossible feat, but one we nevertheless embraced. For eons of time we have continued in this fallacious reasoning. We are weighed in the balances now, and are found wanting. *We*, at this juncture of time, this new age upon us, find ourselves wanting. And in that wanting we also find ourselves wanting to return from that seeming separation, to God, our Source.

The scales of love include hate, because hate is considered the opposite of love. Love, being everywhere and all-powerful, can have no opposite. Therefore, there is a continuum of love which means that love can be denied, but never destroyed. The further we get from feeling love the less we feel and understand it. At the opposite end of the sliding scale is where hate prevails *in our minds*. Hate is only perceived by mere humans; unconditional love is known by us, when we become the awakened children of God.

The great awakening has begun. Many books are being written to guide us, such as *A Course in Miracles, A Course of Love, The Aquarian Gospel of Jesus the Christ,* and other, more recent books. Only those who are open-minded will read and learn and live the new ideas set forth. The others will someday be guided by their forerunners, but we all will return to our Source eventually. When, like the Prodigal Son, we find ourselves figuratively eating pig swill, we will turn to unconditional love and find it within, where it has always been.

## Chapter 72   Moving Mountains

*"And though I have the gift of prophecy, and understand all mysteries, and all knowledge; and though I have all faith, so that I could remove mountains, and have not charity, I am nothing."* I Cor. 13:2

Physical mountains have been topped off for mining purposes. Paul was not speaking of physical mountains; he was speaking of the obstructions we create which keep us from growing spiritually. These emotional mountains, which also seemed impossible, could be moved. Faith was, and is, the essential ingredient for moving our mountains of anger, of judgment, of resentment, of sadness, of grief, of suffering in any form. When we find ourselves in a state of despair we think it will last forever. It will last a very long time if we cling to it, feed it, and tightly hug it to us. It can even become the totality of what we are, over time. This need not be. When we cannot or will not turn to a higher thought it may be necessary to seek someone who will help us look away from our misery.

Anger can and often does overtake us. Sadness can overwhelm us if we let it. Any emotion can overcome us if we allow it to. It is good to remember Archangel Gabriel's definitions of feelings and emotions. Feelings are wavelike in their appearance, if we could picture them. They are gently rising and falling within us all day long. Love is a feeling; the agape love of Jesus the Christ. Spirituality is a feeling. We weep when we feel sad. Emotions are out of control feelings, and if we could picture them as waves, we would see high, sharp peaks and deep, sharp valleys. Annoyance turned to anger and rage is a feeling becoming an emotion.

Feelings are normal; emotions are a strong indicator that a person needs help to understand how to deal with life and her reaction to it. The drug-addicted person who is under the influence may fall into a depression, build into a rage or destroy things, others, or self. The addiction itself is a form of insanity. Some seek help on their own; most have to be mandated or physically taken to a recovery setting. Unfortunately many will not participate in recovery. Denial is an example of the ego's severity. Some people may complete a mandate, and then relapse. They may learn the slogans of recovery, and then return to the drug. The most devastating drug on earth is alcohol. It has destroyed bodies, lives, families, and careers.

Faith is a belief in the unseen. Emotional mountains are felt but never seen. They are part of a 'secret' life in many people. For those who have become drug free, testimony is shared about the miracles and blessings that come with that life. The recovering person will appear to be normal, but no one can see or know the emotional mountains that have been moved; the addictive behavior that has been overcome; or the lingering guilt which leads to relapse. Vigilance is required for lasting sobriety.

Paul, in speaking to the Corinthians, was aware that the earthly mountains could not be moved, but using this analogy he got people's attention and made them think. In Paul's time the words 'feelings' and 'emotions' did not exist, yet his peers felt them and saw them in others. We still live by our feelings. We still think of ourselves as bodies. We are so much more. Paul knew we were so much more; Jesus knew we were - and continue to be - so much more - or he would not have come to save us, to teach us, to help us, to show us the way to salvation. His example life is the indicator of our potential life. In dispersing our emotional mountains we find a way to live a more accepting life. In that new way of living we do not create new mountains to conquer, to move, to eliminate. Acceptance of others and of life erases the need to move mountains, but faith must remain.

When a mountain of despair comes at us - and it seems to careen toward us unbidden - we must rely on our faith in a Creator Who provided us with the tools and equipment necessary to deal with despair and to overcome it. Faith is the answer and only faith provides the solid foundation for a sane life.

# Section X
## Jod


## Chapter 73   My Father's Business

*"And he said unto them, how is it that ye sought me? wist ye not that I must be about my Father's business?"* (Luke 2:49)

An earthly father, when his son follows him in a trade, often advertises as 'John Q. Public and Son'. This is a commonly accepted business title. This combination of entrepreneurs offers a client a double benefit. Two people instead of one can give double the time in every hour. Also, two generations imply the benefit of experience combined with the benefit of recent research.  A child will proudly state that he or she helps their father in his business. As we compare this with Jesus' comment, we would logically ask what his Father's business was.  There is no indication in scripture that Jesus worked a forty-hour week. Even if time clocks were available then we can hardly imagine him punching in and out daily.

Some would answer that miracles were his business, because he performed so many of them: changing water to wine, healing the sick, raising the dead, walking on water, etc. And even after the crucifixion he appeared to many in form. Because of the many miracles the early church fathers placed him on a pedestal, proclaimed him the *only* son of God and worshipped him. Church fathers 'put the fear of God' in adherents. Jesus, who taught and exhibited love, was seen by early Christians as having come from a fearful god.

It would be many centuries before God was accepted as a God of love. We began to see Jesus as our elder brother because he said, *"Verily, verily, I say unto you, He that believeth on me, the works that I do shall he do also; and greater works than these shall he do; because I go unto my Father."* (John 14:12) Jesus would not lie to us. He came to remind us of who we are; to tell us the truth of life and the truth of ourselves. The truth about ourselves is that we are all children of God. Humankind is one great family of God, although we have become scattered on earth: *". . . he prophesied that Jesus should die for that nation; And not for that nation only, but also that he should gather together in one the children of God that were scattered abroad."* (John 11:51-52)

Jesus did not say that he was the author of his works. He said *". . .my Father hath taught me."* (John 8:28) Our earthly father teaches us much, perhaps even about the Bible, but we need to consider now what our Father in Heaven teaches us, His children. We can begin with the Ten Commandments but Archangel Gabriel (visiting Earth 1987-1999) reminded us that they were cast in stone; a rigid, unyielding set of rules impossible to achieve. When Jesus came to earth 2,000 years ago, it was the beginning of a new age. It was the beginning of the Age of Pisces. He taught us mercy and justice, love and peace, forgiveness. He did not judge others but prayed for them. On the cross he prayed to his Father - our Father, to forgive his accusers and persecutors because of their ignorance. They did not realize that a person cannot be killed, for the spirit lives on forever. They did not realize they hated him for doing only good. Rome feared him, the rabbis were jealous; and the Pharisees denied his holiness because he was not one of them.

Jesus sometimes addressed his audience as children. No relationship is more precious to us than that of our children. He knew that we all were his spiritual siblings. He came as a mighty teacher to instruct us to follow him; not worship him. Paul, in the eighth chapter of Romans, speaks of us as children of God, and as such, joint heirs of God. To be about our Father's business here and now, on earth, is not to spend our lives on our knees in prayer, or to join the ranks of the clergy, or to become missionaries. It is not an either/or decision we must make about living our lives. Our Father's business is to be like Jesus, as we perceive him to be in our lives: *"But every man in his own order: Christ the firstfruits; afterward they that are Christ's at his coming."*

We are *Christ's at his coming.* We are standing at the doorway of yet another age. Now we are at the start of the Age of Aquarius. Jesus said, "And then the man who bears the pitcher will walk forth across an arc of heaven; the sign and signet of the Son of Man will stand forth in the eastern sky. The wise will then lift up their heads and know that the redemption of the earth is near." (AGJC, In.10)

In this new age it is incumbent on us to live our daily lives as we have been, with one exception: let our thoughts and actions be permeated with our love of God, Self, and others. As Jesus led an example life, let us apply all his attributes to our own daily lives. As children of God we can choose to do less; as children of God we are able to do more.

## Chapter 74   Neighborly Love

All major religions speak of loving our neighbor - as well as ourselves. For some reason there seems to be a social endemic of self-denigration. Some people do feel 'less than' in the presence of financial wealth; others feel smaller in stature and importance because they lack a title or a college degree. Uniformed officials sometimes scare us. One wonders where we got the idea that we are unworthy to have abundance of love, health, comfort, and friends. When Jesus said, "*For ye have the poor with you always.*"(Matt. 26:11), he did not mean that God chooses some of us to live in poverty while others have abundance. God does not ordain us to poverty. Those who experience poverty are those who *expect* to live that way. By our God-given free choice we make our own bed; think our own thoughts, create our own expectations. Too many parents fail to encourage young ones to think for themselves, to question authority and listen to their hearts. This is not to suggest we should revolt or resort to violent reactions to life. But in our hearts - not minds - we know that we are God's own. We know this in and out of the religious tenets of our faith.

Moses knew he had to look for the Promised Land, Jesus knew he had to live and teach love and forgiveness. Isaiah knew that the 'Prince of Peace' was coming someday. They knew because they had a revelation; a truth was revealed to them from God Himself. Each had the opportunity and the power to fulfill his destiny. Each chose to listen to God. Since God is love and God spoke to these beloved entities, we also can listen to God.

In meditation we do. Yes, these individuals from the long ago were special people on earth. We are *all special* in that we are all loved by God, and all are capable of listening to God - every moment of every day. Every day we do listen to God: when we respond to an angry person with gentleness, when we do a kind deed for others, when we give to charity, when we guide a child in a proper path, and in a thousand other ways. God whispers to us constantly, but we listen only when we have time, or seek 'divine guidance', as though we had to name it such so angels would know how to respond! Our ability to hear God's Voice is limited only by our own belief in the possibility. Guided by our Creator, our only choice is when we will seek to know His Will for us. Every moment we have the option. Every moment He is available. We opt to not listen because we do not feel worthy, or disbelieve He listens, or we simply cannot find the time to meditate. A rigid sense of independence tells us we ourselves have the power. We have none. *A man can receive nothing, except it be given him from heaven.* (John 3:27). God is the greatest power on earth. Its name is Love.

To love self is an option without cost; to love another is also a *free* choice. When we give over to others our power of free choice, they jump in and use it, sometimes against us. We assume the victim role and oftentimes content ourselves with it. Even from the role of victim we can emerge by choice and re-take our power. The only requirement for having and expressing our power is the admission it is not *our* power, but God's, operating through us.

Jesus himself said, *"I can of mine own self do nothing: as I hear I judge: and my judgment is just; because I seek not mine own will, but the will of the Father which hath sent me."* Only by listening and doing the will of God could Jesus endure his experiences. Please note he said the Father, not my father. Jesus gave us the Lord's Prayer; it begins *"Our Father. . ."* because it includes all who pronounce the words. Everything Jesus did we can do (John 14:12). This includes listening to God, and following His directions. Only by our free choice can we do this; only by choice can we accomplish God's Will through us. All of us have the ability; all of us. To know God loves us and all His human family is to feel a true connection with all our brothers and sisters on earth. Only a fear of God prevents us from accepting this wondrous truth.

This is the age when we must awaken to our truth: we are all children of God. We never left Him; He knows this - now we know it, too. This is the age of rousing from our eons-long slumber. Asleep to our own divinity we have chosen to be victims of others. Awaken we must, and seek God's loving guidance. In doing so we can and will assume the power of God in us, ask direction for life and implement it. And it costs nothing! The only cost is to give up our ego. That is a high cost for most of us, but it is possible.

Saying 'my way or the highway' is one example of the ego being in charge. The truth is we alone can do it, but we cannot do it alone. This is not a contradiction. Moses needed Joshua to get to the Promised Land. Jesus needed John to publicly baptize him; Isaiah would not have been born if Amoz had not fathered him. Our greatest leaders are those who have listened to God, including Joan of Arc, St. Francis of Assisi, Mahatma Gandhi, Nelson Mandela, Rev. Martin Luther King, Jr. Jesus spoke plainly and taught with passion. He said everyone can accomplish anything, having faith as a grain of mustard seed, believing in God. ". . . *and nothing shall be impossible unto you."* (Matt.17:20). He was speaking to his disciples. But what he said to them applies to us all. If he rebuked his followers for having insufficient faith, no wonder we, two thousand years removed, and again having Jesus among us, (1995-1999) also have too little faith. Believe we must - as all religions tell us - have faith in a Creator of all life, in Love as Creator, and in ourselves as His Own. Then live by that faith.

## Chapter 75   Nicodemus, Johannes and Me

The three of us have one thing in common, which is also found in many other people: a curiosity that extends beyond the beliefs of the world; a search for truth which few others understand. We succeed, for *no one can fail who seeks to reach the truth* ACIM W pt. I: 131

Nicodemus was a leader of the Pharisees, a Jewish sect which opposed Jesus and his teachings because he was not one of them. Nicodemus went secretly to Jesus by night to inquire into his teaching. He believed that there was a higher truth to be known. His curiosity led him to Jesus because he believed the miracles he performed indicated he must be from God. Jesus told him that a man must be born again. This was beyond the comprehension of the learned rabbi, because the thinking at that time was very pragmatic, and so he asked Jesus how one could be put back into the mother's womb. Jesus replied, Except *a man be born of water and of the Spirit, he cannot enter into the kingdom of God.* John 3:4

The kingdom of God is within, so Jesus' words do not mean a person will not go to a Heaven above, but he will be unable to go within and *have a conscious connection to God.* That conscious connection is what occurs when one awakens to her Christ Self. *A Course in Miracles* is the book that teaches us how to awaken. Nicodemus went by night, which represents spiritual darkness. There is no value to intellectual learning; it is only spiritual regeneration that leads to awakening us to our higher Self.

Apparently Nicodemus continued to seek out Jesus' teachings for the remainder of Jesus' life, because John mentions him again in Chapter 19, when Joseph of Arimathea takes away the body of Jesus for burial:: *And there came also Nicodemus, which at the first came to Jesus by night, and brought a mixture of myrrh and aloes, about an hundred pound weight.* John 19:19

+++++++

Johannes Greber was a Roman Catholic priest in Germany in the early 1900s. One day he was asked by a parishioner to attend a séance. He

refused on the grounds it was against the church's teachings. The man kept asking Greber to attend.

Greber finally relented when the man reminded him that to be aware of this anti-Christian practice would enable him to defend the church's beliefs. The experiences of Rev. Greber from that point on can be found in his book *Communication with the Spirit World of God.* It was translated from German into English, and published in 1974. It contains 432 pages. As a Catholic priest he knew that to listen to an unseen entity, speaking through a boy in trance, could lead to enormous losses. Nevertheless, after receiving instructions from the entity, Greber said, "I resolved to follow the directions I had received, even though it meant the greatest personal sacrifice, the loss of my position and my means of support. This, then, was my decision. No sooner had I taken it than I became inwardly calm and able to confront the future with the utmost confidence." p.30 Hesitant at first to attend a séance, Greber found the truth of life and himself from entities on high. It changed his life and probably his book will change the lives of many others.

Greber closes the book with:

> "There is one more word which I wish to say to the reader of this book, in answer to the question whether it is *imperative* that everyone should strive to enter into communication with God's spirit-world in the manner herein described. It is not. Whoever believes in God and relies upon Him, whoever obeys God's will according to the best of his knowledge, will arrive at God. This end can be achieved without a palpable communication with His spirit-world. But whoever harbors any doubt as to God's existence, whoever wishes to be assured whether or not the doctrines of his religion are true, whoever seeks enlightenment upon the great questions involving the Here and the Hereafter can learn the truth in one way only: by communicating with the world of good spirits."

+++++++

My own experiences began before I even was aware that I was seeking truth. When I was 50 years old and working in the north country of New York State, I visited a medium on a whim. Before the visit I thought I wonder if my father will come to me. (He passed over when I was five years old). After the medium's opening prayer, she immediately described my father, standing behind me with his hands on my shoulder. He said

171

that he could not catch his breath. I wondered what he was talking about, and then it came to me: he was describing his last moments on earth forty-five tears earlier! He died suddenly of a heart attack. He then said that he was waiting for me, to show me around. "The light is different here; the colors are different." I became a believer in spirit communication. In subsequent visits to the medium she described several past lifetimes I had been on earth. I became a believer in reincarnation.

Five years later I attended my first séance. I had never seen spirit entities before, nor believed they existed. But now, at this séance in a private home with about five others, the Master stood before me in a white robe. His auburn hair was shoulder length, and his eyes a striking blue. His hands were outstretched, palms up, toward me, and on his hands laid a huge Jewish loaf of bread. He said, "Lay down your life for me, and I will give you the bread of life." Then he was gone. I was stunned. I had not consciously sought this experience. I did not know what to make of it. I did not know his meaning until a few weeks later; I stopped drinking alcohol, which had been the bane of my existence for many years. This message from Jesus was not understood for several weeks. Then, as if instructed, I had my last drink, and made a decision to turn my life and my will over to the care of God as I understood God. Credit must also be given to Rev. Myrtle who asked all her guides to help me stop drinking.

Three years into my sobriety, I was sitting in a small church in Albany when the Pastor began channeling an entity who we later learned was Archangel Gabriel. He told us he would come for twelve years, and he did (1987-1999). Also, Jesus the Christ channeled through Rev. Penny (1995-1999). Now, thirty years later I can say, and rejoice, that God has indeed given me the bread of life.

Three seekers, across the centuries, joined by thousands more who have learned the wisdom of the ages from the spirit world of God. Gabriel told us that concurrently with him, eleven Master Teachers also visited earth, at various centers of light where a channeling spirit entity was welcome. Their message was the same and was directed to all humanity. In my own words of the universal command: Wake up, children of God. You are not victims. You are creations of God. You are innately sacred and all-powerful, for love is the greatest power. As Gabriel put it: "Walk you in the light; you are the light."

## Chapter 76   Not Seeing is Believing

We have been carefully taught that 'seeing is believing'. In this sad world in which we live we are, therefore, inclined to not believe in anything we cannot see. We cannot see God with our mortal eyes. This does not mean we do not believe in Him. Many do; many do not. Perhaps that is why we find in the Bible, *"Jesus saith unto him, Thomas, because thou hast seen me, thou hast believed: blessed are they that have not seen, and yet have believed."* (John 20:29) Thomas - original 'doubting Thomas' - did not believe he was actually seeing Jesus materialized after his resurrection, until he had touched with his own hands the wounds inflicted on Jesus' body.

Faith comes very slowly to those who insist on seeing with their physical eyes before they will believe. Faith in God, that is. If someone said to us 'do you believe in love?' chances are we would say of course. But we cannot see love. We can only see its effect; its manifestation. We see love manifested every day.  Smiles, kind words, hugs, kisses, and helping hands all manifest love. We may not say to ourselves these are manifestations of love, and yet when we think about it we realize they are.

If someone said to us, 'do you do believe in the wind?' we would probably say of course. We all believe in wind, but none of us has seen it. We have only seen its effect on trees and flags, etc. When we behold a blowing wheat field, bending trees, drifting clouds, birds struggling against it - all manifest the wind's existence. In extreme examples we see hurricanes and tornadoes. It is only the manifestations of wind that convince us that it exists.

To believe in God we must accept the manifestations of His power. What we call coincidence is in truth a miracle. Coincidence is non-existent. We have all had miracles in our lives. Healing can be a miracle, such as when a terminal sickness is suddenly cured, or a planned surgical procedure suddenly becomes unnecessary. What we often call a coincidence is really a miracle. Forgiveness is sometimes seen as a miracle. *A Course in Miracles* tells us clearly "Miracles occur naturally as expressions of love. The real miracle is the love that inspires them. In this sense everything that comes from love is a miracle." (ACIM T 1: I: 3: 1-3).

Jesus performed many miracles, but that was not the primary message that he brought to earth 2,000 years ago. People became astounded at his miracles and that is how we best remember him. We have forgotten the message. The message is love and forgiveness. We fall in love and we fall out of love. That is not the love Jesus manifested. The love he manifested was unconditional love. Most of us do not love others unconditionally. Most of us do not love ourselves unconditionally. Our parents love us unconditionally. We love our children unconditionally. But it ends with family, until we meet a special someone and fall in love.

The unconditional love of God is felt when His Presence surrounds us or infuses us. Sometimes we feel the Presence of God when we meditate. Sometimes extreme weather conditions remind us of the Power of God in nature. The Will of God is complete peace and joy. "If God's Will for you is complete peace and joy, unless you experience only this you must be refusing to acknowledge His Will." (ACIM 8:4:1)

We cannot see peace; nor behold joy. They are invisible to our eyes, just as love and the wind. The peace described in the Bible is something we not only cannot see, but we cannot even understand. It is not the peace before the storm, nor the peace between battles in a war, but the peace *"that passeth all understanding"*. Phil. 4:7. We recognize joy when we see it manifested but for too many of us several days go by between the manifestations. That is the sorry truth.

What a perfect time this is to review Jesus' teachings, and begin living them. Now, in this inception of the Age of Aquarius, we are invited by Jesus the Christ himself (in *The Course*), to begin living from our Christ Selves. It is fine to acknowledge miracles, and more miracles are coming. But now we are asked to take responsibility to seek and find peace in our lives, and joy in our lives. Not seeing and yet believing is the foundation of faith: faith in God, faith in ourselves, faith in others. Like Thomas we can continue to not believe unless we can see. Or we can know that what we cannot see - God, love, peace, joy - will always reveal more than what we can see with our mortal eyes. We are all the Will of God or we would not be here. We cannot see the spark of divinity in each other, but that does not mean it is not there.

## Chapter 77  One Candle's Light

In the early days of television Bishop Sheen presented a weekly show to offer his faith and religious teachings to the public. His slogan was "It is better to light one candle than to curse the darkness." It was a memorable phrase and worth remembering. Cursing the darkness, or at least getting angry with it, is human nature. Today most homes have candles in case of an electric failure. Sudden darkness when we sit in a lighted room with a computer or a television on enrages us briefly, or angers us at the interruption. We assume the electricity will be off for a long time. Sometimes we are wrong, and in a few minutes we can resume our keyboard work or a TV movie.

Sometimes we wonder how previous generations survived without electricity. Benjamin Franklin is credited with 'discovering' electricity. Archangel Gabriel explained to us that all discoveries and inventions - as well as all art - come from the world of spirit. Then he said "You think the man with the key got lucky?" Usually we are grateful for electricity and only when deprived of it do we realize the vast extent to which we rely on it. Candles seem so archaic now. We see candles more as a decoration in our homes than a necessity. For a moment the reader is asked to think about the light of one candle. It could be a taper candle, or a candle of any other shape. The flame thereof will be the same.

A flame has four qualities which we see if we take time to observe it. It gives us light. The flame has colors: white, yellow, blue, green can all be seen with a studied look. The flame gives us heat, and it gives off energy. The energy is not seen but it is there. It can be equated with the energy we do see coming off a hot distant pavement in the summertime. We can feel the heat and our hands cannot come very close without being burned. The colors depend on the distance the flame is from the wick. The light can be doubled if we put a mirror behind the candle.

One candle can make a great difference without electricity. It can give us enough light to navigate from one room to another, to help us cook, play a card game, read, or just to help us see each other. The light of one candle can turn us philosophical. So can a campfire. It, too, has four qualities. As the flames flicker and pop our minds seem to be consumed with the gaze. It offers a special moment; a special feeling; a comforting aspect. Perhaps it is the same feeling cave men had when sitting by a fire. Perhaps there is something of spirit in the flame, as well as the other attributes. Archangel Gabriel told us that entities from another planet gave us fire. Knowing in our ancient memory that this was its origin, maybe we thought fire itself was holy and from God.

An analogy can be drawn from the flame to a teacher who brought the light of truth to a group of seekers, such as the students of Archangel Gabriel when he visited us in New York State (1987-1999). The archangel is the spiritual candle which lit up the room with love, peace, joy. He is the truth-bringer, the Announcer of the Ages. We were, and are, ignorant of the truth of us: spirit in nature, here to learn how to get by in a dualistic world in this current lifetime. Gabriel, as a flame of truth, is lighting our path to a waking state. It was a miracle and a blessing to sit at his feet. Gabriel explained that we, like Jesus, are children of God and now he and eleven Master Teachers came to earth to awaken humanity to its sacred Self. One candle; one great archangel. We can 'see the light' or deny its existence. Jesus came to show us the way Home. Gabriel came to remind us of what we already know, but have forgotten.

We can blow out a candle at will. We can deny an archangel at will. We do not do so at our peril, but going Home will be postponed yet again. We are at two thousand years and counting. It is past time to remember Jesus' words: *"He that believeth on me, the works that I do shall he do also: and greater works than these shall he do; because I go unto my Father."* John 14:12

## Chapter 78  Oneness

"If you feel far from God, guess who moved." When and where I first heard this is not recalled by me now. There was a time when God seemed to be very far away; very unreachable; very uninterested in me or my problems. That was years before I heard Archangel Gabriel (visited earth 1987-1999) tell us that we are all children of God; all humanity. When Jesus the Christ came two thousand years ago his intention was not to start a new religion, but to awaken all humanity to its divine Source and essence. When he said "The kingdom of God is within" no one of that time could comprehend its true meaning. The thinking of the time was prosaic. The daily life was centered on household, family, crops and herds. Jesus knew this, of course, but the seed of truth was planted then. We are still trying to understand it.

Now we have reached a point in our thinking when the esoteric meaning of his words is beginning to make sense to us. Now we understand what he meant, because Gabriel explained that the nucleus of every body cell is spirit! This truth indicates we are permeated with spirit. This is not any different than saying we are all children of God. A human father passes on to his offspring certain aspects of him - eye and hair color; shape, temperament, but they are inherited qualities. God's qualities of love, peace, joy were passed on to us at the moment He breathed us forth into being. Perhaps it was a Big Bang moment; perhaps not. The scientists can research, argue, confirm or deny that theory. The truth of creation will be known to us when we are ready to know it.

No one can question that we exist on the planet Earth and at some time in the past we came to inhabit it - sometime after the beasts walked the earth. The more archeologists dig the more extensive becomes our history. The Bible story of creation in six days has become accepted as a day's equivalent to a million years. Whatever the time of the beginning we do know we exist now. Like Descartes, the 17th century philosopher said, "I think; therefore I am." This ability to think is what differentiates us from the beasts, which live by instinct. Other differences are that humans have free will and imagination.

There is no way that the ability to think materialized in us out of thin air. Imagination and free choice are also part of our inheritance, and if not from our Creator, wherefrom did we inherit them? God is love, therefore we are love. We deny it now, but the day soon will come when we know it to be true. In this new age upon us - the Age of Aquarius - we will awaken to our Source. In that awakening process we will comprehend our need to express our imagination and free will. This awakening will lead us out of the darkness of ignorance and away from the herd mentality which has afflicted us for so long.

To believe we are one with God seems blasphemous to some, but we will not forever deny the connection. It is more blasphemous to deny God within, for in that denial we preclude our spiritual evolvement with a belief in matter as our only truth. Believing we are one with God is not boasting, it is confirming. When we accept the oneness of ourselves and God our imagination will focus only on good, productive ideas. In that oneness we will not be required to solve problems; we will intuitively know any answer we seek. Problems will not exist, because Revelation will be ours. Creativity will know no limits. Relationship with the rest of humanity will be accepted, for fear will be no more. Fear and love cannot exist together.

Jesus was only fearful once, according to scripture. That was in the Garden of Gethsemane, when he foresaw all the persecution to come. But then, as the child of God that he knew himself to be, he called on his spiritual Father. He said, *"Not what I will, but what thou wilt."* (Mark 14:36)

And he went forth as a physical prisoner, but spiritually he rose above the body and consciously resided in his Higher Self for the duration of the abuse. He did not suffer on the cross, but some insist he must have; some believe that to be spiritual we must also suffer. God is love and disallows suffering.

Jesus came to live a life of forgiveness and love. He demonstrated *for us* that example life. He gave us a pattern to follow. He was, and remains. our elder brother. When he said "I am with you always", he meant it literally. I have seen him in my lifetime - once. I have heard him lecture many times, from 1995 to 1999. He came to 'straighten out the crooked places' in the Bible about him and his journey.

When we awaken to our sonship with God we will be able to do all that Jesus did. He promised it. (John 14:12) But we must accept the possibility and then live it, be it. A new Heaven and a new Earth will be ours. God's Will will be done through us forevermore.

## Chapter 79   Only What is Acceptable

When Jesus the Christ came (1995-1999) to teach us about the errors in scripture, he said many of his words were altered to fit the expectations of the people of the time; only what was 'acceptable'. The early church fathers told the scribes what to write, and they decided to write only what was 'acceptable' to the people.

Jesus came to teach and awaken all humanity. He came to Jerusalem because it was the crossroads of the world at that time. He came by free choice, and said so: *"Therefore doth my Father love me, because I lay down my life, that I might take it again. No man taketh it from me, but I lay it down of myself. I have power to lay it down, and I have power to take it again. This commandment have I received of my Father,* (John 10:17-18). This same power is in us, or Jesus would not have told us to follow him. He said it often. He also reminded us that everything he did we also can do, if we believe in him. (John 14:12)

Every society has its particular set of social mores - what is acceptable and what is not. These manners prescribe socially acceptable behavior. However, over time and often as a result of protest, these habits are altered. I believe it was Mahatma Gandhi, when he led a revolt against England, who said, "First they ignore us, then they laugh at us, then they fight us, and then we win." It seems that this list of criteria can be applied to any minority group and its final recognition.

The African-American revolted in the 1960s, the homosexual revolt began with the Stonewall revolt in New York City, in 1969. Women have revolted for decades against discrimination. Voting rights came in 1920, after a long struggle seeking it. Sexual abuse was once 'acceptable' behavior, and only in recent years have laws been instituted against it. Men, and many in high places, have admitted such crimes. Now our society is becoming more 'civilized'. Or is it? Violence now permeates the social scene. Daily homicides are becoming commonplace.

If this is acceptable behavior, humanity has a long way to go. As long as we accept violence as entertainment, violence on the streets will be acceptable. Every person is responsible for this behavior, because on-lookers are responsible to act to stop it. Our apathy and complaining will not stop it. Violence is retaliation against something or someone. Recently we have instigated groups for anger management. It is a start. The lack of acceptance and patience leads to violent reactions. Road rage now besets us. We often react violently against an innocent bystander, or a person unrelated to the original cause. Perhaps it starts in the home; perhaps it begins in school. Most likely it begins in each of us, and only in each of us can the violence end. Suicides are becoming more common, especially among the young. The very word 'suicide' repels us. It is not socially acceptable. Someone once said, 'If we kill one person we are murderers; if we kill hundreds we are heroes.' War was socially acceptable for ages; now people flee the devastation, and others seek negotiation.

In some places the idea of communication between the spirit world of God and humankind on earth is unacceptable. Public libraries are full of literature that is socially acceptable, but they rarely stock on their shelves religious, spiritual or supernatural literature. The Best Seller list- which readers create - tells us what we should read, no matter how immoral or violent the contents might be. Looking back at past wars is the focus of re-enactments. They are socially acceptable. Archangel Gabriel said that such re-enactments keep the negative energy in the area of the original battle. We seem to be intent on hanging on to the past, as though it were worth repeating. We wonder how it can be socially acceptable to review in print or on screen the horrors of the past.

Socially unacceptable is the idea of communication between earthlings and the spirit world of God. When we finally accept the possibility of communication between the spirit world of God and the earthly world of humans, we will have access to truth - only truth. Emanuel Swedenborg wrote a great deal about his interaction with entities in spirit. Johannes Greber, a Roman Catholic priest in Germany, wrote about the experiences he had with spirits. His book was translated into English. It is entitled *Communication with the Spirit World of God.*

As long as we humans decide what is acceptable, we will stay bound to earth. When we begin to listen to those in the spirit realm we will be ready to accept truth and truth itself will then become socially acceptable, and set us free.

## Chapter 80  Our Father's Words

When the Master Jesus taught us the truth of God, he was channeling words from the Father and said so in John 14:24: *"He that loveth me not keepeth not my sayings: and the word which ye hear is not mine, but the Father's which sent me."*

Jesus the Christ taught love and forgiveness. Not keeping his sayings, which flow through him from God, means not following the precept of love. The love of God flowed through Jesus as did the words of God. He came to show us the way back home. It is our choice to follow him or not. Some choose to follow him in one way; others another. When we accept this saying of Jesus, we can accept all his words as also coming from God. Those who believed that Jesus was the *only* son of God have been followed by many generations of humans believing it. Jesus did not come to be worshipped, but followed. He did not come to form a church but to wake us up to the divinity within all of us.

The reader is urged to hear/read the lessons brought to earthlings from 1987 to 1999. Gabriel's words, given us through Reverend Penny, reminded us that the original wording of "Jesus Christ, the only begotten son of God" was 'Jesus Christ, begotten son of the only God." Who or why the translation was written as it appears only God knows. It does not matter. It only matters that now we know the truth. There is a vast difference. The difference is that worshiping Jesus means we can only pray to but never emulate him. Jesus often said, 'follow me'. He also said, *He that believeth on me, the works that I do shall he do also; and greater works than these shall he do, because I go unto my Father.* John 14:12 .

To follow a leader is not to do exactly what he did, but follow the precepts he believed. Abraham Lincoln freed slaves. We cannot re-free them. But we can continue to offer freedoms Lincoln believed they all deserved as free men and women. Perhaps, if Lincoln had foreseen all the continuing bigotry toward the African American, he would have been more specific in the wording of The Emancipation Proclamation. Even today laws exist to limit the voting rights of our African-American kin.

We cannot 'eat the body of Jesus' but we can symbolically ingest the precepts of a Christ that taught love and forgiveness. The act of Communion does not automatically make us believers or followers of Jesus the Christ. There must be a decision and a dedication to live a life of love as he did. *'Love thy neighbor as thyself'* was one of Jesus' commands. He embodied the love of God; he channeled God's words from God to us, the rest of God's children. Jesus came to demonstrate love and forgiveness. His short but powerful life exuded love and forgiveness. Even on the cross he asked God to forgive his tormentors and crucifiers. He asked God to forgive them *for they know not what they do.* (Luke 23:34). The Romans thought they could kill Jesus and he would stay dead. They would be greatly surprised later when the resurrected Jesus appeared before the Council. (AGJC Chap. 177)

What we have learned from Archangel Gabriel is that we are all children of the Living God. Jesus came to show us the way back home. He was the way-shower; the example; the first fruits of an awakening humanity. The days of the 'old rugged cross' are over, and we turn now to our elder brother, Jesus for guidance. He said, '*I am with you always*'. Many have seen him; many have heard him. He visited Earth for four years (1995-1999) to '*straighten out the crooked places in scripture.*'

Some people use sleep as a retreat from the world, some use it as an escape from life. Sleep is an essential ingredient for a healthy human life. The Bible speaks of Adam as falling asleep in Eden, but nowhere in the Bible does it say he woke up. For centuries we, like Adam, have been asleep to our God-given divinity. It is way past time to wake up and live life as children of God - with love for our higher Self and love toward all our neighbors as siblings. All humanity is the great family of God; call Him what you will. He is not an anthropomorphic being. The Mother-Father God of Creation is the Pleroma of life in all the universes.

Creation is an on-going action and we are all part of it, whether we are aware of it or not. Earth is the only planet that still practices disease and death. Gabriel told us so. God has sent us Gabriel and the Master Jesus *again*. He will send teachers until we accept the truth of ourselves and turn homeward at last, knowing we are children of God, and Heaven is our natural habitat. We can listen to Our Father's words and obey them.

# Section XI
## Caph

## Chapter 81  Our Free Spirit

Our spirit is free in that it was given us by the Father at our holy birthing. God is a spirit. (John 4:24). Our spirit is free in the sense that there is no cost to sharing it, which is what we do when we offer unconditional love. We are all children of God, of the same spirit (*in His own image*. Gen. 1:27). Free in the sense that His love and His power are without limit. Such unlimited love and power were demonstrated by Jesus the Christ when he walked the earth. He *knew* that he was the son of God. He also knew that he was walking among his brothers and sisters. He came to show us the way Home. Many times he said, '*I am the way, the truth and the life.*' (John 14:6). He also said, many times, 'follow me.' If we believe that God sent Jesus to demonstrate unconditional love, we often fail to show it to self and others. Perhaps it is because we see Jesus as the *only* begotten son of God. If that were so, why would Jesus say, 'Follow me', knowing that we could not?  He also said that everything he did we could do! (John 14;12)

In this wondrous New Age of spirituality Archangel Gabriel came (1987-`1999); Jesus the Christ came (1995-1999); eleven Master Teachers came to Earth (concurrently with Gabriel, to light centers all over the earth) to reveal the truth of us: to awaken us to our Source and Creator-God. Two thousand years ago Jesus came to Earth of his own free will (John 10:18) - the same free will which God gave us all. He came as an example (John 13:15) that we might emulate him. He often disappeared before the Roman soldiers could grab him and arrest him, for he was a threat to the government, since he was outspoken regarding his kingdom. He was a threat to the rabbis, because he could perform miracles and they could not.

When Jesus was finally arrested in Gethsemane he willingly yielded to the soldiers. Gabriel told us that Pilate offered Jesus a means of escape, but

Jesus told him it was his time. He had preached unconditional love for three years. He taught it by words and actions. He also taught and demonstrated forgiveness. At the end of three years he had spoken to thousands in his travels. He was only in his thirties and ready to leave the earth. But only on the cross - and who could know this but an angel? - he looked over the dark scene of anger, fear, hate, and realized that he had only saved himself. Gabriel explained this true scene to us.

In John 8:32: *'And ye shall know the truth, and the truth shall make you free'.* Jesus spoke this to his followers, but all his teachings are for all of humanity. Christians love to say Jesus came for them only, but Gabriel said that Jesus grounded the light of truth to earth for all people, for all time. The truth of us is that we are, in essence, spirit. Thus we can do whatever we desire to do, when we know that we can. As Jesus, we too can still a storm, heal the sick, raise the 'dead'. We simply do not believe we can, and therefore we do not even try.

The Kingdom of God is spirit. We are His Own. We are spirit. We have the same powers that Jesus had, but we are asleep to that love; that power. *'But seek ye first the kingdom of God, and his righteousness; and all these things shall be added unto you.'* (Matt. 6:33) Jesus here referred to food, drink, and clothes. But he also advised us about communication: *'Settle it therefore in your hearts not to meditate before what ye shall answer. For I will give you a mouth and wisdom, which all your adversaries shall not be able to gainsay nor resist.'* (Luke 21:14-15)

Seeking the Kingdom of God simply means to go within, to our center, and touch consciously the spirit inside of us. It is there. It is eternal, powerful, and accessible to those who accept it. We are powerful, light beings. We are not merely small, vulnerable, weak bodies. *Now* is the time to awaken to our innate divinity. *Now* is the time to live from the Lord God of our Being. Denying its existence will only continue to keep us locked into our sleeping state.

# Chapter 82   Our Transformation

*"And be not conformed to this world: but be ye transformed by the renewing of your mind, that ye may prove what is that good, and acceptable, and perfect will of God."*
Rom. 12:2

Jesus spoke these words to a generation which believed that the body was the only life; that death was a reality of existence. After all, Jesus had not resurrected and ascended as yet. The Master Teacher who walked the roads of Palestine exhorted followers to transform themselves. What did he mean by 'the renewing of your mind'? Some of Webster's definitions for 'renew' are: to make like new; restore to perfection; to make new spiritually; to begin again.

To make like new implies oldness. To restore to perfection is the very truth of us, as Archangel Gabriel explained. God breathed us forth as spirit; eternal and perfect as Him. We must restore ourselves to that truth of us. To make like new spiritually is a reference to the fact we have drifted away (in our consciousness only) from our spiritual center and become grounded in earthly concerns. To begin again means it is within our power to do so.

This generation is steeped in conformity. Anyone or anything that deviates from the norm is seen as anomalous - and often dangerous. Conformity is seen as a safety measure. Sameness is monotonous, and unless we watch the news for those 'unusual events' life can be boring. Archangel Gabriel told us once that if we are bored, we are boring.

To renew our minds means to change our thinking. When Jesus said these things he was providing guidelines for changing our thinking:

*Judge not.* Matt. 7:1
*Forgive seventy times seven.* Matt. 18:22
*Follow me.* Many times
*Everything I do, you can do.* John 14:12
*The kingdom of Heaven is within.* Luke 17:21
*Seek ye first the kingdom of God.* Luke 12:31
*Love thy neighbor as thyself.* Matt.19:19

Reading scripture from this standpoint we find many more references to how we should transform ourselves. We have the power to do it, or Jesus would not have said so. We have the easy power to change our minds. We do it constantly throughout every day. Changing our minds about our spirituality seems insurmountable. What blocks the willingness to change is the age-old premise that we are sinners; that God requires us to beg forgiveness; that unless we declare certain phrases we will go to hell.

Gabriel said there is no hell or devil; that we are children of God; that like the Prodigal Son we shall all return some day to our Father in Heaven. This is the generation for that lovely migration to begin, or as Gabriel said, he would not have come. We do not require an intermediary between us and God, but someone said we did and others believed him. Christianity got off on the wrong foot when an elaborate ritualistic set of rules and regulations were put in place. Pomp, apparel, ritual which required an ecclesiastic leader became our 'norm'. Millions seek to be told what to do, and what to believe, and who to follow.

Only those who dare to question will open their minds for renewal. Only by each one of us seeking guidance from the Holy Spirit will we learn the truth of us and follow the Christ that was in Jesus and that is in us all.

Jesus the Christ came not to form a church or its elaborate hierarchy of power. Mark 7:14-15:

*'And when he had called all the people unto him, he said unto them, 'Hearken unto me every one of you, and understand: There is nothing from without a man, that entering into him can defile him: but the things which come out of him, those are they that defile the man."*

Great courage is required to question old beliefs. This is a New Age. It is the Truth Age; we are the receivers of truth from on high - from Gabriel and Jesus the Christ, who came again - this time to clarify our misunderstandings and mistranslations of the Holy Bible. These spirit entities came not to teach us something new, but to remind us of what we have forgotten - our divinity; our power; our connection to God.

New guidance is now ours to transform our lives by the renewing of our minds. We renew our minds by thinking anew of ourselves and others.

## Chapter 83   Our True Heritage

Our ancestry consists of the many generations which preceded our current life. Our inheritance comes from the generation immediately preceding our own. We may have inherited wealth. We may have been born to a family living in poverty. Sometimes diseases are inherited, such as heart problems, diabetes, seizures, etc. Our heritage is based on our physical life on Earth. We see ourselves as temporary residents in this unstable world. This is not the whole truth of us.

If we are defined as only a physical body, we cannot explain where our capacity for love comes from. If we are merely flesh, blood, and bones, we cannot understand why we desire to marry and have a family. Nor can we identify any body part which makes us want to donate to charity. We cannot name the part of our physical form which loves and forgives others. The heart is a pump for blood. We use it as a symbol for our loving nature.

Genealogies are fun to explore. Especially when we find we are distantly related to a war hero, or a famous statesman. We are fascinated with our past, as though it could validate us now. We hope to find someone there who was more gifted, more important than us, perhaps to justify our current lives, or give us bragging rights. We cannot put their achievements on our headstone when we pass over. Everyone wants to be recognized for what they have done or for who they are.

Our Creator recognizes us for what we are *just the way we are.* He is no respecter of persons (Acts 10:34). The street person who guzzles wine from a bottle in a paper bag is equal in God's eyes to the wealthy man with his own jet airplane and several expensive homes. Our physical parents pass on to us hair color, eye color, race appearance, etc. We do not think about our spiritual inheritance - if ever - until we reach the age of thirty or so. By then we have probably experienced enough of life's challenges to ponder why we are here at all.

Of the billions of humans now living on the planet Earth, a miniscule segment will be known in future history books. Generations to come will ponder the same questions about our origin and destiny. One wonders if we ever going to awaken from our sleep and know that we are God's creations. The Bible tells us that Adam fell asleep. Archangel Gabriel reminded us that nowhere in the Bible does it say Adam woke up; that Adam is symbolic of humanity; that we still sleep to our own divinity. Gabriel likened us to the Prodigal Son, but like that wayward boy, all humanity will return Home.

Our true heritage is the spirit of us; the love of God in us. Our true heritage is the wholeness of good from which we sprang forth. God breathed us forth eons ago and told us to multiply - not in birthing many babies, but in birthing expressions of love, in birthing creative ideas, in birthing compassionate understanding. We inherited love. We are love, loved, and loveable. We choose to split up love into 'kinds', and reserve one kind for partners, one for children, one for parents, one for neighbors, and one for those in other countries we will never meet. But we love them enough to want to help them in times of tragedy. And they help us when tragedy comes to our door.

Two thousand years ago a man came to Earth to show us what love is like; how it behaves. He taught it; he lived it; and he went to Calvary for it. It is called unconditional love. Jesus the man came to show us the way, and often said, *Follow me.* God and the Christ Light in Jesus know who we are; what we are, and what we have within us. Love is the quality we all possess. Love is the answer to all our questions. Love is the greatest power there is. Love overcomes. This exquisite heritage is ours. Adam is a symbol of humanity. Humanity must awaken to its sacred Source. To love everyone as much as we love our children is an easy task when we receive our true heritage.

Gabriel and Jesus came to Earth, joined by eleven Ascended Masters, to remind us of our true heritage: spirit in form; love in essence; eternal in life.

## Chapter 84   Packing for Home

'You can't take it with you' is the common slogan for those who accumulate monetary wealth. It applies, of course to many things which we believe   must be left behind when we go back Home to Heaven. (We call it death, but Jesus the Christ demonstrated for us that life is eternal). For those who believe Jesus was the only son of God, Archangel Gabriel said that we all are sons/daughters of God. Jesus came to show us the way, and told us we can do all that he did. (John 14:12).

Heaven is our natural habitat. Of our demise we may say that we are going Home to God, but in truth we never left Him. Heaven, like Earth, is a state of mind; a state of consciousness. When we are in pain we think Heaven would be a place of succor; when grieving we think Heaven would be a place of comforting. When maimed we think Heaven would be a place of healing. When sad we think Heaven would be a place of joy. Heaven is all these things, and so much more. Lest it is thought that some individuals will descend to hell because of their behavior on earth, Gabriel said there is no hell, nor is there an entity we have named devil. Humans made up these fictions. To deny hell is to know no one ever deserves such a place. To deny hell also denies a person in charge thereof; hence there is no devil, either.

To deny Heaven is to deny our original Home. God breathed humanity forth and in that splendid moment we all were endowed with a spark of divinity, as His begotten children. That spark is our eternal Self. We can no more leave God than the clay can leave the ceramic bowl. What, then, can we not take with us when we return to Heaven? Certainly we do not take our bodies, although Jesus took his. The day will come when we all will ascend with our bodies. Gabriel said some already have. Some of them have become Ascended Masters.

Upon arriving in Heaven - what we call the Astral Plane - our astral form is visible. The astral form is with us on earth, but is not seen until we lay down our physical form. Angels and loved ones who transitioned previously are there to greet and welcome us. Our pets, too, will be there with us. We take our soul with us for it is, in part, our memory. That memory goes all the way back, through every incarnation, to our Source. The soul longs to return to God, our Source. It is our soul that urges us to pray, to meditate, and to attend religious services.

On the other side life is significantly different from life on earth. There is no night there. (Rev21:25). Mrs. Springer (in *Intra Muros*) described the light as constant, except for a 'softening of the glory' at the end of a day, which is much longer than an earth day. When the glory softens, birds and creatures become still, and the residents rest. One might say 'rest from what?' Over on that side of the veil there is much to do. Besides the temple on the hill there are fields and cities. Libraries, museums and factories are available to visit. Builders are erecting homes for new arrivals, young children and babies are seen in a nursery which has small buildings and trees.

For those who have arrived suddenly, healing angels attend to their needs and gently comfort them. It is difficult for them to accept they are in Heaven. It must be explained to them that the 'accident' was their idea and by their own choice. There are no clocks in that lovely setting. What we do is up to us, for our free choice on earth remains our free choice in Heaven. Upon our arrival, once we have adjusted to our new environment, we may choose to take a tour. The grass, we learn, stops growing at a certain height, so mowing is unnecessary. There is a river, and a lake on which boats are seen.

The lack of ball games is evident, and we learn that they do not exist, for there is no 'gravity' as we understand it. Everyone wears a white robe. There are no 'professionals, 'blue-collar' workers; there is no status of any kind. Eating and drinking are not required by our astral bodies, so no 'restrooms' are needed, either! The freedom we enjoy is the freedom to engage in any occupation we choose, without clocks, time, schedules, or appointments. Whatever we dreamed of doing or learning while on earth, we can now do. We can learn to play a musical instrument, paint, sculpt, study the writings of the past; read, teach, build. We are Home at last!

## Chapter 85   Peacemakers All

We are all peacemakers at some time or other in our lives. School mates who fist fight are met with interceders, whether schoolmates or teachers. College students require a peaceful setting while debating. Debating is one of the most important tools in the learning experience. In the workplace, whether a factory or office, peace is necessary for productivity. It is the task of supervision to maintain the peace. When labor unions were formed to demand fair wages and hours, the goal was to afford a home environment of peace and comfort. We learn and grow in a peaceful setting.

History, with its pock-marked face of ravaging wars, now looks exceedingly bleak. Now we have experienced some periods of peace, when nations have reached out to nations with a common desire for Earth peace. Wars continue in spite of this. There will always be those who selfishly desire war because they can profit greatly by production of military machinery. There are also those few who see war as a cloak for their negative deeds. Peacemakers are now forming groups, and they are growing.

When domestic violence came to the public's attention, a solution was sought. Counseling, intervention and legal action all were used to stem the tide of family violence. Alcoholism, once considered a moral fault, was addresses as a disease - and treatment became the response. Social programs of the past 80 years, beginning with Social Security, have enabled many to live a comfortable life after their working years. Today there are social programs for those in physical, emotional or mental need.

Much still needs to be done. Prisons are filled with men and women who, if they received adequate education and care, would become 'productive' citizens again. We value people on their productivity instead of their civility. Maybe that is why we have the terms dis-abled and in-valid. Humans are valid, sick or not. We have finally learned that wars - whether religious, geographical, resource-bound or political - are wasteful. Groups are forming to support and promote peace on Earth. Margaret Mead once said, "Never doubt that a small group of dedicated people can change the world. In fact, it is the only thing that ever has." Small groups of peacemakers are being formed everywhere, to bring peace to local venues or nations. War-mongers would laugh at their tiny groups and seeming insignificance.

In the heart of most humans there is a longing for peace; a peace in which one can grow and learn, and raise children in a safe and secure environment. Home is where it begins. Home is a small group of people. The task of providing a setting for peace falls to the parents. Growing up in a home of peace and love is the cornerstone of a happy life and a successful career. Peace begets peace in the sense that how we raise our little ones will usually direct their parental path.

We sing hymns to celebrate the birth of the Prince of Peace, Jesus the Christ. We do this once a year! Then we return to our daily lives; daily lives that are permeated with thoughts of judgment, labeling, prejudice and fear. If these are the products of our thoughts, then we need to change our thinking. We change our minds all day long about trivial things. Setting our mind to it, we can begin to think in terms of allowing instead of judging; accepting in lieu of labeling; including instead of excluding - the carrot which drives prejudice's goal. When we find peace, even if it is for a moment, we discover there is no fear there. Peace and freedom from fear go hand in hand.

Fear engenders war; peace engenders freedom. Everyone is free to pursue their dream when conflict does not interfere, whether at home, at work, or from a national standpoint. The United Nations was formed with the concept of world peace. Seventy years later in survives, with 192 nation members. It is a start in the right direction. "The author of peace and lover of concord, in knowledge of whom standeth our eternal life, whose service is perfect freedom." *Book of Common Prayer*


## Chapter 86   Perceiving and Knowing

Perception is deception because it is based on what our senses tell us. We perceive everything based on our personal belief system. We see a sunset and perceive its beauty. Another sees it through drugged eyes and it is an oncoming time for hidden behavior. Another is filled with dread because the next day will bring surgery. Some hear a train and have nostalgic memories from the past. Another hears the same train and anticipates with joy the arrival of a lover. Another hears the train and sobs because a loved one will board it and travel away. Perception is unstable because it varies with the perceiver.

This is life as we know it - putting faith in our perceptions. "We believe it when we see it" only confirms our reliance on perception. Webster defines perception as 'a physical sensation interpreted in the light of experience'. Relying on our physical sensations for anything indicates how important we consider the body to be. How important can the body be when it has such a short life? Life expectancy is less than a hundred years; a blink in the scheme of eternity.

We often think the body has a 'mind of its own', but it does not. We tell the body what to give us, and it does. We feel tired; the body yawns. We run a marathon and stretch the body's limits; it collapses. We say we are sick and tired - and that is what we get. Our shoulders ache when we think we are bearing the world on them. Our lower back hurts when we think we are not getting the support we want. Our legs bother us when we refuse to move forward in life. We breathe with difficulty when we think we do not deserve the breath of life.

Cancer invades our body when we do not value ourselves. In this fast-paced life how many feel valued? The rich, the famous, the heroes, the CEOs are all worthy and well-known people, but we common ones get lost in the shuffle. Abraham Lincoln said, "God must have loved the common people, for He made so many of them." To God we are all important. *"What God hath cleansed, that call not thou common."* Acts 10:15; 11:9. As our human children are so dear to us, so too are we very dear to our Father. He patiently awaits our return, which is inevitable. The time we do so is in our hands; is by our choice. First, we must recognize (know again) that God is. Second, we must come to know (not perceive) that we are His children. Third, we have to accept the truth: we came from God and will, as surely as did the Prodigal Son, return to Him. Our soul longs for that return. Our soul urges us to pray, to *'be still and know'* God. (Ps. 46:10)

True perception is the basis for knowledge, but knowing is the affirmation of truth and beyond all perception. Unlike perception, Knowledge is power because it is certain. Webster defines for us: Knowledge is the fact or condition of knowing something with familiarity gained through experience or association. Acquaintance with, or understanding of, a science, art or technique.

Another way to know something is by revelation. What we seek will be revealed to us. It is an immutable law. *"Ask, and it shall be given you; seek, and ye shall find; knock, and it shall be opened unto you."* Matt. 7:7. All knowledge is available to us. Once we understand the basics of anything, we will be given more knowledge as we seek it. The part of our brain we have activated in this and previous lives will respond to additional knowledge in that field of knowledge. The 'child prodigy' has learned tempo, rhythm and notes in past lifetimes (AGJC). Knowing this truth does not make their music any less enjoyable.

At our spirit level we know that we are precious to God; that we are forever one with Him. We think it blasphemy to announce it. In truth, it is blasphemy to denounce our holiness, instilled by God. *A Course in Miracles* was described by Gabriel as the Bible of the New Age (Aquarius). It is the best resource for understanding the fruitlessness of perception and the value of right-side-up thinking. The book explains the difference between perception and knowingness.

# Chapter 87    Perception as Deception

Perception: 'a physical sensation interpreted in the light of experience.' is one of Webster's definitions, and appears to be the most accurate. Perception is not an art; it is a sensation. It is not universal; it is personal. The reason it is personal is that we all have different experiences. Two people, or a hundred people, observe a scene. Everyone perceives it based on their own experiences in life up to that point. Even memories from past lives may affect the observation.

Perception is determined by our experiences and our physical sensation. We see with eyes of a child, a youth, or an adult. Without eyesight we see nothing. The sightless now have only four senses to perceive the world around them and rely on others for interpretation or learn to trust a canine guide or another person. Deafness leaves a person dependent on only four senses. Those who lack one of the five senses are fully capable of living and functioning in the world. Helen Keller lacked both sight and hearing but completed an advanced education, traveled the world, and authored books. She became known worldwide.

The senses of taste and smell do inform us of our surroundings, but lack of them does not require special learning. The sense of touch tells us so much about our surroundings, and lack of it through accident or illness necessitates an adjustment in functioning. All five senses bring to our awareness the world in which we live. In a world of eight billion souls, everyone looks different; everyone perceives differently. God's imagination is immeasurable, for He created us in His image. Must be He is not white, black, yellow or red. Must be He is not human at all! His image is spirit; not human. His image is Love, not fear. His image is forgiving; not judgmental. His image is eternal; not worldly. His image is eternal; not time-bound.

Archangel Gabriel explained we are *not* made in His image because we are an essential *part* of God. 'Image' means reproduction or imitation. God created us from Himself, therefore we too are spirit, eternal, and exist in spirit at the same time we exist in human form on earth. Our spirit Self is not judgmental or hateful. We have learned these negative attributes through our experiences and perceptions. The experiences and perceptions we have had while residing on Earth. We call this planet home because it is the only home we consciously remember. We call it home because it provides us with all our human needs.

Gabriel said that Heaven is our natural habitat. When someone 'dies' we say they have 'gone home'. We say this because at some level we know it is true. Our soul's memory contains all lifetimes and our Origin. At birth we forget what we planned for this incarnation; we forget all the errors and accomplishments of past lives. They do not matter now. This lifetime is the only one we need concern ourselves with. This is the only one we can effect change in. This is the only one we can accept the truth in, and live by it.

If perception is so personal, so variable and so unstable, what is left? Only truth. Only truth is unassailable, immutable, and unquestionable. We heard the truth from Gabriel. Some of his lessons were rejected because they did not 'fit' a listener's perceptions. Of course Gabriel knew this. He came because he said we are ready now to hear truth. Our belief in it or denial of it does not alter truth in any way. Truth is truth forever. Jesus knew the truth of us when he came. He knew us as his spiritual siblings. He wondered why we did not know the truth of us. He came to show us all the way home - all of us.

Jesus said, *"I am the door: by me if any man enter in, he shall be saved, and shall go in and out, and find pasture."* John 10:9 Jesus used the analogy of sheep because sheep were such a common commodity, and sheep follow. He said many times, *"Follow me."* We are all part of the great 'sheep' population which follows the Master Jesus. Finding pasture means finding nurture. Jesus brought us truth 2,000 years ago because he loved us. From 1995 to 1999 Jesus came again, to clarify 'the crooked places' in scripture. He teaches us still, and he still comforts us when we call on him. He always keeps his promise.

# Chapter 88   Perfect Communication

*"And after the earthquake a fire; but the Lord was not in the fire: and after the fire a still small voice."* I Kings 19:12

Elijah was desolate and asked the Lord to take his life. An angel of the Lord beckoned Elijah to eat and drink, then spend forty days and forty nights on Mount Horeb. Elijah was instructed to stand before the Lord. A great wind blew and rocks were broken, but the Lord was not in the wind. Then came an earthquake, but the Lord was not in the earthquake. Then the fire; the Lord was not in the fire.

When we are at the nadir point of our patience or understanding, we seek guidance from an unseen God. We know God is mighty and we may expect Him to appear in a great wind or a quake or a raging fire. As mighty as God is, and as all-encompassing as He is, His guidance comes softly and gently to us. The secret to hearing Him is that He only speaks to us in the silence of our hearts. The silence is contrary to the shouts of the ego.

Every time we hear praise from a friend, achieve a personal victory, view a personal accomplishment, walk across a stage to receive a diploma, our ego yells "I did this; I am *good.*" The ego's loud voice rises over any quiet voice, prevents us from being humble in the sight of God, and we wallow in self-praise. The ego is joyously happy; it is victorious! Friends join us in celebration. Yes, we are *very good!*

There is nothing wrong with celebrating, but any accomplish is impossible without help from a higher power. *"I can of mine own self do nothing"* (John 5:30). This is Jesus speaking! If he can do nothing without help from the Father, how can we, except in our arrogance. There was a time when I sat for a college exam in biology. I was high on alcohol and impaired with prescription drugs. Something kept me in the seat; although I had dreamed the week before that I failed the test with a score of 38. Days later the scores were posted and I passed with an 83! After that I told friends that the angels sure know biology.

It would be many years before I experienced the greatest blessing of my life - the twelve glorious years when I sat at the feet of Archangel Gabriel and learned the wisdom of the ages. It was the period of 1987 to 1999. One of the many lessons he taught was that meditation is a daily (or more often) essential to receiving holy guidance from God. When our minds are full of worry thoughts for others, or thoughts of our own desperation and frustration, we block the door to holy guidance. When we worry ourselves awake at night, we turn our backs to the still small Voice of God.

Asking for God's assistance is like asking a human father for help. The help is always there. Gabriel told us not to take his word but rather put his teachings into practice. As a student counselor I sat in on groups of patients to co-facilitate. One day my supervisor told me the next night I would facilitate the group alone. I went home concerned about my ability, reached for the Bible; opened it at random, and read: *"Settle it therefore in your hearts, not to meditate before what ye shall answer: For I will give you a mouth and wisdom, which all your adversaries shall not be able to gainsay nor resist."* Luke 21:14

The next evening I presented the treatment group with a task called Lifeboat, in which the participants decide who can remain and who must be evicted from the boat, which can safely carry only six of the twelve occupants. It is a good exercise in helping identify one's value system. The exercise went well until I ran out of ideas to pursue all options, and there were several minutes to the end of the group counseling session. I literally stood at the blackboard, facing fourteen patients, and said silently, 'What now, Lord?' Immediately the door opened and a co-worker introduced a new client to the group. He was asked his name and then I told him we were just discussing the Lifeboat exercise. He said he had just had that exercise at another facility, so I asked him to share his experience with it. The balance of the group's time was filled.

A year after I graduated with an M.A. in counseling, I was asked to present an eight hour workshop on spirituality in alcoholism recovery. A recent journal had published an article about the Old Testament in recovery. When the article had been expounded upon by me at the workshop it was lunch time. Wondering what I would offer the group in the afternoon, I wandered into the college library. Perusing the various journals I found an article by the same author, in a subsequent issue of the same journal, about the New Testament in recovery! I quickly took some notes and joyously returned to complete the workshop.

As an ordained minister I was appointed to be assistant pastor. The pastor and I alternated Sunday services. Before every sermon I studied a Bible quote writing notes to refer to from the altar. One day as I began taking notes something told me I did not need to. By then I was listening to the inner hunches (which I learned was the way God speaks to us). So I chose a Bible verse, approached the microphone that Sunday and said to my angels, 'You better give me the words.' I do not recall the topic, bur the words came. As I hugged and shook hands with the departing congregation, a young man approached me and said. "That was a good sermon. It must have taken a long time to prepare." I told him it did not.

Later I realized that young man never attended the service before or afterward. He must have been an angel. He came to remind me that I could indeed be an inspired speaker, and I was. Serving two churches in later years, I never again wrote notes for a sermon. Today my writings are all inspired. Blessings continue to flow into my life.

Listening to the still small Voice of God is the perfect communication. It is always available; wherever we are. In the peaceful silence we merely await God's guidance. It is a holy instant. *"You can claim the holy instant anytime and anywhere you want."* ACIM T 15: IV: 4:4

# Section XII
## Lamed

## Chapter 89 Planned Accidents

"No one ever wounds you without your permission, because God would not allow it." Archangel Gabriel

This is one of the many phrases spoken by Gabriel that sticks in my mind like glue. Upon hearing it the first time my mind shrunk back in disbelief. Then I examined my faith in a God of Love. Of course a loving God would not allow us to be harmed in any way. Also, God created us with free choice. What God grants cannot be annulled, even by God Himself.

It is customary to blame someone or some event for all our pain and suffering. Gabriel made it plain that we plan our entire lives, including every relationship in them. Even our demise is planned - the where, when, how and with whom of it! These lessons in truth were given by Gabriel because this is the time for us to wake up to our personal responsibility. We are on the cusp of the Age of Aquarius - 'the truth age', Gabriel said.

We believe in accidents because they come suddenly and unexpected. They are sometimes extremely painful and take months or years to overcome. We forget that we planned them. We forget we planned them to teach ourselves a lesson. On the other side, prior to birth on earth, we gather to plan our next incarnation. Gabriel said it is interesting to watch us do so. We agree on who will be the husband and wife; the children and grandchildren. and how each person will treat us. Each person chooses by free will how they will participate in our lives - to fulfill their own experiential choices.

The 'accident's' suddenness and unexpectedness is only at the conscious level. The eternal spirit of us knows our plan, but consciously we do no remember it. Perhaps we could call that spirit level super-consciousness, but naming is not required; understanding is. How we respond is the lesson planned. In our free choice we can respond with anger or acceptance. We can resent for a lifetime or we can courageously face the outcome. The experience is the lesson we choose; the response will be whatever we choose. The lesson we planned will be learned or not. An unlearned lesson will come to us again - by our choice, again.

This truth about seeming accidents is a truth we must accept some day; the sooner the better. Each lifetime on earth we are setting the stage for our next time on earth. The karmic wheel has trapped us for centuries by our choice. Gabriel said we have come to earth so many times for worldly experiences that we have met every person now living on earth! God is love and loves us for what we are - spirit in essence; children He created; eternally His. We live by time on earth; eternity has no time.

We could go on forever like this, and that is why God sent Gabriel at this time. As the Announcer of the Ages, Gabriel came to explain us to ourselves; to save us from ourselves; to wake us up to our inborn divinity so we can return to our Sacred Source. The world we live in and everything in it are temporary. When we awaken to our divine Self we will have no more need of this planet. This Age of Aquarius is the first age of evolution as we commence our way back Home. Pisces, the age which began when Jesus walked the earth, was the last age of our devolution.

As for our transition from earth life to the Heaven world, Gabriel told us our spirit Self knows for three days that the 'end' is near. Our spirit knows; not our conscious mind. When we reach the end of a long life, the body 'dies'. It is physical and we have no more need of it on this physical plane. Our spirit is eternal and continues on in the spirit world. When Jesus the Christ said, *The Kingdom of God is within you* (Luke 17:21), we took it to mean something mysterious and incomprehensible. Now we understand that he meant it in a literal sense. Gabriel explained that every cell of our bodies contains a spirit nucleus!

When our 'time comes' to depart earth, suddenly or slowly, our spirit remains forever with God. On the next plane of our existence we have a form for our spirit there, also. God is wondrous indeed. Whatever realm we abide in, God provides us with an appropriate 'form'. When we reach the seventh Heaven we will know we are Home at last, and require no form in that glorious Heaven World - the seventh Heaven.

## Chapter 90   Precious Metal; Precious Mettle

We can name the precious metals. They are gold, silver, diamond, ruby, and pearl. Once a symbol of power, they now have also industrial uses as well as esoteric beauty. We continue to mine them because they can be exchanged for money. Money and precious metals are considered valuable by humanity. It is said that money is power. Power and wealth have been synonymous throughout history. Now there are those with great wealth and others with great power. Power, of course, can be misused. So can money.

The power of precious metals and money has become the epitome of wealth. Those who own them are also highly valued. This being so, we can fairly suggest that money and power have become gods to some. We may not agree with the concept of worship, yet those who toady to the wealthy come very close to that adoration. The rich and famous are the ones who make the news; the powerful we follow in interest. What importance we put on the ruler of a small country, compared with the person who has billions in the bank. The former is unknown; the latter everyone has heard about.

We value some of our brothers and sisters more than others. We adore the hero, the soldier, the rescuer. We do so because they have mettle. 'Mettle' means vigor and strength of spirit; stamina; quality of temperament. Let us attend to these definitions. Webster's dictionary defines 'spirit' as 'a supernatural being or essence'. The precious metals can be confirmed by our senses of sight and touch. Modern usage confirms their strength. Eyes are unable to see the precious mettle of the hero. Courage, or stamina, is a human quality unseen by mortal eyes. Stamina is strength of character, which also defies our bodies' senses.

The day will come when we will place a higher value on human mettle than 'precious metals.' Mining the human spirit means having the stamina, the courage, the fortitude to seek *until it is found*. Until the 'pearl of great price' is found: the Kingdom of Heaven within us.

*"Again the kingdom of heaven is like unto a merchant man, seeking goodly pearls; Who, when he had found one pearl of great price, went and sold all that he had, and bought it.* Matt. 13:45-46

Fishermen will always seek the pearl of great price, as will miners always seek precious metals. Many would sell all possessions to own a valuable pearl from an oyster. The highest good; the pearl of great price, is within, where we *find* the Kingdom of Heaven. The great and wonderful news is that the Kingdom of Heaven is, in a monetary sense, *free*. It's only cost to us is surrendering our self-will run riot; giving up our ego.

The only 'cost' to surrender our ego self is to have faith in a power greater than we are, and humbly pray to It for guidance. This is an exorbitant cost to some people. The screeching ego constantly reminds us that we should be busy at all times; be with others as much as possible; pursue success at all costs. 'Success ' to the ego means our acceptance of it as our ruler. It tells us we can die, that we are unimportant, tiny, dependent, and helpless - unless we listen to its guidance. The ego takes us down a rosy path to nowhere.

The spirit of us, on the other hand, takes us always on an upward path, a positive path, a path that leads to the exquisite pearl of great price: the kingdom of Heaven. It is within each of us. Within is the only place we will ever find the Kingdom of Heaven. What of the criminal, you may ask. God in His Love did not create criminals. With the free choice God gave us, we choose our path in life. The path does not determine our spiritual essence; we merely choose it by our not-good behavior. Many individuals in prison leave and integrate into society, become responsible citizens, have families, and live a positive life.

Faith, courage, stamina, determination will lead us within to our very core, and that is the eternal location in every human being. That is the eternality of life which extends forever. The earthly grave accepts our transformed body, but our spirit is of God; it is God. Children of God that we are, we can and will join in that grand adventure of mining, discovering, and living in the glorious Kingdom of God.

## Chapter 91  Proof of Oneness

The belief in separation is no mystery. We can see different bodies, different colors, and different homes. We can hear different languages, read of different religious tenets, and hear different religious songs. We each have favorite aromas and food tastes; songs and movies. We have individual preferences in occupations, partners, and vacation sites. Every day we see and know these differences. All experience comes from our senses, and each of us perceives life as an individual experience. When two or more people feel or know the same thing a connection is seen or felt. There is a special relationship.

When, at some point in our lives, we turn our attention to a Creator, we see It as different, too. Not only is the Creator seen as different, but better, brighter, wiser, and far *above* us - physically and spiritually. He is better because He is seen as faultless. He is brighter because we think of God as a brilliant, unreachable entity. He is wiser because we see ourselves as learners - and we must learn because there is so much we do not know. Perhaps we perceive the Creator as above us because our ancient myths are all based on our view of the sky. Untouchable stars, unreachable planets prompted us to use our imagination. So we envisioned characters in the heavens and named them; they are the constellations. The zodiac was born - in our minds.

Perhaps we perceived the Creator as a sky-being because in ancient, pre-historic time, beings came from space above us and brought us fire. Much later, they brought us language. Archangel Gabriel (1987-1999) told us these facts. After eons of time on earth we finally came up with a method of telling time. In 46BC Julius Caesar gave us the Julian calendar, and in 1582 Pope Gregory III introduced a revision and today we still track our days and years based on the Gregorian calendar.

Written history is a blink in time compared to the centuries we have occupied the earth. Written religious history also spans a very short period of time. All religions proclaim a Creator, and call It by different names. The differences we have seen, heard and felt are now losing the aspect of 'different'. The original tribes have become nations, and the 'different' nations have now come together in one building, in one room, to share and cooperate with each other. We call it the United Nations.

Since WWII travel has accelerated. Communication discoveries make translation of all written languages possible. Citizens of all countries are inter-marrying with each other. Trade across all oceans is commonly accepted. Electronic devices enable us to hear and see each other around the globe. Some define this as 'the earth is shrinking'. As this 'shrinking' takes place in distance, our minds are expanding in acceptance of others.

We insist on learning the language and cultures of our partners from other continents. Even the various religions have now been viewed as having some common basic themes, like honesty, justice, freedom, honoring parents, forgiveness, love, etc. (refer to *Oneness*, by Jeffrey Moses). Differences are still perceived - clothing, habits, and daily activities. The differences are explainable by our senses, but we know our senses deceive us. We know this because we demonstrate it daily in the choices we each make and how they are perceived. Perhaps the sameness we have come to accept, as the world shrinks, is sourced in the Creator we believe in. We cannot consciously identify the reasons why we have become so accepting of others around the world.

From one perspective, the Creator is love and He created love; we created fear. As fear subsided through time, we came to accept and love others more. As we reached out to others we realized there is nothing in them to be afraid of. We could shake a hand; embrace a neighbor. As we translated other languages to our own we came to understand a common thread of acceptance is possible. Then we cultivated ways to increase our outreach. Perhaps this is the love of God coming into its own through us.

The nations join now against a small group of fighters who are still fearful, untrusting and intent on destruction. The united ones are those who have learned from history that conquering others is not the function of rational and loving human beings. Peace and prosperity beget peace and prosperity. With this current trend of peace we can accept Gabriel's prophecy that the world will end in peace. He said we are just beginning our thousand years of peace. Our lying senses will be replaced with the truth of us. We came here on an adventurous external journey. We will discover internally the God in us. We will know our oneness with each other and our oneness with God. Back Home to Heaven we will go. Then we will realize we never left the oneness, except in our consciousness.

## Chapter 92   Renunciation of Reincarnation

Many people refuse to accept the idea of reincarnation. The Bible makes only one reference to reincarnation. In Matthew 16:13-14, when Jesus asks his disciples *"Whom do men say that I the Son of man am? And they said, Some say that thou art John the Baptist: some, Elias; and others, Jeremias, or one of the prophets."* Nevertheless, most people discount the concept.

Archangel Gabriel said that all references to reincarnation were purged from the original texts of the Bible. When the Bible was first put into Greek or Hebrew words, there were no rules of scholarly literature; no copyright laws; no proofreaders or editors to verify authenticity or regulate authorship. Few people could write and few others could read. The religious rulers who directed scribes to print out words of the Bible dictated their own rules. Gabriel told us much of the Bible was altered to print 'what was acceptable' at the time.

We now have the truth from Gabriel. He said we have lived so many lifetimes here on Earth that we have *'met every person now living on Earth.'*

Considering there are eight billion people on Earth now, the simplest calculations will reveal that we have come here thousands of times, or perhaps millions. Today we experience lifetimes of eighty to a hundred years or so, but this expectancy has only existed for a few decades. Most of our human history we lived only twenty to fifty years. Aged individuals, such as Socrates, were a rarity. The reason we must renounce reincarnation is not to discount its truth but to get off the karmic wheel on which we rotate. We must ask ourselves why we come back again and again. Gabriel answers for us, and to us.

We review each lifetime when we transition to the other side. We see that we wounded another or others physically, emotionally or mentally. We may see that we have stolen things or murdered others. We decide we have to recompense for our behavior, so we plan a lifetime to do so. We sometimes ask our previous victims to return with us so we can 'make up' for our transgressions. We find people on the other side to help us accomplish our plan.

This is *not* predestination, because at any point in our earthly life we can change our mind about our plan; tell the others and then they must alter their plans, too. All this information is necessary because we must come to understand that none of our pre-arranged lives are necessary. Gabriel also taught us about free will. He said when God gave us free will He said he would not interfere with it. So any decision we make we ourselves are responsible for; not God.

In addition, Gabriel told us that because we all have free will *no one ever hurts us without our permission and we never hurt another without theirs - because God would not allow it.* Now we can see that returning to make retribution is unnecessary. Forgiveness is. We can go Home to the Father and not return again to Earth, The decision is ours; the time we do it is ours; the decision to accept the truth is ours.

It is time we knew the truth. That is why Gabriel came at this time. The truth will set us free. Gabriel did not come to seek followers for himself or his beloved channel. He did not come to start a new religion. He told us that he came to teach us nothing new, but only to remind us of what we already know but have forgotten. We know we are children of God; but we have forgotten that divine connection. We know we have all the powers Jesus had/has; but we have forgotten.

We can choose to remain in the darkness of our ignorance; our poor memories - or we can choose to walk toward the light of truth and join our Father again. He patiently waits, with an infinite patience, as we continue to struggle on Earth asking questions we already can answer ourselves. We have a million questions. All answers are within. Seeking first the Kingdom of God within us, we can find all the answers. Listening to the still, small Voice of God we surely will awaken to our glorious, immutable truth.

## Chapter 93   Restoring Our Memory

On May 18, 1996 we gathered to hear Archangel Gabriel. Instead we heard a softer, gentler voice speak to us. It would be years before we knew who the speaker was, because he said, "Call me The One". Now we know it was Jesus the Christ. On that day in May he said, "I come this day to bring to your attention the necessity on your part to release for ever and ever your idea of who you are concerning the earth. You are on the earth but not of the earth." It seems unwise to paraphrase an archangel. As I do so here, I also implore you to hear/read Gabriel's original lesson. The following is the essence of his message that day:

We are on a sacred journey. This sacred journey requires our commitment. Our only commitment should be to seek and know that we are one with God. Unless we have that commitment our journey is meaningless. The things that we concern ourselves with, such as work, housing, pleasure-seeking are meaningless. They are meaningless because they are not part of our commitment to know our at-one-ment with God. Every part of our being is holy. Every part of our being is love.

There was, and remains, a great power that joined with the totality of humankind's mind. This joining created what we know as life. From this joining came a great love; a great love. This love came to be known as the Christus, [Christ in us; God] and in that love we were born; we came into being. We stayed in that Christus, that love. It was the totality of us. Then, by our own free will, we chose to come into spirit. Spirit was the combination of that love, that mind, and that power. We were all one in spirit. While in spirit we came to believe that we were separate individuals; separate particles of the whole.

In that belief in separateness we each and all decided to go forth and create a world of our own. We joined all our creations together and created this universe. We found many homes (planets) here, and went from one planet to another. We created in our minds the idea that we were no longer one, but individual entities. We began to see each other as separate. We saw each other as 'other', and we became 'the other'. In becoming the 'other' we no longer heard the Voice of God, we no longer saw the Face of God, and we embodied all the concepts we had of what a non-god would be. We stayed in that belief and did not stir; we remain in it to this day.

In the ethers [air] there is a great vibrational rate which consists only of what we have created. That creation is our belief in non- godness, a non-Christness, a non-eternalness, and here we remain. Beyond these ethers there is all life, all truth, of what we truly are. Our bodies are only shadows of the unreality we have made. From the perspective of our body we create the scenes we walk through which bring us pain, illness, and death. We believe that we are temporary because we believe what our form tells us. We see our brothers as enemies, and we imagine that God is far away, and that Jesus the Christ does not exist. We look in the mirror and see a face, but we do not see the Son of God that we are. Instead we see this tiny, individualized particle that is so temporary, and so beleaguered. Jesus came that day to tell us the truth of our being, that we might know the truth and thus to become free. Jesus reminded us that he went before us:

"Brothers and sisters, I have known what you know, and I have walked where you walk, and I have known pain, and I have known death. And I can tell you they are not real; they are shadows of the shadows you have created, and nothing more - nothing more. I have walked in your shoes, and so I am qualified to tell you." We spend much time, money, and effort on our bodies: How we look, what we wear, how we feel, what we can do, what our limitations are. The truth is that we are limitless. We are more than this body, more than our brain, more than our emotions. Our emotions tell us that we are victims; that we are persecuted, we are ill, we are poor, and we can die. The shadows in which we believe will disappear in the light which we are when we allow that light to shine. We must by our own free choice allow that light to shine, instead of reasoning it away; instead of saying "I cannot".

Jesus could do all things, and so can we, because the same light, the same God is in us all. We think the body tells us it has pain, but all the body can know is what we tell it. When we *know* that we are Sons of God then our body has to know it too. In that knowing we are transformed, and in that transformation we realize that we are mightier than anything in our body or our mind. We must allow that Son of God of us to flow through us in power, in mind, in love. The body will obey, and we are well.

Nothing that we do or say makes us less in the eyes of God. The Son of God knows no defeat, no illness, and no death. The Son of God is all of us, even the least of us. When we release the shadows and know we are Sons of God the Christ power comes through us. Like Jesus, our Master Teacher, we can do all things. We must believe who we are. We must believe the truth of us. If we choose to walk in truth and light, then we must actually do it. The thoughts and feelings of others are not our concern, for as Sons of God the thoughts and beliefs and feelings about us are our truth. Our truth heals, restores, and remembers our Source. Our truth leads us to *know* we are the Sons of God. That is the truth that sets us free.

There is no place, no space, no time when we are not the Sons of God. This is the truth of us all, even those who disbelieve it. There is no place we can go that God is not. In our being the Presence of God dwells. It came forth in light and truth and it never leaves. When we can behold Christ and know He is within; when we can see our face and look at

Him, we will be assured that indeed we are the Sons of God. No place we have ever been, no deed we have ever done, no word we have ever spoken separates us from the Love of God.

The day will come when the heaven world will open to our consciousness, and when it does we will say, "Why did I stay away so long? Where could I go that I would find what I have found here? Where could I have found such joy as this?" It is then we shall know the manner in which we were created. We will know God loves us. We will know, just as Jesus the Christ knows, and we will be as He is - the I AM.

"I come this day to lift you into light because I know who you are. You are one with me and God, and there is nowhere else that you have ever been. Nothing can ever separate you from that. Everywhere is God and you." The One (Jesus the Christ)

## Chapter 94  Searching for Answers

There are ancient questions which humans have asked since we first gazed at the night sky and began naming the constellations. It seems interesting we would name things which we could not touch or explain. Perhaps even then we knew somehow we had a connection to the stars. Now we have the answers to the ancient questions, for Archangel Gabriel has come to provide us with the answers. From 1987 to 1999 Gabriel channeled his lessons in truth to a small, curious group of truth-seekers.

Gabriel explained how God breathed us forth in the beginning, and then Gabriel said there is no beginning or end to God. We have existed, on some realm, since Creation. We, like God, are forever. We came to Earth after co-creating it with God. It was our manipulation of energy which enabled us to manifest this planet. Analogous to the Prodigal Son, we came to Earth; this 'far country'. Like the Prodigal Son, we are 'wasting our substance' with our lifestyle. We are children of God, and in our

Higher Self we know that truth. But our conscious minds tell us we cannot go back because God has forsaken us.

God cannot nor would not forsake us; any more than human parents would willingly forsake their own children. Our current lifestyle is absorbed with the belief we are a body and nothing more. The soul of us remembers our inception and longs to return to the Father/Mother God that created us. We are all destined to return. It is an immutable law. Each one of us is our own savior. Gabriel informed us of the truth of the crucifixion. It was Jesus' choice because he wanted to save the world and being crucified would cause the populace to be aware of his resurrection. He knew if he died quietly no one would know about it. Also, Gabriel told us that Jesus did not suffer on the cross, because when he prayed '*Thy will, not mine, be done.*' in Gethsemane, his consciousness went to his Higher Self; his consciousness remained there until he 'died' at Calvary. Gabriel then startled us all when he said that indeed Jesus came to save the world, 'but only on the cross did Jesus realize he had only saved himself.'

On the cross Jesus conversed with his fellow prisoners. One of them was bitter and angry. The other asked Jesus if he was the son of God. Jesus responded, 'Yes, and so are you.' When the suffering man denied it, Jesus mentally showed him a vision of Heaven. Then the man said to Jesus, 'We are the sons of God.' The Bible states, *And Jesus said unto him, Verily I say unto thee, To day shalt thou be with me in paradise.* (Luke 23:43)

How insignificant our earthly questions become when we know the answer to the ancient questions. We are all on our way back home to Heaven, God's holy realm and our Home. Gabriel reminded us that we have planned our lives and every relationship we have. Our intent was to have experiences which taught us important lessons. The lessons we refuse to learn now will be chosen again for the next incarnation. This karmic cycle will only end when we accept our truth. We ought to learn forgiveness, which Jesus demonstrated and taught. But, since we plan all our earthly experiences *there is nothing to forgive.*

Jesus knew this truth, but he also knew that until we learn to forgive everyone we will not be ready for the truth that forgiveness is unnecessary. Learning is growth and we are growing closer to God in our awareness. The Age of Aquarius is upon us. It is the first age of our evolvement up to God. The previous age, Pisces, was the last age of our devolvement. This is a grand time to be alive, for it is the cusp of the New Age. This is a grand opportunity to learn love and forgiveness, and then in turn teach love and forgiveness to others. When we awaken to our sacred Selves and return to Heaven we will have no need to search for answers, for there will be no questions.

## Chapter 95  Seeking the Kingdom

*"And seek not ye what ye shall eat, or what ye shall drink, neither be ye of doubtful mind. For all these things For all these things do the nations of the world seek after: and your Father knoweth that ye have need of these things. But rather seek ye the kingdom of God; and all these things shall be added unto you,"* Luke 12:29-31

Our elder brother, Jesus, reminded us that God knows our every need while on earth. Therefore we need not ask Him for those things, for He will supply them. Instead of asking for worldly needs we ought to instead seek the kingdom of God. The Kingdom of God is spirit.  One cannot describe something that they cannot see. Few people have the talent of seeing spirit; most deny its existence just because they cannot see it. The denial does not eliminate it. God is spirit, and cannot be eliminated. God is our Source; the Author of all life. Because describing the kingdom of God is not possible, Jesus taught in parables to help people understand. So he likened the kingdom to a mustard seed, a planter, leaven, ten virgins, and a travelling man. These can be understood by anyone now, as then.

This variety of definitions reminds the writer of Archangel Gabriel's teachings. About ten years after his first visit he told us that he came to teach only one lesson: that we are children of God and must awaken to it and live it. But he had to give us many lessons to help us all learn, because we all learn in different ways. Jesus, Master Teacher, would not advise us to seek something we cannot find. That would be an insidious game. We can find it, therefore. The Bible tells us where. *"Neither shall they say, Lo, here! Or, lo, there! for, behold, the kingdom of God is within you.* Luke 17:21

We are walking around every day oblivious to the Kingdom of God within us. In order to access it, first we must believe Jesus' words and know he is telling us the truth. Second, we must bestill ourselves. *"Be still and know that I am God."* Ps. 46:10. The problem is that we have such a problem with being still. It is so because our lives are so full of busy ness. Family, friends, work, hobbies all consume our waking hours, and sleep, of course, is required to rejuvenate ourselves. Where is the time to be still? Only each one of us can decide if the seeking is worth it to find time; to make time for seeking. *"And I say unto you, Ask, and it shall be given you; seek, and ye shall find; knock, and it shall be opened unto you."* Luke 11:9 Finding is guaranteed; our willingness to seek is an individual decision. It is so simple to just ask, to mentally seek, to simply knock, and enter the Kingdom of Heaven within, by free choice.

We must learn who enters the kingdom. We *all* shall, eventually. *"Know ye not that the unrighteous shall not enter the kingdom of God?"* I Cor. 6:9. This question put by Paul suggests there might be another place for the unrighteous to go. It is not so. There is no hell; there is no devil. Gabriel explained they were both made up by humans. The unrighteous do not enter the kingdom because they do not seek it. They do no seek it because they are unaware it exists. We do not seek what we do not believe in.

The unrighteous come to earth again and again until we get it right; until we finally acknowledge the Kingdom within, seek it, and find it. We are all righteous. We simply have become unaware of our righteousness. Asking for enlightenment we find it; we then seek the kingdom of God. Then we find it. Then we return to our original Home: Heaven, where God breathed us forth from Himself, in the act of Creation. Creation is not static; it creates forever. We are co-creators with God, as His children. We have chosen many wayward paths on our earthly adventures. Like the Prodigal Son we left Heaven (we thought). And like the Prodigal Son, we shall return Home. When we seek guidance from our Guardian Angel and walk the path back Home, angels will gather to celebrate with us upon our arrival. Until then, all our worldly needs are met, as we set our spiritual sights on finding the Kingdom within.

## Chapter 96   Self-esteem and self-esteem

We esteem ourselves based on our accomplishments and possessions. These things do not define who we are. We esteem others based on their accomplishments and accumulations. These things do not define who they are, even if they believe so. Those individuals who have extreme limitations - physical, emotional or mental - have another set of goals. What they accomplish and possess may seem quite minimal. Learning to walk, to cope, to read are still great accomplishments. Our attention to their needs may give them self-esteem. What defines us is not our abilities. What defines us is our spirit Self. God knows He created us and loves us all - just the way we are. If others discount us or ridicule us - or ignore us - their treatment of us does not determine our worth. But it can be so felt. We all desire to be acknowledged as having some value.

When low self-esteem afflicts us, we need to be treated by others as though we are worthy of life, of attention, of love. Low self-esteem is a sense of valuelessness. When others, or even one other, treats us as having value, we begin to believe it is true. Self-esteem takes root and others value us. Self-esteem grows until finally we feel comfortable in our own skin. Once we esteem ourselves we learn to set boundaries when others enter our personal space. We learn to say 'no' - without guilt. We learn to live and let live. We learn to help others who have low self-esteem. We easily identify them - their body language shouts low self-esteem.

All this is based on our belief that we are a body that lives a short time and dies. It is a false belief, for it is based on the five senses which show us the world - a world which is temporary. Perception is deception because all our senses are limited, and they are all based on one's personal experience. Our eyes show us a limited view. We cannot see beyond the horizon. The sounds we hear can be loud enough to burst our ear drums, soft enough to require earphones. Some sounds can be heard only by dogs. Sour and bitter tastes, though relative, can offend our taste buds. Skunk musk and other odors offend our nostrils. Air temperatures that are too low or too high can freeze us to death or dehydrate us to death.

These bodily limitations do not define us, either. Archangel Gabriel made it very clear to us that we are all - all humankind - children of God, because God breathed us forth *as spirit* long before we took flesh on earth. We knew we were His and we loved God and each other. When we came to this planet and took on a physical form, we came to believe in form as our only reality. We accepted all the limitations which the body has. We felt less than spirit because of our limitations. We esteemed ourselves as unworthy to be God's children because we forgot our way Home. We accepted the idea that God would never take us back. Over time; much time; we came to feel at home here on Earth.

Our parents give us physical life. We plan that life beforehand. We bring to each lifetime our personality, our ego and the script we wrote. We also have, eternally, free choice, so we can change the script at any time we choose. No matter how many times we have chosen to incarnate on Earth, ever and always within us is the original spirit imbued by God.

We can, and do, find self-esteem here on earth, as forms. The Self-esteem we are all reaching for and destined to find is the valuing of ourselves as the only begotten children of God. Self-esteem with a capital 'S' is what we all are striving for, consciously or unconsciously. The Self of us is the spirit of us, that sacred space within. We have quick glimpses of it at times. It comforts us and we wish it could stay. It is a moment in time when we feel and *know* that we are at one with God. It is a split second when we remember our Source and an ancient time when we were in truth at one with God. The sense of Self has come into our awareness. We begin to learn that love and forgiveness are more than options. They define the path of our return. We *can* go home again. We can and will ascend when all our error perceptions are transformed into true perception.

When we learn that perception is deception, that what we perceive with our five senses deceives us to the truth of us, we will open our minds to know the truth of us. We will listen to Gabriel's teachings and know they are only truth. We will accept all others as our spiritual siblings. We will find Self-esteem as children of God. The final step in that personal journey is ascension. God reaches to us and we return. Jesus the Christ did it, and he often said, 'Follow me'. Jesus told us that everything he did we too can do (John 14:12). We will ascend when we know it is possible and know our value as God's Own. We will have paid off all our debts when we finally learn we never really incurred them. The self of us awakens to the holy Self of us; children of the Living God, and we esteem ourselves as the sacred offspring of God, as He created us.

# Section XIII
## Mem

## Chapter 97   Spiritual Decisions

Every decision we make affects other people. Depending on what the decision is and our position in life (homemaker, laborer, executive, and world leader) we affect a few or millions of others every time we choose an action or activity. That is a given. Our decisions are based on our personal experiences, our education, our goals and our aspirations. Experiences are so varied between individuals that there is no 'standard' or 'ideal' experience. Education varies according to discipline, ability to learn and quality of memory. There is no 'perfect' experience that fits all decision-making. Individual goals and aspirations depend on the childhood teachings and role models we admired throughout our youth.

With all this in mind, and desiring a positive outcome, we would want to choose the best option for all concerned, if we could only know it. But we cannot know it. God knows it; angels know it; but we cannot possibly *know* what would be the best option for all affected. All our decisions are based on our limited human view of things. Our ego insists that we are qualified to make any decision we are called to make - at home, in the workplace or as the head of a governing body. The more people affected by our decision the less qualified we become to decide the best outcome for all. When we humbly ask God to help us make spiritual decisions He answers us. We must yield the human impulse to listen to our ego. First, we should resign as our own decision-maker. Secondly, we must choose one who knows all possible outcomes. The Holy Spirit is our best teacher. Then we must listen to the decision. Finally, we must apply that decision to the problem. Sometimes it does not seem to fit our ego-based decision, but we must be vigilant.

Anyone can review history and see how many have been adversely affected by wars, racial prejudice, or an argument between neighbors. Only when we do not care about who 'gets hurt' do we run headlong into decisions and actions that wound or destroy another's life, reputation, or well-being. Such individuals are not seeking a common good or a positive outcome for the most people. They listen to their egos which have one goal: keep the ego in charge. These people say, in effect, I know what is best for me.

When we take the high road of wisdom and listen only to the Holy Spirit, every decision is the best. The Holy Spirit is the best teacher and guide we will ever listen to and obey. He is God's Comforter, promised by Jesus the Christ himself. He will never misguide us, never let us down, never refuse to supply us with the best answer. We cannot go wrong seeking, listening and following His direction. His is the still, small voice for God which is constantly available to all who seek His guidance. But he *must be asked*.

A great world leader, before WWII, was given information and guidance by the Holy Spirit. The leader listened to some of the guidance and followed it; the rest he ignored. Had he followed all the guidance there would not have been a second world conflagration. This exemplifies how essential it is to wholly trust the Holy Spirit's guidance. He is not named because I am listening to the Holy Spirit which guides my fingers here. Hearing Archangel Gabriel's lessons one can learn the name. The lesson now is not to point fingers; not to 'blame' someone. We are drenched in the waters of blame-seeking. All of us have made mistakes. We have all made decisions which have hurt others - sometimes intentionally; sometimes unintentionally. Listening to the Holy Spirit we would have made all decisions without hurt to anyone. This is an amazing and comforting truth. The Creator created us to create. We have made some terrible errors in judgement. We are not here to judge others, but rather to accept, acknowledge and love them all, as we desire to be accepted, acknowledged and loved. Our fear is we might love someone who does not deserve it; that is the judgment call we seem destined to make. Free choice and love will guide us to true spiritual decisions. To every question, love is the answer.

# Chapter 98   Spiritual Genetics

Everyone is familiar with the idea that the genes of our parents produce characteristics in us. Much scientific research has developed this genetic composition and prediction. That doesn't explain though why siblings are often unlike each other or their parents. We see the genetic component of our parents as indicating not only eye color, hair color and stature, but also attitudes and behaviors. Much of what research has discovered is true.

Many questions were put to Archangel Gabriel regarding this topic. Surprisingly, he told us that before our birth on earth we choose our parents. We choose a particular malady or body shape, we plan our lives and we choose our parents in accordance with our God-given free will. We know we have free will, but seldom think about *when* God gave it to us. The other option would be to believe that God chose to put us in a body we did not like, inflict on us a disease we had to battle, give us a deformed body which others would shun. Can we believe in such a god?

When we choose any deformity, disease, or addiction, we choose it in order to learn a lesson. If we do not learn it in this lifetime we will return again and try again to learn the lesson. Sometimes we choose a negative situation for others to learn a lesson. We have all been amazed at those individuals who rise above their particular situation gracefully and in full acceptance. They learn their lesson well. Sometime in just being around someone like that we learn from them our own lessons of acceptance and courage.

Responses given to us by Gabriel were more than interesting, they were amazing. Gabriel was once asked why some women have a short labor in birthing and some mothers have many hours of difficult labor. He said it was not the mother, but the infant that creates the long and difficult labors. Just before birth we know what we plan for our life. Sometimes we vacillate, asking ourselves 'should I or should I not?' It is that in decision which extends the birthing process.

Regarding organ transplants, Gabriel told us that a body rejects the implanted organ because of an imbalance in the spiritual development of the donor and recipient. This exemplifies the truth of us: that we are spirit in essence, and our spiritual path will be maintained in the event of an organ replacement. Gabriel did not pass judgment on the either the donor or the recipient, he merely pointed out the fact that we are each on a spiritual path which varies from individual to individual.

When we choose our parents before birth we base our decision on what we aspire to accomplish, what lessons we desire to learn, what obstacles we think we need to overcome. If we desire to become afflicted with a terminal illness, we will choose parents who carry that gene. If we choose to come in a deformed body we will choose parents who have patience to raise us. It must be remembered that when we choose our parents they are agreeable to the relationship because they also have free choice. It is often said that we choose our friends but not our family members. That is not true. Gabriel said it's interesting to watch us on the astral plane discussing who will be the parents and who will be the children in our next lifetime. He gave an example of a woman who desires to raise a child but does not want to go through childbirth. Another woman might say I will have a baby and put it up for adoption and you can adopt it.

This might be a good time to mention walk-ins because it is an example of our free choice before coming to earth. Before coming to live on earth, a person might choose a life to begin as a young child instead of a new-born baby. He thus 'walks in' to life on earth without going through the birthing process. He must find someone on the other side that is willing to participate in this decision by agreeing to 'die' young. It is not common, but it does occur. I once knew a walk-in who exchanged bodies at the moment when the other child drowned in a boating accident. My friend's parents said that their son was never the same after the boating accident. Indeed he was not the same. It is very interesting to me that he *remembered being* a walk-in.

# Chapter 99 Spiritual Gifts

As we approach another Christmas season we make lists for gift-giving. We try to think of something unique that the recipient will remember all year, or even beyond. We must keep within our budget, too. Whether we give clothing or jewelry, gift certificates or food, we make every effort to wrap all gifts with love, and hope they will be appreciated and enjoyed. At one time Archangel Gabriel told us, (when he described the world of angels, I think), that there are two times when angels come closest to earth: Christmas and Easter. It is no surprise to Christians because these holy days celebrate the birth of Jesus the Christ, and the Resurrection of Jesus the Christ. The message Jesus brought was love and forgiveness. He also said that we can follow him. He said it many times. And we can do everything he did (John 14:12). He, in fact, told us we are all like him and can be everything he was.

As we celebrate Christmas this year. Let us accept this sacredness of our being, and see Jesus the Christ as the mighty way-shower, the example (John 13:15), for us to emulate. He is our elder brother, our pattern (I Tim. 1:16). With all the joys of receiving Christmas gifts, we must not forget the reason for our celebration of this holy day. A child was born, as prophesied by Isaiah centuries before: *"For unto us a child is born, unto us a son is given: and the government shall be upon his shoulder: and his name shall be called Wonderful, Counsellor, The mighty God, The everlasting Father, The Prince of Peace. Of the increase of his government and peace there shall be no end . . ."* (Is. 9:6-7).

All life will be lifted up as the result of Jesus' coming. Wild beasts will become tame creatures. Children will become our teachers. Later, Isaiah (11:6) said, *"The wolf also shall dwell with the lamb, and the leopard shall lie down with the kid; and the calf and the young lion and the fatling together; and a little child shall lead them."* At one time Gabriel was asked about this, and his answer was (paraphrased): As all humanity becomes aware of its divinity, so too will the wild creatures become tame and domesticated.

Let us recall, with reverence, our Origin and Jesus' holy journey on earth to show us all the way back Home to Heaven, our natural habitat. We can consider the spiritual gifts noted by Paul when he wrote his first letter to the Corinthians (12:4-11): *Now there are diversities of gifts, but the same Spirit . . . the same God which worketh all in all.* These are the gifts of the spirit, as listed by Paul:

*The word of wisdom*
*The word of knowledge*
*Faith*
*Gifts of healing*
*Working of miracles*
*Prophecy*
*Discerning of spirits*
*Divers kinds of tongues*
*Interpretation of tongues*

All are gifted; all are talented; all are children of God. It is our purpose and our function to follow Jesus by living as he lived, with love and forgiveness for all. He did not obey all the rules of religion, but he listened constantly to the Voice within, and obeyed it. The Father of us all guides us all. It is an immutable law. Now we are beckoned once again to let a little child lead us; to let the Christ Love enter into our lives. Every day is Christmas, when we make it so.

Once we live our truth we will create a world of peace, a peace that will have no end. Our choices are to rail against the unjust, the unfair, and the cruel, or to pray for them. Our choices are to hold grudges and resentments from the past or let them all go and move forward with confidence in self and faith that God will show us the way. In choosing our spiritual gift and employing it daily we have the capacity for an everlasting peace. The only one we can change is our individual self.

People balk when they hear that 'everything is just as it is supposed to be', but it is so, because with our God-given free choice we have populated this earth and expressed a variety of negative attitudes and behaviors. We can change it; we can change our outlook and actions. The Christmas season is an excellent time to make a new beginning.

Chapter 100  Spiritual Nourishment

There is no better example of symbolism in scripture than the references in the New Testament to the word 'meat'. In all the New Testament there are only four references to 'food', but many references to 'meat'. Many uses of 'meat' clearly refer to food, but some uses of the word are just as clearly symbolic of something other than food.

Jesus said, "*I have meat to eat ye know not of. Therefore said the disciples one to another, Hath any man brought him ought to eat?*" (John 4:32-33) Obviously they are speaking of food, yet Jesus then responds with (verse 34): "*My meat is to do the will of him that sent me, and to finish his work*". Here Jesus proclaims that he is on earth to do the will of his Father. As the son of God, Jesus' holy task is to obey his Father, Creator of the universe. Then we wonder what the will of God is. If we believe that we should fear God, how can He instruct us or Jesus? If we accept God as a God of Love, his instruction must be good - eternally.

Much has been learned through science and technology; inventions are currently entrancing us with their grand services. The problem is that our scientific advances are out-stripping our spiritual progress. It is time for us to learn the Will of God so that we can do what Jesus did: listen to the Voice of God and follow it. This is not to say Jesus did not do his job. The failing is ours. Jesus taught the wisdom of God. Few listened; fewer understood. The miracles Jesus performed were so stunning that we forgot the message of love and forgiveness that he spoke of and lived by.

When we align our own will with the Will of God we are spiritually nourished because we allow ourselves to be guided by the Author of all life, God is our Father. God is our Creator. God's realm is the spirit world. We cannot see it even though we are submerged in it. God is everywhere present. "*Wither shall I go from thy spirit? or whither shall I flee from thy presence? If I ascend up into heaven, thou art there. If I take the wings of the morning, and dwell in the uttermost parts of the sea; Even there shall thy hand lead me, and thy right hand shall hold me.*" Ps. 139:7-10

Most modern humans do not think of God as an anthropomorphic being, but the concept still holds that God is omnipresent. In this ever-present holiness we are nourished by God. We are unaware of the nourishment until we seek to know the Will of God and align ours with it. We were given free choice by God and only by our free choice will we seek God's Will for us. This is the inception of the Age of Aquarius. Archangel Gabriel said it is the truth age. Now we have, from Gabriel, all the answers we have ever asked about our existence on earth and what it means. This is the age we are to awaken to our own divinity and know the Will of God. The Will of God is described by Jesus, in *A Course in Miracles:*

"Would you know the Will of God for you? Ask of me who know it for you and you will find it. I will deny you nothing, as God denies me nothing. Ours is simply the journey back to God Who is our home." T 8: V: 5:1-4

Jesus said he would never leave us, and he meant it literally. Through a dedicated servant of God, he came in the last century to re-state his task, to clarify some of the early errors in the Bible, and to re-assure us that the Kingdom of Good is indeed within us all. His lesson long ago was love and forgiveness. It still is. The *Course* is our spiritual nourishment to find our way back to God. In it we find truth, guidance and direction for our holy journey. In fact, Archangel Gabriel told us that *A Course in Miracles* is the Bible of the New Age.

Thirty years after *A Course in* Miracles, our Master Teacher, Jesus the Christ, brought to us another book for our continuing spiritual guidance and nourishment. Its title is *A Course of Love*. Accepting God's Nourishment and Will we help Jesus fulfil God's work.


## Chapter 101   Sunset; Son rise

The world we live in is described in *A Course in Miracles* as a world of shadows, illusion, sin, sacrifice; a world of scarcity, pain, darkness sleep, limits. It is not a pretty picture, but many of us can relate to one or more of these descriptions. This is not to say that we do not have happy times, good relationships, successful careers, and long, productive lives. But we all know someone who has had some kind of adversity in their lives. Or we can identify with an adversity in our own. Some people seem to have an entire lifetime permeated with difficulties in their own life or the lives of dear ones. We do not understand this but we have no choice but to accept it. Or do we have a choice?

God gave us all free choice, and imagination, unlike the beasts and the birds. Our baggage consists largely of guilt, and Archangel Gabriel explained that all guilt, in whatever form it takes, is based on the belief we hold that tells us we left God and He will never take us back. In the first place we never left God because that would be impossible. If we were not part of God we would not exist. Guilt itself is manufactured by us. We think we deserve some kind of punishment for a wounding of another last year or last lifetime. God loves us all equally and His Will for us is love, joy, peace, harmony, abundance. God would not give us anything but a blessing. Anything else is self-created. It is time to listen to the teachers coming to us from the spirit world. They come at this time to awaken us to the real Self of us, the eternal Self of us, the perfect Self of us. This time is the beginning of a New Age - the Age of Aquarius. That is why Archangel Gabriel came from 1987 to 1999. He is the Announcer of the Ages.

We are children of God, made in His Image, and therefore we are spirit in essence. With our free choice we can accept this wonderful news, or we can choose to stay in the darkness of this world where we live. We have grown accustomed to the negative experiences. Even when our lives seem to be going well, we expect something negative to come along. And it usually does. We bring it on by our own expectations. Thoughts are very powerful, Gabriel explained, and by our thinking we create our experiences. By our thinking we also influence Mother Nature.

We endure flooding, forest fires, earthquakes and call them acts of God. A God of love would not allow these disasters. God would not inflict pain and suffering on His children. We think only in Heaven we will be free of such disasters. Scripture mentions a new Heaven and a new Earth. "*And I saw a new heaven and a new earth: for the first heaven and the first earth were passed away; and there was no more sea.*" (Rev. 21:11)

When we 'pass away' ('die') it is not the end of us. We pass away from the earth but we remain alive in spirit. Our bodies have lost their usefulness; our eternal spirit thrives eternally. The earth as we know it - physical form - will pass away when it has lost its usefulness. The last sunset will be seen from earth. That time will come when our minds open to truth and our hearts open to unconditional love; the love demonstrated by the son of God. Jesus came to tell us of the way that we should go. *"I am the way, the truth, and the life."* (John 14:6). As Jesus came to teach, and Jesus resurrected, we too shall resurrect someday.

This is the time to love and forgive. This is the New Age of truth, of spirituality, of light, for us all. Some of us will choose it now, some later. But eventually all will accept the love of God within us and live a life of love and forgiveness. And when all have accepted the light of truth there will be no need of this planet earth. We all will have returned Home to the Father Who created us and we will live in a place of light, peace, joy, and harmony forever. We will never lose our individuation but we will know we are part of God forever.

The spirit self of us knows that what Gabriel teaches is true, for some part of us longs to return Home to God. *A Course in Miracles* was written as a spiritual guide for everyone, when each is ready to be spiritually guided. It says 'the light has come' (ACIM WB I: 75 h). And the light is the Christ Light that was embodied in Jesus the Christ who came to earth 2,000 years ago. His lesson then is the same lesson now.

## Chapter 102 Talking Angels

"The angels could hear me talk, and they talked to me, encouraging me." Alex, in *The Boy Who came back from Heaven*, p.115

We can readily accept the possibility of angels attending to a very sick boy as he lay in a hospital bed. If anyone needed angelic help, it would be him. What is more difficult for us to accept is the notion that angels can talk to us when we are healthy and awake. Yet many times we have felt like we were at the end of our rope, without help of any kind, and someone or something happen which pulled us back from the abyss.

Angels help us constantly, even though we are not aware of them. In recent times more and more people are speaking of angels and more people are seeing them. Archangel Gabriel told us that angels often take on a human form briefly to help us. We merrily go through life, running it as we choose, not seeking angelic aid because we think we don't need it. Then, like Alex's dad, we find ourselves amazed when angels are actually heard by human ears. Here is the possible difference. Our all too human ears do *not* hear angels, but the spirit of us does.

Perhaps angels constantly talk to us, but their soft and gentle voice is unheard amidst the loud shouting of our own minds. Heaven forbid that we all must lie in a hospital bed, very ill, in order to hear angels from on high. It may just be in the realm of possibility that we can make a conscious decision to listen to them. It is very likely we listen to them without 'hearing' a voice, when we call a friend who says 'I was just thinking about you.' Or a person we once knew but have not seen in years comes to mind and then we receive an email from them, or they knock on our door.

Stranger still is the instance where we gather in a group and pray for healing, and then the healing manifests. Most people believe in the power of prayer, but give little or no thought to the process of the response. Only God can heal, and then only when a healing is *desired*. Raphael is the Healing Archangel, and he has a plethora of angels who do his bidding. Healing angels came to Alex, and he said so. When we seek, we find. Whether we seek knowledge by reading books and hearing lectures or seek wisdom by meditation, or seek healing in prayer, we find response.

Gabriel said that angels are now making themselves known now because we have ignored them too long. When we accept them as our reality we can ask their assistance in all things. We each have 144,000 angels at our command! They are ready to help at our slightest request. They help us find parking spots for our vehicles, help us decide what outfit to wear every day, what car to buy, what courses to take in college, etc., et.

Gabriel told us that our angels do not hesitate or ponder if they should respond to us. Our wish is their command. We would be wise to carefully consider what we desire. At one time Gabriel told a woman at the seminar that if she asks for a man in her life she may get a plumber. He said we must be specific about our request. If we desire a relationship our angels would appreciate some defining features.

The interference which keeps us from hearing our angels is our self-created egos. The loud and persistent voice of the ego overcomes the angelic whisper. That raucous voice in our head drowns out the softer voices of angels. We can choose to be still and listen, or turn our backs on angels' voices until such time as we really *need* them. It is our choice.

We can know that in meditation, when all is quiet, the voice we hear may come to us as just a thought. Angels work that way. Angelic words or ideas do not come to us in the traffic's roar, or when we are absorbed in our occupation. They come in the stillness of our hearts and minds.

The Bible says *"seek and ye shall find"* (*Luke 11:9*). It does not say hope you will find without seeking. We get no answers from angels unless we ask the questions. Miners find gemstones because they are looking for them. Students receive answers when they mentally ask for them. Young mothers get help with new infants from their angels - angels of the mother and angels of the infants. Angels are here for us in vast numbers. They await our requests. Disbelieving in them does not eradicate them. They wait until we acknowledge them, ask for help, and then it is imperative that we say Thank you' to them. Angels are all around us to do our bidding. They also laugh with us.

## Chapter 103  Teachers of God

*"And ever since man took his place in form of flesh the Christ has been manifest in flesh at first of every age."* (AGJC Intro, 13)

Time as we know it is marked by days, months, and years. We measure days by hours, minutes and seconds. From a distant perspective, such as seen by the angelic realm, Earth time is measured in ages. We are at the onset of the Aquarian Age. It is also the Truth Age, for wisdom comes from on high now to awaken us to our origin and destiny. Archangel Gabriel and eleven Master Teachers came to various places on Earth at the end of the twentieth century to teach us. Jesus the Christ also visited us, to 'straighten out the crooked places in scripture'. Their lessons were all the same and intended for all humanity: Now is the time for us to wake up and know that we are eternal in spirit. There is no death.

'Aquarius' comes from the Latin 'aqua', or water. Aquarius is the water bearer. "And then the man who bears the pitcher will walk forth across an arc of heaven; the sign and signet of the Son of Man will stand forth in the eastern sky. The wise will then lift up their heads and know that the redemption of the earth is near." (AGJC, Intro, 10) This is a most wonderful time to be alive on this planet we call home. Now we are learning that this home is temporary. Because we are eternal, Heaven is our true home; our natural habitat.

The Piscean Age commenced with the appearance of Jesus the Christ. The word Pisces means fish. Two thousand years later Jesus' followers still symbolize Jesus with the image of a fish. The lessons he taught were forgiveness and love. He not only taught these lessons but he lived them. Even on the cross he asked God to *"forgive them, for they know not what they do"*. (Luke 23:34)

Jesus the Christ proved there is no death when he resurrected to show all humanity that life is forever. But we have misunderstood in two ways: We placed this miracle-worker high on a pedestal, named him the only son of God, and proceeded to worship him. This, in spite of the fact that he told us many times, *"Follow me"*. He also said that we could all do everything he did. (John 14:12) He came as a pattern (1 Tim. 1:16), an example (John 13:15). In effect, he was saying that we all are sons of God, and he came to show us the way back Home. More importantly, Archangel Gabriel now tells us that the Bible's scribes mistranslated the original words. Originally the words were: *"Jesus Christ, begotten son of he only God."*

Also, we have focused through the centuries on the miracles Jesus performed. From turning water into wine to raising the dead, we have envisioned him as a god of wonder instead of God manifest in flesh who in fact was the firstfruits of an awakening humanity (1 Cor. 15:23). The

Master Jesus, our elder brother, came to show us the way to live in the knowledge of our own divinity. As children of our Creator, we are all sacred offspring of the Living God.

The age before Pisces was the Arian Age. The onset of Aries saw the time of Abraham. Abraham means 'father (source, founder) of a multitude' (MBD, 17) and is described in the Old Testament book of Genesis. In the book of Exodus we read of Moses, which means 'drawing out (of water)'. (MBD, 460)

The Taurian Age began with the time of Adam. Taurus means bull. We equate the bull with strength. Archangel Gabriel explained that the story of Adam and Eve is an allegory. We know from archeology that humankind has lived on Earth for millions of years. But the true meaning of the Garden of Eden is that we once existed in Paradise with God. We loved each other and knew God loved us all equally. He still does. We manipulated energy and brought ourselves down, down, down, into physical form, below which energy cannot be slowed. We think God is 'up there somewhere' because we have forgotten our Source.

The ages roll and we have convinced ourselves that we are dinky, unimportant people. Except those who have acquired wealth and fame. God is not impressed with wealth and fame. From His perspective we are beams of light. As light beams we are perfect and eternal. We are love, loved and loveable. This Age of Truth, the Aquarian Age, is the time for humanity to awaken to our divinity. All humanity is the only begotten Son of God. The time has arrived when we no longer require an intermediary between ourselves and our Creator. We are asked to teach each other how to awaken to our Higher Self. We all have the potential of being teachers of God.

*"A teacher of God is anyone who chooses to be one. His qualifications consist solely in this; somehow, somewhere he has made a deliberate choice in which he did not see his interests as apart from someone else's. Once he has done that, his road is established and his direction is sure. A light has entered the darkness. . . . The call is universal."* (ACIM, MFT, 3)

# Chapter 104  Teaching Only Love

*"The great peace of the Kingdom shines in your mind forever, but it must shine outward to make you aware of it."* ACIM T 6: II: 12:8

If the peace of God can shine outward it must be the same as the light within us. God established His Kingdom in us. If He did not, Jesus would not have verbalized it. Our choice in the matter is to express the light outward to others or we can attempt to hide it 9under a bushel). Hiding it is what we strive to do every day. Jesus, in comparing us to a candle, warned us against hiding it, in Matthew (5:15), Mark (4:21), and Luke (11:33). The ego, to which we have given much of our power, constantly strives to thwart us from revealing our light.

The ego's function is divisiveness; its favorite tool is fear. We listen to its commanding voice, which tells us either that we are special and better than anyone else, or it yells in our ear that we are tiny, unimportant things without purpose or function. Both messages are false. The ego thrives on the fear of failure and insists that death is real. The ego is a liar. We are all children of God, regardless of the many adventures we have chosen in this life. God loves us just the way we are (spirit) no matter what we think, say or do.

We still fear death, although Jesus overcame it two thousand years ago. Some will insist that he was, after all, the only son of God, and that explains his resurrection and ascension. In the late twentieth century Archangel Gabriel came to tell us that Jesus came to show us the way because we are all one in God, of God, from God. The Light of God is in us all. Pretending this is not so will never make it false. Gabriel came to wake us up from Adam's sleep. Adam represents humanity. Nowhere in scripture does it say that Adam woke up.

*"Ye are the light of the world."* (Matt.14). It does not get clearer than that. Any beginning student of the Bible, in employing its concordance, will note the many references to the light within us and the importance of expressing it. God is Light. We are the lights of the world. We may attempt to hide it, but we can never extinguish it. The ego will try to deny

it. Gabriel, the Announcer of the Ages, came to tell us how important we are to God and how important we are to God. Gabriel told us how necessary it is to express our light to others. The great peace of God is the light in us all. It is our content, our function and our purpose. The ego loves darkness and hiding truth from us. We must now turn away from its hollering and decide on expressing our light. We are constantly teaching others by our attitudes and behavior. So many people live by their ego that we feel quite at home doing the same. This is a new age. Gabriel called it the truth age; the Age of Spirituality. He brought his message because we are ready to hear it.

We have denied our light for so long that the idea we are light seems foreign to our thinking. Gabriel's lessons awaken us to the truth of us. We may argue against the truth but truth needs no defense. When Pilate asked Jesus, *"What is truth?"* (John 18:38) Jesus did not answer. If he did answer, it is not in the Bible. Perhaps Jesus thought Pilate could not comprehend truth; perhaps we ourselves cannot. Truth is and thinking cannot alter it.

Every day we make a thousand choices about our activities, our bodily needs and pleasures. The body is temporary, and will have an end to its need. The spirit of us is eternal. Our new choices will bring us closer to the truth of us. These new choices will inform us of our true nature. Our decision to let our lights shine will bring us closer to God *in our awareness*. In truth we cannot get any closer to God than we already are. Awareness of God in us can be ours. The choice must be made to open our minds to truth and then live from the truth of us; to let the light in us shine outward. When we do that, others will learn how to do it. At some point in time all our lights will join as one and God's expression of Love will be complete on Earth. In spirit they never parted.

# Section XIV
## Nun

## Chapter 105   The Absent Biographer

When we desire to learn about the life of a famous person we seek his or her biography. There is no one in history who is more famous than Jesus the Christ. Archangel Gabriel said that there is not a human on Earth who has not heard the name; regardless of their opinion of him. Josephus (37-100 AD) wrote his own biography. Jesus himself wrote nothing, as far as we know. Matthew, Mark and Luke all wrote synopses of Jesus' life after the Master Teacher Jesus died and resurrected. John also wrote after Jesus left, but provided us with more detail about Jesus and his teachings.

Who among us would be satisfied to read of Abraham Lincoln his birth, an event when he was twelve and the last three years of his life? Historians would scramble through all writings of the time to gather a complete biography. In Jesus' time writing was not common. Scribes were rare, and they scrolled onto parchment only what they were told. It is interesting to note that we are satisfied to know so little about a man who changed the world so profoundly. Humanity has chosen two views about Jesus: some place Jesus only in Heaven as son of God. In this belief we can never hope to emulate him, but the early church fathers told us we should try, because we were 'born in sin'. Others view Jesus as an elder brother who came to show us the way. A careful reading of the Bible shows us that Jesus was the 'firstfruits' (Romans 8:23, I Cor. 15:23). Jesus came to show us he way: *"I am the way, the truth, and the life."* (John 14). He came as an example: (John 13:15, I Peter 2:21); a pattern: (I Tim. 1:16).

We also have the benefit of the Apocryphal books of the Bible. Unless we accept, as the early Christians, that they are spurious and unworthy, we can learn much more about Jesus' life. The following quotation is from the title page of *The Lost Books of the Bible.* (World Publishing Co, New York, 1971)

*"Christ was the joyous boy of the fields. We are not permitted to think that the shadows of Calvary darkened His pathway as a youth, and the Apocryphal Books of The New Testament show a great deal of the early life of Christ not to be found in the four Evangelists."* Dr. Talmadge

The reader can find more insight into Jesus' life on Earth. A few excerpts will suffice. Eye witness accounts of the virgin birth of Jesus are found in Chapter XIV of The *Protevangelion*. Jesus, as an infant, performed miracles on the journey away from Bethlehem to Egypt. Many people were cured of leprosy and other afflictions simply by the power of the water in which Jesus had been bathed. See book *I. Infancy*, Chapter VI. In Chapter II *Infancy*, Jesus causes clay sparrows to fly. All Christianity's original writings contain some false information. Gabriel informed us that the slaughter of the innocents (Matt. 2:16) never took place. Asked why anyone would manufacture such a story, Gabriel did not know. Apparently angels do not comprehend the terrible depths of imagination into which men's minds sink.

In the Introduction to *The Forgotten Books of Eden:* "It is not too much to say that no modern can intelligently understand the New Testament, unless he is acquainted with the so-called 'Apocrypha," and with the "Pseudepigrapha" as well. The very words of Jesus were in many instances, suggested by sayings current in his day, more or less as unconscious quotations from the Testaments of the 12 Patriarchs." In *The Second Book of Adam and Eve* we find an exquisite description of life after death: "When Enoch had ended his commandments to them, God transported him from that mountain to the land of life, to the mansions of the righteous and of the chosen, the abode of Paradise of joy, in light that reaches up to heaven; light that is outside the light of this world; for it is the light of God, that fills the whole world, but which no place can contain." (XXII: 8)

Sadly, the Book of *Nicodemus* relates a story of Christ's soul going to hell. Thanks to God the truth told us by Gabriel is that there is not, nor ever was, a place called hell; nor an entity which we call satan or the devil. *(author note: spellcheck tells me satan should be capitalized; I gladly refute it, for a*

236

*non-existent entity*). Jesus was a man in bodily form; Christ was the light in him. Christ is the light in all of us. We are children of light, but by choice we left that heavenly realm in which we knew we were light and we knew God loved us. He still does; we still are light beings. We are sleeping our earthly life away in our abject ignorance of our holy beginning. Jesus came to awaken us twenty centuries ago. From 1995 to 1999 he visited Earth again to teach us the same lessons of love and forgiveness. This time he performed no miracles to thwart our attention away from the truth he brought; the truth that he is; the truth that we are.

## Chapter 106  The Air We Breathe

We send astronauts into space inside a capsule which contains air to breathe. Upon landing on the moon, and walking on the moon's surface, the space travelers had to wear masks to survive, since there is no breathable air on the moon. We might wonder how all this breathable air manifested on the planet Earth, and what keeps the air around this planet which is spinning on its axis; and revolving around the sun. I suppose the scientists who study such things will simply reply 'gravity'. We know that gravity is what keeps us humans on the earth's surface - in spite of its speed on its axis and in spite of its rate of acceleration around the sun. I wonder if the aerospace scientists take gravity for granted. Certainly it is an element in calculating the trajectory of rockets into space.

We non-scientific people may not understand what the scientists know; perhaps we have no interest in such things. We merely care that we have air to breathe. We take it for granted constantly. We think about the air we breathe only when smog, fog, or contaminated air impedes breathing. Or when the rarified air on a high mountain makes us gasp. Otherwise we take air for granted. The dictionary tells us that air is 'the mixture of invisible, odorless, tasteless gases (as nitrogen and oxygen) that surrounds the earth'.

We are unable to see, smell or taste air, but we also cannot hear it or feel it, except when it moves swiftly around us. Therefore all of our five senses are incapable of discerning air, yet it is essential to our earthly lives. The word 'spirit' has its source in Latin *spirare*, meaning 'to breathe'. We cannot see spirit, either. We cannot only because we think we cannot. Some people have the ability to see spirit. It is one of the spiritual gifts (I Cor. 12:10). We call them psychics or mediums.

 I have seen spirit only once in my life: the Master Teacher, Jesus the Christ, appeared before me at a séance, in 1984. He stood a few feet in front of me, holding a huge loaf of bread on extended arms, palms up, and said, "Lay down your life for me, and I will give you the bread of life". It was a few weeks later that I realized what he meant: as a victim of alcoholism, I should foreswear alcohol consumption and turn my will over to God. Thirty years later I can say he truly has given me the bread of life.

The air we breathe is necessary for life, yet it remains undiscernible by all our senses. Air as spirit also defies our senses. 'Spirit' is defined by Webster as, 'a supernatural being or essence'. Because it supernatural we cannot destroy it. We can breathe it, pollute it, compress it, and use it. But we cannot destroy it. As air is required for physical life, spirit is required for our spiritual essence. Air is essential to us both physically and spiritually. life.

Those who do not understand spirit make of it something fearful, and speak of ghosts, malevolent spirits and controlling spirits. Turning again to Webster, spirit is also defined as 'the immaterial intelligent or sentient part of a person'. There is something, we must admit, that is beyond our five senses. Call it supernatural, metaphysical, immaterial or something else. But it is in us, as we breathe. Some may call it conscience. It makes us want to do good things. If we desire to do negative things it is because, like belligerent children, we choose to rebel. We rebel because we listen to the ego. We have 'a mind of our own' and stubbornly insist we know best. We are rebelling against ourselves, our spirit, our essence.

Given free choice we have the option of choosing positive or negative every moment of every day. Sometimes the narrow, fearful, judgmental life is cozy, predictable, and easy to settle into. We seek others of like mind and thus confirm our negativity as we conform to theirs. Then an experience comes into our life which wakes us up to our basic - not base - selves. We hear people say, 'That's the spirit!' when we forge ahead on a positive path. Over time we find life to be more comfortable and rewarding. We seek others of like mind. We form friendships. We see others as being on the same path of a positive life.

All this comes from the air we breathe - that 'essential combination of gases,' that spirit in us, that keeps us spiritually alive and physically breathing. We are spirit beings, and our spirit keeps calling us to do good, to love self and others, to wake up to our spirit selves. Scientists search and research facts of space and air, but everyone can, without understanding why, become all we are intended to become, just by the air we breathe. Just by seeking our unseen spirit selves. Our bodies will transform when we no longer need them. Our spirit Self is forever, and continues through eternity without the nitrogen and oxygen necessary for earthlings.

## Chapter 107  The Beautiful Temple

In the third chapter of Acts, in the New Testament, we find a story about Peter and John giving a healing. The two apostles are about to enter the temple called Beautiful when they see a man, lame from birth, seeking alms.

*And Peter, fastening his eyes upon him with John, said, Look on us. And he gave heed unto them, expecting to receive something of them. Then Peter said, Silver and gold have I none; but such as I have give I thee: In the name of Jesus Christ of Nazareth rise up and walk.* (Acts 3:1-6)

The man does stand up and walk. He leaps with joy and praises God. We can read this story and assume that the words alone are the causative factor in the man's healing. But words alone do not have the power to heal. Neither did the words spoken by Peter do the healing. It was Peter's Faith in God which opened to God's healing power. It was Peter's knowingness that as he asked God to heal, God would surely do so. Peter represents faith. With faith in God we can accomplish anything we desire, because faith is the door which opens to the power of God. Peter had faith in the unseen, knowing in his heart of hearts that God *is*, and God would respond to his request.

When the man asked for alms he expected money with which to buy his food. Instead he was given the precious gift of mobility. It is of some interest to note the healing process described. Peter said to the man Look on us. In other words, focus on faith (Peter) and love (John); keep your attention on faith and love; block out everything else. Peter was not going to toss a coin into the man's hand; he planned on something far greater for him. He did not ask the man if he wanted to be healed (but he may have mentally asked him). Peter assumed that walking would be the greatest gift he could give, and walking would preclude his need to beg.

John represents love. Peter told the man to Look on us, because faith and love combine to bring about a healing. Faith in God, the Unseen and love for God, the Unseen, make a powerful combination. We know also from scripture that faith without works is dead. (James 2:17). So Peter desired to heal the man rather than simply donate money.

In recent years such faith and love has been employed to heal. A woman named Myrtle Fillmore (1845-1931) healed herself by applying faith and love to her dying body. She recognized the life in her body and talked to the life force in her liver, eyes, abdomen, heart. She told her organs that they were full of energy and strong. Myrtle would close herself in a room and study the Four Gospels. She focused on her faith and her love of God. Her healing process:

"I did not let any worried or anxious thoughts into my mind, and I stopped speaking gossipy, frivolous, petulant, angry words. I let a little prayer go up every hour that Jesus Christ would be with me and help me to think and speak only kind, loving, true words; and I am sure that He is with me, because I am so peaceful and happy now." (*Myrtle Fillmore Mother of Unity*, 42-43). Mrs. Fillmore, with her husband, Charles, founded the Unity Church.

A church is not required to love God and have faith in Him. Jesus reminded us that the Kingdom of God is within us. Finally, in this inception of the Age of Aquarius we have the ability to comprehend the meaning of his words. Jesus' peers could not. The Kingdom cannot be seen by mortal eyes, nor described. It is faith in the Unseen Creator of all life which opens every door to the seeker of truth. Healing, wisdom, all answers, are available to us. Faith in God and love of God combine to manifest our every request.

We know that within Jesus was the temple: *"Destroy this temple and in three days I will build it up.* John 2:19. His listeners scoffed and said the temple took many years to build. Later it was understood that he meant himself as the temple and his resurrection as the 'building up'. We all contain this beautiful temple; this holy temple: *Know ye not that ye are the temple of God, and that the Spirit of God dwelleth in you?* (I Cor 3:16).

## Chapter 108   The Blind Reader

When driving up to an ATM a few years ago, I noticed that the keyboard included brail information. I wondered how many blind drivers benefitted from it! It reminds me now of the many people who read the Christian Bible, or any other religious writing, and see only the words. Thanks to Jeffrey Moses, we have a book in which he reveals the commonality of all major religions. He chooses not two or three but twenty-nine basic religious tenets, and quotes various religious writings to reveal a world quilt of common threads of faith.

One of the threads is the concept of a meaning behind words. Some of our Christian brothers and sisters choose to see the letter, not the spirit, of the Word. Other religions have their own religionists. What is the difference between the letter and the spirit of the law? When Jesus spoke of the ninety-nine sheep who were found and the one which was missing, his words were meant for shepherds; the underlying meaning was for all of us. Sheep represent thoughts. "Sheep are the most harmless and innocent of animals. They represent the natural life that flows into man's consciousness from Spirit. It is pure, innocent, guileless, and when we open our mind to this realization of Spirit life we open the gate by the sheep market." MBD, 597

Paul says, *The letter killeth but the spirit giveth life.* (II Cor. 3:6) Mr. Moses provides us also with a tenet of Judaism: "Rather let a letter be uprooted than the Torah be forgotten." The spirit of a word has a meaning which cannot always be described. We cannot know the *feeling* of love when reading the words 'I love you'. Islam gives us, "The Koran was sent down in seven dialects, and in every one of its sentences there is an outer and an inner meaning." 'Seven dialects' might indicate the desire of the writer to put into print words which would be understood by *all* readers of that sacred text. Turning to Hinduism we have:

"Study the words, no doubt, but look
Behind them to the thought they indicate,
And having found it, throw the words away
As chaff when you have sifted out the grain."

How interesting to note the fact that 'grain' is found here; like the mustard seed, the smallest grain, that Jesus spoke of. 'Throw the words away' could mean not to destroy the book but rather to forget the words but always remember their meaning.

The Christian Bible has been translated many times since the original writings on papyrus in Aramaic language of Jesus. In recent years the *Dead Sea Scrolls* were discovered. Perhaps someday another ancient writing will be found. The truth of the matter is - as given us by Archangel Gabriel - much of our Bible was changed to write 'what was acceptable at the time', and some words were changed and some were purged entirely. Jesus visited us for four years (1995-1999) and was asked if he would tell us the true, original words of the Bible. His reply was "It would take about three minutes."

Bible students study, discuss and memorize Bible passages. If that is what they are drawn to, so be it. To seek and understand the meaning behind the words enhances the understanding; increases the ability to know and *feel* the intent of the writer. We can hardly imagine what it was like to stand in a field and *hear* Jesus preach the Sermon on the Mount. Nor can we place ourselves at the table of the Last Supper and *feel* what the disciples felt. In Sufism scripture we find:

"Let not scholars scrutinize
The language of the wise too closely;
The seers think more of the thought
Than of the words in which 'tis caught."

Of course we ought to read the religious books of our choice, but it is equally important to know the meaning behind the words. When Jesus washed the feet of his disciples, it was not to bathe them. It was a symbolic gesture. The feet represent understanding. Jesus was demonstrating the need for his apostles to understand the lessons he had taught them.

## Chapter 109  The Bread of Life

We think of the ritual of Holy Communion as instituted by Jesus the Christ. In truth the symbolic gesture began in the Old Testament: *"And Melchizedek king of Salem brought forth bread and wine: and he was the priest of the most high.* Gen 14:18. Abraham received the ritual from Melchizedek. Three angels appeared to Abraham, and he said, And *I will fetch a morsel of bread, and comfort ye your hearts; after that ye shall pass on . . ."* Gen. 18:5. All the first four gospels recite the story of Jesus presenting Communion. (Matt. 26:26-28, Mark 14:22-24, Luke 22:19-20). They all describe Jesus giving his disciples the bread and wine which represent his body and blood of the New Testament. John devotes Chapter 6 to describing Jesus' intent and promise of the ritual of Holy Communion.

Fast forward 2,000 years, and we find: "The Holy Spirit's messengers are sent far beyond the body, calling the mind to join in Holy Communion and be at peace." (ACIM 19: B: 3:1)  One time in my life I saw Jesus in person. It was during a séance in Schenectady at the home of a medium,

Rev. Myrtle. She was my first Bible teacher. It was my first séance. As I recall there were about eight people present. Before the séance I told Myrtle that I had never seen spirit. She heard and saw them constantly. Shortly after the séance began Jesus appeared a few feet in front of me, with arms outstretched and holding a Jewish loaf of bread on his palms. He said, "Lay down your life for me, and I will give you the bread of life." And he was gone. It was in the spring of 1984, and on July 25 I stopped drinking alcohol which had led me to a life of tragic errors. Myrtle told me she had prayed for my sobriety. Only in a sober life did I understand the meaning of Jesus' words.

This author was blessed to hear several seminars presented by Jesus the Christ, from 1995 to 1999, concurrently with seminars by Archangel Gabriel. His lessons in truth were given through a dedicated and spiritually evolved woman of the cloth. Many times I asked Jesus questions, as did others of the group. At one of these seminars I limped to the microphone to ask Jesus a question. Before I could ask, he said, 'Why do you walk thusly?" I told him it was a problem with my hip for which surgery was required, but I thought I could heal myself, as a student of Gabriel.

He asked me if I knew the story about the one lost sheep and the ninety-nine safe ones. (Matt. 18:12) I said, "Yes." The answer he gave - and I must paraphrase it - was basically that there was a problem I had and when I dealt with it honestly I would no longer limp. Never having identified the problem, I had surgery a few weeks later. But the message was clear: every illness is self-determined and can be self-healed. "All forms of sickness, even unto death, are physical expressions of the fear of awakening." ACIM 8:9:3:2 This 'awakening' refers to the fact we are all asleep to our divinity as children of God. Adam slept and nowhere in scripture does it say he awoke. We must awaken.

Archangel Gabriel came to wake us up at the beginning of this Age of Aquarius. He is the Announcer of the Ages. In addition to Gabriel, eleven Master Teachers came to various locations on Earth with the same message. One of them was Ramtha, in California. All humanity is 'the only begotten son of God.' Gabriel emphasized this was the original wording instead of the Bible's injunction "Jesus Christ, only begotten son of God."

This generation awakens to a realization that we do not need the symbolic gesture of communion to feel at one with God. Already one with Him, we can know this oneness in meditation. Those who disdain or fear the act of meditation are among those who fear awakening. The fear of awakening comes from our belief that (like the Prodigal Son) we think our Father has turned us away for leaving Him, and He will never take us back. But, like the prodigal's father, He will welcome us with open arms and celebrate our return from a journey we never really took.

Gabriel gave us a new version of the Lord's Prayer, part of which is, "Cause me this day to be aware of the bread of life: thy Presence in my consciousness."

## Chapter 110   The Carpenter's Ax

'We use the ax to cut away the knotty, useless and ungainly parts and make the character symmetrical.' (AGJC 20:16)

Jesus had just returned from the Synagogue when he was twelve. He spoke of the carpenter's tools as representative of the characteristics to be developed as we journey through life on Earth. The ax, as the sculptor's chisel, strikes off the sharp edges (such as impatience) of our nature, to reveal the inner child of God.

Impatience is spawned by the desire for control. In our arrogance of believing we are the only ones who know the best way of life, we make plans - from our ego's perspective. It does not occur to us that there could be another, superior way. We are convinced that we must climb high mountains, cross raging rivers and battle with wild tigers to arrive at our desired goal. We insist on believing the false premise 'no pain; no gain'. We continue to stumble and fall on this chosen path - until we acknowledge a Higher Power, Which is accessible always, Which will guide us on a smoother path.

Another sharp edge is judgment, which leads to prejudice. It never crosses our mind that judgment is a terrible indictment. Someone once said that anger and hatred married and begat prejudice. Anyone who speaks a different language, wears different clothes, eats different food, worships differently, is often judged to be less than us. The person who suffers the most is the one passing judgment. The judged one is rarely aware of the label. Prejudice is a narrow, tight little path which leads nowhere but discontent. The option is acceptance. God is no respecter of persons.

Selfishness is a sharp edge in our character because its message is that we deserve everything we can acquire, and others are not entitled to anything. Hoarding is its method. Fear is its motive. Sharing is our alternative. Dishonesty, which beckons us all at one time or another, captivates us. Every time we use a 'little white lie' to avoid blame and get away with it, it confirms the value of deceit. Then larger lies are acceptable and a spiraling down manifests as we pile one deception on another. When we are caught in a deception, or when we feel the awful weight of guilt, or when a mentor points out our failing, we begin to act in an honest way. It is a lighter journey when we unload the guilt and speak, act, and think honestly.

A very sharp edge is the one we create as victims. We often come to think of ourselves as victims of 'fate' beyond our control. When a person uses speech or actions that intimidate us, we fall victim to them. We may feel victim of the government, our employer, our neighbor. In all cases we see ourselves as less than. We are not less than another or others. As children of God we have the power, the love, and the gentleness, of God within. Seeking His guidance, awaiting His direction, implementing the answer, gives us awareness of our inner Light and strength.

The habit of living a joyless life is a sharp edge, indeed. We are created in joy; it is our innate nature. Angels bring joy when we laugh - they laugh with us. They do not even understand what the opposite of joy might be.

Traumatic events turn our joy into sadness. We rarely if ever ask God to help us understand the lesson therein. Hindsight will always show us the lesson, unless we drown ourselves in sorrow. 'Death' is not the end of life, only life as we know it. This short-term existence on Earth is nothing to the eternal existence of spirit and the Heaven world.

Distrust is another sharp edge. Trust comes slowly to most of us. When others 'hurt' us in any way we often generalize and hate every one of the same race or culture. When we learn and accept the lessons of Archangel Gabriel, we understand that no one ever hurts us without our permission, and we never hurt others without theirs - because God would not allow it. We have free choice to crucify ourselves or trust others. We have free choice to love and accept everyone, as God wills. A sharp ax does its work easily and cleanly. As sharp instruments of God, we can be just as efficient.

## Chapter 111   The Carpenter's Tools

*"We use the compass to draw circles round our passions and desires to keep in the bounds of righteousness"*. AGJC 55:15

To draw circles around means to set boundaries. The boundaries required around our passions provide us with access to the world around us. We need to be aware of and interact with those who make up our support system, including family, friends, church family, and co-workers. Sometimes our ardent desires also consume us at the expense of social interaction. What becomes a passion for us depends on who we are, our experiences, who affects us and, of course, the plans we have made for this incarnation. These plans are the culmination of all the experiences and lessons from our past lives.

To compass our passions does not mean that passions are not valid. We simply need to keep them within the bounds of our ability to express them. The bounds are made clear to us as we seek divine guidance. As well as the 144,000 angels that Archangel Gabriel said we each have, there are masters, teachers and guides in the spirit world available to us. All the helping entities know our plans. We have the responsibility to ask, to listen, and then to perform the tasks we have set before us. Sometimes we struggle to know our path, but once we find it, passion takes over.

Likewise we can be consumed by desires. Infatuations can become obsessions. Attractions can become possessiveness. Boundaries are required in these cases because they can envelop us with clouds of denial, the smoke of blindness, or the unwillingness of denial. Others can help us see through the clouds, the smoke and the unwillingness. That is what friends are for.

*"We use the hammer to drive home the truth, and pound it in until it is a part of every part."* AGJC 55:17

It is interesting that Jesus uses the words 'drive' and 'pound', yet they are fitting. We engage so often in little lies, then greater deceptions that we accept them as true. Prejudice, labeling, discrimination are only some examples. Truth is truth and needs no defense. We staunchly defend our 'right' to judge and discriminate. Then truth is brought to our attention somehow; often driven into us until we recognize it and change our thinking. Truth has to pound us by coming at us from several different directions, until we finally accept the unalterable truth. That truth then is expressed by us to others. Like a rippling pond, our truth affects all around us. Every aspect of our being is changed. Friends notice the change. Friends validate us when we are truthful.

*"We use the plane to smooth the rough, uneven surfaces of joint, and block, and board that go to build the temple for the truth."* AGJC55:18

Not a crack, not a rough spot, not an opening on our surface - the face and character we express to others - is left for relapse or return. We are a finished product and fully prepared for eternal truth.

*"The chisel, line, the plummet and the saw all have their uses in the workshop of the mind."* AGJC 55:19

The chisel reveals the inner Self of us; the line is for straightening our path, the plummet to identify our progress, and the saw to whittle away the unneeded scraps of negativity.

*"And then this ladder with its trinity of steps, faith, hope and love; on it we climb up to the dome of purity in life."* AGJC 55:20

Purity in life does not mean constant prayer - after all, we *are* a constant prayer throughout our lives, as children of God. Purity in life means living honestly, patiently, tolerantly, compassionately. It means accepting everyone else as our spiritual siblings. With faith, hope and love we can accept all others as God's huge and magnificent family. Faith in God and Self, hope for all humanity to awaken, and love unconditional. It seems a tall order in today's world. It is. But we can do it, with dedication, determination and most importantly, with God's guidance.

*"And on the twelve-step ladder we ascend until we reach the pinnacle of that which life is spent to build -- the Temple of Perfected Man'"* AGJC 55:21

Jesus demonstrated by his very life Perfected Man. He came to show us the way back Home. He would not have come unless we were ready. Twenty centuries later we still do not follow him. We continue to turn our backs on God, denying our divinity. Jesus said that the Kingdom of God is within. He would not lie to us. Many centuries have passed and we still cannot understand the simple phrase: "The Kingdom of God is within." We are all perfected now, because God willed us this way. Like the expert carpenter we must take inventory of the tools of our lives. When we use them properly we will wake up and live our holiness, as God intended.

## Chapter 112   The Center of the Universe

From our physical world we see the Milky Way in our universe. Since humans began traveling in space, we now see that the Earth is on the suburbs of the Milky Way. The fact is that our universe travels around a Central Sun, just as Earth travels around the sun we see rising and setting. The sun is the center of our universe and earth revolves around the sun. The sun seems to be setting and rising, but what actually occurs is the earth turns away from the sun (the sun sets), and the earth turns into the sun (our sunrise).

Before it was discovered that the sun is the center of the universe, Earth was considered its center. As our view of space has expanded, by virtue of new telescopes, we have come to know a universe far vaster than our ancestors ever dreamed. Today astronomers have become aware that our universe actually revolves around a Central Sun. This revolution takes about 26,000 years. The years are divided into segments called ages. Each age is about 2,100 years of earth time. (See Intro., AGJC)

Jesus the Christ lived on Earth at the beginning of the Piscean age. To this day the image of a fish represents followers of Jesus. Abraham lived at the inception of the Age of Aries. Adam lived around the beginning of the Age of Taurus. This vast zodiac reflects on a huge scale the zodiacal signs of our annual calendar. In ancient times astrology and astronomy were the same. Astronomy became the physical observation of our physical universe. Astrology became the study of the planetary influence on humans based on the time and place of their birth. The astrological chart of any given person is based on one's birth sign. This study is very complex as it takes into consideration the revolution of the planets at the time of birth. Extensive knowledge is required for this occupation.

All of this knowledge is based on our *physical* universe. Perhaps the Central Sun is the center of the spirit world of God. Perhaps the Central Sun is the light without heat which lights the heaven world to which we rise to at our so-called death. Scripture tells us *'there is no night there'* (Rev 21:25). The heaven world is eternal, yet unchanging. What God creates is eternal. What God creates is love, because God is Love. Creation creates from itself. Humans who create give something of themselves into the created object. When God creates, some of the love He is goes into His created entities, humankind.

God is a spirit, (John 4:24) and spirit, though invisible, is real. It is as real as God. We would not exist as human beings if we were not spirit. A body provides us with movement on earth. Spirit is eternal. We are eternal in spirit. There is no death; only physical transformation. Perhaps God's realm is all the universes (Gabriel said there are many), and the center of God's realm is the Central Sun. *"Heaven and earth shall pass away, but my words shall not pass away."* (Matt. 24:35). Archangel Gabriel came as the Announcer of the Ages two thousand years ago. He came to earth then to announce the Age of Pisces, when he told Mary she would give birth to Jesus. Gabriel came to Elizabeth to announce John the Baptist's birth. Pisces was the last age of our devolvement from the Heaven world of the Father. Jesus the Christ came to wake us up to our innate holiness.

In the late twentieth century Archangel Gabriel came to announce the new age upon us. This time on Earth is the beginning the Age of Aquarius. Aquarius is the first age of our evolvement back to our Source. It is the age in which we shall begin to awaken to the truth of our being. Finally we will begin to comprehend the meaning of the words *"the Kingdom of God is within you."* (Luke 17:21). We will come to realize that humanity is the only begotten son of God; that we are one gigantic family of God. This awakening will bring us the truth of our being. We will learn to communicate mentally with each other. We will learn that love is everywhere and in everyone. We will learn that war is obsolete because it is violent, destructive, wasteful and meaningless.

Peace on Earth will become a reality. Light beings, aware at last of the light in us, we will illumine our surroundings. In that illumination is our awareness that love is everywhere - now and forever. God the Creator is the center of our universe. Awakening to Him in us is our goal in this coming age.

# Section XV
## Samech

## Chapter 113  The  Elevated Self

There is a common expression we hear when dealing with life's problems. A friend might say to us, "You need to rise above it." What are we 'rising' to? Perhaps we are rising to our elevated Self. The elevated Self is our connection to God, as His children. When an artist creates a painting, a sculpture of any material, there is within it a kind of stamp of herself. If we study art, we can readily recognize a Renoir from a Rembrandt. Students of classical music easily recognize a Chopin from a Beethoven score. Likewise when God created us His 'stamp' in us was-and remains - spirit. *God is a spirit* (John 4:24) God created us in His image (Gen. 1:27). Gabriel told us we are not the image (likeness) of God but in truth we are *part* of the Father. We are His but in denying that connection we came into physical form. God patiently awaits our return, just as the father of the Prodigal Son awaited the return of his wayward son.

Accepting our elevated Self as spirit, it means that we can pluck the fruit of the sprit and enjoy it. *"But the fruit of the spirit is love, joy, peace, longsuffering. Gentleness, goodness, faith, Meekness, temperance: against such there is no law."* (Gal. 5:22-23)  This is quite a long list of fruit! With this list in mind we might wonder why we do not enjoy love in our lives all the time. We 'fall in love' and we love our families and friends; others are outside our space. Jesus the Christ was and is love. He knew it. He lived it. He loved everybody. His life is our example life.

Happiness comes and goes, in moments of time. We cannot seem to hang onto it, for some reason. Jesus was a man of joy. His life is our example. Peace is what we accept between our incessant wars. The peace enjoyed by Jesus was *the peace that passeth all understanding.* (Phil. 4:7). The Prince of Peace knew peace at all times. Jesus never suffered. Contrary to the church's teachings, Jesus did not suffer on the cross. When he said, in Gethsemane's Garden *"Thy will, not mine be done."* he went up to His elevated Self and remained there throughout the arrest, the whipping, the abuse, and the crucifixion. If today an ordinary person can have an 'out of body' experience, surely the Son of God could do so then.

Gentleness comes easily to some people; others have a hard time with it. That may be the case because our current society is permeated with action and violence. We have come to see violence as a form of entertainment. When the Romans wanted to kill the Christians they put them in the coliseum with lions and the lions killed them all. People shouted with glee at the slaughter. We don't do that any longer, thank God. But we still relish the violent acts on the screen when a human stabs, shoots, strangles or blows up other humans. It is news. It is in books. It is on the cinema screen. Why have we become so enamored of violence? It is diametrically opposed to gentleness. Jesus was a gentle man. We have come to see it as weakness. Jesus was not weak.

Goodness toward those we love is easy to express. Others we may lie to, discount or label. Jesus was a good man; he treasured goodness in others. His life is our example. Jesus was also a man of faith. He did not *believe* in God; he knew he was God in flesh. He had the power and knowingness of God and well knew it. Archangel Gabriel and Jesus the Christ both told us that Jesus is our elder brother. He came to show us the way to live. His life is our example.

The meekness that Jesus showed was not a weakness; it was strength. To remain meek at the hands of torturers was the stunning response of Jesus when captured and arrested. He knew it was his time. He knew he had planned the crucifixion so the world would remember him. He knew he would not suffer, as long as he stayed in his elevated Self. On the way to the cross he continued to heal his followers in the crowd.

In everything Jesus did he was temperate, if temperate means mild; not over-indulgent. He was, indeed, a mild-mannered man. His life is our example. This seems like a tall order. It is no wonder that we wanted to see him as the only Son of God and worship him forever. That would excuse us from trying to emulate him. Gabriel said Jesus came to save the world; to wake us all up to our elevated, holy Self. But, Gabriel said, *only on the cross did Jesus see that he only saved himself.* From that high cross Jesus looked out over a crowd that was in the darkness of ignorance, fear, and hatred. He had been crucified for nothing.

So, two thousand years later, at the beginning of another new age (Aquarius), Jesus came *again,* this time with Gabriel, to wake us up to the sacred elevated Self of us. His life was an example. We have no excuse to not emulate him. His life was and remains our example. Many times in the Bible Jesus tells his listeners "Follow me." He did not mean to the cross; he meant emulate him and awaken to our own elevated Self.

## Chapter 114   The Essential Messenger

Many individuals deny the possibility of angelic messengers bringing to humans a picture of the future. We need only to look in the Bible to know that prophesying is a gift: *"Though I have the gift of prophecy . . ."*   I Cor. 13:2 Again, in I Cor. 12:10, as Paul recites the gifts from spirit to men: *"To another the working of miracles; to another prophecy . . ." This* tells us that some of us will be given the gift of foretelling the future. The gift is the ability to *receive* the prophecy, not to make it. *"For the prophecy came not in old time by the will of man but holy men of God spake as they were moved by the Holy Ghost."* II Peter 1:21

Prophecy comes from God; humans merely transmit it to others. The person who transmits is the messenger, the intermediary, the go-between. Prophecy is foretelling of the future. No human being knows it unless she has the gift of prophecy. The idea of angels communicating to earthlings is not new. History is filled with examples: Moses, Joshua, the Blessed Mother of Jesus, Joseph, Jesus' earthly father, Elizabeth and Zachariah, John the Baptist, Jesus the Christ, Joan of Arc, Emanuel Swedenborg, Johannes Greber, Nostradamus, Edgar Cayce, are only a few.

"Prophecy is a phenomena that for thousands of years has sunk deep roots into the  consciousness of humanity . . . the belief in prophecy cannot wholly die out anymore than the belief in goodness, or spirituality, or culture," *The Story of prophecy,* 11. As in any art or endeavor, there are some people who use such a power as prophecy in negative ways. That is an awful truth. But they cannot detract from the majority of psychics and mediums who honestly and faithfully channel spirit entities. These entities in spirit may be loved ones, Ascended Masters, or angelic beings.

Archangel Gabriel did not come to earth to provide us with answers to our questions about our daily problems. He told us he would not because "You have psychics and mediums for that." Gabriel came to wake us up. He reminded us that Adam fell asleep in the Garden of Eden, but nowhere in scripture does it say he woke up. He came to tell us that we are holy, powerful children of God. We have forgotten our holiness inn the mists of the centuries and we have given our power over to our egos. Gabriel said he did not come to find followers, to start a new religion, to find followers for beloved Reverend Penny (the dedicated channel who brought his lessons). It took five hundred years of earth time to teach Reverend Penny how to channel an archangel, the vibration of which is exponentially finer than the vibration of humans.

During the twelve years that Gabriel taught us, Rev. Penny was instructed before every seminar what to eat, when to sequester herself for prayer and meditation. While she channeled, angels constantly monitored her body to maintain a healthy balance. Water was always available to Gabriel, and one time Gabriel asked for a banana. It would be impossible to put into words the gratitude we all felt for Rev. Penny. It took an incredible faith for her to willingly sit for an hour or two and allow an archangel to use her vocal chords, saying words unknown to her. She was in deep trance as Gabriel taught us.

Gabriel told us there are many entities on the other side who would love to bring us information, but there are few people on earth that are willing to cooperate with spirit in this way. All the wisdom known to God which we are capable of understanding will come to us as we sincerely and honestly seek it. "*Beloved, believe not every spirit, but try the spirits whether they* are of God: because many false prophets have gone out into the world. Hereby know the Spirit of God: Every spirit that confesseth that Jesus Christ is come in the flesh is of God." (I John 4:1). We have the ability and the capacity to discern true from false. This ability and capacity must be used to discern good spirits. There is a wall of disbelief and denial about spirit communication. Until that wall is removed we will have to rely on our own decisions. Only our egos tell us we are wiser than God. "Notwithstanding this, rejoice not, that the spirits are subject unto you; but rather rejoice, because your names are written in heaven." (Luke 10:20).


## Chapter 115   The Example Life

"For I have given you an example, that ye should do as I have done to you." John 13:15

It does not get much clearer than that. Jesus came to show us love and forgiveness; compassion and mercy; acceptance and justice. Then he told us to do the same. He also said, "I am the way the truth and the life." (John 14:6). A pattern is a model for imitation. In his first letter to Timothy, Paul advised, "Howbeit for this cause I obtained mercy, that in me first Jesus Christ might show forth all longsuffering, for a pattern to them which should hereafter believe on him to life everlasting." ( I Tim. 1:16)

Somehow the early church leaders focused singly on John 3:16, and placed Jesus on a pedestal. Thereafter we worshipped him as the *only* son of God instead of the way-shower which was Jesus' intent. Archangel Gabriel, who came to bring truth to this blessed generation, told us about the mistranslation of John 3:16 - The original words were "Jesus, begotten son of the only God." In worshipping Jesus, instead of seeing him as our elder brother, we have every excuse for not being like he was. We can only pray to improve but can never emulate him. Logic says this would then be a frustrating life of trying to be something we can never be. A God of Love could hardly intend for us a life of frustration. God is Love. We are the children of the God of Love. Even speaking to his disciples, Jesus called them 'little children'. (John 13:33). He knew they had much to learn; as do we.

In Jesus' time, the people of Israel were under the harsh rule of the Romans. When Jesus came as a savior they thought he would overthrow the Roman rulers. Barabbas and others expected Jesus to gather an army and overthrow the Romans by military power. But this calm man could do such a thing. When he preached love and forgiveness he was not seen as a warrior. In truth, Jesus did not come to earth in order to overtake the Romans, but rather to overcome the world. And he did. Archangel Gabriel told us there is not a human being on Earth who has not heard the name Jesus Christ, however they may think of him.

*"These things have I spoken unto you, that in me ye might have peace. In the world ye shall have tribulation: but be of good cheer; I have overcome the world."* John 16:33 His message was inspiring. People longed to be what he told them they were. They thought, probably, 'wouldn't it be nice if it were only true?' The Jewish people then could not comprehend the idea of the Kingdom of God being within. It was an esoteric truth beyond their understanding. It is a truth we still struggle to comprehend.

Many times Jesus said, *"Follow me."* And enough people did in order to bring his message to future generations. Gabriel and Jesus both came in the 1990s to give us the wisdom of the ages. We are on a grand journey back home to God. We have the power of choice to consciously step upon a spiritual path, and finally to ascend to the Father, just as Jesus did. It is a given. As children of God we can do everything Jesus did. Jesus himself said it: *"Verily, verily, I say unto you, He that believeth on me, the works that I do shall he do also; and greater works than these shall he do; because I go unto my Father."* John 14:12

This is the Age of Aquarius, the Age of truth. Gabriel came to announce it; for he is the Announcer of the Ages. He announced the Age of Pisces when he told Mary that she would bear Jesus and Elizabeth, that she would bear John the Baptist. Fish is the symbol of Pisces, and two thousand years later we still accept it as a symbol of Jesus. Now, humankind is heading home, at last. We prodigals have been away from

Home a very long time. God awaits our awakening to Him in us. Adam, as a symbol of humankind, will wake up. The truth will set us free. This world will end gently, as we become our true Selves and no longer have need of her. On the other side of the veil Heaven awaits. Jesus will rejoice that we finally followed him Home. He will welcome us, as angels sing greetings. This is a blessed generation. We are on the cusp of the New Age. The adventure of realizing our holiness in God has begun. We are on our way Home.

## Chapter 116  The Falsity of Duality

"Everything is dual; everything has poles; everything has its pair of opposites; like and unlike are the same; opposites are identical in nature, but different in degree; extremes meet; all truths are but half-truths; all paradoxes may be reconciled." (*The Kybalion*, 119)

We see opposites all the time: hot and cold; up and down; back and forth, etc. Archangel Gabriel addressed this topic of duality at one of his lessons in truth. He used the example of hot and cold. It was wintertime when he spoke. He asked us if it was not warmer where we were (Albany, NY) than at the North pole. We had to agree although our weather did not feel 'warm'. He asked us at what point on the thermometer - the scale of temperature - does 'hot' stop and 'cold' begin.

This example led us to understanding the phrase that opposites are 'identical in nature, but different in degree'. The thermometer is the nature of the temperature, the temperature itself is the degree of difference. Another example Gabriel mentioned was love and hate. Where, he asked, does hate stop and love begin? He then explained that God is love and God is everywhere, and what is all-encompassing can have no opposite.

When less and less love is felt, the emotions slide away from the feeling of love and in its absence hate is felt. Gabriel also told us that we think of love and hate as opposites, yet love is all there is. This is not an exercise in logic; it is one of the ancient axioms of life. By some it is called Polarity, one of the Hermetic Principles. We constantly believe in opposites, but our Source is God; God is One, and we are part of God. We are all an idea of God and ideas never leave their source, as Gabriel often reminded us. There are many examples of this principle of polarity. Lightness and darkness are ranges between black night and brilliant daytime. The musical scale has its highest and lowest note with a given range of notes expanded by flats and sharps. It is all music. Colors have their range; Noise has a range. So does dullness and sharpness. These are physical examples.

A mental example is courage and fear. Because it is mental, we can mentally make up our mind whether to be fearful or courageous. The interesting thing is that "The tendency of Nature is in the direction of the dominant activity of the Positive pole". (*The Kybalion*, 124). Our mental states can vary from high optimism and joy to deep depression. We are not influenced by anyone else unless we choose to be. Courage and faith strengthen our self-confidence. Jesus was an ordinary man, containing the Christ Light. He had great self-confidence because he knew that what he taught was only truth. It was only truth because he listened only to the Voice of God. He broke all the rules of the synagogue, but was confident that everything he said and did was alright; was all good.

"'All truths are half-truths." When Gabriel came to teach us, his lessons often contradicted the accepted wisdom. Gabriel did not bring half-truths; he brought only truth. We had the choice to accept truth or not, but we cannot change it. Coming to know and accept truth is our function while on Earth. All truths will be ours when we are ready to accept them. "All paradoxes may be reconciled." A paradox is 'a tenet contrary to received opinion. seemingly opposed to . . . common sense.' (Webster). Based on Gabriel's lessons in truth, common sense is now seen as fallacious reasoning. Simple examples:

We 'tell time' by our clocks. Gabriel told us we don't tell time anything; it tells us when to rise, work, etc.

We see our feet as appendages which enable us to walk. Gabriel said they *represent understanding.*

We perceive death as the end of our life. Gabriel explained we have lived here many times (reincarnation) and have 'died' many times. It is called 'karma.' The truth is we are spirit in form and eternal spirit life is ours.

In our arrogance we think we discovered fire, language, electricity. Gabriel told us they all came from the spirit world of God. 'As above so below.' is a truth.

Turning our will and our lives over to the Holy Spirit (part of the Trinity of God) is the only way to live a free and joyous life. We have the choice of doing so. We are blessed with free choice and we are exposed to a huge variety of options in life. In truth, the only choice we will make, someday, is to listen to The Holy Spirit. He must be asked, but upon hearing our request, the Holy Spirit answers. His guidance never fails. He, and all of us, are part of the Oneness of God.


## Chapter 117  The Farmer's Lot

Every farmer knows that when he plants corn wheat will not come up. When the truck gardener plants tomatoes he will not harvest cabbage. This is just plain logic. Human behavior is like this, too. When we act in dishonest ways, as sowers, we expect others to be dishonest. Or we first see others dishonest and then justify our own dishonesty. Taking pencils home from the office is alright 'because everybody does it.' Instead of sowing and reaping 'good' and 'bad', we can opt to travel the high road of life - live by a high moral standard. Parents are our first teachers and they lay a firm foundation of accepted behavior - or they do not.

Growing up through our teen years we are tempted on every side to mimic those around us, because it is 'acceptable'. It is, in truth, a herd mentality. It is also known as mass consciousness. What earlier 'masses' did is what we all continue to do, believing it is right simply because so many ancestors acted that way. History has not really taught us much that has lasting value. Historically humankind has accepted war as inevitable.

*"Whatsoever a man soweth, that shall he also reap."* (Gal. 6:7) Paul wrote this to the people of Galatia. He was reminding them of the natural law. All major religions speak of this eternal truth. Confucianism states, "What proceeds from you will return to you. Modern vernacular says "What goes around comes around." We use it mostly to comment on a person 'getting what's coming to him.', and we often rejoice at the 'justice'.

How we treat others exemplifies how we see others. If we see them as separate from us we treat them any way we choose. If we see them as part of us, or connected to us, we treat them with consideration. The view of separateness may be due to skin color, language, custom, or religion. Opinion only is often our excuse for seeing others as separate. We focus our attention on the differences. Our vision becomes blurred and without warrant. Judgment and prejudice often result.

If others are related to us we are likely to see them with compassion, overlook short-comings and forgive hurts. When marriage joins two families we open our arms in accepting embrace. In recent decades, for several reasons, inter-marriage has become more common. Marriages once forbidden by law are becoming socially acceptable. Different religions, nationalities, colors, are inter-marrying. Homosexuals can now marry and parent. Some of us refuse to accept 'foreigners' and become critical of their social mores or customs. Some of us may not only accept those 'others', but may desire to learn their language, understand their way of life and even participate in their customs. Most of us expect them to assimilate into our culture and many do.

However we treat others is the way they will treat us. Honesty, acceptance, compassion and love will bring from them the same qualities. If we withhold trust until we see them as trusting, our attitude will create distrust. Our openness, willingness to understand and an optimism that the 'others' are just like us in many ways will open a welcoming door to them. We seem just as much 'different' to them as they seem to us. An open hand to join another brings more closeness than a fist of fear or a heart of doubt. Open arms to embrace bring one closer than turning one's back.

The sameness of all people is not hard to identify. Red blood, salty tears, disappointment, laughter, fear, doubt, and regret are common features of all humanity. We are the fruit of God's creation, whatever we call Him. We are one diverse and huge human family. We were created from love. We all live on a gorgeous planet. We are all the blessed custodians of our earth home. What we plant we shall reap; how we treat others is exactly how they will treat us. Chasing them away will not draw them to us. The farmer's lot is a joyous one of simplicity. Honesty, plain-speaking and focusing on the furrow ahead takes him to the end of the day. Perhaps he is physically weary, but he is in touch with the earth which has nourished him. Mother Earth provides us with all our needs: food, clothing, housing, medicine come from her. God created her to house us until we return to our original Home. We ought to plow furrows of love.

## Chapter 118   The First and Great Commandment

*"Jesus said unto him, Thou shalt love the Lord thy God with all heart, and with all thy soul, and with all thy mind. This is the first and great commandment."* Matt. 22:37-38

The heart is a blood pump, but it represents to us the emotion of love. To love only God and the good He is should permeate all our thoughts and actions. Instead of a 'mind of our own' (ego) we ought to choose instead to acknowledge our minds as being part of the Mind of God. The soul contains our memories; all things we ever said or did through all our incarnations. To love God with all our soul means we should forgive ourselves for all wounds we inflicted and forgive everyone who ever wounded us. And in that forgiveness we replace wounds with love.

Love is what we were commanded to do, long ago, by the great Master Teacher. We were commanded to love 'thy God'. For those of us who value these words and the idea they represent, we must ask ourselves if we truly love our God. When we are very young we believe that God is 'up there, somewhere', and will 'get us if we are bad'. Some parents say to their children they would 'put the fear of God' in them. As we grew into our teen years we could begin to comprehend an all-powerful Creator, even though we could not see It. We were told that God is everywhere. Religious tenets became our belief system, depending on our parents and their influence. We began to question whether God should be feared or loved. Fear seemed so popular, in religion and all areas of life. Love seemed rare and constantly sought after.

Our concept of God changes over time, but God never changes. God is everywhere, and unchangeable. God gives us our daily life; our daily bread. Our daily life is full of wonderful things, but we often fail to see them. As we busy ourselves with life, activities divert our attention from the loveliness of nature. God is love, and we proclaim it; yet He seems to bring us tragic events and accidents. If He did all the things we lay to his charge, He would be a fickle god. We proudly announce that we have free choice. In our free choice we cause the accidents, the tragic events. It is far easier to blame an unseen Creator than to look at our part in life's experiences.

The 'acts of God' which we rage against are hardly possible from a God of Love. This Earth we reside on was and is a green, lush, and beautiful planet. Mother Earth, before and now, provides us with all our needs. Then came humankind to hunt, first for needed food and clothing. Indigenous people - Native Americans - mentally asked a creature if it was ready to give itself for food, clothing and housing. If the answer was positive, the kill took place. If the creature bounded away, the response was 'no'. Mother Earth was loved and respected because she provided everything necessary for life. Then 'civilized' men came and hunted only for the pleasure of the kill. What kind of pleasure comes from killing? Love turned to fear and hatred. God became a god of fear. If we suffered we thought it was God's doing. We believe we are victims of what we call fate; that an unpredictable, judgmental God is in charge. We believe He will 'take us' when we choose when He chooses.

To love God with all our heart means to honestly accept a God of Love and be compassionate toward God at all times. To love God with all our soul means to have undying faith in Him. To love God with all our mind means to ask for His Guidance at all times, knowing we receive it. Every thought, every action is brought to us by choice. We can choose God's Guidance or our ego's guidance. The former will never fail. The latter will never succeed. God is a spirit and created us in that image, providing us with imagination and free choice. Our egos tell us that we created ourselves and are in charge of our lives. We all are spiritual; we all are part of the Oneness of God. We are a variety of races, languages, colors, beliefs, but God has a great imagination. There can be, and is, variety in oneness. The beauty of a rainbow is the combination of the entire palette of colors. 'Commandment' seems like a strong word for the gentleness of love, but the truth of the matter is that love is the greatest power there is. That is because God is love. And God is omnipotent. His commandments are worthy of heeding.

## Chapter 119   The Five Thousand Year Gap

Before the Old Testament time there was a Goddess that was worshipped. Archangel Gabriel made that quite clear. The female sex reigned. There were no wars. The reason for this was that the earthly male was inactive. (All creation has two energies. On earth we name them male and female.). Peacefulness reigned. Women could produce life and men could not. She had a power that men could not accept, and men thought she had reigned too long. The story of the Beginning had to start with an error by a female, so the Garden of Eden became the story of the beginning of mankind. Then came writing and this myth was put in print, by men. Eden is an allegory of humankind. Only when we understand our journey from God and our destined journey back will we accept Eden as a myth; an allegory. We can understand now and that is why Archangel Gabriel came at this time - to awaken us to the truth of us; the truth of our journey.

For five thousand years the female gender has been described as subservient. In the Old Testament even clothes worn were dictated by the author: *"The woman shall not wear that which pertaineth unto a man, neither shall a man put on a woman's garment: for all that do so are abomination unto the Lord thy God."* (Deut. 5:22). No reason is given why it is abomination, but one can readily see that even then such garb was worn; perhaps there was a problem of sexual orientation then, too.

Paul wrote much of the New Testament, even though he never met Jesus. In the New Testament we find: *"Wives, submit yourselves unto your own husbands, as unto the Lord."* (Eph. 5:22). Also, *"Wives, submit yourselves unto your own husbands, as it is fit in the Lord."* (Col. 3:18). The power of the statement is enhanced by using the Lord as part of the command. It appears that a subservient position is required because the male is afraid of the latent power of the female. Fear and love are antithetical.

The old phrase 'a woman's place is in the home' eventually became, 'a woman's place is in the House (of representatives) - and Senate', [said by a female in the U.S. government]. Over time we have made some inroads to equality, but much still needs correction to place us on an equal footing with the men in society. Some men and women do not believe there is equality - that men must always be the ruler of the home, and the women serve him. Some may quote scripture in order to support their position. I recall a question Gabriel put to his audience one day: "How many men here believe that women are equal to men."? A few hands went up, then Gabriel said, "That is not a good question because there are probably three men on Earth who believe it!" That shows how far we have to go.

Late in the nineteenth century suffrage was the drive for women's right to vote. Susan B. Anthony and Elizabeth Cady Stanton spearheaded the suffrage movement in the U.S. They did not, however, live to see the law passed. Personally, I was unacceptable as a candidate for an accounting job in the 1940s. My dream (then) was to become a CPA. But one had to have working time in an accounting office before the CPA exam could be taken. Therefor all doors were shut to me. In my lifetime I met the first female CPA in Vermont. I still cheer when I see a woman wearing a hardhat directing traffic.

Considering that women were once owned by men and women had no say, we have experienced some acceptance in more and more areas of society - albeit the speed is at a crawl. Sexual abuse and rape continue in colleges, military branches and the workplace. Government at all levels has a disparate proportion of female presence. Since the male-dominated world has existed for five thousand years, it will take a long time for us to regain a place of recognition; of worthiness by the male population. As mothers, sisters, grandmothers, great-grandmothers, foster mothers, perhaps we can do more to educate others about the topic of sexual balance and respect. We are on the way, and someday the gap will close. Closing the gap is not to return us to a ruling goddess, but to have both sexes on an equal plane. God has always viewed us as equal to males. Equality negates myth.

## Chapter 120   The Fourth Dimension

*"That Christ may dwell in your hearts by faith; that ye, being rooted and grounded in love, May be able to comprehend with all saints what is the breadth, and length, and depth, and height . . ."* Eph. 3:17-18

Upon reading this we see that Paul's letter described four dimensions. But we live in a three-dimensional world. We can easily measure the length, depth, and height of boxes and buildings. But then what is 'breadth'? Mr. Webster's dictionary tells us it is synonymous with width. But he also gives 'scope' as a definition. This comes a little closer to what is probably the fourth dimension - spirit.

Referring again to the dictionary, 'breth' is a Middle English root of 'breadth'. If we add an 'a' or drop a 'd' we get 'breath'. And 'spirit' means breath. 'Spirit' is defined as 'an animating or vital principle held to give life to physical organisms'. Without breath we are not physically alive. Our breath comes from the very air which surrounds us. God is everywhere; we breathe in the essence of God. The concordance of the Bible reveals that the word 'spirit' appears hundreds of times in that holy book, in both the Old Testament and the New Testament. *"God is a spirit"* is found in John 4:24. In his second letter to the Corinthians, Paul describes a man he knew but did not know if the man was *"in the body or out of the body"* (v. 2-3). What could 'out of the body' refer to except an out-of-body experience, with which today's psychics are familiar. Paul's letter to the Romans, verse 8:11, mentions the *"Spirit that dwelleth within you."* (See also I Cor. 3:16)

The One spirit is God and is in us all, and God therefore knows us as spirit. He created us as spirit (in His Image). Our problem lies in the fact we are not *aware* of the spirit within us because we live life by the laws of the world. Paul tells his listeners *"But we all, with open face beholding as in a glass the glory of the Lord, are changed into the same image from glory to glory, even as by the Spirit of the Lord."* (II Cor. 3:18)

What changes us into an *awareness* of our spirit? First we need to acknowledge that we have in us that spirit which is also the Spirit of God. Some may call it 'conscience'. It is that drive which urges us to be honest, to be fair, and to accept others as they are instead of judging and labeling them. Little children are so trusting, friendly and out-going. They are fearless, and we need to protect them until they know the dangers of vehicle traffic, hot stoves, etc. When Jesus said we should allow children, and even to emulate them, he saw children as curious, open-minded, friendly, and trusting. He did not mean we should (as some people do) view kids as ignorant, uneducated, unruly, vulnerable.

Children are not born fearing those of a different color. They are taught it by prejudiced parents. Children enjoy play with anyone who will play with them. Prejudicial parents inflict their own judgments on their offspring. Hopefully, in the days to come, parents and guardians will teach the young ones to be trusting and forgiving. Parents will dare to teach their offspring that they are children of God, and in them is the same spirit.

This will come about when adults accept the spirit within themselves, and listen to the 'still, small voice of God'. It is God calling to us, as He always has. In the stillness we can hear His Voice, but in the clanging of traffic it eludes us. It also eludes us when our ego is loudly shouting things like 'be like everyone else; do what they do; think like them'. That is the herd mentality which so many follow. The ego does not want us to pray, meditate, seek God's Will, walk a spiritual path in life. So it tries continually to keep us distracted.

All this is in accordance with man's laws. But God's Laws are as unlike man's laws as day is unlike night. The Old Testament prophet said it well, when he reminded us of God's gift to us all: *"He hath shewed thee, O man, what is good; and what doth the Lord require of thee, but to do justly, and to love mercy, and to walk humbly with thy God?"* Micah 6:8

We all desire these qualities, but we do not always live them in our daily activities. We seek justice for those we love, but do not always seek it for our 'enemies'. If we love mercy we should be merciful to all. When we pray and meditate we are humble in God's Presence. What we forget is that we are *always* in God's Presence. *"Whither shall I go from thy spirit? or whither shall I flee from your presence? If I ascend up into heaven, thou art there: if I make my bed in hell, behold, thou art there. If I take the wings of the morning, and dwell in the uttermost parts of the sea; Even there shall thy hand lead me, and thy right hand shall hold me."* Ps. 139:7-10

Fortunately we can safely say that there is no hell. Gabriel told us he has been around forever and has never seen a place called hell or an entity we call devil. However, the ancient people did believe in both.

# Section XVI
## Ain

## Chapter 121   The Great Amnesia

When we disbelieve in God, for whatever reason, it does not mean we define the truth of His existence. We have made God in our own image, assigning to Him all our shortcomings and limitations. When and if we come to believe in a God that is all-good and knows only good, we find faith in a majesty beyond our imagination; a faith that brings tears of gratitude. The gratitude is deeply felt when we review a life of blessings. We then know we could not possibly be the determining factor of God's existence. Humanitarianism is a philosophy which rejects religion and stresses self-reliance through reason. It appeals to many.

For those of us who believe that God is the Author and Origin of all life, we find not only solace in our faith, but also knowingness that life is eternal and God is Love eternally. Such a faith began with Moses, the first human to believe in one God instead of the many gods of the previous ages.  Amenhotep IV was the Sun God, or so he proclaimed to be. But he could not make the rain or create clouds. He saw the Sun as the god of all. Then Moses came and accepted the idea that God could not be seen by humans and yet He was powerful enough to help us all.

God is. God is Love. Eons ago God breathed us forth and we were - and remain - children of God. That origin was so long ago we have forgotten our beginning. When Jesus the Christ came he taught us that the Kingdom of God is within. This symbolic definition was beyond the pragmatic thinking of the shepherds, carpenters, merchants and housewives of the time. We still struggle with the concept.  It became more easily understood when Gabriel taught us that every cell of our human body contains a nucleus of spirit!

At one of his seminars Gabriel said, "You have only one life." Gasps from the audience could be heard. Then Gabriel explained that the one life is the life of our spirit Self. The great amnesia is that we have forgotten that origin of our spirit's beginning. Gabriel reminded us that the spirit Self of us is the Self that is one with God. Jesus said, *"I and my Father are one."* John 10:30

Only a few times in the twelve years that Gabriel visited us (1987-1999) did he mention reincarnation. Some of his words were,

"You have lived so many lives on earth that you have met every person now living."

"You cannot remember your past lifetimes; you cannot even remember events of your childhood."

"This is the only lifetime that is important."

"This is the lifetime you will remember."

Everything Gabriel taught is for everyone who reads his words or hears his voice. (See Bibliography). When we hear the truth we *know* it is truth and we can never forget it. The truth will make us free, as Jesus promised us, in John 8:32.

As we read and listen to Gabriel's words, we are impelled to take his advice and meditate regularly. In that exercise we will come to know that we, as well as Jesus our elder brother, are the way, the truth and the life. (ACIM 7: III: 1:9). The great amnesia will end when we remember the truth of our being. The truth is we made a decision to come to earth briefly and return Home, where we had knowingness of our oneness with God. But one day we stayed here on earth too long, and forgot our way Home. We came to believe that our only existence was in form; in physical matter. We stayed so long that we forgot our origin in the Father. We forgot the truth of our being. We forgot that a spark of God's Kingdom is within us.

Upon remembering the truth, it will set us free. Free of the separateness we now deem ourselves to have from each other and God. We will know that we - all humanity - are one giant family of God; that Jesus was truly the first fruits of our awakening. (I Cor. 15:23). Jesus came to show every human the way Home, not to start a new religion. His example life is the pattern for us to follow. Heaven is our natural habitat, Gabriel said.

Concurrently with Gabriel eleven Ascended Masters came to various locations on Earth. Their message was the same; to wake us up to our innate divinity so we can return Home. Jesus the Christ also visited the earth - to correct some of the errors transcribed falsely in the Bible. Jesus' lessons and Gabriel's teachings combine to reveal the wisdom of the ages. With an open mind, listening to them or reading them will show us how to awaken to our truth. The great amnesia will end. We shall begin our return journey to God Whom we never really left.

## Chapter 122  The Great Awakening

*"And as they did eat, Jesus took bread, and blessed, and brake it, and gave to them, and said, Take, eat: this is my body."* (Mark) 14:22

The symbolism is clear: Jesus knew the apostles could not; would not, participate in cannibalism. The bread was symbolic of the Christ in him.

*"And he took bread, and gave thanks, and brake it, and gave unto them, saying, This is my body which is given for you: this do in remembrance of me."* (Luke 22:19)

Forever we are to remember Jesus the Christ as a man of love and forgiveness; a man of infinite patience and understanding; a man of faith in God his Father. These attributes were not of the man Jesus, but of the Christ in him. The man Jesus was a human being. He ate, drank, laughed and wept. He died and resurrected to show what we can do, also. He proclaimed that we, too, could do everything he did! (John 14:12)

*"For the bread of God is he which cometh down from heaven, and giveth life unto the world."* John 6:33

Jesus was the bread of God. Jesus thus proclaimed himself to be the vehicle which God sent to earth from Heaven to show, by his resurrection, that life is eternal. We continue to take the communion sacrament to celebrate that moment of the Last Supper. The bread is symbolic; it represents the substance of life.

This author was blessed indeed to hear and speak with Jesus (1995-1999), as he came concurrently with Archangel Gabriel, to clarify scripture. Once in my life I saw Jesus in person. It was the spring of 1984, at my first séance. He stood in front of me, his arms outstretched with palms up. On his palms was a huge Jewish loaf of bread. He said (in words or thoughts; I do not know): 'Lay down your life for me and I will give you the bread of life." I was stunned. I knew it was Jesus, though my knowledge of the Bible was scant.

A few weeks later I abstained from alcohol; the addiction to which had taken me away from my family and my home. Looking back then I believed that 'turning my life and my will over to the care of God as I understood God' was the meaning of Jesus' words. Years later, Gabriel gave us the female version of The Lord's Prayer. In part it says,

"Cause me this day to become aware of the bread of life, Thy Presence in my consciousness." The bread of life is the Presence of God in an awakened consciousness; the constant presence of Him in us. The bread is now understood to mean the living Presence of Christ in our consciousness.

*"According to my earnest expectation and my hope, that in nothing shall I be ashamed, but that with all boldness, as always, so now also Christ shall be magnified in my body, whether it be by life, or by death. For to me to live is Christ, and to die is gain."* Phil. 1:20-21

The Christ in us is the life in us; the very air we breathe and, without which, our body cannot survive. Paul said to the Colossians: *". . . But Christ is all, and in all."* (Col. 3:11) Also, to the people of Corinth Paul said, *"But now is Christ risen from the dead, and become the firstfruits of them who slept, For since by man came death, by man came also the resurrection of the dead. For as in Adam all die, even so in Christ shall all be made alive."* (I Cor. 15:20-22; II Cor. 5:17)

The reader is directed to Paul's letter to the Ephesians (3: 12-22). Without a doubt, Paul's words in 5:14 must also be recalled: *"Wherefore he saith, Awake thou that sleepest, and arise from the dead, and Christ shall give thee light."* The sleep of Adam signifies the sleep of humanity. Awaken we will, and confirm the Christ Light placed there by God in the beginning. We do not create ourselves or the light in us. We merely awaken in our consciousness to the truth of us; the light *in* us.

## Chapter 123  The Great River

*What is man, that thou art mindful him? And the son of man, that thou visiteth him?* Ps. 8:4

The religionist may read this and believe that question continues to pose a mystery. To the metaphysician who accepts the symbolism of the Bible, he is delighted to read an explanation of what man is that he is awakening to. The first few chapters of the Old Testament provide the explanation of what man is, and Archangel Gabriel explained what we are awakening to.

When Gabriel gave a detailed interpretation of the Book of Revelation (See Bibliography), he told us that the entire Bible is symbolic. Now we look at Genesis, Revelation, and the other books with new eyes and see what God told us, in code. To assist the reader in her quest, *The Metaphysical Bible Dictionary* is recommended. Generations have slept through centuries of reading and memorizing the Holy Bible of Christianity. As we become willing to learn and accept its symbolism we find the treasure Jesus spoke of, in  Matt. 13:44: *Again, the kingdom of heaven is like unto treasure hid in a field; the which when a man hath found, he hideth, and for joy thereof goeth and selleth all that he hath, and buyeth that field.* Now we are blessed to have the treasure revealed to us, through Gabriel's lessons in truth. *With God all things are possible* (Matt. 19:26). It is now within our imagination, then, to accept that God inspired men long ago to write the coded text of scripture. The Bible also contains a prophetic code, as described in *The Bible Code.*

*There is a river, the streams whereof shall make glad the city of God, the holy place of the tabernacles of the most High.* (Ps. 46:4). The *Metaphysical Bible Dictionary*, page 560, defines 'river', in scripture: 'a current of thought or a current of vital forces, of life. 'The 'river' of Genesis 2:10 symbolizes the current of life in the organism (garden).' The first river mentioned scripture (Gen. 2:11) is Pison/Pishon: *'fully diffused, carried to its highest degree.'* MBD, 532

The second river (Gen 2:13), Gihon, 'means *formative movement*. It represents the deific breath of God inspiring man and purifying his blood in the lungs. It flows through the darkened consciousness (Cush)'.

The third river, Hiddekel (Gen. 2:14), now known as the Tigris: 'symbolizes the spiritual nerve fluid that God is propelling throughout man's whole being continually, as the electro-magnetic center of every physically expressed atom. . . Man ever cries out for a higher, fuller way of life and will continue to do so until his full redemption into spirituality is accomplished.' (MBD, 278)

The fourth river, Euphrates, 'represents the blood stream. The circulatory system receives and distributes the nutrients contained in the food we eat. The blood stream is charged with the food substance for bone, muscle, brain, teeth and hair. Every part of the organism is supplied with substance through this wonderful river Euphrates,' (MBD, Addenda II). With all these fine definitions we see that in these few chapters man is described: The circulatory system, the blood stream, the nervous system, and the holy Breath of God in us; all define our bodies as we seek to become fully diffused, carried to our highest degree, which is spirit.

In Chapters 13 and 14 of *The Aquarian Gospel of Jesus the Christ* Matheno (Egyptian priest) instructed John, and then baptized him in the river Jordan. "Matheno taught the harbinger, and he explained to him the inner meaning of the cleansing rite and how to wash himself and how to wash the multitude." (15:27). Gabriel confirmed that Levi received the AGJC from spirit. Levi also tells of Jesus' many travels prior to his three years of ministry. In those days a teacher was not recognized until he reached the age of thirty. In India Jesus taught the multitudes. "And all the people were entranced, and would have worshipped Jesus as a God; but Jesus said, I am your brother man just come to show the way to God; you shall not worship man; praise God, the Holy One." (AGJC, 26:23-24). Jesus taught by the river in Katak (26:1), and at Behar (27:2) "on the sacred river of the Brahms, he taught many days."

## Chapter 124   The Greater Zodiac

The word zodiac (*Angels A-Z*, 421) means 'circle of animals' from the Greek *zoion*. There are thousands of constellations in the heavens, but the signs of the zodiac "are arranged around the ecliptic. The planets, all orbiting the Sun on the same plane, appear to travel against the background of these twelve constellations"(*The Book of Divination, 16*). The ecliptic is the earth's orbit around the sun. "The zodiac is an imaginary band in the heavens centered on the ecliptic that is divided into twelve constellations or signs each taken for astrological purposes to extend 30 degrees longitude." (Webster). We know these signs as Aries (the ram), Taurus (the bull), Gemini (the twins), Cancer (the crab), Leo (the lion), Virgo (the virgin), Libra (the balance), Scorpio (the scorpion), Sagittarius (the archer), Capricorn (the goat), Aquarius (the water bearer), and Pisces (the fishes). We have all become accustomed to the horoscope in the daily newspaper. Some people live by it, others read it for fun, and still others would not be found dead reading it - believing they are anathema to God.

Using this small example as a reference point, we now turn to the greater zodiac in the heavens. This greater zodiac is the orbiting of our entire universe around a Central Sun. Our universe circling around a Central Sun defies our imagination. It takes approximately 26,000 years for this orbit around the Central Sun, which means that each sign of the greater zodiac takes about 2,100 years. (*Aquarian Gospel of Jesus the Christ*, Intro). Astronomers know of this Central Sun. Archangel Gabriel told us that we live 'in the suburbs of the Milky Way'; that there are several universes.

Critical students of this discipline agree that the sun entered the zodiacal sign Taurus in the days of our historic Adam, and the Taurian Age began. Abraham lived at the beginning of the Arian Age. When the Roman Empire arose, the Piscean Age began. It was early in this age that Jesus the Christ walked the Earth; hence the fish represented his followers, and still does to this day. Pisces is a water sign, and baptism is one of the Christian sacraments. At the Jordan River John baptized Jesus. At the last supper, Jesus washed the disciples' feet because feet represent understanding. After his resurrection, Jesus appeared for the third time to the disciples, by the sea of Tiberius and cooked the fish they had caught for them to eat. (John, Chapter 21). Gabriel told us that Jesus cooked the fish but did not eat it.

Now we are embarking upon the Aquarian Age. Aquarius is an air sign. Many inventions have already been brought to light. Air travel, communication methods, electricity, and magnetism, have all contributed to a new and more comfortable way of life. Jesus referred to the beginning of this age: "And then the man who bears the pitcher will walk forth across an arc of heaven; the sign and signet of the Son of Man will stand forth in the eastern sky. The wise will then lift up their heads and know that the redemption of the earth is near." (AGJC 157:29-30)

It was at the very beginning of this Aquarian Age that Archangel Gabriel and eleven Master Teachers came to earth. This is the Age of Truth; the Age of Spirituality, Gabriel said. Jesus the Christ also visited the Earth, to correct some of the transcribed errors of scripture. Scribes were told to print 'what was acceptable' to the readers of the time.

Now is the time for all humanity to awaken to our Source, and learn to live from the Lord God of our Being. Gabriel said we are ready to do this, or he would not have come. The eleven Master Teachers visited various locations on earth, where centers of light accept channeling from the spirit world. Gabriel came to upstate New York to a center of light; in a small church. The founding pastor and minister for thirty years was the dedicated channel. Gabriel said that it required five hundred years of (earth time) study for her to be able to channel him (1987-1999), as well

276

as to channel Jesus the Christ (1995-1999). Gabriel said his teachings will be translated and disseminated across the world to awaken all humanity. We find new comfort in the words of Paul:

*"Therefore judge nothing before the time, until the Lord come, who both will bring to light the hidden things of darkness, and will make manifest the counsels of the hearts: and then shall every man have praise of God."* (I Cor. 4:5)

## Chapter 125  The Greatest Commandments

When Jesus was asked by one of the scribes *"Which is the first commandment of all?"* his reply was, *"The first of all the commandments is 'Hear, O Israel; the Lord our God is one Lord: And thou shalt love the Lord thy God with all thy heart, and with all thy soul, and with all thy mind, and with all thy strength: this is the first commandment. And the second is like, namely this, Thou shalt love thy neighbor as thyself. There is none other commandment greater than these'."* Mark 12:28-31

Jesus makes it crystal clear that these are the primary commandments, never mentioning the commandments of Moses. Much later (1995-1999), Jesus reminded his audience that the Ten Commandments, cast in stone, are rigid, unchangeable, and unyielding. This first commandment seems to be similarly impossible to abide by. It seems to suggest that we should pray constantly. This is a misinterpretation. When we establish for ourselves a basic commitment to act in all ways from our love of God, we can then routinely act as His beloved children.

That is, when we 'turn our will and our lives' completely over to God because we love and worship Him, our every thought and action stems from that love. We understand that our spirituality is not *part* of our daily life but that it births every thought and action. Turning 'our will and lives over to the care of God as we understand God' means loving Him with all our heart, mind, soul, and strength. We set the standard of love; we commit to that fundamental feeling of love; we live by it. Jesus' life was lived by his love of the Father.

The second commandment Jesus speaks of also seems an impossible order. To love our neighbor as we love ourselves suggests that loving ourselves is a given. Few of us truly love ourselves. We deem it egotistical. Jesus means we should love ourselves as children of God. He knew he was God's son and lived out his entire life from that central knowingness. Archangel Gabriel reminded us that God loves us just the way we are. He created us perfect spirit, and we are perfect spirit forever. Not one thought of ours, nor one act of ours, alters in any way that perfect Self of us. That is the Self we are to love, because it is God in us.

In loving others we see that Self in them, also. God sees us as His perfect, sacred ones. We see our own children as perfect and very special, although we may not like what they say or do. We love them for who they are, and so does God love us for who we are - eternal spirit, as created by Him.

The person who truly loves Self is the person who is comfortable in their own skin, as they say. Their secret is one of acceptance. When we accept ourselves as we are, we speak and act from our heart, knowing God is in us, and turning within to Him, He guides us every step of the way. When we accept all other people just as they are, it is unnecessary to judge them or decide how we want to act toward them. Our response to everyone is honest, clear, and unambiguous. We have nothing to hide. Everyone can attain this love of Self. Regardless of past behavior we can forgive ourselves and move on with self-acceptance, then Self-love, as God's Own.

In the above Bible quotation, Jesus specifically states that there is no greater commandment than these two he cites. Jesus, this holy child of God, came in flesh two thousand years ago to show us the way by his own example, and lived the truth he taught: love and forgiveness. He was the pattern and way-shower for us all. He had no hidden agenda or pretense. He spoke as one in authority, and he led us then as a caring shepherd leads his sheep.

In the 1990s, Jesus came again, to teach the same lessons: The Kingdom of God is within us; we can and will follow him; God is love and He loves us. We can follow him as he as asked us to do, or we can continue to carry our heavy load of guilt and remorse from the past, and slow ourselves down from progressing as sacred offspring of the Living, Loving God. Jesus said long ago he would never leave us, and he never has. Jesus said he would send a Comforter, and he did. The Comforter is the Holy Spirit. As we ask the Holy Spirit to guide us, He does.

## Chapter 126  The Greatest Generation

This generation, from which I will soon depart, has been called the Greatest Generation. Perhaps it is so called because we lived through the Great Depression and the Second World War. Has anyone thought to consider it the worst generation because it spawned these horrors? From a larger perspective we can view history in greater depth. Perhaps then we might view the first generation of the Age of Pisces to be the greatest generation. That was the time in which Jesus the Christ lived. It was the beginning of a new age: the Age of Pisces. To this day a fish is a symbol for Jesus the Christ followers. Now, as the twenty-first century dawns, we are at the beginning of the Age of Aquarius. These ages are depicted by the larger zodiac in which our universe travels around the Central Sun every 26,000 years. (AGJC, Intro)

The message brought by the Master Teacher Jesus, was the message of love and forgiveness. The first example on earth of forgiveness was Joseph's (coat of many colors) forgiveness of his brothers, for leaving him on the desert to die, then lying to their father about Joseph's death. Jesus came to teach love and forgiveness by demonstrating these qualities in his daily life. He also performed many miracles. His miracles attracted more attention and therefore he was considered - and so named in scripture - as the only son of God. Archangel Gabriel told us that there was a serious mistranslation regarding this. Originally written, the manuscript read, *"Jesus, begotten son of the only God"*. As a result of this mistranslation, we placed Jesus on a cross of suffering and saw him as the only son of God. This made him worthy of worship and made us unworthy to emulate him. Jesus was considered something that none of us could ever be. We also find in the Bible Jesus saying that we can do all things that he did (John 14:12). This is a grand truth.

Gabriel is the Announcer of the Ages. The same archangel that announced to Mary the coming of Jesus through her, and to Elizabeth the coming of John (the Baptist0 through her - that same archangel came to earth to announce the Age of Aquarius! Or, as Gabriel called it, the Age of Truth. From this viewpoint we may decide that in the past two thousand years the greatest generation was that one in which Jesus lived. It was his birth that heralded the very time designation that much of the world lives by, with our calendar of days and years. Gabriel said there is not one person on the earth who has not heard the name Jesus Christ, whether they believe in him or not. Gabriel also reminded us that it takes humanity two thousand years to learn something new! Many have learned the lessons of love and forgiveness; many have not.

This is the first generation of the Age of Aquarius. Gabriel said he told us nothing new; he said he came to remind us *of what we already know but have forgotten.* Our Higher Self, the Christ in us, already knows that we are children of God. Consciously we have all forgotten that truth. Eons of time on earth have brought us to the belief that physical form is all there is - even all that there is to us. God created us like Himself, spirit. In our early years we came to earth occasionally to view it and returned to the Father. Then one day we forgot our way Home. Like the Prodigal Son, we have ventured down the path of vibration to its lowest interval of expression. But unlike the prodigal, we have forgotten how to 'go back' to God. The very word 'religion' means 'to tie back'. We created a variety of denominations within Christianity, instead of focusing on the great lessons of Jesus. He came not to begin a new religion, but to awaken all humanity to itself, as one vast family of God's beloved children.

These early years of the twenty-first century perhaps make up the greatest generation, because it is the time when Gabriel came again. This time to tell us what we all are: holy children of God. At the same time in which Gabriel came, eleven Ascended Masters came to other countries around the world bringing the same message. Gabriel asked us if we remembered the Bible story of the Garden of Eden, when Adam fell asleep. We did recall it. Then Gabriel shocked us with the revelation that nowhere in the Bible does it say that Adam woke up! Adam represents humanity. Gabriel told us to wake up and live from the Lord God of our Being.

## Chapter 127  The Greatest Invitation

The greatest invitation is to those who desire to get off the karmic wheel and return Home to God is found in the Book of Psalms:

*"Be still, and know that I am God: I will be exalted among the heathen, I will be exalted in the earth."* Ps.46:10

When we become still, which is not very often in this busy world of ours, we can know that God is. There are many people who fear being still, for whatever reason. Some believe it demonstrates we are being lazy or unproductive. Some fear the stillness because they fear their own thoughts when they become still. Others fear stillness because they fear to know their true selves. Perhaps, at some level, we all know we are children of God but we don't want to acknowledge it because we believe we cannot go back Home. Gabriel said our greatest fear is that we *are* children of God.

The term 'heathen' means 'strange; uncivilized'. Webster's Collegiate gives a second definition: 'an unconverted member of a people or nation that does not acknowledge the God of the Bible'. Probably Webster means the Christian Bible, but there are other religions which have their own holy writings. When the white man descended upon the New World he arrogantly called the natives heathens. Native Americans worshipped the Great Spirit and honored all life. Indians hunting would mentally ask the buffalo or deer if it would give its life for the benefit of humans, and only kill it with the creature's permission. The natives did not kill for pleasure. Every part of the beast's body was used for practical purposes: food, clothing, housing, personal care. Now we call it reverence for life.

Archangel Gabriel explained this respectful attitude of our predecessors in America. God is a Great Spirit, the Author and Creator of all life. He created all humanity to continue in the act of creation. We created much beauty. We also have brought about much harm and disharmony to our earthly home. As God's children we are spirit, also. Eons ago we were aware of our divinity, but century upon century we have become enamored of physical form, including our own. In the forgetting process we forgot God, our Source.

What beckons us to seek the stillness is our soul, as it longs to return to its remembered Source. Gabriel said our greatest fear is that *we are children of God*. If we accept this truth we must also accept all the negativity that we have made in contrast to the love we are; our spirit Selves. Gabriel provided us with a female version of the Lord's Prayer, which begins: "Our Mother, who art the sacred space within, holy is thy name. Thy Kingdom be manifested on all levels of my being, as it is manifested in the sacred space of my spirit Self."

Here is the invitation pronounced yet again, for the Age of Aquarius generation. Gabriel came, as he does at the beginning of every age, to announce the coming age. Every two thousand years the earth enters a new age in its circular movement around the Central Sun. Jesus lived at the inception of the Age of Pisces, and the fish still designates his presence.

Psalm 46:10 could also be read as: 'Be still, and *know* that I AM, [that] God [is in you].' Jesus said, *"Before Abraham was, I AM."* (John 8:58). Gabriel made it abundantly clear that we are a human family of God, that the words in the Bible that say Jesus was the only son of God were mistranslated in the early days of Christianity. Correctly written, the original words were, "Jesus, begotten son of the only God." This makes a great difference. Now is the time to know the truth of the original words of Jesus the Christ.

In us, all of us is the sacred space which has been there since time began. The bread of life - the Communion bread for Christians - represents a *conscious awareness* of God's Kingdom within us. By rote we often take Communion. By a conscious choice we can be still and know that sacred space within is God. In that awareness we are able to follow Christ's way back Home. That is what Jesus meant when he said, 'Follow me.'

## Chapter 128   The Hardest Lesson

The lessons taught by Archangel Gabriel in his earthly visitations (1987-1999) were many and varied. One of the sweetest lessons I recall was "You are children of God." Something in me whispered, 'yes, it is so', as if an ancient memory from an ancient time had been confirmed. Now, with deep conviction I know I am, and everyone is, a child of God. We are as eternal as God Himself. He created us from spirit, and that is our true, eternal Self, unseen by mortal eyes but clearly visible to the angel realm of God. We can acknowledge the truth of it, but we fail somehow to know it with every fiber off our being. If we did know it we would not still be here on earth learning.

Gabriel explained the truth of many false beliefs we hold, and gave us the wisdom of the ages - not to believe in, but to *know* as truth. For me, the hardest lesson to hear and accept was the truth of our life on earth. Somehow I had no problem believing in reincarnation, but when Gabriel said that we plan our lives, including every relationship and every experience, my mind immediately rebelled. Why on Earth, I thought, would I plan a life in which my loving father would die when I was only five, and my mother would become an alcoholic, emotionally out of my reach thereafter? Later in my own life, I myself became an alcoholic. Upon recovery, forgiving my mother became not only possible but logical. Now I understood the disease and its terrible ramifications. I had abandoned my own offspring under its horrible power. Some of the lessons I learned were temperance, acceptance, forgiveness, love.

We can all rebel at this idea of planning our lives. We are so accustomed to blaming God. We accept loss and suffering as a God-given reality. We complain that so many people come into our lives that we did not *want to know*. In hindsight we see that each one taught us a lesson. We wonder why a child would choose to be born with a debilitation handicap. We also wonder why a child is born dead or dies at a very young age. We wonder why some become afflicted with cancer, heart disease, and other diseases. On the other hand, we also can wonder why and how more people now are living a hundred years or more. The magnificent machine we call a body can live without repair a longer time than any machine made by humans. We cannot know the answers while on earth. Only the person's Higher Self and God know them. Only our spirit Self remembers what and why we plan as we do. On the other side we do recall. In that recalling we also see whether we did or did not learn the lessons we planned.

There is one infallible truth, and that is that God gave us all free will. Every day we make a thousand choices, from breakfast food to clothing worn, route to work, how to treat another. We choose if, to whom and when and where we shall marry. No one questions this variety of choices. If we break the law - no, if the law breaks us - our free choice is limited severely in jail or prison. Incarceration, too, is a choice we make. Even there we choose how we will behave, what we learn, who we will speak to, etc.

The script we write for each lifetime is not in our conscious memory, but our Higher Self, spirit, knows it well. So does our Guardian Angel; so does God. We choose all our experiences based on lessons we failed to learn the last time around, on the karmic wheel. We have made the karmic journey, to and from Earth and the Astral Plane, that we have *met* every person now living on Earth, Gabriel said.

This New Age upon us, the Age of Aquarius, is known to the angelic realm as the Truth Age. Not only did Gabriel come to Earth to awaken us, but eleven Master Teachers came to various locations on Earth to wake up all humanity to its divine origin. We are ready to get off the wheel of karma by forgiving ourselves and all others for every seeming injustice. We are sentient beings on Earth, and love is the finest feeling we can know. Also, love is the greatest power in all creation, because God is love and He is the only Creator of life; all life.

The time to deny reincarnation is over. The time of seeking someone to 'blame' is over. The time to turn our backs on God is over. The time to seek peace is now. The time to forgive is now. The time to love is now.

# Section XVII
## Pe

## Chapter 129   The Heavenly Depot

Pulling into the station I know I have arrived in Heaven. This is the way I chose to take my last ride. I always loved trains. I loved riding, sleeping or eating in them. I loved watching them chug in from a distant place or chug out to yet another destination. When my traveling days were over, I still loved to hear the distant whistle blow and the mighty engine noisily roaring by. I am not alone in this love of trains. That is probably why there is a heavenly depot. The depot is crowded with men and women and children. Everyone is dressed in white; everyone is smiling in joyous anticipation. With me several others detrain and we all are greeted by loved ones who have left earth before.

We look to watch the train leave the depot, but as soon as the depot is cleared, the train disappears in the mist. But, oh, here comes another train! The scene repeats: new arrivals detrain and join their loved ones; the train disappears; another train arrives etc. and on and on, like an endless stream of passenger trains. Beloved family pets also arrive on the trains. Such happy family reunions! Into another room each family moves silently and there we share experiences - ours on earth and theirs in Heaven. In only minutes (it seems) we have shared our lives and dreams, then each heavenly resident leaves to resume their chosen tasks. The newcomers are greeted by angels who help us adjust to the heavenly realm. They explain that the only communication is by thought. That explained why the depot was so silent! Universal understanding prevails because language is not necessary.

Just before we leave the depot I see a sitting train and people on stretchers are borne by carriers. Angels explain they passed over in sudden accidents and need to be nursed by healing angels for a time. But among the stretchers we see tiny ones and very young ones. Angels tell us they will be taken to a nursery in Heaven, where everything is small to suit their needs and comfort.

Angels explain that when soldiers 'die' in battle they require extra care, for many believe they gave their lives for country or cause. They soon learn there is no death and they merely experienced a chosen passing based on their beliefs. The atmosphere in the station is joyful, no matter the moment of transition. Heaven is our Home now, until we choose to have another earthly adventure. The principle lesson to learn here is that 'death' does not exist, except in the minds of humans who have come to believe in it. In this peaceful place called Heaven our astral bodies are not animated by the breath of life as we have known it on earth. No air here! God is spirit. Spirit is our Essence; it is the Light in us. The Light is eternal; our spirit is eternal. No breathing is required here.

In the heavenly depot we see all races and cultures mixed together. There is no judgment or animosity here. Heaven is a place for further learning. Here, in peace and without fears of any kind, we can pursue every interest we ever had on earth. We can do this without interruption, for we need neither food nor rest. This heavenly quest brings to our awareness all things necessary to supply us with every need. Libraries, museums and art galleries disclose the past. Laboratories, workshops, art studios, factories provide us with the tools we need to bring to fruition our dreams of accomplishment.

We have no need to 'rush about' here, for time does not exist. There is no need to become comfortable, wealthy, or famous here. All our needs are met before we perceive a need. Money is non-existent. Everyone is equal; none are more 'famous' than others. There is no time here; no clocks or calendars. We are informed of all this before we leave the depot. It is too much to take in - and yet we know it is all true. We know it is true because we suddenly remember that we have been here before.

People we knew on earth are coming into the depot now, inviting us to visit their heavenly homes. Our angels gently remind them that we first need to rest and acclimate ourselves to our latest arrival in Heaven.

# Chapter 130  The Highest Authority

When we allow the ego to control our life we think our highest authority is ourselves. In truth it is our ego directing our every thought. Ego-oriented thoughts lead to actions which result in turmoil, pain, and confusion. Even when we know an action is not-good, our ego shouts so loudly we pay no attention to the still, small Voice of God which points us to a positive path. In retrospect we see the harm our decisions caused. Regret fills us. We decide to change, but we continue to listen to the fear-oriented ego. We know what is best for us; we know the road we want to take. This life of living from 'a mind of our own' may continue several years; or an entire lifetime.

If we are fortunate, a situation, an experience, or a person comes into our life from which we awaken to some grand truths. Honesty is the best policy. Others respect honesty. We are not alone in our experiences. Others deserve respect, just as we do when we are honest. We seem to be guided by another, higher Voice in us. When we begin to listen to that inner Voice for guidance we come to know that it never lets us down. We depend on it more and more over time. What is that inner Voice? Perhaps it is our conscience; perhaps it is God speaking to us. Every time we accept its reliability we become more and more aware that it is unfailing in its guidance. Does it matter what we call it? We can safely say it is the highest authority that we can call on in every instance.

It is not likely that we can name the year that we had the greatest realization of this highest authority. It may have been a miracle or an epiphany. It becomes and remains the one authority that would we count on constantly. The truth of the matter is that it is our higher Self that we are listening to. Our higher Self is part of the oneness of God. We are awakening to the fact that we are all children of God. Our physical parents pass on physical and mental characteristics. Part of what they are is part of us. Our heavenly Father passes on spiritual characteristics. What God is is part of us. That part of us that is the best of us; that part of us that is eternal; that part of us that is love. Love is the highest authority. Love never fails, as explained by Paul when he spoke to the people of Corinth (Chapter 13). Love is eternal.

Our highest authority, God in us, goes with us wherever we go. It is as dependable as the sunrise. It is comforting. When we take the time to listen to the highest authority the Answer is always forthcoming. If it is not forthcoming immediately we must patiently wait for it. The phrase 'when in doubt do nothing' is a proper response. When we go to bed at night we can seek an answer, and we should. Sometimes we awaken with the answer. Sometimes we read the answer, sometimes we overhear a conversation and therein is our answer. We will get the answer, and every answer received confirms that the Source is the best - the only good choice.

When our faith in the Voice of God increases, we finally realize that there is no choice to be made. Listening to the Voice is no longer an option. It is a basic requirement. It is God's Power echoing in our very nature. God in us directs us. The ego must be dealt with head-on. Its destruction is unnecessary. We need only relegate it to its proper place. We created our ego to warn us of pending dangers, but over time we gave all our power over to it. Fear is its greatest weapon. We have come to fear many things and many 'other' people. Humanity is the wondrous family of God. We are all spiritually connected because of this holy paternity.

Having listened to our ego for many years we believe that we are not worthy of love. The ego is not worthy of love; the God in us is not only worthy of love, it *is love*. We are love. We are loved. We are loveable. Love is the Answer to every question. When we ardently seek an answer and it seems unanswerable or it seems to take too long coming, we can recall the rule, 'when in doubt do nothing". Sometimes patience is the answer, but our ego seeks instant gratification. The ego will fight for its life because it is afraid. As we listen to the Highest Authority we have the best and only true Answer.

# Chapter 131   The Incomparable Moment

Life is full of special moments; special events; special celebrations; special accomplishments. Yet, from my perspective - that of looking back from eight and a half decades - there is no moment which compares to that of seeing a newborn baby for the first time. My own incomparable moments numbered four. The song titled *When a Child is Born* captures the thrilling event. (Lyrics by Manolo Otero):

*A ray of hope flickers in the sky.*
*A tiny star lights up, way up high.*
*All across the land dawns a brand new morn.*
*This comes to pass, when a child is born.*

The entire world seems to take on a new brilliance and a new dimension. Perhaps this miniature human brings with it a spiritual aspect that cannot be seen but is felt by all observers. I believe that William Wordsworth had it right:

*And not in utter nakedness,*
*But trailing clouds of glory do we come*
*From God, who is our home:*
*Heaven lies about us in our infancy. (Ode on Immortality)*

This brand new infant captures our spontaneous and loving attention. We love it because its helplessness invites our protective arms. We love it because we know it began with an act of love. Whatever demands our love and attention makes us feel love all around and within us. This newborn is unique. This moment cannot be duplicated. The feeling of this moment cannot be captured in print or film. It is unique and uniquely lovely.

Of all life's experiences, the birth of a children ranks at the top of the list of joyful moments. It may be that upon first sight we not only behold a tiny replica of ourselves, but we also know in our souls that here comes a brand new sibling in the world family of humankind. That would explain why friends and neighbors, too, enjoy beholding our new human prize. We find the greatest of pleasures in counting fingers and toes. What joy when we see the first smile - as though they were accepting us and the world as they debuted into their new home. So many 'firsts' are ahead of us.

With the unmatched joy of newborn comes a responsibility for this helpless tot. We take on the responsibility with joyousness. The responsibility is more than offset by the thrill of watching this infant grow, learn, and become a teen, and then an adult. We have a front-row seat for this event. We teach this child all the do's and don'ts of social life. Somewhere along the line the glow of the birth dissipates. We immediately assume that we know what is best for our offspring - as though having been down the growth road ourselves we now are experts at the journey!

Of course, we do want to raise a child to become part of the social world, even though we often long to keep them home longer than necessary. They will let us know when they are ready to leave the nest. There was a time when Archangel Gabriel described the parenting of the eagle, whose cliff home is very high. Gabriel said when it is time for the fledgling to leave the nest the parents begin to remove the soft feathers in the nest. When the nest becomes too uncomfortable, the eaglet tries to fly. Gabriel said the bird parents do not teach their young how to fly; they teach them to *remember* how to fly. Knowing how to fly is instinctual.

Perhaps we could consider that our little ones know how to behave from their past lifetimes. Of course, they will test us when two - or thirteen - but we can set some reasonable rules of behavior. When our own children were small we decided they would not rule the household as some parents allowed at that time. Our lives would have been chaotic if we had let our two year olds make family decisions. Watching young children at play can teach us about cooperation, in spite of their selfish actions at times. Children of all colors play without prejudice if given the freedom to do so. If we teach our young the basic rules of behavior they will recall them, even if for a time they wander down a destructive road. We need to instill in them a code of behavior, but we must always remember that their blueprint came from God.

As the precious newborn grows and becomes we treasure every 'first'. We treasure every accomplishment. This is the child we gave a life to. This is a child of God who chose us as parents.

# Chapter 131   The Inspired Life

From the very beginning of my writing career, in 1998, I have been an inspired writer. I was being inspired even before I knew it. It was inspiration that started me on this great adventure. When I realized this, I began to thank God for such a blessing every day. At this time I have written several books, all inspired. Ideas and words flow through me from God, my Source; everyone's Source.

Recently in meditation it came to me that I should be aware of spirit guidance all the time, not only when I write. Strangely enough, this seemed like a revelation to me. I know that we each have 144,000 angels, because Gabriel said so. However, my writing which stems from and is permeated with Gabriel's lessons, I consider the inspired words to be divine guidance. Now it seems very logical that as a child of God I can be inspired constantly in my life. God sends his messengers to talk to me constantly, because I know I am His Own.

We are so accustomed to thinking that we have a life on earth as humans and God has a life in heaven with all those angels in that heavenly realm. To begin to live in this way (consciously in contact with God), would take a great deal of practice. But before the practice begins we must make a decision to begin the practice. This sounds like a serious commitment, which it is. Only one who is dedicated to such a task will succeed. What will happen if we do not? Nothing different from what we have. Nothing different from what we've already planned for our lives.

We begin to practice by asking our angels to assist us in this effort. And they will. Gabriel reminded us that angels do not sit around and wait, or decide if they want to answer our call. They jump joyously to the opportunity to serve us. Several things will happen as we turn within to our Christ Light. Firstly, we will turn our thoughts to positive and away from negative. This alone will provide us with some peace of mind. Secondly, we will find ourselves accepting others more readily. This too will provide us with a degree of peace of mind.

This conscious decision to practice being inspired means that we need to keep our minds uncluttered with extraneous thoughts. When we fill our mind with thoughts about yesterday or tomorrow, or pass judgment on what is in front of us now, our mind is not open to guidance. This is part of the early practice for inspired guidance. Scripture tells us that we should limit our speech to yes and no, which suggests that we should eliminate things like gossip, worry, frustration, hurt feelings, and specially anger thoughts. Negativity plagues us only if we allow it to.

The greatest benefit of this practice is peace of mind on a regular basis. In this state we are open to guidance which cannot come to us when our thoughts are filled with other things. It's like trying to open a door which is blocked with clutter on the other side. Practicing open-mindedness also takes a great deal of faith in a higher power. Open-mindedness has two components: it means keeping an uncluttered mind and keeping a mind open to new thoughts. Inspired thoughts are new thoughts.

At any given time throughout the day, an inspired thought may come, but only to an uncluttered mind. It will come when a flash in a moment of time, and it is important to write it down at the time. Like a dream not recorded, it can easily be forgotten. Inspiration comes from the Heaven world to our consciousness for a reason. The reason may be to make a phone call. The reason may be to write, to paint, to cook a special meal.

It is amazing what kinds of inspired thoughts we have. They seem to come from nowhere, yet we know their guidance is true. We can choose to dismiss the inspired thought, if we are busy at work or at home. But it only takes a moment to write a word or two as a reminder. Inspiration brings to us calmness, joy, and self-confidence. In addition to these good feelings we have the knowingness that we are following God's Guidance. This practice will help those around us; those who share our daily lives. They will see the difference in us. Perhaps they too, will recognize the benefits of inspired living. If so, they in turn will inspire others to be inspired. On earth we are not perfect, but we know the perfect Source.

# Chapter 133   The Invited Guests

One of Jesus' parables (Matt 22:1-10) relates to a king who made a wedding feast for his son. Briefly, the king sent servants to invite tradesmen and merchants. They all made excuses, declined the invitation because they were too busy with their business affairs. Angry, the king told his servants to go out in the streets and invite everyone. This story is also found in *The Gospel According to Thomas*, 36-38: *Tradesmen and merchants shall not enter the places of my Father.* These quoted words do not mean that tradesmen and merchants are not worthy of Heaven nor does it mean that they shall not see Heaven. But, if they do not *believe in* a certain place, why would they *want* to go there? We become so absorbed in our daily routines that we will not find time to pray to - or even acknowledge the existence of - our Creator. Some religious groups require weekly attendance; some require several visits to church every week. It is interesting to note that Islam requires prayers five times every day.

The number of hours is not the important measure of our faith. The *focus* of our time is the essential factor in measuring faith. When we disallow time for meditation, we simply are denying God our attention. God does not demand attention. Love never does. Attention on God and His works bring to the believer a comfort and an assurance that He and we are one. The busiest person, who suddenly finds herself stopped in her tracks by circumstance, will not only find time to pray but will have nothing but time to do so. Our hectic world demands action, activity, and competition. To be busy means to be productive; to be productive means we are valid. The person who cannot work is seen as unproductive. The person with physical or mental limitations assigned lesser tasks. A bed-ridden person is called an invalid (in- valid?). We are masters at labeling each other: the poor, the wealthy, the laborers, the professionals, blue-collar workers, clerks, supervisors, management, mid-management, executive, CEOs, founders, bag-ladies, etc. In our current economy we have a new designation: 'the working poor'. Only in recent decades have we seen a person 'poor' who is employed. To the writer this is incomprehensible. The truth of humanity is that we are all children of God. Gabriel explained that 'the only begotten of God' is *all humanity.*

I have read much about the 'other side' of the veil we call death. There is no status there. Someone once said that tragedy is a great leveler. In a disaster we are all cooperative human beings, striving for mutual survival. Perhaps, like the king in the parable, we should ask 'the man in the street' to come to our feasts. *When thou makest a dinner or a supper, call not thy friends, nor thy brethren, neither thy kinsmen, nor thy rich neighbors; lest they also bid thee again, and a recompence be made thee. But when thou makest a feast, call the poor, the maimed, the lame, the blind: And thou shalt be blessed; for they cannot recompence thee.* Luke 14:12-14

In this blessed generation we are beginning to see the value of bringing to the feast those who are unable to return the favor. Giving a true feast is inviting those to the table who we invite from the love of our neighbor, not for the possible benefits we might glean. This is an example of the agape love; the unconditional love shown by Jesus the Christ. There was nothing that could have been given Jesus that he did not already have. His love was offered first to those who could not pay him back: children, lepers, blind beggars, lunatics (mentally ill). Jesus was derided for mingling with the publicans and sinners, but he responded that he came to save the sinners; for the righteous needed him not. (Matt. 9:13).

In Jesus' time there were many who went to hear him speak. They were all busy people in those days: shepherds, farmers, merchants. But they found time to listen to the wisdom presented by this itinerant preacher who spoke of love and forgiveness. It was a new lesson. There were many traveling rabbis, but none offered these lessons. Parables, analogies and straight talk came from this Prince of Peace. His speech was plain and easy to understand. His message was inspiring. He repeatedly said, 'Follow me.' He still does. When Gabriel taught we went and listened. It seemed the right thing to do, without a doubt or question. Perhaps God invited us because it was our time to learn.

# Chapter 134   The Kingdom, the Power, the Glory

Archangel Gabriel provided us with a female version of The Lord's Prayer. It ends: "For Thine is the Kingdom of my Being, the Glory of my Light, and the Power of my Spirit, now and forever." Amen.

It is interesting to note that after two thousand years the spirit world still uses the term 'kingdom'. There was no dictionary in Jesus' time, but today's lexicon gives the following as one of several descriptions: 'the realm in which God's will is fulfilled'. Surely all of God's kingdom cannot be within any one person, but just as surely we cannot prove that every person does not contain a spark of that realm. Gabriel knows who we are. He told us we are children of God and we must wake up to that truth so we can live from the Lord God of our Being.

Our human eyes do not perceive the inner Kingdom; only spirit entities can discern it. We are light beings. The Light in us is a spark of God within. It is more brilliant than the sun, yet beyond our ability to see. Our mortal eyes are not equipped to see the Kingdom or the Light within. Only by faith can we know the light is within. Our ability to discern it does not determine its existence. This Light is the Glory of God in us. 'Glory', the dictionary tells us, as one definition: 'the splendor and the beatific happiness of heaven: eternity.'

In this world we do not see or comprehend how we could contain eternity within us. We are in this world but not *of it*. Earth is not our real home; we are strangers here. Heaven is our natural habitat. Very, very long ago we lived in Heaven, with our Creator. We all loved God and we all knew that God loved us. We loved each other. We communicated with our thoughts, which made language unnecessary. In His creating, God gave us free choice, unlike the angels. God gave us free choice across the board, but to angels he gave free choice only within the realm of good.

Our sight is so limited here on earth that we cannot see anything that is spiritual. We have taught ourselves to see only material things because we have accepted physical form as our reality. The more solid the form the more we accept it as real. A fifty-story building is more real than a newspaper; a marble statue is more real than a pair of shoes. The truth, which we are now learning, is that none of these things are real.

We have been living on the earth for so long that we believe only what our senses perceive. We are learning at last that all the forms we see are temporary. The Earth is temporary. The light we see from some stars is still travelling to us, even though the star no longer exists. Astronomers tell us this. So, stars are temporary, too. Our hearing is limited. Some sounds are too soft for us to hear, like a tree screaming when chopped down. Our nose is offended by some odors, such as a skunk's spray. We live in this box of limitations when all around and *within us* is the Kingdom of God, flourishing for eternity.

The only real world is the one we cannot see. As we learn Gabriel's lessons (see Bibliography) we understand that God has no need of physical form. That is why Jesus the Christ said, *"Heaven and earth shall pass away, but my words shall not pass away."* (Matt. 24:35). This statement means they will not continue to exist as separate states. "My word, which is the resurrection and the life, shall not pass away because life is eternal." (ACIM T - 1: III: 2: 1-2)

Now, in this twenty-first century, we have Jesus' word that what he said in the first century is still true. For eons of time we have resided here on the earth and accepted our littleness and our guilt as the truth of us. We are so much more. Two thousand years ago a man came to teach us a new way; a way of love and peace. We did not listen. We placed him on a pedestal and fell on our knees in worship. Now we must stand up, acknowledge him as our elder brother, and put his teachings to work.

Being still in meditation we can know God; know that we have the Light of God within us. Vision must replace sight. Knowingness must replace faith. Eternal life must replace death. We will all ascend, when we decide to, and re-join our Father in Heaven once again, with the Kingdom, the Power and the Glory.

# Chapter 135 The Last Awareness

We, as a human race, love to think that we have progressed to where we are, in 2016, by virtue of our own ingenuity. We accept the idea that each generation teaches the following generation how to live better. We call it progress. Perhaps that is true. Or, perhaps, we have simply become *aware* of what we can do. We still do not know exactly why or how. The people who are imbued with intelligence seem to lead us progressively through the centuries. The rest of us follow with our labor, and gratefully accept the fruits of the combined efforts. Before recorded history the human family lived on earth for millions of years. Archeologists have proven this. Perhaps our first awareness was how to survive. Or perhaps we first became aware that we could reproduce ourselves. Archangel Gabriel informed us that in the earliest of times we did not value newborn infants. They were helpless and not helpful to primitive survival. A father might even devalue them to the point of terrible abuse, kicking them around like a football. Then one day a father looked at his offspring and realized it looked like himself. From then on, babies were seen as valid and were raised to maturity. The lifespan then was only about twenty.

Gabriel told us that for a long time there was no awareness that the act of intercourse was related to the birth of a baby! A newborn was seen as a gift from the gods. The female was seen as having separate power from the male. He was jealous of the female, and at some (much later) point, wrote (in Genesis) that the male was greater, and described the female as a by-product of the male. That idea persists today. In the course of time the male offspring was treasured, especially by royalty which required a male successor to the throne. China has only recently lifted its ban on multiple children. Only recently have female babies there been allowed. We became aware that tribes and nations could be formed - with military might. Boundaries were formed to designate the countries. We became aware that we had the power to rule others or enslave others. Some societies revolted against the rulers and freedoms were instituted.

With the Industrial Revolution we became aware we could manufacture products, with the hard physical labor of others. Almost in imitation of a beehive, a 'queen bee', or President, could employ many 'workers' to sustain the hive; the society. Workers revolted at low wages and long hours because they became aware there is power in numbers.

Now we are finally becoming aware that we can help others help themselves. Societies have become more caring, more humane, more interested in peace than in war, We can see these modern choices as being more civilized. Or we can become aware that all we have accomplished thus far is only the recognition of our innate ability to love others. Over the centuries religions formed because of a Founder, a holy leader who preached certain rules of behavior; tenets of faith. From Moses on, humanity became aware of One God in place of many gods. All religions formed around a nucleus of ideas that profess love of others, worship of God (by whatever name), forgiveness, valuing of life, etc.

Today ecumenical councils seek to find common ground to become aware of the oneness of life. 'As above so below', the ancient axiom, has not lost its validity. All inventions, all art, all creative ideas, come from above. The last awareness of humanity, it seems, will be when we have an awareness that we are one human family of God. In that awareness we are seeking peace in our nation and all nations. The United Nations exemplifies our ability to cooperate and assist each other. It exists in order to seek peaceful resolutions instead of revolutions. War must become obsolete. Not because we can wipe out thousands of people with one lethal weapon, but because we have become aware that war is senselessly destructive and wasteful. It is unproductive and unnecessary. It destroys instead of building. People suffer without cause or reason.

Peace is not a sign of weakness; war is. Defense is only required when we fear each other. The Prince of Peace came to remind us that the kingdom of God is within - within *all* of us. This truth will be our final awareness.

# Chapter 136   The Longest Journey

The longest journey the body can take is measured by time and distance. We have learned how to circumvent the Earth. We have learned how to fly into space; visit the moon; set up a space station. We have sent cameras into space to photograph Pluto. We aspire to continue our journeys into space to explore our universe. We wonder if there is life 'out there' in space.

Archangel Gabriel, Announcer of the Ages and Teacher of God, told us that entities from other planets come to visit the Earth. They watch us bury our dead and wonder why we are so wasteful; why we do not ascend with our bodies as they do. They do not understand that we have not learned how, yet. We believe that only Jesus could ascend. This is the age - the Age of Aquarius - that we shall begin to remember many things, including how to ascend. Gabriel told us that he did not come to teach us anything new; only to remind us of what we have forgotten.

The longest journey we have ever taken is the journey we *thought we took* away from God. We cannot make such a journey; we are part of God; we are his spirit offspring. In our consciousness only we left God; feel adrift away from Him; long to return. The journey of the body is measured by time and distance. There is no distance between God and us. There is no time in the spirit world of God. We cannot measure our longest journey by time, for spirit knows no time. God's only time is eternity and we are in it. We invented time on Earth to keep track of our activities and each other. We are spirit; timeless as God; eternal as God.

Measuring this longest journey in terms of life on Earth, we can measure it only through the many lifetimes we have been present on this planet we call home. Only recently have we begun to accept reincarnation as fact; many still consider it anathema; an 'evil' concept. We accept the idea that we can come full-blown to earth and quickly learn language and customs without any prior teaching. We believe that some individuals are child prodigies. Everything around us discloses a need for growth and development - flowers, plants, trees, and creatures.

The prodigy is the one who has spent many lifetimes studying tempo, timing, harmony, etc. The genius is the one who has studied background courses and came to Earth to 'discover' something new. All discoveries come from above; all inventions; all art. We have experienced so many incarnations on Earth that we have *met every other person now living!* Gabriel told us this; he would not lie. He brought only truth, for we are ready now to hear it, to learn it, and to live it. The only important lifetime is the one we are now living because it is the only one in which we can effect change. It is the result of all past lifetimes. The cycle of life on Earth and the Astral plane again and again, is called the karmic wheel. Gabriel came to tell us how to get off the karmic wheel. The way to get off the karmic wheel is simple to hear but difficult to achieve. Jesus the Christ taught forgiveness and love. These rules still pertain. It is time to realize we must forgive ourselves and others. Not because the wounds were alright, but because we caused them all. In truth, no one ever hurt us without our permission and we never hurt anyone without theirs. So, in the final analysis there is nothing to forgive!

Regret is the deepest pain we have ever known. There is nothing we need to regret. It benefits no one to reminisce. Looking back derives no benefit. Remember Lot's wife. Now is the time to focus on now. We can plan but we must not project. What we do and what we think at this moment will determine our future moments, and what we so sow we shall surely reap. That is an immutable law. The issue we need to face is the power we have given the ego. It tells us constantly we belong to it, and fear is necessary. Love and fear cannot sleep in the same bed. It is time to arise and meet truth head on. It is time to live life knowing we are eternal.

This journey in our consciousness has taken us far from our innate divinity as children of God. Our journey has been mental, emotional and physical. All these levels must be redeemed. There is a seventh Heaven awaiting us. We can shorten the journey by heeding instruction, such as is found in *A Course in Miracles* and *A Course of Love*. (See Bibliography)

# Section XVIII
## Tzaddi

## Chapter 137  The Longest Movie

Archangel Gabriel presented us, in his twelve years of visitations (1987-1999), with a great deal of information. In explaining to us about our Source, our earthly journeys and our varied experiences, he told us many lessons. To help us understand our sacred nature and our tendency to deny it, he gave the example if seeing a movie. We enter a theater building and take a seat. On the screen we see people acting out a story, either a love story, a war story, an adventure, a mystery, or a comedy. History comes to life on the screen when some past period is the theme. Our attention is totally focused on the story line. We become absorbed in the content. It may have a personal meaning. Our emotions are roused. We identify with the actors and their plight, their pain, their frustration or any other emotion which they evoke. We laugh at the comedy, cry with the victim, cheer for the hero. When the story is intense we feel drained at the end. Once in a while the story is too brutal or too painful to watch, and we leave the theater early. But most of the time we sit until the end, horrible or not. We give our attention totally over to the happenings on the screen ahead of us. Today's movies are extremely graphic and we forget that it is all 'staged'.

Finally, the story ends, credits for the workers scroll down the screen, then the screen goes blank. We leave the building and return to the 'real world'. We have enjoyed this short escape from the reality of our daily lives. Gabriel likened this experience to our earthly existence. The world is our theater and we are the actors. There are no 'credits' because the script writer, the visual artist and the choreographer are all *us*. We act out our play: We travel the world, marry and have children, study in schools, find occupations which invite us. We live a short time or a long time on earth, depending on our script. When we leave the planet (theater building) we return to the real world which truly is real and eternal. It is eternally real. It is the world of spirit; the world of God. The spirit world of God is our natural habitat; God is our true Source. The human family puts on shows all over the world, but there is no audience. Angels know we do not belong here. Angels are assigned to all of us. Gabriel said we each have 144,000 angels to assist us in life. They help us whenever we ask, but they can never interfere with our free choice. That is a gift from God and even God cannot interfere with our choices.

Just as our full attention is on the theater screen, our full attention is on our daily life. We have come to believe that our bodies are our real selves. They are not. They are very short-term envelopes to house our sacred spirits for a time on earth. When we return to our Home, Heaven, we review our lives and see what lessons we learned and what lessons we did not. In our 'review' we see which short-comings we did overcome and which ones we did not overcome. We then proceed to plan our next adventure in the world. Gabriel told us we have come to earth; the world of form so many times that we have *met* every other person now living. That fact, like many others given us by Gabriel, staggers the imagination. Gabriel came to announce the coming Age of Aquarius. He is the Announcer of the Ages. He came with only one lesson. He came to remind us that Adam fell asleep in the Garden of Eden, but nowhere in the Bible does it say he woke up. Adam represents humanity. We are still asleep to our own divinity.

Sometimes, in meditation, we touch into our sacred core and know we are so much more than our bodies. Jesus knew he was a son of God. His life was dedicated to showing us the way Home. He came when he was greatly needed. Jesus came again, in the 1990s, to clarify errors in scripture which were made deliberately or by scribes' ignorance. Gabriel came to explain what we all truly are - children of the Living God; sacred beings visiting earth repeatedly and unnecessarily. As we awaken we will leave our theater (life on Earth) behind. The screen will go dark on our adventures and we will stay Home where we belong, in the spirit World of Light.

# Chapter 138   The Love of Fear

We seek love and acceptance from others throughout our lives. What we love we seek. One of our greatest loves is that of fear. Loving fear, we seek it. Perhaps all this love of fear keeps love itself away from us Halloween's Fright Night is a tiny example of our passion for fear. We seek thrills to become excited. We seek thrills to know what it is like 'living on the edge'. From the game of hide and seek as a child to scaling Mount Everest, some of us are willing to risk our lives in pursuit of fame or money or just the excitement. Most of these are fearful activities; excitement equates with fear. We fear we will not accomplish something or fear we will.

Some sports offer the opportunity for fear. Mountain climbing, building-scaling, auto racing are some. The tight-rope walker spans The Grand Canyon, or Niagara Falls, seemingly fearless - but all the spectators watch and fear *for* him! Scary movies are the most popular. War movies, disaster movies, vicious monster movies are the most popular. We seem to love being fearful.

Perhaps the reason is because we remember fearful moments longer or more poignantly than tender moments, or because whatever we do has an element of fear in it. We seem to love recounting times when we were fearful in the past. We teach our children to not speak to strangers. We teach them about the bogey-man. By our own actions we often teach them to fear the dark; to fear thunderstorms. Our daily fears are fear of poverty, want, unemployment, sickness, unforeseen accidents - and sometimes even our neighbors.

Too many of us fear God, and believe that God will 'get us' if we are not 'good', although we cannot define the ways He will 'get us'. Like so many other things, 'good' is relative. If God were a judgmental god he could have destroyed us long ago for our 'sins'. Only a loving God could continue to accept us with all or frailties and short-comings. We exist here for a reason. It makes no sense to believe we exist to be fearful human beings. For those of us who believe in a God of Love, we persist in believing that we are more than a body. As spirit, and created by Him we have a spirit, also. Just as a child bears a resemblance to its parents because of physical genes, it is possible that we have within us spiritual genes from our Father. These spiritual genes are love, light, peace, and joy; for these are the attributes of God.

Two thousand years ago we were told that the Kingdom of God is within us. The minds of his (Jesus') time could not comprehend that esoteric concept. Their lives were all about family, crops, and animals - earthly subjects. Word of mouth was the only communication means. Today our mental capacity has stretched to include the sciences and philosophy. We can imagine things beyond our senses. But the idea of the Kingdom of God within still escapes us. Only those who turn within can begin to accept this truth.

Without going within we continue to see only what we expect to see; experience only what the past has experienced. The past is full of fear. We re-enact wars to assure us of the chaos. The reality of war is pain and agony. Do we really want to re-enact *that?* We continue to hold memorials for past wars and atrocities; 'lest we forget'. Perhaps it is time to forget war's horrors. Fear must not forever rule our lives.

We can choose to eliminate fear by turning to love, and only love. We have the potential for that. Given that the kingdom of God is within and that we are able to tap into it, we can begin the *process* of becoming humans loving, instead of humans simply being. Five thousand years of ignorance and fear are coming to an end, thanks to Archangel Gabriel and eleven Master Teachers who visited Earth late in the twentieth century. Jesus the Christ visited us also, explaining some of the errors of scripture. These heavenly messengers came all around the planet, with the same message: to awaken us to our divinity, as children of God.

This is the Truth Age, and the truth of our being is that we are holy offspring of the one God of us all. The time for thinking, analyzing, calculating are over. As God's Own, we must listen to our Father. We never left Him, any more than the Prodigal Son left his true inheritance. God has patiently waited for us to wake up from our long, long sleep. Adam fell asleep and nowhere in the Bible does it say he woke up. It is the sleep of forgetting our origin. As we awaken to our Higher Self - our God-self - we will become more willing to listen to God whisper in our ears. This inward journey is meditation, where we listen to God in the stillness. God will never let us down. He will never point us the wrong way. He will never leave us without comfort and joy. He sent the 'firstfruits' of awakened humanity in the form of Jesus the Christ (I Cor. 15:23). Scripture describes Jesus as an example, a pattern, to follow. Jesus himself said many times 'follow me'.

Love is the greatest power there is. It has transcended royalty, wars, evil acts for centuries and has not lessened one iota. God is. God is eternal. We are His eternal kids. How much longer will we hit the snooze alarm and stay asleep? This is the hour to wake up and live from the Lord God of our Being. This is the time to know we are love. This is the Age of Truth. Our time has come to come out of our self-created shell of darkness and re-take our true power, which we turned over long ago to our ego.

There is nothing to fear. Love will prevail on Earth. Gabriel's lessons are all available in English and in decades to come they will be translated. Someday all the centers of light will join - the twelve centers where Gabriel and the eleven teachers came. Then peace on Earth will prevail. Each and every one of us is important to God. We all can learn how to take responsibility to become fully awake, and fully live a life of love instead of nameless, useless fear.

## Chapter 139  The Multitude of Disciples

*"And believers were the more added to the Lord, multitudes both of men and women."* Acts 5-14

Jesus chose his twelve apostles as his students and followers. As he walked and preached, many others joined his group. Many women were included in that multitude. Archangel Gabriel told us all references to these women followers were purged from early religious documents. It was, after, all, a male-oriented society. It still is, Gabriel pointed out, and has been for five thousand years. Prior to that humanity worshipped a Goddess, but that is another story.

It is interesting to note that although one of the first four gospels was written by Luke, the physician, he is not named in Matthew 10:2 as one of the apostles. Most of the New Testament was written by Paul, a convert who had been Saul, friend of the Romans. Paul never saw Jesus until Jesus manifested to him after the resurrection. Jesus' words led Paul to convert. Most of the apostles could not write, for reading was not an available option except to the priests who read the Old Testament, the Jewish Bible. The twelve apostles were named in Matthew 10:2: the two brothers Peter and Andrew, the two brothers James and John, sons of Zebedee, Phillip, Bartholomew, Thomas, Matthew, James, son of Alpheus, Thaddeus, Simon, and Judas Iscariot.

Each apostle represents a human faculty. Simon' name was changed to Peter by Jesus. Peter represents a rock of faith, a firm foundation for spiritual growth. The Bible says Peter was told by Jesus he was the rock upon which the church was to be built (Matt. 16:18). Gabriel corrected this story, and told us that Jesus' actual words were that if Peter remained unyielding (as a rock) in his beliefs, he would live to regret it. Peter did not accept women as worthy to follow Jesus.

Andrew represents strength, James, Zebedee's son, represents judgment, and his brother John represents love. Philip is the power faculty of man, Bartholomew is imagination, and Thomas is the understanding faculty. Matthew represents the will, and James, son of Alpheus, represents the faculty of order. Simon the Zealot represents the zeal, or enthusiasm of our character. Juda represents life - the unredeemed life forces of man.

Of course these symbolic meanings were not stated by Jesus. The teachings of Jesus were easy to understand in his time. He used parables in terms of the everyday life of his peers. He also knew that the symbolism of his teachings would not be accepted nor understood for many generations to come. The entire Bible has symbolic meanings. If this were not so, The *Metaphysical Bible Dictionary* (1931) could not have been written.

For two thousand years much of humanity has taken up Jesus' teachings and represents more modern multitudes of followers of Christianity. It is the saddest thing that Jesus' teachings have been interpreted in so many ways. This diversity of interpretation has resulted in a vast number of denominations in the Christian faith. Christians range from fundamentalists, who accept the words of scripture literally, and deny symbolism of any kind, to the most liberal sect which believes in communication with the spirit world of God. Christianity is one of the world's largest religions. One wonders if this magnificent multitude would be even greater if we had only striven to find a common ground of faith, instead of segmenting into denominations.

At this inception of the Age of Aquarius, Jesus the Christ came again (1995-1999) to correct errors in the Bible. Much was purged; some was mistranslated. This time he performed no miracles, which detracted us before. Now he tells us to take him off the old rugged cross, follow him and become like him, a child of God. Created by God as spirit, Jesus and all humanity are the only begotten sons of God. Jesus knew he was that holy offspring; we forgot it in the mists of time. We invented time and here we are, stuck in it. Eternity is forever; we are forever. In eternity 'now' is the only time. As large as the human family of God is, all will return Home. Heaven has plenty of room for the multitude.

## Chapter 140   The New Bible

The Old Testament was quoted often by Jesus as he walked and preached. He was raised by his devoutly Jewish parents. As a child he performed miracles and he questioned the rabbis in the temple. His parents knew why, because of his astonishing birth. But his behavior was not always appreciated by the neighbors. According to the apocryphal *Infancy* chapters, Jesus once fashioned mud birds and then brought them to life, and they flew away!

The New Testament of Jesus the Christ was written many years after Jesus' life and resurrection. As far as we know, Jesus himself wrote nothing. He has been quoted and misquoted by the apostles, or by the scribes who printed what they were told. Perhaps one day we will discover the original writings of the Bible. Or perhaps we shall have to read them in Heaven, where all writing and painting are available as originally written. Archangel Gabriel told us (1987-1999) that authors read their works in Heaven and then have the opportunity to re-write them based on knowledge received in Heaven! Gabriel also told us much about Jesus' life in two of his (Gabriel's) seminars, *Master Jesus* and *Master Jesus II.* (See Bibliography). The Bible contains misquotes of Jesus and words were put in his mouth that he never said. Also, there is a lack of information about the many women disciples who followed Jesus, as well as the many references to reincarnation. Gabriel informed us of these errors. This wondrous archangel gave the symbolism of the Book of Revelations, also. See Bibliography.

In the 1960s Jesus began dictating to Helen Schucman, a professor of medical psychology, a multi-page book. Helen was a Jew and was chosen by Jesus because she had no set ideas about Jesus. He thought that was 'wonderful'. It took several years for the four part book to be dictated and written down. The parts include a 600+ page Text, a section with 365 Lessons, and a Manual for Teachers. There is also a section Definition of Terms. In that last section it says: "A universal theology is impossible, but a universal experience is not only possible but necessary." The universal experience is the message of the book, entitled *A Course in Miracles*.

Gabriel told us that this book, *A Course in Miracles,* is the Bible of the new age, the Age of Aquarius which is now upon us. At the start of every age Archangel Gabriel comes to earth to bring good news. He is the archangel known as the Announcer of the Ages. He came to more people this time because more people are now open to spirit communication and are willing to hear him. We were in awe of his early visitations. We never took Gabriel for granted. His lessons often shocked us. Especially amazing was the lesson in which he said that we plan our lives and every person, every experience therein!

Today Bible students study scripture, both the Old Testament and the New Testament. Memorization may help a student but living the precepts Jesus taught is the task at hand. The new Bible, the Bible of the New Age, offers basic explanations about our error perceptions and how to overcome them. Study and application are necessary. One year or more is the prescribed time for the workbook. The reading order of the parts is optional. The Manual for Teachers does not require a college degree.

Anyone is a teacher of God who chooses to be. It is this 'calling' that is the only requirement. The book is not a book on theology. It is a universal text for any human who chooses to read it, learn from it, and apply it. Chapter I defines fifty Principles of Miracles. The first principle is, 'There is no order of difficulty in miracles. One is not "harder" or "bigger" than another. They are all the same. All expressions of love are maximal.' (Text 1: I: 1)

The third principle is, "Miracles occur naturally as expressions of love" (Text 1: I: 3)


## Chapter 141  The New Freedom

When Jesus visited Earth (1995-1999) he corrected our thinking about the 'straight and narrow ' path we have accepted as our only way to God. Our gratitude should know no bounds when we read his words: "People think that if you follow God you have to restrict yourself and be narrow, and not allow, not do, and not be. God, to be expressed from within, is a freedom that you have yet to come to know." (*Master Jesus III*, 1/17/98)

Expressing love will give us a new freedom. Few people live a life of love. We have the tendency to judge, label, compartmentalize everyone we meet. We use our own bar of judging that always fails us. We are not made to judge others. Judgment is not a requirement of love. It is entirely foreign to love. Love accepts, cares, nurtures, and protects. Expressing love then becomes a little freer. We embrace in public; we kiss in public. Not long ago this was seen as exhibitionism. When Jesus speaks of love now, he means it as he meant it two thousand years ago: unconditional love. What is 'unconditional' love? Mr. Webster tells us that 'unconditional' means 'not limited, absolute, unqualified'.

Archangel Gabriel told us that motherhood is the closest humans have come to unconditional love on Earth, but he said it truly is so much greater than that. There are those individuals who say they would love us if only we would be someone else or do something else. That is a clear 'condition'. We might wonder why, if love is eternal, we separate and divorce from another after marriage. Gabriel informed us that even if we separate or divorce, the love we once shared continues forever.

Gabriel said that when we fall in love it is not us that causes it, but the other toward whom we are attracted. He said the other person awakens in us the love that is our essence. The glow is unforgettable for those of us who have experienced it. That is the love that God created us from. It is the truth of our being. When the glow subsides some of us love without conditions and enjoy long years of marriage. When we find ourselves differing in decisions it probably is a battle of the egos. But we can, with honest communication, reconcile differences. This reconciliation deepens our love for each other.

Jesus provided us that day with a description of our true selves:

> Within every human being there is a living spirit that is the truth of your being and that spirit is the child of God of you. That spirit in you is pure and holy. It knows no sin; it knows no error; it knows nothing of anything that would make you bad or wrong, or not what you should be. For that spirit is cast perfectly; absolutely perfectly, in the image and likeness of God. Around that spirit you have the personality that you yourselves have created. And that personality is the Roman soldiers around the Hebrew people, if you will . . . Because you have this holiness

within you; because you are a sacred, precious emanation of all that is you have this truth laying latent there.

Then, in his brief time with us that day, Jesus compared us to the vibration of a sounding fork. When one spirit speaks out loud, the spirit of all must respond. "Within you is the same spirit that is within me. Lying asleep, curled up in the boat of your consciousness, is the Christ." Jesus knew the power of his words; the power of his life. "I spoke a truth and it resonated throughout eternity, and it will always resonate because I spoke with the Voice of Christ. I spoke with the authority of my Father. Everything I did I did because I was told to by the God within my breast. Everything I did."

We pray and meditate and seek to know the Christ within. This generation will learn how it is done. This generation will learn to understand and accept its truth; the Christ within. This generation will find the new freedom of knowingness. To know ourselves as expressions of the Christ Light will bring us unspeakable joy and irrefutable freedom.

## Chapter 142  The Ones Who are Dead

*"Jesus said unto him, Let the dead bury their dead: but go thou and preach the kingdom of God."* (Luke 9:60)

This Bible phrase confounded me until I was fifty-one years of age. At that time I had my first psychic reading, and my father and mother both came to me, expressing through a well-known medium. My father passed into spirit when I was five years old, and my mother when I was thirty-seven. The night before the reading I wondered if my father would come to me. The first thing the medium did was bring my father! He said "I could not catch my breath". I pondered that remark, and then realized he was describing his heart attack forty-five years earlier! He also said that he was waiting for me. He said, "I want to show you around. The light is different here; the colors are different."

The first thing my mother said to me was, "You are the ones who are dead, you know." It was like the Bible phrase had come to life. This sounded wonderful, for I understood that Jesus did indeed demonstrate eternal life when he resurrected. But my complete understanding came years later, when Archangel Gabriel explained to us the story of Adam and Eve in Eden. *"And the Lord caused a deep sleep to fall upon Adam, and he slept . . ."* (Gen. 2:21) Then to his startled listeners, Gabriel said, "Nowhere in scripture does it say that Adam woke up". In effect, Gabriel reminded us, all humanity is still asleep to its own divinity.

*We* are the ones who are dead! Now I fully comprehended Jesus' words in the book of Luke. This is a profound teaching, for it strikes at the root of Christianity; even all faiths. The truth, Gabriel told to us, is that Jesus came *not to start a church* but to wake up the entire human race. What can we do with this lesson in truth by Gabriel? For starters, perhaps it would be a good idea to see ourselves not as victims but as powerful offspring of God. The Master Jesus said that everything he did we can do. (John 14:12) When was the last time anyone walked on water? I know several people who have walked on fire. They meditated and accepted the fact they could do it. And they did it. Perhaps meditation is a first step in performing miracles.

"'Rest in peace' is a blessing for the living, not the dead, because rest comes from waking, not from sleeping. Sleep is withdrawing; waking is joining. Dreams are illusions of joining, because they reflect the ego's distorted notions about what joining is. Yet the Holy Spirit, too, has use for sleep, and can use dreams on behalf of waking if you will let Him." ACIM T- 8: IX: 3:5-8

The great awakening from being dead will begin for each one of us in our own chosen time. This is true because God gave us free choice. By our free choice we are living out our own scripted and choreographed life. By our own free choice we will seek truth when we are ready to hear it; ready to know it. Then we can live from the Lord God of our Being and rise above the walking dead who seem to be alive. We can learn the truth of us: we are children of God and He will direct us. The Holy

Spirit, *when asked,* will whisper every word of guidance in our ears. Listening to Him, we shall walk the road back Home to God. Only then will we understand that Heaven, in truth, is our natural habitat.

This road back to God is not a mystery. Jesus the Christ came to demonstrate it. Two thousand years later he came to correct old errors in scripture. Please read or hear *Master Jesus, Master Jesus II and Master Jesus III* (Sacred Garden Fellowship.com). Jesus also wrote a new Bible for the New Age, Aquarius. Its title is *A Course in Miracles.* We have journeyed a very long time away from Home; but only in our consciousness. In truth we never left Home. We never left God. The journey is an inward journey. That is why it is unique. That is why it is personal. That is why it is a personal journey.

## Chapter 143   The Only Savior

When Jesus the Christ came to earth his intent was to save humanity. He said as much: *"And if any man hear my words, and believe not, I judge him not: for I came not to judge the world, but to save the world."* John 12:47 Archangel Gabriel told us - and who else would know - that only while hanging on the cross did Jesus realize he had only saved himself. He looked out over a dark scene of fear, hatred, anger, and vengeance. The only light was his radiant spirit, which mortal eyes could not behold.

Jesus came to save us. If Jesus had actually saved us from our sins, why have we not been sinless ever since? Jesus knew he was a child of God, through all his incarnations. He did not understand why we could not see our own divinity. So he came to save us from our ignorance; to shed the light of truth on the darkness we had created on earth. He came to awaken *all humanity*, not just his fellow Jews.

Early on, the founders of Christianity chose to see Jesus as the only son of God, basing that view on an error in the Bible which, originally written, stated that Jesus was the begotten son of the only God. Those first rabbis also placed Jesus on a pedestal to be worshipped. We cannot emulate what we worship. Many continue to worship and adore that idol.

Jesus saw us all as his brothers and sisters. Clearly Jesus stated, "*I have given you an example, that ye should do as I have done to you.*" John 13:15. An example is a pattern to be imitated. Jesus came to save us, his siblings, from ourselves. "*For the Son of man is come to seek and to save that which was lost.*" Luke 19:10. The desert Moses crossed represents the wilderness in which humanity got lost. How lost did we get! We forgot our birthright which is the power and love of spirit. We gave our power, over time, to the ego. The ego lives by fear. We have let the ego convince us that we do not need God. It wants us to believe that we are independent and can do all things on our own.

The Bible tells us, "*The son can do nothing of himself, but what he seeth the Father do: for what things soever he doeth, these also doeth the Son likewise.*" John 5:19

There is nothing we cannot do, when we seek to do good. We are good by nature; our ego denies our good and shouts loudly in our ears. It is the still, small Voice of God that whispers 'do good.' In our ego-oriented days we hear all the shouts of the ego readily. We think we must be busy doing something, being with someone or listening/looking at something. All these 'somethings' distract us from our inner Self; our Higher Self, our sacred Self. Only when we are still ourselves can we hear the still, small voice guiding us.

It is in the silence that we hear and learn, and *know* our truth. Patiently God awaits our awakened state. For in that awakened state we will rush to re-join God in our consciousness. He will take the last step to raise us up where we belong. Heaven is our natural habitat. We will recognize it when we arrive there. This is an immutable truth. Gabriel was asked how we would be recognized when we arrive in Heaven. He said, "They will know by the look on your face!"

We each are our own savior. Denying it will not change the truth of it. Denying it will merely postpone our awakening. To save ourselves we are given a roadmap, so to speak. The map is set before us by Jesus the

Christ. Following him, emulating him and becoming as him is the task before us. We can do it. We will do it. Then we will be saved. It is time to see Jesus as our elder brother and know we can follow him. His message was not the crucifixion, but the resurrection. His life and his message were the same: love, forgive, pray, and worship only the one God - the Holy Father of us all. In the twentieth century Jesus provided us with a new roadmap: *A Course in Miracles.*

## Chapter 144  The Pearl, The Seed, and Us

*"Again, the kingdom of heaven is like unto a merchant man, seeking goodly pearls: Who, when he had found one pearl of great price, went and sold all that he had, and bought it."* Matt. 13:45-46

Jesus did not speak of an ordinary pearl, but an exceptionally valuable one (of great price). This was a parable that everyone could relate to because fishing was one of the primary methods of employment in his time. Pearls, then as now, were easily recognized as having a high value.

It is interesting to note that the Bible does not contain the word 'oyster', yet the pearl found within it is likened to the heavenly kingdom within us. A merchant is a person who sells goods for the highest price possible; monetary gain is his primary goal in his occupation, if not his life. Because of his appetite for profit, the merchant here is aware that the one great pearl has a value exceeding all material wealth. And in his awareness he sells all his property to gain it. The time will come when we, too, will find that pearl of great price - the spiritual awareness that the Kingdom of God truly is inside of us. Matthew is the only apostle who mentions the pearl of great price.

Matt.13:31, Mark 4:31 and Luke 13:19 all noted the comparison Jesus made between the Kingdom of Heaven and a mustard seed, the smallest seed. Farming was another major occupation two thousand years ago, and probably everyone knew that the mustard seed was the smallest seed that could be planted *(least of all seeds)*. The parables still make sense to the twenty-first century mind. Something which seems as insignificant as a tiny seed is likened to the most significant part of our being. The most significant part of our being is our spirit Self; the Kingdom of Heaven within.

Why does Jesus compare our spirit with something extremely valuable and another thing which appears so tiny? The value of our spirit self - our higher Self - is of inestimable value. No one can put a price on God. No one can put a price on His Kingdom within us. As for the tiny seed, it grows and becomes a tree which provides all the birds with a roosting place; a resting place; or a place of nourishment. Unlike the pearl of great price which human eyes can behold and see the value of, the minute seed does nor even attract our attention. Then the Son of God came to tell us that no matter how valuable the great pearl is, it is of less worth than the value of the Kingdom of Heaven.

He also taught us that an insignificant little thing like a mustard seed has the potential of producing a tree of much value to the birds. This is not a puzzle. It is the truth of us, as children of God. Our spirit, unseen self, has a worth unknown, unacknowledged, and unremembered by us. Archangel Gabriel came to awaken us from the Adam-like sleep of the centuries; to wake us up to the Kingdom of Heaven *which has always resided there.* Gabriel also reminded us that birds represent our fleeting thoughts.

We are the bringers of light to the world when we honor ourselves - and others - as children of God. Too long we have imagined ourselves as a tiny, insignificant resident of earth. God's Kingdom is far vaster than this tiny planet we live on. By expanding our thinking and imagination we will be able to encompass more of the universe in which we live, move, and have our being. Gabriel spoke of 'the universes'. Our minds cannot even attain an awareness of this universe.

As we enter the Age of Aquarius some will hear or read Gabriel's lessons. We are the blessed bringers of truth. Others must be willing to listen and read. Gabriel and eleven Ascended Masters came to Earth in the late twentieth century to wake us up. The unseen alarm clock keeps ringing.

Many reject a new way of life; many refuse to hear anything new. There are none so blind as those who *will not* see; none so deaf as those who will not hear. This is the age of truth and Archangel Gabriel said he brings only truth. This the age to open our eyes and ears to the ageless truth Gabriel brought.

# Section XIX
## Koph

## Chapter 145   The Pull of Addiction

Webster's dictionary: 'addiction is a compulsive need for and use of a habit-forming substance (as heroin, nicotine or alcohol) characterized by tolerance and by well-defined physiological symptoms upon withdrawal'. Behavioral addictions have also been identified, such as OCD, gambling, and sex. Treatment is available for all of the known addictions. The keys to recovery are acceptance of the problem, a little willingness to be treated and a decision to apply one's continuing efforts. Most addictions provide an escape from the world around us. We believe we can find a better world than what we see. Removing our conscious thought from the world around us we seek and find what seems to be a solution.

The world of addiction shuts out the world around us, but the new-found world of obsession is a very lonely place. Friends, family, co-workers have all turned against us. Others join us in our obsession. We find them, and they confirm for us the 'reality' of our tiny addictive world. This small place becomes devoid of true friends, of honesty, of peace of mind, and in some cases, of moral standards. This tiny world offers only loneliness, anger, guilt, remorse and self-hatred. We deny we have a problem and defend the denial. Denial keeps us imprisoned in our little world. Others are incapable of understanding the deep and abiding need for the addictive substance; the addictive behavior. They therefore reinforce our feeling of need. There is no breaking of the destructive habit except abolishment. Abolishment must be complete and forever; it takes vigilance. The trigger for the abandonment comes in various ways. An automobile accident, an arrest, a lost marriage, a lost home, etc. may emotionally shake the addict enough to stop. That is just the beginning, for the ego will pull and pull stronger to keep the addict in bondage.

If there is anything the ego does not want it is for us to have a sense of well-being that does not require its power. We are without our own power when we submit to the addiction. The substances, the behavior now have power over us. Only yielding to another power, a strong power, a certain and eternal power, can we hope to find release from addiction's horrible grasp. Whatever name we give that power, we must value it above all else. Some people call the power God, some Creator, some Allah, some Great Spirit. Others cannot identify a name, but find a support person or support group to rely on for abstinence.

Someone sees in us a valid, viable human being who is worth saving from addiction's prison. We begin to see that the escape we sought gave us nothing of value. We begin to see the insanity of addiction. We begin to sleep better. All aspects of our lives improve. The permeating guilt from our behavior begins to loosen its grip. Some individuals revert back to the obsession. Vigilance is essential to maintain abstinence. Oftentimes this vigilance includes meeting with others and/or sharing with others, the continuing problems of life.

Addiction has been conquered. We believe that life in the real world can begin. Then we read the lessons in truth that Archangel Gabriel taught. There is a *real* world beyond this one. It is not a tiny world of exclusion, but rather the vast world of Creation; the eternal world of God. This world that is revealed to us by our eyes, ears and feelings is a temporary world. It has held us in its grip for centuries. Freedom from its grip is triggered by a thought that something better than this world is possible.

Like the Prodigal Son we came to this 'far country', Earth. This 'far country' is a place we have retreated to in our consciousness, forgetting our Source and Creator. Eventually we all leave this far country, Earth - not in 'death', but in awakening to the God-Self of us. Vigilance is not required; only acceptance of the Love of God; only the realization that *we are the love of God made manifest.*

Surrender is the key to awakening. First the addict must surrender to the Will of God and awaken to her sober self. Then surrender to the Higher Power of us all. Angels assist us all the way.

# Chapter 146  The Revolving Door of Life

The life we know on earth ends with what we call death. We bury the physical form, and loved ones grieve their absence. We are coming to know this is not the end of us. Now we celebrate a life instead of grieving the 'dead'. We have become convinced that life continues on after our body loses life. Many people have received help from angels in human form. Many people have read about or experienced near-death episodes. Many have heard about spirit entities channeling through earthlings. More and more people are accepting the idea of communication between earthlings and humans. We can deny no longer the continuity of life.

When Archangel Gabriel came to earth in the late twentieth century (1987-1999), he told us that we go on to the astral plane at 'death'. There we review our lives and we decide that the perceived harm we had done must be recompensed. So we return to balance the scales of justice. We do this over and over again. We have revolved from Earth to the Astral Plane and back so many times that we have met every person now living on planet Earth! Gabriel gave us this stunning fact. With eight or nine billion people on earth, and lifetimes of ninety or a hundred years, an easy calculation discloses the astronomical number of times we have traveled the karmic wheel.

Nothing will get us off the wheel except our awareness that we plan our own lives. The following precepts from Gabriel are the eternal truths of us all:

1. We never harmed anyone without their permission.
2. No one ever harmed us without our permission.
3. Love is the greatest power there is.
4. Jesus the man came to demonstrate the Christ Light - love.
5. Our eternal spirit, which is love, has never been harmed or altered in any way by any experiences, words or thoughts of our many lifetimes. Created from love, it is and always was, perfect and eternal.

Once we accept and understand this wisdom provided us by Gabriel and other teachers from the spirit world, we enable ourselves to see life in an enlightened way. We see Mother Earth as the beautiful, nurturing living entity that she is. We must care for her to heal her from the ravages of the centuries. We will see everyone as our spiritual siblings. We will see all humans as one huge family of God. And we will do whatever we are inspired to do in order to demonstrate the love of God. We will demonstrate love as Jesus the Christ did, and have no enemies. We will see all life as creations of One God; a God expressing growth in infinite variety of color, size and range of abilities. We will seek unity in life on Earth instead of focusing on differences.

Centuries have rolled along and we have rolled back and forth on this endless karmic ride. Gabriel came to Earth to remind us of what we already know; not to teach us anything new. Concurrently with his visits, eleven Master Teachers came to other centers of light on Earth; all with the same message: we are children of God who have forgotten our Source and birthright. God is our Source; love is our birthright. We are eternal; we are perfect in spirit.

When we finally get off the karmic wheel we will return to God. There are other realms beyond the Astral Plane. Gabriel explained that we can only know the next plane up in our evolution, so the Astral Plane is all we can know while here on earth. Remember the phrase 'seventh Heaven' and let us all be assured of Shakespeare's words: "there is more in Heaven and earth than this world dreams of."

## Chapter 147   The Rewards of Knowing

In any occupation the rewards of knowing are increased salaries, promotions, titles. With the rewards come increased responsibilities. But there are rewards for knowing ourselves, why we are here, and where are we going. There are rewards for knowing how we got here, and what life really is all about.

Such rewards; such knowledge, comes to us by revelation. Revelation comes to us directly from God. Our Creator knows all answers to all our questions. It has no questions of its own, for it always knows the truth. Archangel Gabriel imparted to his students the wisdom of the ages and answered our every question.

Gabriel told us that he came not to teach us anything new, but only to remind us of what we already know. He came not to be worshipped, not to start a new religion, nor to invite followers of his beloved channel, Reverend Penny. His students were few but dedicated. We gathered bi-monthly to hear his lessons in truth. He also gave short lectures and occasionally he offered question and answer sessions. The rewards of his presence were peace, permeating love, the sense of a holy presence. He took all questions, accepted the 'motley crew' (his own words) which constituted his student body: male and female, ages from thirty to eighty, various occupations. The common thread between us all: seekers of truth. Though we did not then identify ourselves as such.

Regardless of what we call God, He is the Creator and Author of all life. The rewards for me were many. The reward of knowing that *God is* has given me an assurance that my faith in God has not been misplaced. The reward of knowing that God is Love confirms for me that, as His child, I too am love. The reward of knowing there are not 'bad' and 'good' people is the awareness that some children of God are more aware of their spirit Self than others. People who perceive themselves to be 'bad' are simply unaware of the God light within them. Those who we perceive to be 'bad' are perceived as such because of our ignorance. We, too, are unaware of God's Love within them and us.

The reward of knowing that we all - every race, culture, color, and language - are children of God is the feeling of connection to all humanity. That true connection is keenly felt by those who have endured such tragedies as war, fire or flood and have been aided and comforted by 'others'. The reward of knowing that we are spirit beings, not mere mortals, was a truth that stunned, then excited, and then made me worship the Father more ardently than ever before.

The separation which we perceive ourselves to be is of our own making. God created us one with Him. We fall from grace only by our free choice. Grace is consciously ours as soon as we accept it as part of our divine nature. The reward of knowing life is eternal is to gain a new perspective of life on all levels and in every relationship. The reward of knowing that creation is on-going rather than a seven day event is the belief that everything we can imagine is possible to manifest.

Love is God expressed. Love has no attributes; it simply is. The reward of knowing we are all connected and we are all love in essence is feeling that connection. In feeling that known connection we find it easy to pray for and forgive all the ones who choose to behave in negative ways. They are most in need of our prayers, for they have turned away completely from their Source and essence.

The reward of knowing that we plan our lives has been, to me, a startling truth. In reviewing my life I can honestly say that the bumps in the road have taught me much, such as acceptance, forgiveness, tolerance, mercy, justice, humility. The grandeur of life is our spiritual nature, but our perspective is muddied by our ego selves. Perception is deception; knowingness is freedom. Freedom means being ourselves without concern about others, or their opinions. Freedom is expressing ourselves as children of God, knowing that only positive creativity will come into our thinking. Freedom is knowing that what we manifest benefits all of humankind.

## Chapter 148   The Sacred Space Within

*"The kingdom of God is within you."* Luke 17:21

*"But within ye are full of hypocrisy and iniquity."* Matt 23:28

How can we reconcile these two statements in scripture, given us by the first apostles of the Master Teacher, Jesus? Surely they did not preach different teachings of Jesus the Christ. Hypocrisy comes from our judgment and judgment comes from our perceptions. Now, thanks to *A Course in Miracles* we know that perception is deception. This is so because our senses all deceive us. They deceive us because they accept the physical world as our home. It is not. God created us eternal as Himself; earthly lives are temporary.

The Kingdom of God is as vast as the skies. It is more varied than we humans can imagine. Tiny examples of God's domain are the things on Earth we hold in awe: towering mountains, roaring oceans, deep mysterious canyons, and arid deserts. The weather and its variety of expressions also amaze us. This is not God's domain; it is the home of humans for a small span of life.

When God breathed us forth we knew we were His Own. His 'stamp' of spirit was in us. When we came to Earth in human form we continued to be His Own. Unseen by humans but as real as God, we live our daily lives unaware of our holiness. We live our lives as described by Matthew, thinking hypercritic ideas; behaving in iniquitous ways because we could do so. Our imagination throughout the centuries has conjured up every kind of injustice, bigotry, and hateful thoughts. Our bodies acted on them. None of these actions impinged on the sacred space within; the domain of God placed there in the Beginning.

The physical forms we call our bodies have no connection to our spirit selves. One is physical; ephemeral. The other is eternal. One is seen by mortal eyes; the other by sacred vision only. Archangel Gabriel said that the spirit Self of us never touches the earth. Our constant denial of our holiness does not diminish its existence nor cancel its truth. The existence of God is not determined by our belief or non-belief in Him. God is. God is love. God is our Creator. We are not flotsam and jetsam of a big bang eons ago. If that were so, we could not explain the synchronicity of the heavenly planets; the rhythm of the seasons. We ardently seek to know if there is something more to us; for us.

Like Thomas Didymus in the Bible, we doubt what we cannot see. Thomas would not believe that Jesus resurrected until he touched and saw Jesus' wounds. We deny everything we cannot see or touch. We are so grounded in what is unreal - physical form; physical matter - that we are unwilling to accept what we cannot discern with our five senses. This denial of truth does not alter the truth; it merely postpones our acceptance of it.

The soul's memory of our beginning calls us to return to God. We kneel in prayer; attend religious ceremonies; worship the God of our understanding. Then we wonder if He hears us. Our little faith will become a greater faith when we *know* how holy are spirit Self is. The answer is within us: a little willingness to know; an honest searching for truth; an open mind to all possibilities will open the door to unassailable truth. The truth, then, will make us free. Free to go home where we will know that we belong. Heaven is our natural habitat.

Doubters will always say there is no God, but they are not in touch with truth. Neither are we. Archangel Gabriel brought us truth. He brought the truth because, he said, we are ready to hear it. Deniers will postpone accepting it, but their denial will never alter it. The freedom that truth brings is ours but for the asking, and God is awaiting our questions. From the sacred space within we can hear and know the Will of God for us.

## Chapter 149   The Seven Servants

When the number of Jesus' disciples increased greatly, it came to their attention that some of their number should be appointed to handle the distribution of food to the rest in order that the majority could focus on teaching the Word of God. Seven were chosen: Stephen, Philip, Prochorus, Nicanor, Timon, Parmenas, and Nicolas. Most of these names have been lost to time, but Stephen stands out as a martyr in the early days of Christianity. (Acts, Ch. 6 and 7)

We might wonder how a servant of his fellow disciples could become a martyr, just in taking care of provisions, or waiting on table. If we can consider a modern experience in a restaurant, a waitress or an owner might express a profound truth that stays with us forever. A believer in Jesus Christ has a way of speaking that includes basic tenets of faith, like honesty, sincerity, kindness, compassion.

Because of his deep and abiding belief in what Jesus taught and its effect on Moses' teachings, Stephen found himself expounding in detail about all of it. He might not have been stoned to death if he stopped there. But he finished his talk with, "I see the heavens opened, and the Son of man standing on the right hand of God." That did it. No one, they believed, could see God and live. This was what the listeners considered blasphemy, and they stoned Stephen to death. As they threw the stones, Stephen "kneeled down and cried with a loud voice, Lay not this sin to their charge."

The story is even more memorable when we read that one of the witnesses to the stoning was Saul, at whose feet the witnesses laid Stephen's clothes. We know Saul of Tarsus as St. Paul today. But immediately following Stephens death, Saul "made havock of the church, entering into every house and haling men and women he committed them to prison." Perhaps it was his guilt - at allowing a fellow preacher to be stoned - that he reacted in such a way.

What do we know about the other six servants? Philip went down to Samaria to preach (Acts 8:5), the others, as explained in the *Metaphysical Bible Dictionary,* have a meaning to their names:

Prochorus - joy; harmony; leader of the dance
Nicanor - steadfastness of victory
Timon - honorable, sound
Parmenas - enduring, permanent
Nicolas - conqueror of the people

There is much to learn from this story. Courage to speak our minds is one lesson. We must learn to speak truth instead of saying what is acceptable to our peers. Stephen spoke of the church's history for all to hear. He gave a synopsis of Christianity's beginnings. That might have stirred the crowd. But to relate to his listeners a supernatural experience was too much for them to accept; it was anathema.

Today we seem to be more tolerant of another's beliefs, as well as their openness in speaking it. Recently I told my writers' group that for twelve years I was blessed to hear lessons in truth from Archangel Gabriel as he channeled through a devout believer. Some of the listeners are born again Christians and probably thought I had lost my mind - but they did not stone me!

The other six servants apparently lived out their lives and died a natural death. Only Stephen saw fit to speak out what he knew to a group of people in the street. This does not mean the other six servants were not true Disciples of Christ. We all are teaches by the way we are, not just by the words we speak. What we are means the way we treat others, the way we treat ourselves, the way we deal with life and its experiences.

If we can relate to the crowd's reaction then we might stone someone we hate - if it were possible to do so. Before the hatred would come judgment, and we know scripture says, Judge not. Tolerance is another lesson to be learned. Obviously those who heard Stephen could not tolerate the idea that he could see spirit, much less describe the experience. Few people today who have seen spirit tell about it to others, and only when the 'others' are known to accept the possibility.

Open-mindedness is a lesson Stephen's listeners could learn. If we close our minds to new ideas we are doomed to repeat the past - over and over again. Can we honestly look at our past and say it cannot be improved upon? We can improve on the past only if we open our minds to the new. Gabriel wondered at one time why we *number* our wars. He certainly had a point. Do we want to kill each other to infinity?

Reading this story in the book of Acts in the New Testament might bring to the reader's mind more lessons. Certainly we needed the new teachings of Jesus or we would still be living 'an eye for an eye'. Mahatma Gandhi said that if we all live by the rule of an eye for an eye, we shall all become blind. We are blind indeed if we are close-minded.

# Chapter 150  The Spirit of Man

*"The burden of the word of the Lord for Israel, saith the Lord, which stretcheth forth the heavens, and layeth the foundation of the earth, and formeth the spirit of man within him."* Zech. 12:1

These words are similar to the words of God, when he asked Job, *"Where wast thou when I laid the foundations of the earth . . . who laid the measures thereof . . . who hath stretched the line upon it . . . whereupon are the foundations thereof fastened . . . who laid the cornerstone thereof?"* Job 38:4-6

Believers accept that a mighty Creator brought forth this planet Earth. Here the prophet is saying that the same Creator brought forth *the spirit of man within him.* We produce, through copulation, a human entity, and see ourselves as our own creations. That human entity is our physical form. The spirit of us is invisible to the human eye. This does not mean it does not exist. Our spirit takes its residence within us at birth, but our spirit is eternal and contained our body every lifetime. Some may call it our conscience; others something else. It is the 'something' in us that seeks to do good, to forgive, to love.

Jesus resurrection was planned to prove to humanity that life is eternal. Jesus appeared to the apostles in physical form to show Thomas, the doubter, that Jesus had in fact resurrected. Jesus, and all humanity, has a physical and a spirit form. Jesus could transform the molecular structure of his body, and did so, in the cave, before his resurrection. When he ascended he took his physical form with him. He knew that he had lived his last lifetime on earth. He had demonstrated to us that life is eternal. We shall all ascend when we are ready.

Archangel Gabriel made this truth clear. He said we are not ready yet to resurrect, because most of us do not like our bodies; and why would we want to take with us a body that we disliked? Our spirit Self is the eternal essence of our Being. God is Creator of our spirit. Adam forgot his Source and fell asleep to it. Scripture does not reveal an awakening of Adam. It does not reveal it because it has not as yet occurred. Humanity, represented by Adam, remains asleep to its Source, and the spirit which God placed within us.

Gabriel also made it clear to his listeners that Jesus came not to start a new religion - he was raised a Jew - but to bring the truth to all humanity that we are, every one of us, God's children. *"There is neither Jew nor Greek, there is neither bond nor free, there is neither male nor female; for ye are all one in Christ Jesus."* Gal. 3:28

When we wake up to the spirit Self of us, then the awakening is ours. Too long have we pretended we are merely human. Too long have we been denying our sacred center. Too long have we denied the fatherhood of God; the brotherhood of man. Angels are making themselves known like never before. They come to remind us of the glorious world of spirit, the domain of eternal life. This is a new age. It is the Age of Aquarius. It is, Gabriel said, the Age of Truth.

The truth that Gabriel imparted to us is the truth that will make us free. Free to be and free to do all that our spirit is capable of doing. "When spirit's original state of direct communication is reached, neither the body nor the miracle serves any purpose." ACIM 365: V: 2

The future of humanity lies in our hands. It lies in our willingness to make only good choices. We know what choices are good, but many times we have chosen poorly, like a defiant child. As we mature we become compassionate and understanding. Maturity comes when we disavow the ego and its power over us. We gave it the power and so we can take it back. It is our choice to retake our power and live as God's Own.

## Chapter 151  The Spiritual Race

We readily define the population of planet Earth as the human race. We have occupied the earth for many centuries. There are records of 'early man' in archeological digs. The more digs we engage in the older we prove the human race to be. For a very long time we moved about the planet on foot, then horses, then wheeled vehicles. Now we travel extensively all over the globe with various methods of transportation.

Because we humans are a curious lot, our curiosity has taken us into space. Early planes, then rockets and now we boast of walking on the moon. Our next goal is a journey to Mars. It seems there must be a reason for this insatiable curiosity. Perhaps we are constantly searching for our own origin, as though we have a source not yet identified. Many scientists accept the theory of evolution, pointing to the similarities of the physical structure of apes and humans. Darwin himself said there is a 'missing link'; a link in which the transition from ape to human can be identified. Now we know there is no missing link. We did not evolve from apes.

Archangel Gabriel came to explain our true Source. He is the Announcer of the Ages. This is the inception of the Age of Aquarius. Gabriel spoke through a dedicated channel to awaken us to our origin - not the physical form but the eternal spirit Self of us. Pisces was the last age; the age of the fish. Jesus the Christ is still identified with the beginning of that age. When Jesus came it was the beginning of Pisces; it was a new age then. Jesus brought to earth a startling new idea. Instead of 'an eye for an eye', he taught love and forgiveness of our neighbors. Gabriel came to announce that new age. He told Mary that she would birth Jesus; Elizabeth that she would birth John, who became the Baptist. In this new age, Gabriel brings a startling new idea; the truth of us.

These ages are segments of a larger zodiac than our calendar year. The larger zodiac is the revolution of our universe around a Central Sun. This revolution encompasses a journey of 26,000 years. Each age takes about 2,100 years. Before our feeble beginnings of writing on cave walls and cuneiform, there are few human records except the bones and buildings archeologists find. From a broader perspective, a far more objective view, Gabriel knows our history as a race of spiritual beings. Gabriel came to earth to explain our true origin and how to awaken to it. He said we are ready to hear and know it now.

As co-creators with God we created this world on which to live. Then we created the beasts. We were co-creators because God breathed us forth from Himself, Spirit. The Spirit that is God is the same spirit that is in us all. That is why we are children of God. Earthly creators leave their imprint on all their works; God's imprint is in the entire human race, as The Kingdom of God. God gave us free choice.

We are responsible for all our choices. Our spiritual origin is God's Creation. As children of God we have free choice. We also have imagination and abstract thought. With this free choice we decide our every lifetime. We choose what lessons we need to learn 'the next time around' and seek others on the other side to assist us. We are not a race of humans groping in a world of violence to become more. We are reaching to become more because, at our spirit level we *know we are more.* We know we are more because our soul remembers our beginning. Originally we knew and loved each other; we knew God loved us with unconditional love. We knew then that we were all children of God, with the love and power of God within us. We still are children of God, but have left the conscious memory of it in the mists of earthly history.

Human history goes back much further than our writings. The reader is encouraged to read/hear the truth lessons brought here by Archangel Gabriel. In this Age of Aquarius, the spiritual age as Gabriel called it, we are taught the truth so we can awaken to it. We are a spiritual race of children of God. Now we are ready to hear this truth. Now we are ready to wake up and live our truth.

Only a few are ready now, but there will come a time when all are ready. Gabriel did not come to earth alone. He had many angels with him as helpers. Also, around the globe eleven Master Teachers came also, to various locations on earth - to teach the same lessons. The locations were where there was a belief in communication between Heaven and earth. The centers are known by angels as centers of light. Orthodox religions deny such communication. Perhaps that is why more and more people believe in mediums and psychics. When Gabriel was asked an earthly question he reminded us that we have psychics and mediums for that. He brought us the wisdom of the ages; he told us so many things that we could not otherwise know. He knows our spirit Selves, and saw us in his seminars as 'beams of light', not human forms.


## Chapter 152   The Theater of Life

The stage of life seems eternal, but at some point in Earth's time we shall end this stage play ---- when *we* decide to finalize it. The great playwright Shakespeare spoke of this fantasy well, in his insightful words:

"Life's but a walking shadow, a poor player,
That struts and frets his hour upon the stage,
And then is heard no more; it is a tale
Told by an idiot, full of sound and fury
Signifying nothing." Macbeth v. iii, 16


The stage is Earth. We have selected the actors and written the scenario. We are producer, choreographer, and director. We are in total charge of our lives, whether we think so or not. We fret (worry) our lives away or strut in grandiose ways. Fear is the cause of both behaviors. When we 'die' our loved ones remember us until they also pass on, and we are known no more on Earth, but God recognizes our eternal spirit. It is insane to believe that we created ourselves. The sound and fury is our daily experience. All kinds of sounds fill our days. Fury is expressed by domestic violence, road rage, border disputes, and wars. In the end they all mean nothing, for all we see and hear shall end, also. Then only peace and love will continue forever. Most people hate silence. It is only in silence that we can listen to the Voice of God whispering to us.

The perception that creates our suffering is our strong belief in guilt, shame and retribution. The perception was spawned in our ego eons ago; too long ago for us to remember. We took it upon ourselves to think, and then believe, that we created ourselves, since we are physical, and all our senses confirm it, and our mother birthed us. Yet, in truth we are so much more. The purpose of our physical form is merely communication; its function is to move our eternal Self from one place to another.

Prior to an ego, God created us in His Image. God is Love, and from His Love He breathed us forth, and gave us free will. This Creation occurred so long ago that it is not in our conscious memory. It can be found in mythology, and it is in our soul's memory. God's Creation of all his children was in what we call the 'beginning', though God has no beginning or ending. We are all the only begotten sons of God, and God only begets Love. This is such a difficult concept only because for centuries; for many lifetimes, we have focused on the belief that we are physical in form and that is all we can see with mortal eyes.

Our personality has no form; we only identify it by its expression. Other 'parts' of us (astral, mental, and *spiritual*) are also out of our eyesight's range: our subtle bodies (The only real, eternal one is our spirit, described by Jesus: T*he kingdom of God is within.* Luke 10:9. In recent years angels and Master Teachers have come to earth - in form of humans or in a voice channeled through a human, as Archangel Gabriel channeled through Reverend Penny Donovan. As a devoted and highly evolved teacher of God, she brought us Gabriel's lessons, from 1987-1999. Jesus the Christ also channeled through beloved Penny, from 1995-1999.

Gabriel told us that concurrent with his visits, eleven Master Teachers came to 'centers of light' around the Earth. They did not come to threaten us. They did not come to scold us. They did not come to injure us in any way. They came to awaken us to our holy Source. We have become victims of a 'fate' we cannot define; victims of others; victims of nature's fury. The 'victim' roles we play are by our own design. We perceive that we have wounded another in life, and so we come back to 'suffer at his hand' to balance the scales. The scales themselves are our own. *God's Justice warrants gratitude, not fear* ACIM 25: IX: 2:3

These teachers from God have brought us the truth of our being. We are God's own, Love in essence and eternal in existence. 2,000 years ago Jesus the man came forth upon the Earth to teach us that we all are like him, and in him was - and is forever - the Light of Christ. Christ is the

Light of God and is manifest in all His children. We see it not with mortal eyes simply because *the natural man receiveth not the things of the spirit of God: . . . because they are spiritually discerned* I Cor. 2:14

.Jesus' intent was indeed to save the world, as noted in scripture. He always knew - through all his incarnations - that he was a Son of God. He could not understand why we did not see ourselves the same way. So he came to save us from ourselves, to awaken us to our own divinity. Archangel Gabriel told us - and who else could know this - that only on the cross did Jesus realize that he saved only himself. Each of us must awaken to our God-given divinity when we are ready to do so. Now, angels and other heavenly beings are coming to Earth to awaken us to our own holiness. This is not blasphemy. It is blasphemy to believe we created ourselves, thus turning our back on God. God's intent when He said to 'multiply' meant to increase our thoughts in using our creative ability.

We *have the right to all the universe; to perfect peace, to complete deliverance from all effects of sin, and to the life eternal, joyous and complete in every way, as God appointed for His holy Son.* ACIM T 25:.VIII:14: 1

# Section XX
Resh

## Chapter 153  The Trap of Mass Consciousness

It seems that humanity has become obsessed with pleasing others. We dress to please another person; we behave in 'acceptable' ways in society. We want so much to be 'accepted' by our peers, especially when young. When we fall in love we desire to be accepted by the family of our beloved one. In the workplace, the gym, the restaurant, we are constantly aware of our language, our behavior, our tone of voice. We want all these 'strangers' to accept us. We have become trapped in this mindset.

The famous individuals became famous because they were different in some way. They dared to write, or search, or fly, or swim. In this chosen adventure they do not look 'good', whatever that means. Sweating in public is not 'becoming', but the tennis player who sweats profusely is praised for her/his effort of athletic ability. The ironworker, walking on high steel, is admired for his agility, but he must not walk into an upscale restaurant to dine. The downhill skier is seen as a talented athlete, but on the street there are other criteria for his clothing.

Famous people become famous by doing something or thinking something that no one else has ever done. They step outside the 'accepted' rules of behavior to walk their unique path. If they spend too much time in their chosen effort, others wonder what is 'wrong' with them. An obsession with a sport, a scientific discovery, or a new invention is not always seen as 'productive' until the results are in; until the effort has 'paid off' with worldly recognition. In God's eyes we are all holy, talented, beautiful, artistic and worthy to be His. We each have a talent. So few seek to know it and express it. Some people have a variety of talents. What we have learned in our past incarnations we brought with us to this one. The communication routes we now enjoy enable us to learn without traveling; without attending classes; without professors.

The time we take to learn something new is dependent upon our talent, willingness and the time we assign to it.

When Archangel Gabriel spoke of future education, he said what we now take twelve years to learn we will someday learn in two years. Education itself is not our most important venture, nor our primary goal. Our goal in this life is to discover who we are; what we are. We are revealed to ourselves when we express ourselves. We express ourselves best when we identify our 'hidden' talents and bring them to action.

Besides all the books we read and lectures we hear, we must be aware that our guides on the other side of the veil are happy to help us. They cannot teach us what we have no background in. They help us by bringing other people to help us. Our personal angels are one step ahead of us as soon as we acknowledge their existence. We must always thank angels who help us, and they always help us when asked. Sometimes angels take human form briefly to help us - as mechanics, nurses, comforters, etc. Artists and writers often say the painting, the book, came from outside them. This author now confirms my works are inspired. The words are my own vocabulary, but there comes an intuitive higher idea that needs to be presented in print. Angels know it. I listen to them and write.

Before the Industrial Age there were many 'cottage' industries, businesses begun and maintained in a home workshop. Individual expression was common. Today an unknown business in an unknown location mass produces much of what we buy. Few stores remain from the cottage industry. Bakeries are one example; meat markets another. A privately owned hat shop used to be seen, but now fewer people wear hats. Most products, like clothing, toys, etc. are mass produced. Young people today are inventors, creators, artist, and builders. There is a new tendency to self-express. These abilities must be encouraged. Our talents lie dormant until we find and express them. Now is the time to do it; now we can express our unique abilities. We can do this at any age, any time.

# Chapter 154   The Unpalatable Truth

When we are very young we learn to read and all our lives we remember how to read. When we are very young we learn to write, and as long as we live we have this ability. When we are very young we are taught rote prayers and religious phrases that stay with us for a lifetime. The reading and writing seem innocuous enough - after all, we need these talents to survive in the modern world. We constantly use our reading and writing skills thus maintaining our ability. We are strongly encouraged by church leaders to continue using rote prayers and phrases. This habit will insure a happy life and, we are told, our closeness to God.

When someone - even an archangel - comes along with a new message we shrink in disbelief, deny in loud voices or discount the messenger; or all of the above. The new message is unpalatable and most people will not accept it. Unpalatable means distasteful, unpleasant, disagreeable. The old ways are so ingrained we cling to them like a magnet. Only an exerted effort will pull us away from our ancestral ways. When Archangel Gabriel came he told us not to 'swallow whole' his teachings but to put them to use in our daily lives and verify their truth.

There is a saying, 'Don't confuse me with facts; my mind is made up.' If the truth will set us free, as noted in John 8:32, why are we so willing to deny it? We deny it because it does not fit with our past learning, our past teachers or our past experience. Our past learning always came from books, teachers, or experience. It never came to us from an archangel channeling through a woman. Our past teachers always came in flesh; not spirit form. Our experiences were personal in nature and unique to each of us.

Only in the Bible do we read of God speaking to prophets and ordinary *men*. But that was a special time, some say, and today we do not need any further instruction. If that was such a special time, we might wonder why the teachings do not continue to guide us in a holy direction. We might wonder why we read about the Crusades, the Witches Hammer, and the constant wars that plague the earth. Today channeling as such is considered evil by some; impossible by others. I guess you had to be there, when Gabriel patiently, calmly, constantly (for 12 years) explained our reason for being on earth, our journey back Home, and how to travel it.

Our past experiences have not been couched in the belief that communication between the spirit world of God and earthlings is possible. This is because religionists quote some parts of scripture to support their belief, but fail to recognize the phrases that support spirit communication, such as these:

*Try the spirits* (I John 4:1)

*I will pray with the spirit. I will sing with the spirit.* (I Cor. 14:15)

*Spiritual gift of prophecy.* (I Cor.12:10)

*To another discerning of spirits.* (I Cor. 12:10)

It was just in the late nineteenth century that in England and America entities came to show us such communication is possible. Eternal truth must come from God's realm of spirit. An archangel has brought it. Gabriel said that on our spirit level we know we are holy in essence. Believing this, why can we not accept contact, in some way, with the plane from which we came?

Some of Gabriel's lessons were comforting, such as we are children of God. Yet, Gabriel said, we have many fears and our greatest fear is that *we are the children of God.* One of the most discomfiting lessons was the fact that we plan our lives and every experience in them. This was too unpleasant to hear; too disagreeable to accept! Until Gabriel reminded us that God gave us free will, and anything we choose to experience will come into our lives. Couple this with the common phrase, 'What goes around comes around,' and we begin to understand. We can blame God or humans or circumstances for our plights, but we are the responsible ones.

There were a few people who came to hear Gabriel's lessons in truth, then turned away because they did not agree with him! The unpalatable truth that Gabriel brought will be unaccepted to many, for years to come, but inevitably each person will finally acknowledge the truth and begin to live it. All the planning of the entire earth population has brought us to today's world of angst and destruction. All of us must take responsibility for it. We must accept the wisdom of the ages Gabriel taught. When we do, we will live by it, and we will come to know the wisdom of 'the truth will make you free.'

## Chapter 155  The Upward Steps

When we find ourselves perceiving life as something greater than appearance and accomplishment, miraculously teachers come into our lives, friends who support us appear, and books of instruction find their way to us. We have stepped upon a spiritual path. The word 'spiritual' is from 'spirit'. God is spirit. The spirit world of God now informs our thoughts and directs our actions.

We know our self-directed thoughts do not answer all our questions. Inspiration takes over. The inspired artist loves her task. Inspiration comes day or night, winter or summer. It never fails. The word 'inspiration' comes from 'inspire', which means to breathe in. We take in thoughts and then act on them. Writers, sculptures, painters all receive such inspiration. And in turn their works inspire us.

To access this infinite wisdom of God there are steps in life we have taken or are striving to hone. The first step is trust. It is first because it is foundational. Trust in God must supersede trust in our ego. When we trust ourselves as children of God we are aware that only in prayer (talking to God) and meditation (listening to God) can we establish a life style of complete trust. We must seek help from the Holy Spirit, one of the Holy Trinity of God. The Holy Spirit never leads us astray; never. But we must ask.

Honesty, which may or may not have been part of daily living, now becomes an essential ingredient of our character. Not the rigid honesty which hurts others, but a sincere honesty combined with compassion. Too often we have excused a dishonest act with, 'everybody does it'. It is this herd instinct, the mass consciousness that is relinquished when we seek a path of honesty.

If we are totally honest on our new path we will admit we do not know everything and we become open-minded to new ideas. Our brain *processes* thought; it does not think. Ideas come from spirit; our motive determines the source. There are spirit entities who seek negative outcomes. Some call in Black Magic. We must always and ever ask for positive ideas, from positive entities, by praying 'May only good spirits come to me'. We share our thoughts with others, listen to theirs and conclude the ideas that appeal to our reasoning. Open-mindedness is vital to our growth. A closed mind is detrimental to one's self and one's life.

Tolerance does not mean to 'put up with' but rather to understand the person or situation. When we judge we are expressing a lack of trust. Judgment destroys honesty; shatters trust. Gentleness is often seen as weakness, yet the opposite of gentle is harmful, and on the steps of progress, harming has no place. Gentleness has its own strength. The confident person finds gentleness an easy trait. Jesus demonstrated gentleness as well as all these traits.

Joy blooms from the buds of gentleness. Joy is contagious, thank God. Joy differs from happiness, which is short-lived. We have happy moments, but joy is a constant in our lives when we are trusting, honest, and gentle.

Defenselessness does not come easy. 'Defense mechanisms' are accepted options from a psychological viewpoint. But we need to ask ourselves what we are defending ourselves against. Defenses lead to dissension. On a spiritual path defenses are not needed simply because all our trust lies in God, and He can never fail. No one can ever harm us without our permission; God would not allow it. Safety, peace, and joy are the benefits derived from faith in a higher power.

Generosity is seen by some people as 'giving the shirt off your back'; doing without so others may have. When we have eight apples and give away three we have five left. That is simple arithmetic. It is also worldly thinking. Spiritual thinking says giving and receiving are the same. Everything we give is a gift to us in a spiritual sense. We like to list our wants and needs, but they all imply lack. As God's children we have no lack, for what we are and what we have are the same. Innately we have all the attributes of God - love, peace, joy, eternalness and truth. Our 'needs and wants' are only stuff. Sharing what we have of God's gifts can only lead to the spiritual growth of all.

Patience, so foreign to our thinking, is another necessary step of learning on our spiritual path. Instant gratifications, fast foods, faster cars, all satisfy our worldly desires. True desire truly seen brings lasting joy. 'Desire' breaks down to 'de' (from) 'sire' (the Father). When we know that all is well and a positive outcome is sure, we can patiently wait for its arrival. In retrospect we can see and understand that what appeared to be disastrous brought deeper awareness of God's love for us. We establish in our minds an erroneous time schedule, but God has no clock. And being aware of all related circumstances, He knows the right time for the right outcome for all concerned.

Faithfulness to all other steps is the crowning feat of our spiritual path. All characteristics here described require a steadfast, constant, complete faithfulness. Life - not as we know it - but as we are able to *become* depends on our faithfulness to these attributes. We can only prove it to ourselves by living them. We can only learn to live by them with the help of the Holy Spirit. Holy help is ours for the asking.

## Chapter 156   The Voice in the Wilderness

Isaiah predicted the coming of Jesus the Christ, which occurred several centuries later (Is. 9:6). He also prophesied the coming of John the Baptist: *"The voice of him that crieth in the wilderness, Prepare ye the way of the Lord, make straight in the desert a highway for our God."* (Is. 40:3).

When Archangel Gabriel taught us he said the wilderness is where humanity is now. We wander in the desert of unknowing seeking a Promised Land which we cannot define but pray is awaiting us. Jesus came to show us a way, but we misinterpreted his mission. We placed him on a pedestal to be worshipped but never emulated.

His mission was love and forgiveness. We claim to be Christians on one or two days a week, then pass judgment on our brothers and sisters the remaining days. We fall on our knees to adore God then entertain vengeful thoughts against an 'enemy'. We insist we want a world of peace, then war with others and within ourselves.

Two thousand years after his resurrection, Jesus came to a small group of seekers in New York State, to 'straighten out the crooked places' in scripture. He was misquoted when he said, *"Think not that I am come to send peace on earth: I came not to send peace but a sword."* (Matt. 10:34). He was a man of peace and had no use for a sword; a weapon of war.

Gabriel was asked why, in John 18:10, the apostle Peter had a sword? Gabriel answered, "He did not wear a sword; the sword was drawn from one of the Roman guards". Jesus was asked at one time during his visitations if he would tell us what parts of the Bible are as originally written, and his response was, 'That would take about three minutes." We were stunned.

Jesus explained that all the original writings of the Bible regarding reincarnation were purged from the manuscripts. Also deleted were all references to the many women who were among his followers, as he travelled and preached. Jesus told us that Mary Magdalene was never a whore; that she was wealthy in her own right, having inherited wealth. Jesus asked her if she would travel with him and his followers to help find lodgings for them enroute. She agreed, if he would accept her as a student. He did. Jesus told us the truth of the story about the planned stoning of a whore, in John 8:3-8. He said that when he *'stooped down and with his finger wrote on the ground'* he was writing the date of the last time each accuser had been with the woman. Of course, they dropped their stones and walked away.

343

The story of Daniel in the lion's den was clarified by Gabriel: the angels put such an odor around Daniel that the lions pulled back, uninterested in eating such a meal!

I believe the two most egregious errors of scripture are these:

1. Jesus, only begotten son of God originally was written, Jesus, begotten son of the only God.
2. Jesus did not suffer on the cross because he held himself in his Spirit body. Today we would say he had an 'out of body' experience.

The Bible is a great book to study and to live by, but we must be willing to accept the original truth it represents. Literary accuracy did not exist in Jesus' time. The scribes wrote what they were told to write by the early church fathers. And the early church fathers decided to write 'what was acceptable' to the people.

Now is the time for only truth to be acceptable, so that we may live by it. Only by knowing and living our truth will we leave the wilderness of our ignorance and return to our natural habitat, Heaven.

## Chapter 157   The Voice of Strangers

*And a stranger will they not follow, but will flee from him: for they know not the voice of strangers.* John 10:9

Jesus was speaking of sheep refusing to follow a stranger because his voice was strange to them. Sheep were common in Jesus' time and he often spoke of them. Everyone could understand his talk of sheep. Sheep followed their shepherd. They each knew the voice of their master. If there was a large herd of several owners, each shepherd would call out and only his own sheep would respond. Others would flee from the voice. Many times Jesus spoke of sheep. He likened men to sheep. When he told Peter, "Feed my sheep," ((John 21:16) he did not mean Peter's sheep. Peter was not a shepherd but an apostle. He meant that Peter should feed the followers of The Master Teacher, Jesus. He meant that Peter should feed them with the spiritual truths which Jesus taught.

For all their willingness to be followers, sheep do know one voice from another. They follow unerringly their master's voice. It is a learned obedience. It is a taught obedience. When Jesus likened men to sheep he did not mean we were dumb (lacking words) animals; he meant we follow dumbly another's voice without reasoning. He desired that Peter feed (teach) them the lessons Jesus had taught his disciples. He chose twelve men to carry on his lessons of forgiveness, non-judgment and truth to the multitudes so future generations could learn them.

Why did he choose only men? Women were, for the most part, considered chattels. A few stand out in scripture because of their great faith, wealth or daring. Women's opinions were not considered important. They were considered to be totally dependent on men. Because of this, women were never considered teachers and therefore would not be listened to. At one time Archangel Gabriel was asked why a woman did not come to teach us instead of Jesus. Gabriel explained that at that time a woman would not have been listened to or taken seriously.

Jesus knew from infancy what his life would be. He performed miracles as a child (see *Apocrypha*, Infancy chapters)). He could have preached at ten years of age, or fifteen or twenty, but in those days a man was not considered mature until he reached the age of thirty. Thus, when he was thirty, Jesus went to the Jordan River, to be baptized by John and begin his ministry. When Jesus called his twelve disciples they all responded for they knew he was their shepherd; their master; their teacher. They knew his voice and their mission because prior to their birth they all agreed to be his followers, as Gabriel explained. Of course they did not recall this pre-birth decision any more than we recall our pre-birth plans for our own lives.

In our hearts we know the difference between right and wrong because of our innate divinity. But when we respond to a stranger's voice it is our ego that reacts instantly. Our ego thinks that fear, excitement, doing 'bad' things and racing down a road of destruction are all good for us. They are only good for the ego, and its survival. It is easy to listen to the ego because when we do it takes our attention away from our positive goals. This is true because we think we are sinners; are born in sin; are not worth paying attention to.

When we are raised to listen to the still, small Voice for God, we learn to flee from what a 'stranger' tells us. We identify him as a stranger because his voice is contrary to everything we have learned. This is not about learning a man-made religion. It is about trusting the inner Voice of Truth which guides us unfailingly up a road of honesty, justice, mercy and peace. It is The Holy Spirit whispering in our ear. We may learn about it through religion, honest and God-loving parents, or early in life through a teacher in our formal education. Or a neighbor; or a stranger who tells us eternal truths and our heart sings back. Sometimes we learn it sitting in a prison cell. Whenever we hear it we will respond because we recognize our Master's voice. Our soul wants to follow it. Our soul is the memory bank of all our incarnations. It also holds the memory of our beginning; our original Home. Our soul longs to return Home.

## Chapter 158 The Wealth of Life

We spend a lifetime of activity to 'make a living'. Then we retire to enjoy the benefits of that working life. So many of us live a long span of years and yet never learn the true wealth of life. When a person passes into spirit at a young age, s/he has not spent enough time here to appreciate the true wealth of life we do not see. (Maybe they learned this in a previous lifetime.) This is because it seems to take much time and many experiences in order to be appreciative of the true wealth.

Others, though they live long and prosper, fail to comprehend the wealth of life is far more precious than accumulating earthly wealth. The gratitude might begin with a special relationship, a new experience of ownership, like owning a first home. If not before that, certainly beholding one's own first child evokes a deep and profound love of life. Love of life! That is the wealth we desire. Or is it? Perhaps it is more, because so many events can distract us from our love of life: sickness, accidents, divorce, estrangement take our attention away from loving life and point our attention instead toward anger at life, or at self, or at God.

When maturity sets in we understand there is more to life than our tiny world. As our horizon expands we see that a vast number of human beings people the Earth. We begin to understand we all have some things in common. We all bleed red blood; we all have feelings of joy and remorse; we all laugh and cry; we all cherish family and friends; we all want to survive - and more than that - we all want to be recognized as having some value. There is not a Spanish laugh and a French tear; there is not an African hug and an English embrace. There is not an American birth and a German labor prior to birth.

Children are precious indeed to all people. They are part of our true wealth. The true wealth which does not go off to school or marry and leave home is the wealth of God within. We do not usually 'discover' this wealth until we reach our later years, or have a traumatic experience which takes us there. Sometimes a friend will suggest we go within by meditating. We balk at the idea at first. We wonder 'what will I find there'?

If we read the Bible we will see that Jesus and many others meditated. Maybe there is something to it. The main problem with starting to meditate, I think, is the idea that we will not know what is happening in our world. I believe that is why kids don't like to nap, or go to bed ahead of us. *They might miss something.* Also, we are so entrenched in the idea that we should be busy doing something that to be still for several minutes is non-productive and wasteful.

What is within, and what we find there, is the Kingdom of God. See Luke 17:21. Hinduism also states, "God abides hidden in the hearts of all." Even though no surgeon ever saw it there, the Kingdom is there, whether we believe it or not. The sun rises not; it is constant. It seems to rise depending on where we stand on Earth. God is, and is constant. He comes into our *awareness* in meditation, but we do not invent Him. He does not rise and set, nor does He ever leave us. God need not remain hidden. Knowing He is within, we ought to seek Him within. This can only be done in silence and stillness; the silence of our surroundings and the stillness of our minds. "Do not search in distant skies for God. In man's own heart is He found." Shintoism

Christianity does not have an edge on the idea of the Kingdom of God within. All major religions refer to this truth. Confucianism states:

"What the undeveloped man seeks is outside;
what the advanced man seeks is within himself."

The true wealth of knowing that God is within, coupled with the *feeling* of His presence there, is what we can seek. Only when peace of mind in every mind and peace of soul in every soul is found will humanity experience a universal peace on Earth.

"If you think the Law is outside yourself, you are
embracing not the absolute Law but some
inferior law." Buddhism

Jesus asked the people what they went into the wilderness to see. They were seeking John the Baptist because he lived like a hermit. Jesus told the people that John was much more than a prophet, *This is he, of whom it is written, Behold, I send a messenger before thy face, which shall prepare thy way before thee.* Luke 7:24

Sikhism contains the following:
"Why wilt thou go into the jungles? What do you hope to find there? Even as the scent dwells within the flower, so God within thine own heart ever abides. Seek Him with earnestness and find Him there."

Language, culture, custom and color all lose their significance in the face of this truth: The Kingdom of God is within. Finding it is an individual discovery. It is the greatest wealth attainable by humans. It will light our path of salvation and take us into our union with God.

# Chapter 159   The Willingness to Succeed

In order to succeed we need a little willingness. The success I mean is not the success the world perceives. The worldly perspective of success is based on abundance of monetary wealth and material things. This success is temporary and cannot be retained upon our demise. When we pass over to the other side would God ask what our net worth was while on Earth? No, 'You can't take it with you'. True success is a lasting goal. True success is success as a child of God, a sacred offspring. It is a moral success. True success is meeting the challenges we have planned and rising above them. It is overcoming every obstacle we placed in our path in this lifetime.

When we pass over to the other side we have the opportunity to review our lives and our response to every experience. As we go down the list of experiences we chose and the lesson we hoped to learn, we can check off our 'successes' and 'failures'. Hopefully, we can see that we did learn patience in the face of those things we could not control; that we forgave the ones who wounded our bodies or our feelings. Jesus' patience was tried when he saw the holy temple used as a market place. But the patience he showed when beaten and crowned with thorns is unfathomable. Did he forgive those who persecuted him? Yes, because he understood why they did it. They followed military orders. They did not know that humans cannot kill the spirit of a man. He asked God to forgive them for their ignorance *("they know not what they do.")*

Archangel Gabriel told us that Jesus the man did not suffer from his wounds or the crucifixion. In the Garden of Gethsemane, when he said, *"Thy will, not mine be done."* he immediately became his spirit Self which feels no physical pain. This is not difficult for us to accept, when ordinary people today have 'out of body' experiences. In biblical times, also, we find this experience. See II Cor. 12:2

When we arrive on the other side all seeming wounds are forgiven. It is so because no one ever wounded us without our permission. This truth becomes evident in Heaven.  What does all this have to do with true success?  Our journey away from God (our greatest error perception, for such is impossible) has brought us here. And here is our starting point to return *in our consciousness* to the at-one-ment with our Creator. That at-one-ment was our starting point. In our erroneous belief that we are separate from God, we engaged in multiple examples of not-good thinking and behavior.

Now is the time to wake up to our errors and to correct them, one by one. We can list them. Or we can ask our Guardian Angel to help us align our will with the Will of God. We are the Will of God. God wills us to return home. Sometimes we think we heard that ancient call. We must be willing to set our feet upon this wondrous adventure of return. True success cannot fail. True success is as certain as God Himself. A little willingness on our part is all that is required.

Forgiveness is the first lesson to learn. We planned this life and asked others to participate in a relationship which required forgiveness. In truth, therefore, there is nothing *to forgive*. Forgiveness is not believing that the hurt was real and pretending it was not. Forgiveness is not complete unless we also forget. Jesus the Christ said to forgive seventy times seven. The sum is 490. Did he mean we should keep a tally, or did he mean endlessly? We do not benefit from our grudges; our ego does. Our resentments hurt no one but us.

Forgiveness costs nothing, except a wounded ego. And our ego is the perpetrator of all our error perceptions. We are children of God and do not require an ego to protect or control us. Living with the knowingness that we are sacred, now is the time to acknowledge, honor and express that sacredness. True success may simply be our total awareness of our Christ Self, and the Christ Self of everyone else.


## Chapter 160  Things and Life

We pick a blade of grass and hold it in our hands. It is a thing now. But before we picked it, it was a living piece of nature. Nature is all around us and it has a livingness. Flowers, trees, grass, the water in a variety of expressions - streams, rivers, lakes and oceans are all living expressions of the Creator. Most of the earth is covered with water. Flowers and trees have a vast array of expression. Creatures abound on earth, from ants to elephants. Ocean life ranges from whales to snails.

We cut down a tree and although it screams (Archangel Gabriel said) we do not hear it. We have suddenly, and without compassion, ended its life. Sometimes we too scream as our lives are ended - as in a highway, train or airplane accident. Then our bodies, in lifelessness, become things. The memory of us is not so much the body as how we behaved; how we treated others. We are remembered by our smile, our hugs, our compassion and our love of life.

Creation is of God and all that is created has livingness. Creation did not happen once a long time ago. Creation is on-going and perpetual. We create as new ideas come to us. Artists, writers, sculptors are not the only creators. We create every day on the job and in the home. Perhaps a new way of doing things occurs to us, or a new method of manufacture, or a new route for shipping, or a new way of packaging. Perhaps we think of a new way of mopping a floor, washing dishes, hanging curtains. Ideas are our livingness expressed. The use is manmade. God creates and we, as His children, make things. We make things to serve a particular purpose. We have ideas from an unseen source. We take credit for the ideas, and view some of us as being 'smarter' than others because they have more ideas.

There was a time, a few centuries ago, when everyone expressed creativity. What we now call 'cottage' industries were once the only means of making, from creative thoughts and individual endeavor. Then came the revolution in industry, and machines replaced our hand crafts. Hands came to be used in rote ways to run machines. Creative ideas are now told to another who can make things with machines.

We rely more and more on products coming off the assembly line and less and less on creating from ideas. God creates and we are part of the divine Mind of God. A brain processes thought, but the thought comes only from our Creator. He is always available to provide us with a creative idea. There are many reasons why we are not receptive to them. We seem to have 'mind of our own', but that is only the ego taking control of us.

Our busy life of family, home, and employment consume much of our time. We also feel entitled, therefore, to some leisure time. Care and feeding of the body is of primary concern. We must care for our family and we must make a living. We do not find time to have creative ideas, which seem to come in our not-busy time. Only late in life do some people have time for creative ideas. Grandma Moses did not pick up a paint brush until she was ninety years of age. Most famous artists and writers began at an early age. We all have creative ability. We choose not to use it, as we allow the daily chores to monopolize our time.

What does it take to use our innate creativity? A little willingness; a little time; a little faith. Because all ideas come from God, we need a faith in Him. We need to take some quiet time to allow the idea to come. We need to be willing to listen to God's Whisper. We also need to expect results, without doubt or question. All creative ideas come from God; from Heaven. As the old adage goes "As above, so below." All creativity resides in an unseen realm, waiting to be thought and expressed. Every painting exists first in Heaven. An artist 'imagines' the scene and translates it in paint to the canvas. There are 'discoveries' to be imagined and expressed by us. One of the pearls of great wisdom that Archangel Gabriel shared with us was the fact that a new energy will be discovered which will preclude the need for all fossil fuels! Someday a person will be open to accepting that great 'discovery'. It will change the world, of course.

The livingness of Mother Nature is in our care. Animal cruelty is no longer accepted. Dog fights, chicken fights once were common. Rescue animals are constantly being adopted. Shelters everywhere take in domestic animals or all animals. We have been saved from fire by our pets. They love us as we love them. Plants and trees have feelings, also. They even know how unaware we are that communication with them is possible. *Findhorn* describes a garden in Scotland in which the plants communicates with the gardeners.

We are living because we are breathing the air around us. All life requires air; all life is from God and kept alive by His omnipresent spirit energy. We are always alive in spirit; it is our eternal Self. Our spirit shall never become a thing.

# Section XXI
## Schin

## Chapter 161  Things Not Seen

*"For our light affliction, which is but for a moment, worketh for us a far more exceeding and eternal weight of glory: While we look not at the things which are seen, but at the things which are not seen: for the things which are seen are temporal; but the things which are not seen are eternal."* (2 Cor. 4:17-18)

Possibly 'light affliction' refers to our time on earth, which is for a moment in the scheme of eternity. What exists in eternity is far greater because it is eternal glory. Now we are coming to believe more in things not seen with mortal eyes. When Paul wrote this letter to the people of Corinth, he must have known that his listeners were *able* to look at the things which are not seen. He surely meant the temporal things were those which our mortal eyes can see; but he does not explain how we 'see' the eternal things.

Like Jesus before him, Paul knew his teachings were valid and could be accomplished. As a follower of Jesus, Paul referred to eternal things and temporal things. The listeners were expected to understand. We wonder if Paul's listeners knew how to 'see' the eternal things. In this new era (Age of Aquarius) we have become familiar with dreams, visions, and prophecy, near death experiences and communication between earthlings and the spirit World of God. Only in the peaceful, uninterrupted minutes of meditation are we able to 'see' eternal things.

We dream of loved ones who have passed over before us, but in truth we visit with them, when they meet with us on the Astral Plane. We sometimes see in visions the plight of other people. We seek information from psychics and mediums; they prophesy for us. All near death experiences reveal a brilliant light at the end of a tunnel, and someone says, 'not yet'. We have a revelation - an epiphany - and know it is true. These are all examples of eternal things.

There is a Power which is called God. In Him is eternal Wisdom. The Power and the Wisdom are available to us, but only when we accept it, acknowledge it, trust it, and *seek* it. Jesus often called his followers children. He did so because he saw us as having the attributes of human children: accepting, curious, open, and teachable. He desired greatly to be accepted by them, to satisfy their curiosity about themselves, to teach an open mind the truth, and to teach by his own example, that they could do likewise.

Jesus the Christ is with us always. He promised us that. We can sit and have a conversation with him, if we believe we can. This writer had many conversations with Jesus, when he came to visit us, from 1995 to 1999. See website Sacredgardenfellowship.org. Those glorious years also brought to us visits from Archangel Gabriel (1987-1999). Also Gabriel told us that eleven Ascended Masters came to various locations on earth. They all came to remind us of what we already know but have forgotten: we are children of God; the human race in total is the only begotten Son of God.

When we decide to return Home to Heaven, we shall. It is our choice. We must decide first to forego the karmic wheel and put our ego in its proper place. We have given too much power to it. By daily meditation we can listen to the Voice of God and follow it. Then is the inward man [and woman] renewed day by day, as Paul says in verse 16.

If one disbelieves in our ability to 'see'; things eternal, they will not. If one disbelieves that God can instruct us momently, He cannot. If one disbelieves in the earthly visitations of Jesus and an archangel, so be it; their lessons will go unread, unheard. Such individuals have their reasons and faith. So be it. Someday acceptance will come. Free choice is ours to believe or disbelieve. Free choice is ours to seek truth or not to seek it. Everything is just the way it is supposed to be. Billions of people, with free choice, have brought us the world we live today. It is in our power to make it better. Not by repeating history but by accepting things not seen, knowing they are true.

# Chapter 162   This Temporary World

How solid and permanent this world seems. Even viewing it from space, hanging there so precariously, we still feel grounded and secure on her surface. We are well aware of the fact that she rotates on her axis. Scientists have proven that she circumvents the sun every year. These calculations are now relied on. We use them for agriculture, ocean travel, and space navigation.

The Bible gave us a clue: Speaking of God, Job says, *He stretcheth out the north over the empty place, and hangeth the earth upon nothing.* Job 26:7. In this New Age; this age of truth as Archangel Gabriel called it, we have the facts about the earth and our relationship to it. We are prodigals in this far country, and when we have brought ourselves to a point of surrender, we shall return to our natural habitat, Heaven. When all humanity has returned the Earth will quietly disappear for lack of need. We will have all made the choice to return Home. Angels will celebrate with us.

In *A Course in Miracles* we find, "This world was over long ago." ACIM 28: I: 1:6. We are convinced that time is real and our bodies are the whole truth of us. Archangel Gabriel clarified this error thinking. Humans created time to keep track of each other. Time exists only in man's imagination. Eternity, which is of God, has no time but 'now'. In eternity it is always now. Eons ago, way before written history, we came here to live a life we planned based on our belief in karma. Then we 'died', came back again, etc. Every incarnation, or lifetime, was geared to 'paying back' or 'getting even' for a past issue. Without time, there is no 'past'; no 'future'.

We see a vast universe in which earth resides. Outside of that universe is eternity. We live, move, and have our Being here on Earth, but we got 'stuck' here eons ago because we *believed we could.* And from His high place, God watches us 'live out' our lifetimes, choosing pain and suffering, anger, hatred and prejudice. We are totally unaware that we are His beloved children, and Earth is a place we live temporarily. He waits our conscious return. He gave us all free choice. One day we shall all return to Him, but it will only be so when we choose it. We have made many choices. But we have forgotten our connection to our Father.

We know now there is no death. Jesus demonstrated it. He still comes to those of us who know he can and will, to guide us along our path. We walk in darkness. It is the darkness of ignorance as to who we really are. God sent Archangel Gabriel and eleven Master Teachers to Earth late in the 20$^{st}$ century, to awaken us. We have slept the sleep of Adam, and now we must wake up and live life with the knowingness that we can indeed do everything Jesus did - he told us so (John 14:12). We have the power to change much more than our minds. We can change our lives. It all starts with changing our minds about life.

As begotten offspring of the Living God we can change the weather, communicate mentally, and take our body anywhere we choose by the power of thought. These are available talents to all, but only a few know that they possess them. We all ought to be about our Father's business - by living awake instead of sleeping. We can and should pray and meditate for that awareness, that awakening. Angels have come because now we are ready to listen, to learn, and to become.

Perhaps Tennyson knew this when he wrote:

*"A voice spake out of the skies*
*To a just man and a wise --*
*'The world and all within it*
*Will only last a minute."*

## Chapter 163   Those Twelve Wondrous Years

Every day, as part of my prayers and meditation time, I thank God for those twelve wondrous years during which I sat with my fellow seekers to hear Archangel Gabriel. We sought truth, and Gabriel imparted it to us. He answered for us the ancient questions: Why are we here? How did we get here? Where are we going and why?

He came when he did (1987-1999) to announce the coming age, the Age of Aquarius. He had announced the new age of Pisces when he appeared to Mary before she birthed Jesus, and to Elizabeth to tell her of a delivery in her old age of John the Baptist. We have no record of his announcement of the previous age, that of Aries, when Abraham lived. These zodiac signs reflect a larger zodiac in which our universe circles around a Central Sun. (See the Introduction of *The Aquarian Gospel of Jesus the Christ* by Levi). Gabriel referred to this new age as the spiritual age, or the Age of Truth. He explained why he came and why he came where and when he did

Gabriel came where he did, upstate New York, because there was a center of light in that place. In that center of light, a small church, Reverend Penny was the Pastor. Gabriel told us that she had spent five hundred earth years (of Earth time) learning how to channel an archangel. The vibration of an archangel is exponentially higher than that of a human. She was and remains my best friend, minister, healer, teacher, and counselor.

Gabriel is the Announcer of the Ages. We are on the cusp of a new age, Aquarius. "Jesus referred to the beginning of the Aquarian Age in these words: 'And then the man who bears the pitcher will walk forth across an arc of heaven; the sign and signet of the Son of Man will stand forth in the eastern sky. The wise will then lift up their heads and know that the redemption of the earth is near'." (AGJC 157:29: 30)

The very question, Why are we here? Suggests there is another place to be. Gabriel made it quite clear that Heaven is our natural habitat. We are strangers here on earth, like the Prodigal Son. Our soul remembers our Origin, in God, and longs to return Home. We are drawn to prayer, meditation, places of worship in answer to this longing. When we are at the end of our rope we fall on our knees seeking help.

We all (humanity) came here when we decided. We all thought we had left God and believed He would never take us back, like the Prodigal Son. We believed we were separate from God. This is not possible, any more than the clay can leave the ceramic bowl. We shall all return unto the Father. The return is guaranteed. The time of return is our choice. When we decide to live a life of only love and forgiveness; when we recognize ourselves as children of God, we shall all return.

Meantime we live out our lifetimes on earth in a seemingly endless cycle called karma. We do not remember our past lives because if we did we would not be able to focus on growing in this lifetime. We cannot even remember what we did on our second birthday. Jesus lived what he taught, and he taught unconditional love and complete forgiveness. We see them as impossible goals, but Jesus came again, in the 1990s, to re-state the truth of us. Jesus is our elder brother and we are to follow him Home.

When Adam fell asleep in Eden, he represented the sleep of humanity. We are asleep to our sacred selves. Our spirit is as much a part of God as it was in the beginning. It is not for us to create a spirit (only God can); it is up to us only to *remember* who we are, children of God. Viewing Jesus' life as an example and a pattern, we can read the roadmap he provided so long ago. He does not belong on a cross to be worshipped, but on the road ahead of us, leading the way. According to the Bible, Jesus often said, 'Follow me'.

We are blessed to be living at this cusp of the Age of Aquarius. Now is the age on earth for us to learn and then teach the truth of us. We, and our spiritual siblings on this lovely planet, shall return to our natural habitat, Heaven. In reading/hearing Gabriel's lessons we shall know how.

## Chapter 164   Time and Eternity

Time is what governs all our activities. Without time life on Earth would be chaos. Or so it seems. In the spirit world of God, there is no time, simply the one constant moment, called 'now'. I recall Archangel Gabriel telling us about time. He said we speak of 'telling time' and yet, he said, we tell time nothing - time tells us when to arise, when to work, when to eat, when to go to bed, etc.

As earthbound humans we are time-bound in all our activities. Without clocks we would be at a loss in planning and living our daily life. Is it possible that this could change in the future? After hearing Gabriel, I began an adventure in living without an alarm clock. Before going to sleep I would ask my angels (Gabriel said that we each have 144,000!) to waken me at a certain time. For instance, I would say "Wake me at 6:00 a.m.". Then I would picture in my mind a clock showing 6:00 o'clock. I tell you truly it works. It worked for me because I had faith Gabriel told us about their availability and helpfulness. How much nicer to awaken from an angelic nudge than a harsh alarm!

At this dawning of the new age - the Age of Aquarius - we will begin to call on angels more and more, and show others their innate capacity to do so, too. Angels can assist us in other ways to remind us of our activities throughout the day. Gabriel said this is the truth age, or the Age of Spirituality. Although I have been retired several years, I am keenly aware of my angels as they constantly remind me of my planned day's actions. Entering a room and wondering why, they nudge me to remember what I planned to do there. They are one step ahead of me!

I tell people that I don't believe in angels; I *rely* on them. When we rely on angels to remind us of anything we desire to do, it is essential that we *expect* their help. It is also essential to thank them for their help. Even angels enjoy hearing 'thank you'. We know that angels are God's messengers, and as such He sends them to guide and protect us for our entire life. We always have free choice and angels cannot abrogate that.

When the life we have planned is over, at any age, angels cannot interfere. As long as we are on earth they help us accomplish our goals. When we call on them they will always answer. Even though there is no time as we know it in the Heaven world, angels are aware of our reliance on time. Countless times, when driving, I have been reminded about a planned stop just in time. Seeking angelic help is not time-consuming or difficult. The next time you go out for dinner on a busy evening, ask your angels to find a space to park. Ask for answers to your every question.

Angels bring people, places, or things to help us decide on a chosen goal. I thought my first book was the only one I would ever write. Gabriel's lessons, Jesus' teachings, the Bible, the apocryphal books of the Bible and other books I had read were the impetus to start writing. When I began researching for it, all kinds of help came forth on this new journey. All these talented and willing workers - editor, proofreader, internet tech - were in my circle of friends. In retrospect I now understand they had all agreed before we came to earth in this incarnation. Gabriel told us we plan our lives and everyone in them.

What have angels got to do with time? Angels save us time that we consider so precious. With one thought we seek help. It only takes a Nanno-second to have a thought. Angels receive our thought as quickly. We have all been frustrated at finding a parking spot for our cars. Many of us have anguished over choosing a career; buying a house; deciding to marry. Angelic help is there for us all the time, in one split second, day or night. The only requirement is to have faith in them. By starting small (like a parking spot), we learn to rely on them more and more. It still amazes me at how quickly and surely they respond to every request. And the time saved is immeasurable.

The time saved can be used to learn the lessons Jesus the Christ taught so long ago: love, forgiveness, acceptance, patience, and gentleness. He lived what he taught; we can do the same in the time we are here.

## Chapter 165   Time's Illusion

We view our world and everything in it based on time. Archangel Gabriel once noted that we speak of 'telling time', and yet, he said, we tell time nothing. Rather, time tells us everything - when to rise in the morning, when to go to work, when to eat and sleep. Time rules our lives. But time is an illusion in itself, he said. To prove his point he asked the question,

"If a ball is bounced on a moving train, how far does the ball travel?" We suggested about eight feet, round trip to the floor and back to the hand. Then he posed the question about the train's speed. The total distance must take that speed into consideration. Furthermore, from the perspective of an angel, the train is moving on the planet Earth, which itself is rotating on its axis. Finally, he added that we must also consider the movement of the Earth's orbit around the sun. Of course, all of these calculations can be made using scientific data. I leave it to the reader to perform this task.

What has all this to do with Gabriel's teachings about us as children of the Living God? Most of us already believe that God is eternal, but in eternity the only time is 'now', therefore there is no tomorrow, yesterday; no past or future, except as we have invented them. The bouncing ball on the train is a small example of our belief in the illusion of time. Gabriel said that we created time in order to keep track of ourselves and each other.

It takes great imagination to contemplate a world without time. Perhaps we take a vacation so we can enjoy a few days without schedules, appointments and various engagements. When we meditate we are unaware of time. This is demonstrated when we stop our meditation and see by the clock that we spent more time there than we thought. Master teachers can spend several days in a meditative state.

The time we spend in meditation takes us temporarily out of the illusion of time. In such sacred moments we share eternity with our Maker; our spiritual Self with God. It replenishes us for the day. In sharing eternity with God, we are making a conscious connection to our holy Source. We are going within to the core of our Being; to an awareness of our oneness with God. Some people begin their day with meditation, and should a sudden event keep them from it, the day goes wrong at every turn - not as a punishment from God, but because they are not 'centered' in spirit.

The practice of meditation is not new. Biblical characters meditated: Isaac meditated. (Gen 24:63), Joshua advised his followers to meditate for success. (Jos. 1:8) the Psalms contain many references to meditation. In Paul's first letter to Timothy, he advised meditating (I Ti. 4:15). Jesus often went apart from his disciples. Perhaps he did so to take 'time out' to meditate.

We refer constantly to time: we speak of 'time off' from work, 'free time' to have fun; 'down time' is calculated by employers when we are not productive. In sports we measure by time segments: halves, quarters, innings, rounds, laps, games, sets, matches. We also have 'time out'. Because of the Earth's rotation around the sun, we establish time zones. We focus much time on the past, because we value it. Archeology is based completely on the past. Past masters of art, music, writing, architecture are honored. Past wars are re-enacted, past heroes are sculpted, and old battlefields are considered 'hallowed ground'. Regarding this, Gabriel explained that're-enactments' maintain the negative vibrations of war. It is more positive to send peace thoughts across the battlefields.

The greatest illusion of time is our belief it exists. How can we imagine life without time? Very likely we cannot. However, we can know for certain that the spirit world of God is eternal, where time does not exist. The only 'time' in eternity is *now*. Perhaps that is why we call 'now' the present - because it is a gift to us. 'Now' is our greatest gift. Losing ourselves in the now makes us unaware of time. When, at last, we return to our oneness with God, there will be no constraints of time in our sharing, loving, creating. Perhaps we cannot imagine that. We cannot imagine the Pleroma of the universes, either. But in time we shall - and the time then will be 'now'.

# Chapter 166  Today's Importance

*"Between the future and the past the laws of God must intervene, if you would free yourself."* ACIM T 13: IX: 7

Jesus the Christ gave us these words. There is a freedom which Archangel Gabriel spoke of that is beyond our conscious human experience. Gabriel reminded us constantly of the truth of us. He said we are children of God because God is the only Cause, and He created us. God created us in spirit form - God's own likeness and image. We have wandered to this far country, earth, as a result of our belief that we are separate from our Source. God has no beginning or end. Our spirit has no beginning or end. Eons before any written religion we walked the earth. We knew that we could return from our wandering to the Father any time we chose.

Then one day we forgot our way Home, and a long and tedious journey in form began. We came to believe that our physical world was our true home. We came to believe that we could never return to God. We gazed at the night sky and looked in awe at stars we could not touch or explain. We gathered in small tribes for safety and saw other tribes as 'enemies'. Inter-marriage was considered essential for safety. We slew anyone perceived as an enemy, with weapons we designed and made for that purpose. We invented the idea of an ego which would warn us of dangers and offer protection from wild beasts.

In the killing of animals and other humans we felt guilty somehow. Guilt was born. Eons passed. Tribes became city-states, then nations. But always the formed governments had borders, to show separation and to distinguish ownership of land. Many more centuries passed before scribbled images were made on cave walls. Gabriel reminded us that entities from other planets came to give us fire, then speech. This was too long ago for a record to be made.

Then an Egyptian King came to proclaim the sun as God; and himself as a human expression of the sun. Ikhnaton was the Sun God. He had many images to show the people his power. But his successor destroyed all the statues and signs of the Sun God. Indigenous people of all lands worshipped great powers beyond them and believed in many gods. More centuries passed. Great religions of the world came into being: Brahma, Buddha, Judaism, and Islam all answered man's eternal quest for truth.

"Then Jesus came, the last to take his place
In that great line of masters of the race
To shed his radiance upon the saints and sages
Who bowed before the Altar of the Ages." TVC, 270

Jesus the Christ said, *"I am the way, the truth and the life."* John 14:6. Two thousand years later, at the inception of the Age of Aquarius, Jesus came (1995-1999) to correct errors in the Bible which were made accidentally or purposefully. All believers will return Home to the One Creator. God's laws are not man-made. We live by our own laws and make all decisions today based on the past. The past is full of wars. Wars are the result of judgment; judgment is man-made. Why would we want to repeat the past? If we desire change, then we must change today. Today we have the choice to obey the laws of God or continue worshipping the past.

Today is the only time we can exercise our free choice. To choose God's laws does not require a religion. God gave us all the religions, through devout leaders. In this way He gave us hope; hope that one day we would learn who we really are - His children. In silence and reverence we can ask our Creator for guidance. Only in the silence can we hear the whispered Word of God. There is no time in God's world. Now is all He knows. God sends angels, masters, teachers, and guides to help us awaken to the truth. He will guide us *as we ask for guidance*. Faith in our ego; faith in the past, faith in ourselves, keep us stuck in man's laws. God's Will is ours today for the asking. It is not mysterious.

*"He hath shewed thee, O man, what is good; and what doth the Lord require of thee, but to do justly, and to love mercy, and to walk humbly with thy God?"* Micah 6:8

## Chapter 167   Turning Love Away

Archangel Gabriel noted that we have no problem loving another, but we do have problems accepting another's love for us. Many times, he said, we have turned away love from others. Perhaps there are several reasons why. In our sense of low self-esteem we do not believe we deserve unconditional love. So we doubt or question another when they treat us in such a way. In that response our message to the other is reactionary. Distrust takes over and we accept the idiomatic phrase that 'if it is too good to be true, it probably is'.

Suspicion of another's actions makes us snap back verbally which, of course, causes the other to walk away. An act of love seems to be just that - an act. We readily think that the person has a hidden agenda; is seeking something in return. Or maybe they have hit a nerve of pain in us, like remembering abandonment by a previous love. Or we may accept the love, but always wonder what that person wants from us. When we ourselves are incapable of loving, for whatever reason, we expect others to also lack the ability to express love.

Coming from a family where loving attention is not the norm we may show, by our body's reaction, an aversion to another's affection. We do not understand it and we do not know how to accept it willingly and graciously. Regret often follows when we turn away love. We may end a relationship because of the erroneous belief the other has been unfaithful. But when we realize our error it is too late to undo it. Too late, unless both parties agree to reconcile and resume the loving relationship. Often we turn love away simply because we do not communicate with each other. In some instances two people - or one - will shut down, be silent and refuse to verbally interact. This is a deadly response; an untenable posture; an unforgiving attitude. There is no opening for resolution. The door is slammed against the option of communication and mutual understanding. It is all too common.

The love Jesus taught is not limited to conjugal love. Parents, extended family, neighbors, co-workers, friends are all within the realm of unconditional love; the agape love demonstrated by Jesus the Christ. Even strangers on the other side of the planer evoke our love when disaster strikes them. We pray, send donations, maybe even travel to volunteer assistance. That is what unconditional love is about.

Fearing love's expression will send others away instead of drawing them to us. Having been hurt once in a relationship sometimes leads to distrust of all people of the same race, religion, or culture. This generalization can lead to mass prejudice, and that can lead to war. There is no place for love in the violence of war. Unconditional love is what we are by nature; from God. Expressing it toward everyone awakens us to our nature. There are people who think that love can be bought. Financially wealthy persons can easily fall into such error thinking because they have the monetary capacity to seek such a purchase. Money can buy allegiance, duty, slavery. But it cannot buy love. Love - and we are speaking here about unconditional love - exists far apart from sex, attraction, beauty, appearances.

Unconditional love, by definition, requires no conditions whatsoever. None. It is the love which Jesus the Christ expressed in his daily life. It is the Love of God which brought us forth in form. It is our nature. We need only reveal it without fear, without conditions, without distrust. The power of love is, in fact, the greatest power there is. Feeling good about ourselves and believing we are worthy of only good, we accept the unconditional love from others. Turning them away is no longer an option.

## Chapter 168   Understanding Peace

*"And the peace of God, which passeth all understanding, will keep your hearts and minds through Christ Jesus."* Phil. 4:7

Paul tells the people of Philippi that God's peace is beyond our comprehension. We have come to believe that peace is the absence of war. Peace is not the absence of war, although we have come to believe it is. In the times of peace we arm for war. We anticipate war; we expect war, we have a 'standing army' ready for war. We have engaged in many terrible conflicts since the 'war to end all wars' of a hundred years ago.

The terrible conflagration caused by atomic bombs of WWII has shown us that a nuclear war would destroy the planet. We are forced therefore to seek a lasting world peace through tolerance, cooperation and understanding. World peace may still be seen as the absence of war.

A true peace is the peace that begins within each of us. Jesus taught peace for he was a man of peace. *"Peace I leave with you, my peace I give unto you."* John 14:27 Upon instructing his disciples Jesus said, *"And if the house be worthy, let your peace come upon it: but if it be not worthy, let your peace return to you."* Matt 10:13 Jesus calmed the raging Sea of Galilee when a storm arose, frightening his followers: *"And he arose, and rebuked the wind, and said unto the sea, Peace, be still. And the wind ceased, and there was a great calm."* Mark

4:39 It is unfortunate that some of the words of Jesus were altered, as Gabriel said. Archangel Gabriel refuted the quotation of Matt. 10:34: *Think not that I come to send peace on earth: I came not to send peace but a sword.* A man of peace would not have come with a sword. It was at another seminar that Gabriel was asked about Peter wearing a sword (John 18:10). Gabriel said that Peter took a sword from one of the Roman soldiers.

If we mortals cannot understand the peace mentioned in Philippians, what are we to do? The only thing we can do is acknowledge the fleeting moments when a deep peace envelops us. Perhaps it is then that we have a tiny glimpse of what real peace can be. Everyone has a different experience to induce it. We can cherish those special moments but they defy description. The young dislike peace because they have a high energy level and want to be busy expending it.

One sign of maturity is a desire to know personal peace, even for an instant. Over time, two people can enjoy a peaceful moment together which is a kind of bonding experience. It is memorable and the circumstances surrounding it are unforgettable. For those who pursue group meditation, a peaceful moment can be shared by several other people. Gabriel explained that peace is not the absence of war but instead is the realm of consciousness in which war has no place. *". . .to be spiritually minded is life and peace."* Romans 8:6

There are ways to have peace. To be spiritually minded means to maintain a lifestyle which loves everyone, not just some people. We need not like what others do, but we ought to love them all for what they are, and pray for those who have forgotten they are children of God. We can enjoy music and conversation and television, but the talk should be geared to peaceful topics, not gossip or fearful notions. In the busy world we live in peace seems far out of reach. Action and violence permeate our 'entertainment' genre. They are valued by the masses, but seekers of peace will find a way to spend time enjoying peaceful friends, peaceful places and peaceful thoughts.

Even in an active workplace personal peace is available to all. We simply ask a higher power to bring us peace of mind and help us maintain it throughout the day. Should a sudden stressful moment arise, one can opt for a peaceful few minutes in a restroom or outdoors. If this sounds tedious or difficult, we are not ready for peace in life. When we desire a peaceful home, others will find great comfort there; sometimes will not want to leave. When we find a peaceful spot for a vacation time we want to return to it.

The peace that passes our understanding is the peace that is *constant and forever,* because it is the Peace of God. On the other side we can know it, because the other side is Heaven; a peaceful place. 'Rest in peace' should mean enjoying Heaven.

# Section XXII
## Tau

## Chapter 169   Universal Space

We speak of, and usually honor, one's personal space. We set 'boundaries' around us and demand that others respect them. We have our family space in the home. Our office space has become a cubicle. On vacation, we seek the spaciousness of the countryside; or the wide open space of the sea; or the high mountains. The crowded subway and bus are acceptable for a short time, but there is a sense of relief when we disembark. All of our lives we surrounded by space or people, and quite unconsciously we adjust accordingly. In large cities various groups may form a neighborhood, like Chinatown, Little Italy, etc. Originally they were probably formed for protection, but they remain.

We respect another's home area, whether a city apartment or country acreage. Some wealthy folk live in a gated community, to protect rigidly their chosen space. Recently there has been a movement to build and live in tiny houses. This is appropriate for people who do not spend much time at home, and they realize spaciousness is not required in their daily residence. The elderly, also, require little space. They spend much time at home, as a rule, but their space needs have been greatly reduced, by choice.

There is a time when all the boundaries fall; all personal space is disregarded, and everyone is suddenly on a level playing field. It is a time of great tragedy. It can be a flood, a forest fire, a bombing, a tornado. But suddenly everyone is in the same predicament. There is no difference between helper and victim; survivor and first-responder. Color barriers, if there were any, fall. Social status is forgotten. There is a common bond between all those so afflicted - plus those who come to their aid. The common denominator is survival. Then another common denominator prevails: clean-up, repair and rebuild. Someone once said 'tragedy is a great leveler.' This is what was meant.

The greatest tragedy of all is that we need a tragedy to perceive ourselves as having a common bond. The common bond is life itself. Perhaps the day will come when we will not require a tragedy to see each other as equal in every way, not as human beings, or Homo sapiens, but as the children of God that we are. Is a global tragedy required to bring us to a realization of our oneness? There are places in the world where believers acknowledge and pray for that realization. These places are called light centers. Eleven Ascended Masters came to various countries; at the same time that Gabriel came to teach.

Most of us believe in the power of prayer. Accepting a world where we see everyone as having a common bond is the challenge for humanity. Gabriel explained that *'the only begotten son'* in scripture is the entire human family. In truth we are all spiritual siblings. As each small group accepts this truth, it will radiate outward until every person knows of that at-one-ment.

As we acknowledge the oneness that is demonstrated after a tragedy, we can begin to see that such a bond is possible. And if it is possible, why not desirable? It is not necessary to identify what is within us all that embraces the commonality. Whether we call it soul, or spirit, or something else, it is a God-given essence. The final outcome of this unity would be world peace. Our perceived differences invite judgment, and separateness. United we are joined; not only in thought but in love of each other.

Should we, then, pray for a global tragedy, or begin building bridges of connection between individuals, groups, nations, and cultures? The United Nations is a global example that demonstrates all national governments can gather and discuss global problems and resolve them. The League of Nations failed after 26 years, and was followed by WWII, but the United Nations is holding thus far. Begun in 1945, at this writing the UN is 70 years old, with 193 member countries. When Abraham Lincoln said, "A house divided against itself cannot stand", he referred to this country as half free and half slave. Lincoln was quoting the Bible

(Mark 3:25). Possibly the statement holds true for this planet on which we live.


## Chapter 170  Universal Spirituality

A universal religion is impossible, but universal spirituality is essential. The reason universal religion is impossible is that all religions are based on exclusivity. The tenets of all religions insist on certain beliefs for its adherents. In addition, Catholicism, Protestantism, Buddhism, Mohammedanism and Confucianism all have within them denominations varying in specific tenets of faith. Each delineates proper behaviors and rituals. Ecumenical councils have done little to address the common ground of all religions. All religions have their Founders; their named Creator. When, or if, we are able to accept the idea of One God of all creation which is known by different names, the oneness of humanity will be accepted.

Universal religion can be sought, but never found because of the vast scope of beliefs and rituals.  This does not preclude us from respecting others' religion. Ecumenical councils seek to find common ground of respect, if not of beliefs. This common ground exists because all religions share the belief in a power greater than man. We did not create our spiritual Selves, only our physical selves.  We procreate and raise our children in our own religion, if we have not forsaken the religion of our parents.

There is a common humanity that recognizes good from not-good. Religion of itself does not define us; our humanity does. The human family has evolved through the centuries from a joining by necessity to a joining by love. Perhaps this has occurred because God placed within us a core of love. Over time - a very long time - we have forgotten our origin; our Maker. In that forgetting we replaced love with judgment, malice, fear, and doubt. When we set our feet upon a conscious spiritual path these negative attitudes fall away, one by one.

The moment we begin a *conscious* spiritual journey is determined by our experiences and our responses to them. It rarely occurs before the age of thirty or forty; for some even later. There are also individuals who never set their feet upon such a path in this lifetime or any other. They are not less spiritual because they have forgotten their innate sacredness. We have all forgotten us. This explains why we are still here - to remember our core-self which is love. Gabriel's visitations were to announce the new age (Age of Aquarius) and awaken us to our holiness, as children of God. Gabriel reminded us that nowhere in scripture does it say that Adam woke up from him sleep, in Genesis.

A universal spirituality bespeaks of a spiritual human family. Every baby born into this world has the capacity to learn any language. We have a universal ancestry. We have lived on many continents, held beliefs in different religions, learned social behaviors relevant to our social status and country. There are behaviors which are understood by all humanity - laughter, music, love, hands folded in prayer. Love has brought nations closer by bringing individuals of different nations together. The commonality is our humanness. Our humanness is the universal love which God instilled in us.

Universal spirituality is possible; it is inevitable. This is the lesson to be learned by us all. As Homo sapiens we need to accept ourselves as one family of God. Otherwise we will destroy our planet and have to begin again, as Gabriel explained. We cannot be destroyed, for spirit is eternal. We now have the capacity to destroy our home, Earth. We also have the capacity to join. The choices are ours. In choosing joining we choose awakening the spirit Self of us - all of us.

We think of ourselves as an intelligent race of humans; now it is time to see ourselves as loving humans. We 'rescue' beasts but judge our neighbors. We donate anonymously to help the poor but disdain the street person. We give ourselves and each other mixed messages. We live a life of dichotomy. We are all one in a Creator, whatever we call It. It is so easy to accept someone with whom we share a specific problem or disaster. Everyone has some problem; everyone has known or seen a disaster. It is our ego which seeks differences, separateness, and judgment. It is our minds, ad parts of the Mind of God, which seeks love, peace, and unity.

## Chapter 171   The Vestibule of Heaven

When at last we lay down this physical envelope and 'pass on', our loved ones mourn. They celebrate the life that was so dear to them. This is human nature; this is a spiritual honoring ceremony. In truth, we rise to the Astral Plane and there reside in an astral body. It is the plane of illusion, where we experience instant gratification. It sure sounds like Heaven! But it is only our next stage in the progression of our soul's return to the Father. What goes around comes around. We have regressed so far from our origin in Heaven that we have several realms to evolve back through to reach our spirit origin.

The human family has devolved down so much that it now resides in physical form, which is the slowest manifestation of energy. Spirit is the highest manifestation of energy. We have heard the term 'seventh Heaven', and now we have learned from Archangel Gabriel the definition. The Astral Plane has a lower and higher phase. Most go to the higher, but those who constantly dwell in negative thoughts and behavior expect a 'negative place' beyond the grave. So they find themselves in a lonely, desolate place after 'death'. Angels go to them often to remind them they can go to the light of the higher astral. There is no hell, except in our imagination; there is no devil. Each plane has a lower and a higher phase. Gabriel explained that each realm can only be aware of the next realm up. Only when we reach the Astral Plane can we know of what the Mental Plane consists.

The seven realms are; earth, lower astral, higher astral, lower mental, higher mental, lower spiritual and True Heaven, Home of us all. It sounds like a very long journey, but we have all taken the downward path *by choice*. Now we are at the nadir point below which we cannot go. We have bounced between earth and the Astral Plane for a very long time. It is known as the karmic wheel. We have made this round trip so many times that we have met every other person now living on earth!

It is high time to begin our homeward journey, and this Age of Aquarius is the age of such a beginning. That is why there is so much talk now of the sixth sense, angels, karma, divine intervention, channeling of spirit entities, out of body experiences, and near death experiences. As Gabriel explained, it is time to wake up to our divine nature. He reminded us of the Garden of Eden story, in which Adam fell into a deep sleep. Then we were startled by his words, "Nowhere in scripture does it say he woke up!" Humanity's deep sleep is over, and this is the time for our awakening. The 'wilderness' in scripture represents our journeys on earth.

When we reach the Astral Plane, the plane of illusion, we experience instant gratification. First we are greeted by angels who help us become adjusted to our new surroundings. Then we meet family and friends who arrived there ahead of us. We can have the house of our dreams built for us. Although we do not need autos there, we can ask and receive any vehicle we wish. Transportation is unnecessary because when we desire to be in another place, such as the celestial city, we are suddenly transported there. If we desire to pray we are instantly transported to the Temple on the hill.

There is no commerce, but there is manufacturing. Arts are displayed in the museums. The art gallery has on its walls the *original* of every masterpiece. Gabriel told us that all art we see on earth is a duplicate of the original in Heaven. On earth we make paint in colors we know. At one time my own father came to me from spirit, when I was fifty. (he had passed on when I was five). Through a medium my father said, "I'm waiting for you. I want to show you around. The light is different here; the colors are different."

In the library there are all the books that have been written, including books by authors who re-wrote their works after arriving in Heaven! Their new books reflect the truth, to correct their error perceptions on earth. There are musical instruments we do not have on earth. To the dismay of many readers, there are no 'ball games' in Heaven because gravity does not exist. As a matter of fact there is no competition at all. Time is non-existent. 'Days' are longer than earthly days. There is no night there (Rev. 21:25); only a 'softening of the glory' (Springer). Many authors have written about the other side. Swedenborg, Greber, Borgia, Springer, Cayce, and many recent authors have given us insights into life after 'death'. There are waterways on that plane; fields, trees and grass in that lovely place. Grass grows only so far and therefore needs no mowing! Fruit drops from trees when ripe and disappears. There are no rainy days; no snowfall.

Some individuals get stuck in that place of illusion, but others desire to continue on their spiritual journey upward. Jesus the Christ has been idolized and worshipped for generations. In the Bible he tells us that he came to be emulated. Many times he said, "Follow me." He came as an example (John 13:15). He came as a way-shower (John 14:12). He was the first to come and show us life and the resurrection:

*But now is Christ risen from the dead, and become the firstfruits of them that slept.*
*For since by man came death, by man came also the resurrection of the dead.*
*For as in Adam all die, even so in Christ shall all be made alive.*
*But every man in his own order: Christ the firstfruits; afterward they that are Christ's at his coming.* I Cor. 15:20-23

When Jesus said, *"Let the dead bury the dead."* he meant that we are all dead to our divinity as children of God. When my 'dead' mother came to me through a medium, she said "You are the ones who are dead, you know." The Bible and Jesus' words suddenly made sense to me.

## Chapter 172   We Have All Met

Authors and readers; workers and bosses, farmers and executives; sailors and merchants; parents and children - all have met previously on earth. Every member of humankind has met each other before. This was one of the startling truths imparted to us by Archangel Gabriel, during his earthly visitations from 1987 to 1999. We return to this planet over and over again because we think we must. Gabriel told us that we have lived so many lifetimes on Earth that we have met every other person now living here! That is an astonishing number of lifetimes. It is time to get off the wheel of karma we have invented.

Gabriel came to remind us of what we already know but have forgotten. We know, at some level of our being (spirit), that we are children of God. Our soul remembers our Home of origin - Heaven. In our ignorance we think we left God, which is impossible. If it were possible we would not exist. In our persistent ignorance we think God will never take us back because we left His world of perfection. God knows we never left except in our consciousness. He beckons us back.

Our soul, because it remembers, urges us to pray, to meditate, to attend religious places and ceremonies. It longs to return Home. What we already know is everything. God, in Hi omniscience, can and will impart to us anything we desire to know which is positive, uplifting, and productive. We have stopped seeking His guidance, except in prayer. We think He has abandoned us. He could not; He would not. Forever is the only time in Gods world.

Instead, we choose to listen to the ego. As infants we call for help from parents when we are wet, hungry, hurting. They always come. In our early years we are taught that strangers are to be feared; that all we gain we must gain ourselves. This kind of learning directs our attention to our ego selves. The ego tells us we are in charge of our lives. Every private thought is ours alone; every accomplishment is personal and personally rewarding. We invented the ego. The ego is in charge of us by our choice. Fear is the ego's greatest weapon. We can list all our fears.

Gabriel explained that all our fears originate in the one great fear - the fear that God will never take us back. Gabriel came to awaken us to what our soul never forgot - we are children of the Living God and must awaken to our innate divinity and live from the spirit of us, not the ego of us. Gabriel told us that now is the time for us to know the truth of us.

Now we can understand fully what Jesus taught: the Kingdom of God is within. This statement has confounded us for centuries. Now Gabriel informs us the literal truth of it: Every cell of our physical body contains a *spirit nucleus!*

When The Master Jesus said to the man, *"Sell all that you have and follow me"*, (Matt. 19:21) he was not suggesting that everyone live a pauper life. He knew the man's possessions were treasured by him; they had become his god. His ego had convinced him, in effect, that all he had gained was important. We are all entitled to wealth and comfort, but we have made things our god. The things we accumulate are merely 'stuff'. Fire, flood, wind, can destroy it all in minutes. We bemoan our loss but always remark, "We are still alive; that's what is important."

In an hour of catastrophe we suddenly realize what is important to us - life itself. A tragedy may enrage us for a time, but loss of any kind brings stages of recovery, as suggested by Kubler-Ross's book *On Death and Dying*. Denial which, in spite of what we see, tells us it cannot be. Then comes anger (sometimes at God), then a bargaining with God - let this be a dream and I will change my ways. The next stage is depression, then acceptance. We are vulnerable at all stages and can get stuck in any one of them. The final stage of acceptance cannot return us to our former selves, for trauma leaves its scars. What we can do is recognize the eternal truth of us. We *are still alive*, in spirit, and that is what is important.

We are precious to God but deny our holy worth. God loves us, but we seem determined to continue in self-abasement. It is said, 'If you feel far from God, guess who moved?' In us, at our very core, is the eternal spirit present. It never leaves throughout all our lifetimes or all the adventures in spirit between lifetimes. Earth is our transient residence. Heaven is our natural habitat. We are children of God eternally. Getting off the karmic wheel requires only a change of mind. In our acceptance of God as our Source, and an open-minded willingness to *listen to Him*, we can step upon the path that leads Home.

# Chapter 173    We Prodigals

In Luke 15:11-24 Jesus tells his audience of Pharisees and scribes; publicans and sinners, the parable of the Prodigal Son. It is the story of humanity. We are all prodigals. The son who asked his father for his wealth and then squandered it is the human race. As an analogy, let us liken humanity to the son who left home. The family was comfortable and all its needs were met. The sons knew they would inherit their father's estate. As sons of God, we lived in a place of abundance and comfort. It was peaceful and joyous. It was Heaven. We knew that God loved all of us. We loved each other. There was no status; we were equals in every sense of the term. We knew our Home of love, peace and prosperity. We shared God's power, as His children.

The son who was too impatient to wait for his rightful inheritance asked for his share and left home. Humanity was given free choice by God when He breathed us forth. We became bored with this perfection and, using our power, we began to manipulate the energy (vibration) of which everything was created. We slowed down the vibration and created a mental plane. We existed thereon for eons, in a mental body. Then we slowed down the vibration even more and thus created an emotional (astral) plane, living there in an astral body. We continued to slow down vibration until we created the world; land of form; physical matter.

The son, upon leaving home, squandered all his money on wine, women and song - or anything he chose to spend it on. We are busy here on Earth spending time and money on stuff we do not need, things to impress others, and items we know we cannot 'take with us' when we die. The power we had we have given away to others and to our egos. We fear accidents, illness and death. In effect we have become victims.

The Prodigal Son reached a point where he was eating the slop given to pigs, but feared to return home because he believed his father would reject him. All our current fears are based on the belief that we left God and he will never take us back. But spend what we can in money, time, and energy; something always seems to be missing. We long for something but know not what. Our Soul remembers the beginning and longs to return Home to Heaven.

We have incarnated so many times that we have all met on earth before. We have come to Earth many times in the cycle of reincarnation. It is a karmic, useless, endless journey until we decide to get off the karmic merry-go-round, remember our power, our love, and then act. We have forgotten the power God gave us and how to use it. We can remember it.

The Prodigal Son had to muster up the courage to return home and take a chance that he could find there some edible food, if not acceptance. We must gather our courage, too, and open our minds to something new; something better. We have created a world in which some worship other gods, like money, status, education. It is a world where some starve and some languish in wealth. We fail to appreciate the loveliness of our planet which provides our every need. We have sullied the Earth, the water and the skies with awful pollution.

Our power is as eternal as God and as accessible now as ever. We can recall our original power and our innate love for each other and our Creator. What we have learned has come to us with thinking, experimentation, and reasoning. Now it is time to learn through revelation. In Matt. 10:26 we find: *"Fear them not therefore; for there is nothing covered, that shall not be revealed; and hid, that shall not be known."* One thing now revealed to us is the mystery of the pyramids: The pyramids were not made by muscle and blood. Those ancient people remembered how to use vibration (energy) and changed the molecular structure of the massive stones so they could readily be put in place. See *The Emerald Tablet*, 27

For too long we have believed we cannot control our environment. Too long we have accepted the role of victim. We have merely forgotten our power. We can control even the weather, just as Jesus did when he calmed the Sea of Galilee. (Matt 8:26) At an Archangel Gabriel seminar we visualized and prayed for better weather than predicted. We did so to ease the way home for participants who had to travel several miles after the seminar. The weather we sought occurred for that day *and three subsequent days!*

Faith in a God of Love Who shares His love and Power with His children will enable us to awaken to our innate creative ability. This time we must create with love, as our Father did and continues to do. Through us God will create a Heaven on Earth, when we are ready and willing to have Him do so through us. It takes courage, open-mindedness, faith and a little willingness for it to occur.


## Chapter 174   "'What Did I Tell You?"

As a parent, when our children disobeyed we would remind them of the rules we had in our home. Any penalty given met with their grumbling. we would remind them of the rule by saying, "What did I tell you?" Punishments were not severe - an early bed, earlier curfew - or, if the infraction warranted it, 'grounded for a week', which meant they could not leave the yard after school.

When I was a child, I never heard this. My mother never told me anything except "Go play outside." or "Go play in the sandbox." My father died when I was five, and the subsequent years led to my mother's obsession with alcohol. She lived in her own lonely, sad world and shut everyone out. For many years I thought I would never forgive her for her detachment. But then I succumbed to the same addiction and forgave her. She went Home as an active alcoholic. I was blessed with recovery.

Now I understand the Fatherhood of God; the Brotherhood of Man. When God breathed us forth millions of years ago, He said, Go forth and multiply - in good deeds, in creative endeavors, in compassionate sharing. Over time we forgot where we came from. Like the Prodigal Son we spent our entire heritage (power of God; love of God, peace of God) and now we wonder why we have poverty, hunger, and wars. So we blame God for all our misery, all our lack, all our insecurity.

No one can argue that we have free will. Every moment of every day we make choices. We think there are hundreds of choices open to us. In truth our choices lead only in two directions: a road of truth, love and peace, or a road that leads in the opposite direction. When we make a choice that is 'not good' we pay the consequences, and then rail at God for our misery.

We look around at this sorry world and wonder why God made such awful things happen. God does not make awful things happen. Do you really believe that God would give you anything but a blessing? He would not be a God of Love if He brought all this misery to us. By our own free will we have made some terrible choices. We justify anger, we judge others, and we expect that any success in life will be at a high cost. We ask God to bring peace on Earth, and then criticize our neighbors, the media, and the government.

We are giving mixed messages to ourselves. We want peace on Earth but we hate a relative, a neighbor, a co-worker, or others. Peace on Earth will elude us as long as we deny ourselves peace in our daily life. Once a year we join millions of other Christians and ask the Prince of Peace to bless the world with enduring peace. But we fail to see our own responsibility to make it so. The other 364 days we make choices which can only lead to anger, dissension and war.

Perhaps God is whispering in our ear, "What did I tell you?" God knows we have multiplied negativity instead of positiveness. He knows we have made some terrible choices in His Name. He knows we have abrogated our free choice by accepting the role of victim. He knows we have turned our power over to our ego or another person. We have forgotten our Father and our original essence: love. Judgment comes easier than acceptance because it is now habitual. In this New Age (the Age of Aquarius), this spiritual age, we can willingly choose another option and make acceptance a habit.

Realizing that earth is our temporary home, we can learn *now* to respect and love her; to nurture and protect her. Now, as we recognize our divinity, it is time to love and respect all our brothers and sisters on earth. They are all our spiritual siblings. Only with this acceptance will God whisper in our ears, "Well done, my good and faithful servant." He will not scold us, with "What did I tell you?"

## Chapter 175   When Will We Know?

We are so very blessed to be on earth at this time! It is the inception of the Age of Aquarius. Archangel Gabriel, the Announcer of the ages, visited earth to announce it. The age just ended, Pisces, began with his announcing to Mary the pending birth of Jesus, and announcing to Elizabeth the coming of John the Baptist. Joseph also was informed by Gabriel that his aged wife would give birth to John. Pisces was the last age of our devolvement and Aquarius is the first age of evolvement back to our Home in Heaven.

Instead of making brief announcements of babies to be born, this age is blessed with many visitations by Gabriel. For twelve wondrous years Gabriel presented daily seminars bi-monthly and monthly lessons in truth on Sunday evenings. The questions humanity has asked for centuries have now been answered. Gabriel explained why we are here, how we got here and how we shall return to our Father.   Only a few of his lessons are written here. Readers are strongly encouraged to read/hear all Gabriel's lessons in truth.

Gabriel shocked us with some of his messages. For instance, the Bible states that Jesus was the only begotten Son of God. The original words were, 'Jesus was the begotten son of the only God'.  This changes everything we have been taught! All humanity, Gabriel told us, is one great family of God; we are all His begotten offspring. God is spirit and we are His spirit children. It is our spirit which is eternal. Many phrases in scripture now make sense, such as the numerous times Jesus said, 'follow me', Jesus' promise that we could emulate him (John 14:12). His example life is noted in John 13:15; his pattern life in I Tim 1:16 both support the concept that Jesus came to show us the way.

Another amazing truth told to us by Gabriel: Jesus did not suffer on the cross. When he said, in the Garden of Gethsemane, *". . . not my will but thine be done."* (Luke 22:42), his consciousness was elevated to his spirit Self, and there he remained until his 'death' on the cross. Today we hear the expression 'out of body' experience.

When we hear that we are *all* children of God, we wonder, then, why some are poor; some are rich. Some are healthy; some unwell. Some are working; some live a life of leisure. Some live in large houses; some on the street. God gave us free choice, and Gabriel explained that we plan our lives and every experience in them. Our plan is to recompense for past errors - from any past incarnation. Yes, we have been here before; to the point that we have met every person now living!

When we asked God through the centuries why we were here, we thought the questions were unanswerable; that we could not know.  We can accept the truth now because a Master Teacher told us two thousand years ago, they are written in *A Course in Miracles,* and Archangel Gabriel confirmed them. We strive to become, in our own way, what we are as God's own. Jesus the Christ said he would be with us always, and he meant it in a literal sense. The same journey Jesus took we are taking also. It is an inner journey of awakening to our spirit Self.

There are none so blind as those who *will not* see. When Archangel Gabriel taught us, some listeners walked away. Gabriel explained they simply were not ready for the truth. We can pray for their awakening as others prayed for ours. We have been where they are. As Jesus has taught us, we must teach others. Belief in that unity of the human family is our goal. To know, with every fiber of our being, that we are children of God, is our goal.

We did not 'fall away from God'; we did not leave our Source; we only think we did. Like the Prodigal Son who left his father and spent his fortune, we think we left God and we are spending our time and energy in a fruitless pursuit of happiness. We have found some happiness, but happy times come and go. They are experienced between times of loneliness, ill health, and desperation. There is another feeling which we can have: it is joy. Joy is a lasting experience. *". . . weeping may endure for a night, but Joy cometh in the morning."* (Psalm 30:5)

When we awaken from the darkness of our forgetting, we will be joyous knowing and *feeling* that we are children of God. Gabriel reminded us that Adam fell asleep in Eden, but nowhere in the Bible does it say he woke up. It is the great awakening which awaits us. It is promised, and it is lasting. *"And ye now therefore hath sorrow: but I will see you again, and your heart shall rejoice, and your joy no man taketh from you."* (John 16:22)

At last, thanks to Gabriel, we know how we got here, and how to return to our original spirit Self, consciously. Everyone is going Home. Helping each other is our task, accepting each other as spiritual siblings is necessary. The worst criminal needs our greatest prayers, for he has unconsciously roved very far from his God-self. Prayer works. We know how to pray, which is talking to God. We can learn how to meditate, which is listening to God. He will guide us always; we must ask. *"He hath shewed thee, O man, what is good; and what doth the Lord require of thee, but to do justly, and to love mercy, and to walk humbly with thy God?"* (Micah 6:8). These precepts are easy to understand but not easy to express.

Mercy, defined as 'compassion or forbearance by one in power to an offender'. We leave it to court judges to decide on mercy but we all should exercise that quality of character. It replaces quick judgment, accusations and retaliation. We are exhorted to not only be merciful, but to *love* mercy.

To do justly is to be fair; to deal with everyone equitably. Too often we have a kind of justice for a friend, another for a stranger, another for a perceived enemy. Enemy is one of the words we ought to drop from our vocabulary and our thinking. Blame is another. Hatred, revenge, resentment and rage follow; never to be felt again.

In *A Course in Miracles, Manual for Teachers,* several character traits for a teacher of God are defined. A teacher of God is anyone who chooses to be. Jesus chose to be one. He came to save humanity; to awaken humanity. But, Gabriel told us, only on the cross did he realize he could only save himself. Each of us has a journey ahead of us, and that is to wake up to our innate divinity. We are children of God, and therefore we are sacred. In His loving Embrace God protects us all. Nothing ever happens to us that we did not plan. God would not allow it. Our free choice takes us down a tortuous path. Our free choice can take us up a joyous path. In ACIM, Manual *for Teachers, teachers of God have a handbook of behavior:* trust, honesty, tolerance, gentleness, joy, defenselessness, generosity, patience, faithfulness, and open-mindedness. These can all be accomplished when we are ready. Readiness depends on willingness to learn, willingness to do, willingness to become. When we begin the great awakening journey is an individual choice. When is up to each one of us. Only then can each one of us become what we were originally meant to be. Then we can reach back and give a helping hand to those still asleep. Perhaps Wordsworth said it best: "We feel that we are better than we know."

## Chapter 176   Who Can I Tell?

Who can I tell that for twelve glorious years (1987-1999) I was blessed to sit at the feet of Archangel Gabriel? Who can I tell that a few of us gathered every two months to listen to his teachings of the wisdom of the ages? Who can I tell that he reminded us he was teaching us nothing new, but only reminding us of what we already know but have forgotten? Who can I tell that he told us we are all children of God; that we plan our lives; that there is no death? Who can I tell that Jesus the Christ also visited Earth, (1995-1999) to clarify the stories of his life written in scripture?

I can tell the world, but the world will not listen. I have told a few people, but some will not listen because they believe messages from angels ended in Jesus' time. Others have said, when I told them a truth from Gabriel, 'I don't believe that'! The Bible speaks of angels talking to humans, but of course (some believe) they have not done so since. Others think I am delusional. Some listen in disbelief, but do not ask to borrow the recordings or printings of his lessons that I own. Some disbelieve that communication between the spirit world of God and earthlings is impossible; some think the idea is anathema.

So I have had to resort to writing what I heard. When Gabriel told us the story of the crucifixion, some of us wept at the words. He was asked why (he always took questions). His response was that those who wept were at the scene of the crucifixion. He did not tell us what our role then was. This answer and others led to his explanations that reincarnation is factual.

In truth, Gabriel said, reincarnation is impossible because we have only one life - it is the eternal life of our spirit, which is one with God for it is part of God. But we have come to believe we are separate from God; 'left' God and He will never take us back. These erroneous beliefs have persisted for eons of time. Gabriel came to wake us up to our innate divinity. He said in the Bible we read that Adam fell asleep, but nowhere in the Bible does it say that he woke up. Humanity still sleeps and must awaken to the glory that we are.

In the course of twelve years we learned so much from Gabriel about ourselves, about life, about the long journey we have been on, pretending we are apart from God. We learned about what we need to do to return home to the Father. We invented the karmic wheel which swings from astral plane to Earth and back, in an endless circuit. We design a life to 'make up' to others for apparent injuries to them in a previous lifetime. We design a suffering life because we think we 'deserve' it. The truth is we never harmed anyone without their permission and no one ever harmed us without ours. The glorious truth is that no one will ever harm us without our permission, *because God would not allow it.*

If we believe we are separate from God, we might as well believe the clay can leave the ceramic pot. If it could, the pot would no longer exist. If we could leave God (which we cannot) we would not exist. A belief in God does not make God so; a disbelief in God does not negate the truth of Him. The road home is a simple one to understand, but for most of us it may seem difficult, tedious or impossible. The Bible speaks of the Golden Rule. Bibles of all religions contain this basic command. It is the beginning of our journey back. Love self and neighbor. Forgive all. These are the ways to return and get off the karmic wheel forever.

Who can I tell all this to? I want to shout it all from the rooftops, but I would probably be committed to a mental hospital. So I write, and know that those who are willing to learn will find this or another of my books. I am an optimist. I am a profound believer in God and the angel world. I have come to understand that all life communicates. Intra species communication is available to those who believe. Grand adventures in communication await humanity in the centuries ahead!

It has been so exciting to live on the cusp of the new age (Aquarius); Age of Truth; the age when all humans begin their ascension back to Heaven. All will ascend, beginning soon. At one of Gabriel's seminars there was a pregnant woman in the audience. Gabriel said to her, "The child you are carrying will ascend." The Age of Pisces was the last age of human devolution; Aquarius is the first age of evolution back to God.

Jesus the Christ explained that all references to the many women among his followers were purged from early scriptural texts. Also deleted were all references to reincarnation. He came two thousand years ago to teach humanity, not a few. He did not come to start a new religion. He said people put him on a pedestal because of the miracles he performed, and lost sight of his lessons in truth: Love and forgive; do not judge. It is for that reason Gabriel did not perform miracles; he wanted his lessons in truth to be remembered. They are all recorded for future generations.

In the scheme of eternity time does not exist. In the scheme of eternity everything is just as it is supposed to be, no matter how negative or destructive it seems to be. This is true because God gave us free choice and imagination - two abilities God granted only humankind. What we have done with this imagination and free choice is, in some cases, exquisitely beautiful, and in others terribly destructive. Only by free choice - by all of us - will we bring about a world of love and peace. The Prince of Peace has shown us how to accomplish such a world. He does not, nor cannot make us do so against our will. Freedom of choice is ours. Choice alone will bring us home.

Forgiveness of self and others will provide the door to love of all, and we will be on the road to world peace. Who can I tell all this to? I just told you!

## Chapter 177 Women in Scripture

Although many women made up the multitude which followed Jesus, Archangel Gabriel said all references to them in scripture were purged from the early texts. Peter disliked women and, Archangel Gabriel told us, Peter was jealous of Mary Magdalene (who was never a whore) in whom Jesus confided. Jesus loved the women who followed him, as much as he loved the men. When Jesus preached to a crowd, Gabriel said, he invited the women to come down in front to hear, to the dismay of the men present. Peter did not write for the Bible. It is unlikely any of the apostles could write, since writing then was limited to a few learned scribes. It is unfortunate indeed that Paul also disliked women, for he wrote significant portions of the New Testament books, even though he never met Jesus. Even in recent times some Christians still consider a man to be the 'head of the household'. *"But I would have you know, that the head of every man is Christ; and the head of the woman is the man; and the head of Christ is God."* I Cor. 11:3

Gabriel told us that Paul also disliked women, and that is why he wrote that they should be subservient to men: *For a man indeed ought not to cover his head, forasmuch as he is the image and glory of God: but the woman is the glory of the man."* I Cor. 11:7. This seems to say that man alone receives the image and the glory of God, and then he bestows it on woman. This opinion about women is a carry-over from the Old Testament writings. The story of the Garden of Eden says that woman came from man (his rib), not a man from a woman. Of course all men come from women in the act of birthing, but that was not mentioned. Gabriel explained that, prior to the writing of the Old Testament, women ruled. During the reign of the Goddess there were no wars. Also, the centuries in which women ruled and the Goddess was worshipped came to an end five thousand years ago. Then the Bible was written by men. Paul re-states the ancient

389

Garden of Eden story: *"For the man is not of the woman; but the woman of the man. Neither was the man created for the woman; but the woman for the man."* (I Cor. 11:8-9)

Not only were women subjects, but they also ought to be silent. Men were the authority figures and the teachers: *"Let the woman learn in silence with all subjection. But I suffer not a woman to teach, nor usurp authority over the man, but to be in silence.* (I Tim. 2:11-12). However, in scanning the New Testament, in the first four books Jesus refers to women honorably. *"Then Jesus answered and said unto her, O woman, great is thy faith: be it unto thee even as thou wilt. And her daughter was made whole from that very hour."* (Matt. 15:28). Jesus not only honored women, but at least once in the Bible he singled out a woman for her loving behavior:

When Jesus' feet were anointed by 'a woman which was a sinner', Jesus said to Simon: *"Thou gavest me no kiss: but this woman since the time I came in hath not ceased to kiss my feet. My head with oil thou didst not anoint: but this woman hath anointed my feet with ointment . . . And he said unto her, Thy sins are forgiven."* (Luke 7:45-48). Not many places in scripture mention women disciples, but in Acts 9:36 we find: *"Now there was at Joppa a certain disciple named Tabitha, which by interpretation is called Dorcas."* The meaning of Tabitha/Dorcas is the same: antelope, doe, gazelle; signifying grace and lightness. (MBD, 640)

As Jesus hung on the cross he instructed John to take care of his mother in his absence. This demonstrates Jesus' love for his mother as well as his concern for her safety, comfort, and well-being after he left the earth. *"When Jesus therefore saw his mother, and the disciple standing by, whom he loved, he saith unto his mother, Woman, behold thy son! Then saith he to the disciple, Behold thy mother! And from that hour that disciple took her unto his own home.* (John 19:26-27). The unconditional love which Jesus taught, and by which he lived, is most closely reflected on earth by the unconditional love of a mother toward her children. But this unconditional love, which was demonstrated by Jesus the Christ, is much, much greater than that, according to Gabriel.

# Bibliography

*The Apocryphal Books of the New Testament.* Philadelphia: David McKay, 1901.

Archangel Gabriel (booklets):
*The Easter Story*, 4/11/93.
*Your Soul*, 9/5/93.

Archangel Gabriel (Seminars): *Angels, Aliens and Earthlings*, 7/27/91.

*The Book of Common Prayer.* n.c. USA: Pacific Publishing Studio, 2010.

Borgia, A., *Life in the World Unseen.* London: Odhams Press Limited, 1958.

Boss, J., *In Silence They Return.* St. Paul, MN: Llewellyn Publications, 1972.

Bristow, B.O., *The Universal Consciousness.* Ocala, FL: privately printed, 2009.

Donovan, P. and Lee-Civalier, M., *Getting to Know Your Soul.* New York: iUniverse, Inc., 2004.

Emoto, M., *Messages from Water.* n.d.: Hado Publishing, 1999.

Fillmore, C., *Metaphysical Bible Dictionary.* Unity Village, MO.: Unity School of Christianity, 1931.

Findhorn Community, *The Findhorn Garden.* New York: Harper and Row, 1975.

Forman, H. J., *The Story of Prophecy.* New York: Tudor Publishing Co., 1940.

Foundation for Inner Peace, *A Course in Miracles.* Mill Valley, CA: Foundation for Inner Peace, 1992.

Greber, J., trans. from the German, *Communication with The Spirit World of God.* Teaneck, NJ: Johannes Greber Memorial Foundation, 1974(1932).

Holmes, E.S. and Holmes, F.L. *The Voice Celestial.* New York: Dodd, Mead and Co., 1960.

*Holy Bible, AV.*

Levi, *The Aquarian Gospel of Jesus the Christ.* Marina del Rey, CA: DeVorss & Co., 1980 (1907).

Lewis, J.R. and Oliver, E.D., *Angels A to Z*. Canton, MI: Visible Ink Press, 2002.

Littleton, C.S., gen. ed., *Mythology*. London: Duncan Baird Publishers, 2002.

*The Lost Books of the Bible* and *The Forgotten Books of Eden*. New York: The World Publishing, 1971.

*Merriam Webster's Collegiate Dictionary, Eleventh Edition*. Springfield, MA: Merriam Webster, Inc., 2005.

*Mysteries of the Unknown*, Editors of Time Life Books. 3 vols. Alexandria, VA: 1987-1988.

Rodegast, P. and Stanton, J., comp. *Emmanuel's Book*. Toronto: Bantam, 1987.

Sanderfur, G. *Lives of the Master*. Virginia Beach, VA: A.R.E. Press, 1988.

Schul, B. *The Psychic Power of Animals*. Greenwich, CT: Fawcett Publications, Inc., 1977.

Smith, A.R., ed., *My Life as a Seer*. New York: St. Martin's Press, 1997 (1971).

Springer, R. R., *Into the Light*. Shakopee, MN: Macalester Park Publishing, 1994. Originally published as *Intra Muros*, n.p., 1898.

Swedenborg, E., *Heaven and Hell*. Dole, G.F., trans., West Chester, PA: Swedenborg Foundation, 2000.

Three Initiates, *The Kybalion*. Clayton, GA: Tri-State Press, 1988. Originally published by Yogi Publication Society, 1908.

# Discography

## Audiocassettes

Archangel Gabriel, *Master Jesus*, 1/18/97
Archangel Gabriel, *Master Jesus II*, 5/17/97
Jesus the Christ *Master Jesus III*, 1/17/98
Archangel Gabriel, *Revelation I*, 1/25/92
Archangel Gabriel, *Revelation II*, 2/22/92
Archangel Gabriel, *Atlantis Rising*, 8/24/97

# Sitting at Gabriel's Feet

# Sitting at Gabriel's Feet

Inspired essays based on the archangel's teachings

by Reverend Ellen Wallace Douglas

Other books by author,
available from Trafford.com:

*The Laughing Christ*
*El's Rae: A Memoir*
*Homeward Bound: Meditations for Your Journey*
*Be Still and Know*
*The Peaceful Silence*
*Home to the Light and The Beckoning Light*
*Divination Through the Ages*

Also by author
*Concordance of The Aquarian Gospel of Jesus the Christ*

*This book is dedicated to Emanuel Swedenborg, Fountainhead of New Thought, genius before his time, frequent communicator with the spirit world of God*

"The betrayal of the Son of God lies only in illusions, and all his 'sins' are but his own imagining. His reality is forever sinless. He need not be forgiven but awakened." ACIM T 17: I: 1:1-3

# CONTENTS

# Introduction

It was the evening of October 26, 1987, in upstate New York. I remember it as well as my birthday. Rev. Penny, the founding pastor of Trinity Temple of the Holy Spirit, read from scripture as she always did as the introduction to her sermon. She looked up at the audience to speak, and her voice changed. It was slightly louder than Rev. Penny's usual feminine voice; it spoke with authority. It said "Children of God . . .". We realized later that she was channeling in full trance, which means she was not consciously aware of what she was saying. The spirit entity spoke for about 20 minutes and told us that we should wake up to our own divinity because we, and all humanity, are children of the Living God.

When Rev. Penny returned home she demanded to know who channeled through her. The entity said, "I am Gabriel, the Announcer of the Ages. I will only come again if you allow me to." He then reminded her of what she always said just prior to every sermon - 'May only truth come through me' - and said he brought only truth. When she suggested that no one would believe she was channeling an archangel, he said, "Then call me Lucas".

For more than three years we did call him Lucas, as he gave day-long seminars bi-monthly as well as monthly Sunday sermons. The Board of Trustees at Trinity agreed that Lucas could speak one Sunday each month. It became known as 'angel Sunday' and the church filled up to hear him. On July 27, 1991 Archangel Gabriel presented *Angels, Aliens, and Earthlings, in* which he described the angel world, from the seven archangels to the various levels of angels, including principalities, powers, and thrones. He said there are more angels in Heaven than our minds could comprehend. That was when he told us that he was Gabriel and henceforth we should call him that. At one of his presentations Gabriel told us that spirit had been preparing Rev. Penny for 500 years to be able to channel spirit as she did.

I was blessed to hear all Gabriel's seminars presented in the area. He told us that he would come for twelve years, and he did. His last visitation was December 3rd, 1999, which was attended by about 200 people.

All the seminars Gabriel presented began with quiet instrumental music as forty to eighty people gathered on a Saturday at various locations. All his seminars were recorded and are available at Sacred Garden Fellowship.org. It is suggested the reader listen to them all. He spoke on many subjects, including how/why we come to Earth and what we must do to leave it once and for all, instead of 'cycling' between Earth and the Astral Plane on an endless and needless karmic wheel. Some of his lessons were difficult to hear, such as the fact that we plan our lives before birth, including every person (with their permission) and every circumstance. We do this in order to learn a self-chosen lesson.

The most astounding lesson, in my opinion, was the interpretation of the Book of Revelation, the last book of the New Testament. Four of the following 44 essays combine to give an overview of those interpretations. Contrary to popular belief, Revelation is not about the end of the Earth, or the demise of humanity. In truth it describes, in symbols, humankind's journey away from God and back home again. This book, as the entire Bible, is symbolic first to last.

In 1998 I began writing because I was impelled to pass on Gabriel's teachings. After writing my first two books (see copyright page), I felt that I had one more book to write. As I pondered what it would be, Jesus the Christ came to me through Rev. Penny. He told me that my third book would be a book of meditations, drawn from scripture, *A Course in Miracles,* and my own experiences. He told me to be open to guidance and he would help me. As he once said, "I always keep my promise" and he did. Without his help I would never have become an author.

The Master Jesus also channeled through Rev. Penny, from 1995 to 1999, and one day he came in the morning and Gabriel came in the afternoon. Gabriel explained what a momentous task it was for her to do, since Jesus' energy and Gabriel's are vastly different. That is because Gabriel never manifested as a human being on Earth and Jesus often did; as did we all. Reincarnation is a fact which Gabriel confirmed.

It must be noted here that Gabriel told us eleven Master Teachers came to various places on Earth concurrently with his visitations. They all came with the same message: Wake up, humanity, to your divine nature, as created by God, and live from the Lord God of your Being.

"The only miracle that ever was is God's most holy Son, created in the one reality that is his Father. Christ's vision is His gift to you. His Being is His Father's gift to Him". ACIM T 13: VIII: 6:5-7

The title of this book came to me as I recalled one of the very special moments during a Gabriel seminar. One of the women in the audience said to Gabriel that she did not know who her spiritual teacher was. Gabriel told her that when she found that teacher she would know it. Immediately I went to the microphone (they always took questions) and said to Gabriel "You are my teacher." and he looked me in the eye and responded, "And you are my student". It was a thrilling moment that I shall never forget!

Many of Archangel Gabriel's phrases ring in my mind, such as, "Walk you in the light; you are the light". But I could not tell you what seminar, or even what year, he said them. Regarding Gabriel's teachings, Jesus once told us, "Listen to Gabriel; he is a good teacher". In this lifetime I have been blessed in many, many ways. One of the blessings is my willingness to accept the idea that there is a Heaven world and entities therein can communicate with earthlings. Without this belief I could never have heard the wisdom of the ages from Gabriel or Jesus. There are some individuals who are unwilling to accept the idea of communication from the spirit world of God. It is not a new concept, for the Bible relates many incidents of such communication. This phenomenon is necessary if we are to 'wake up' and live from the Lord God of our Being. The Master Jesus is our elder brother who came to Earth two thousand years ago, as the 'firstfruits' (I Cor.15:23) of humanity. He came to show us the way back home, and often said, "Follow me".

# Section One: Personal Lessons

# All My "Mothers"

## Ida

My biological mother birthed me, changed my diapers, fed me, potty-trained me and taught me table manners. In our home both my parents instilled in me a sense of honesty. My Father passed into spirit at 58, when I was five, and soon afterward my mother became an active alcoholic. All but one of my siblings moved away, and I was left at home with mother and Leah (ten years my senior). Once my mother became addicted to alcohol, she withdrew into her own little dark world. Leah withdrew also, and was diagnosed with schizophrenia. She was committed to the insane asylum. The eldest of us was Marcia, who was eighteen when I was born. She moved to New York City to work and live. My second oldest sibling, Ada, was 16 when I came into the world. She became my surrogate mother when I was about 12. Ada, now divorced, got an apartment for herself and me. She also got an apartment for Ida. With Ada constant moves were part of my early life. Ada kept a home for me until I graduated from high school. Then I went to live with my sister Mertice (6 years older than me). She was waiting for her husband to return from the Pacific, in WWII. Then I went to live with a co-worker, Emma.

## Emma

I lived with Emma and her three sons for a few months. I think she was lonely because her husband was living in Iola, a local TB sanitarium. Emma visited him often, of course. She was kind to me and I think I saw her as another substitute mother. We saw movies, ate out, and worked crossword puzzles together. Emma had a live-in housekeeper named Aunt Kate.

## Aunt Kate

Emma and Kate were not related, but we all called her Aunt Kate. She had a heart of gold. Her temperament was even and kind. Her day began at 4:30am when she arose to go to City Hall to clean it before the business day began. She and I had some good conversations, though I do not recall any topics in particular... I admired her for her ability to start her day so early. I also looked up to her as a person who seemed to understand without saying so.

# lAda (Abie)

Ada Beth was my sister's name; we called her Abie. When I graduated from high school, Abie wanted to go to Florida to live; she hated winter. She asked me to go to Florida with her. She wanted company, I guess. I could not drive yet. We went to Florida, experiencing car problems all the way. I still recall the evening in St. Augustine when we arrived there. A brilliant full moon; palm tree fronds blowing in the wind that was coming off the ocean. It was so warm and wonderful. A whole new view, sound, and feeling for this teenager! I stayed in Florida with Abie for a couple months, then decided to return home to what was more familiar to me. The 24 hour train trip was very long, and I happily stopped off in New York City, to visit Marcia. She was recovering from a radical mastectomy. She asked me to stay with her; she would send me to college, but I was not motivated at that time to return to school. Also, in all honesty, I have never been comfortable around people who are sick. I cannot explain it, and never understood it. But that uncomfortable ness made me say "no" to Marcia. In retrospect I can see it was a selfish decision. Here was my sister weak in recovery and I was unwilling to help her out -- education or not.

I returned to Rochester although there was no home to return to, with Abie now in Florida. Both Joy and Mertice had married. So I got a room somewhere in a residential neighborhood and got a job at Hawkeye, part of Eastman Kodak, as a keypunch operator. It was the beginning of the electronic era. I punched a time clock four times a day and worked in a room of about 100 keypunch machines. I felt like a number. I lasted three weeks. When I gave notice I was lectured severely about how much EK had spent to train me. It all fell on deaf ears. I hated living alone, at seventeen. I never learned to make friends and I didn't want to go to bars. Also, I had very low self-esteem. So I called another sister, Joy, and asked her if I could come live with her and her husband and their three children.

# Joy

Joy tried to talk me out of it because there was no city bus service in West Brighton; there wasn't much room in their small home, the roof leaked, etc. etc. But I was determined - stubborn - and she relented. I moved in, found a neighbor to commute with, and lived there for nearly three years. It was while living there that I met Steve, a neighbor of Joy's - and later married him. Joy was seven and a half years my senior. When Evie, my first baby was born, Joy showed me how to change a diaper and give Evie a bath. In fact, she was my role model as a mother. She treated her children lovingly and fairly. Throughout my parenting years it was Joy who got me through all the problems and accidents. She knew when something was serious or not, when I saw disaster in every little accident. The most selfless example of Joy's support in those years was when I was accidentally burned severely and spent 7 weeks in the hospital. Joy took my then three kids until I returned home. I had been at death's door, but did not know it until after the critical time. The only comment she made when I had made a full recovery was that it took some getting used to, to have kids at her dinner table with brown eyes! She was raising her own six blue-eyed children.

## Catherine

When the children were all in school I went back to work full- time. I landed a fine job as a bookkeeper on Gibbs St., and then I worked for an insurance company at East Main and Culver Road. One of my co-workers had an elderly baby-sitter for her nine-year-old son. The sitter's name was Catherine. I met her on her 79th birthday. Catherine and I became fast friends. We would go out for lunch, have a few drinks, and then order food. Total time spent on lunch would be 3-4 hours. Catherine had lived an extraordinary life and she shared her experiences with me. When I left Rochester she had been moved to a nursing home by her absent son (he lived in Florida and visited Catherine twice a year). Because I was so impressed with Catherine's life, I wanted to write about it. She agreed to being taped as she related her experiences to me. But I never did write the story of her life. One day when I lived in Schenectady she telephoned me and said that she had breast cancer and would undergo surgery to have the breast removed. She was 92. I drove to see her the day after the operation. She was sitting up in bed; hair combed; lipstick on. I said "How are you feeling?" She said "Fine; how are you?" Catherine passed over at 95 years of age. No one called to let me know. I learned of her death when I called her and her phone was disconnected. I called the nursing home and was told, coldly, and matter-of-factly, that she had 'expired' two weeks earlier.

# Myrtle

While in eastern New York I kept in constant contact with my children and returned to visit for weddings and the births of all my grandchildren, nine in number. I moved from place to place; always in eastern New York. About five years after I moved to eastern NYS, I met Myrtle, a widowed lady with several grown children, one of whom I met. He lived in Schenectady, where Myrtle also lived. She taught interested people how to become psychic. She was a born medium, herself. She was my first Bible teacher. We would go out for dinner weekly, then park by water someplace - Mohawk River, a lake, a stream, or the Erie Canal. Water is the best transmitter of psychic energy. There, in the car, I would read a portion of scripture that she chose, and then I would read one or two psalms, also of her choosing. I asked her questions about the readings, and thus became familiar - for the first time - with the Bible. Myrtle also held weekly séances, on a Sunday afternoon. These, too, were all new to me. At the first one, although I had never seem spirit before, Jesus the Christ came to me. Standing a few feet away, in the psychic circle, he wore a white robe. His auburn hair fell to his shoulders. His piercing blue eyes met mine. His arms were outstretched, palms up. He held across his hands a huge loaf of bread, and said, "Lay down your life for me and I will give you the bread of life." I have never since seen spirit again. I did not know what he meant by the words, but the vision is engraved in my memory. It was several weeks before I understood. It was when I stopped drinking and realized I had to 'let go and let God' run my life; surrendering forever to a Higher Power. A few years later I became ordained as a Christian Metaphysical Minister. Then I became pastor of Trinity Temple, where I met Olive, called Ollie by all her friends.

# Ollie

This fine woman had attended Trinity Temple of the Holy Spirit church for years before I came on the scene. She and her husband supported the church faithfully. Ollie's husband passed before I met Ollie. She made cakes for all celebrations at the church. Although Ollie did drive, after her husband passed over, she gave up her car. I used to pick her up on a Sunday afternoon for dinner and we took a drive in the country. She told me that when her husband was alive and working she worked with him. He was a binder of libers (legal books) and he traveled extensively in central New York State, to city halls and county buildings to repair or replace bindings on the huge tomes of recorded deeds and mortgages.

## Reverend Penny

Reverend Penny Donovan founded Trinity Temple of the Holy Spirit in the 1960s. I first met her in 1983 and began classes in psychic and spiritual development in 1984. In 1987 I became a certified medium, and decided that I would like to study the ministry. Although Rev. Penny was younger than I, the impact she made on my life cannot go unrecognized here. Perhaps she was, and remains, my spiritual mother! When I asked her to teach me to be a minister, she immediately said, "Yes". I was very pleased. But the next day I realized that she really did not know me. So I called her and made an appointment to see her in person. We met at her home. I told her how much I appreciated her instant agreement to accept me as a ministry student, but she did not know my background. I told her about leaving my husband and family, and my alcoholism. She said that did not matter. I was joyous over her acceptance. It would be many years before I realized that she saw something in me that I did not see; some potential that I was totally unaware of. Of course Rev. Penny is a natural medium and perhaps she did have some inner vision of my future. In recent years she told me that, as a writer, I inspire her! She has inspired me since we first met and continues to be my best friend, minister, teacher, healer and counselor - as well as a mighty channel of Archangel Gabriel and Jesus the Christ, from 1987 to 1999. Since then, she has channeled other entities in the spirit world.

## Dorothy

Dorothy Donovan was Rev. Penny's mother. Dorothy attended every Sunday service and every Gabriel presentation that she was able to. Dorothy was a reader and sometimes gave me books she had read. She loved to go to a market in Sharon Springs, several miles away, for apples, apple cider, and other items. We would have a nice dinner, drive to the market and talk and laugh a lot. Dorothy enjoyed telling me - and others - that she was born in Bethlehem. Bethlehem is a suburb of Albany, NY. That is where she was born, but because of her ardent love for scripture she wanted people to think it was the place where Jesus was born. Before Dorothy passed into Heaven, she told her daughter exactly what she wanted to wear - clothes and jewelry - when laid out, who should get the jewelry before she was buried and who should officiate at her memorial service: Rev. Neal (also ordained by Rev. Penny) and I were chosen. Dorothy also insisted that Rev. Penny *pay* us for the memorial service, although neither of us would have otherwise accepted payment in exchange for this high honor. Dorothy had a dachshund that she name Squeedunk. Before she passed into Heaven, she asked the local cemetery manager if she could be buried with her dog. He told her it was illegal. But she had Rev. Penny hold Dorothy's ashes until Squeedunk passed and then they were buried together.

## Genevieve

The other church in Albany where I served as Pastor was the Capital District Church of Religious Science. One day a woman called the church and left a message. She was looking for a CRS church in the area to attend. I phoned her and we made an appointment to meet at her daughter's home, where she was living. She told me that she had just moved to Waterford from Rhode Island, where she lived alone. When diagnosed as legally blind she decided to move in with her daughter and son-in-law.

Gen, as I always called her, was an interesting lady who had been born in eastern New York State, joined the US Army after WWII, became a 1st Lieutenant, and went to Germany for a time after the war. She saw the terrible devastation in that post-war county. In the service she met the man who became her husband. They had four children, whom they raised in Oregon. They later divorced. To cope with her blindness she attended a special school in Rhode Island. While there she made a caned footstool which she gave me during our friendship. I still use it. Gen was a student of *A Course in Miracles*. I had a weekly group meeting in my home to study it. She always attended. I also would take her to our Sunday service at church. Gen had a great sense of humor and we shared many hours talking and laughing together. She was a steadfast friend and attended the church, my weekly *Miracles* group, and a weekly spirituality group I offered in rented space under the assumed name "The Penultimate Sanctuary".

One evening I picked Gen up for one of my weekly classes. It was snowing but the roads were okay. We stopped to eat on the way. While we ate, the snow came down much harder. I looked out the restaurant window and said to Gen, "I think we better consider the class cancelled", and I took her home. I was amazed and appreciative of her devotion to me. Gen was extremely generous to me. Once I mentioned that I was going to go shopping for a mattress, and she gave me money to buy one! I was asked, rather abruptly, to leave the Capital District Church of Religious Science (the 'retired' pastor returned). Gen took it personally and refused to return to the church for Sunday services. I did not attend, either, since I did not feel comfortable doing so. Gen insisted on tithing to *me*, in spite of my protests.

Gen came from a long-lived family and one time she visited her sister in Pennsylvania who was 93, a little older than Gen was at the time. After I moved back to Rochester, Gen was hospitalized at the VA hospital in Albany. I did not go to see her because I thought (based on her long-lived family history) that it was a short-term situation and she would soon return to her daughter's home. She did not. A few weeks later I rented space in Rensselaer and held a memorial service for her. About 20 people came and shared their memories of this great lady. Because of her friendly, out-going personality she had made many friends in a short time. I still cherish - and use often in my writing - the *Concordance of A course in Miracles* which she game me as a gift. I also have photos of her, as a young woman and more recently, as my dearly beloved friend.

These women all contributed to my life. There is nothing like a companion, a friend, a supporter. They all were wonderful women with whom I shared time, ideas and dreams. I salute and praise them all here and now. I only hope that I made a difference in their lives as they made a difference in mine.

Finally, the Mother of us all - Mother-Father God. I have heard clergy of the Catholic and Protestant churches use this title. And so I offer Gabriel's female version of The Lord's Prayer:

*Our Mother, who art the sacred spaced within,*
       *Holy is thy Name.*
*Thy Kingdom be manifested on all levels of my being*

*As it is manifested in the sacred space of my*
*Spirit Self.*
*Keep me aware of Thee, my Source.*
*For so shall I then be delivered from the*
*Illusion of separateness.*
*For thine is the kingdom of my being,*
*The glory of my light,*
*And the power of my spirit,*
*Now and forever.*
*Amen*

# The Forgotten Holiday

I wonder how many women can identify the very day that their first menses began. It is likely that we can recall our age at the time, or the year, or even the event itself. But the very day that it began seems to have been lost in the annals of time. Is it really so insignificant? How many women were forewarned? How many women were taken by surprise and filled with fear, thinking it might be death itself come upon them?

In my case I was thirteen and, fortunately, I was home. Mertice, six years older than me, was home at the time. I called out to her from the bathroom, 'I think I am dying.' She calmly came to me, holding a napkin in her hand. She gave it to me and merely said, 'Here, use this. You will need these every month now'. I wondered how she could be so calm, but it settled me down. Since that day was 71 years ago, I do not recall the extent of my knowledge at the time about "the birds and the bees". As a mother I admit that I failed miserably to have a serious conversation with my daughters before they reached puberty.

Some women can name the day when they will start and stop bleeding. As for me, I could be a week early or a week late. This irregularity made it challenging to know when I conceived any of my four children. But 'the period' does happen monthly for many years - 'productive years', they call it - when women are physically able to produce offspring. Another unpredictable time is when menses will begin. Some girls are only nine; others can be fourteen or fifteen.

I am not sure where the word 'curse' fits in to this experience, or when in began. From a cynical standpoint I could say that men named it such, because as a rule intercourse does not take place during the menses. Because the monthly event sometimes brings pain, bloating and short tempers, perhaps women named it 'the curse'. For women who do not want to become pregnant but may have engaged in unprotected sex, the onset of menses is a joyous relief, the antithesis of a 'curse'.

Although I did not always have 'cramps', there is no question but that proper personal care is a nuisance. When I entered this phase of my life, pads and belts were common. Later, with internal protection (tampons) the nuisance was lessened. One simply had to remember to regularly change the insert.

The reason it is a 'forgotten holiday' is because this writer believes it is a significant rite of passage that should be acknowledged, informed, and celebrated. It is a singularly important event in the life of every human female. This is the first right of passage in a woman's life. It should be acknowledged to the extent that the celebrant is comfortable with the acknowledgement. The girl should be informed previously just what exactly takes place in her body. It should be celebrated because is means so many things.

It means that even though she has not matured emotionally, her body is telling her that it is ready for conception. Suddenly she is not a little girl, but a blossoming young woman. Now she must take responsibility for taking care of herself on 'those days'. More importantly, now she must take the awesome responsibility of making some serious decisions. Does she know what temptations are in store for her, when she is attracted to a member of the opposite sex? Does she have a clue about the hormonal urges? Can she decide in advance how far she will go in her intimate affection (once called 'petting')? Is she aware of the ramifications of becoming pregnant? Does she not have a right to know all this? Will all this knowledge empower her to control her sexual life? I believe that with all this information she will begin an emotional maturation to accompany her physical changes.

Of course formal education includes information about the 'biological clock', and the physical process can easily be explained. But what of the emotional process? Based on my own experience I believe that it is so important for an older woman to be available to answer questions. Encouraged to talk about it, by a compassionate female, the girl may have many questions about the new challenge. She ought to be made aware of the significance of it. A personal advisor should be available to assist the new young woman as she enters this new and lasting phase of her sexual life.

The celebration can be limited to the girl and her personal advisor - whether her mother (ideally), or another woman who will take the time for explanations and questions. It is, after all, a private matter. And probably the other person will note the date as she relates to the girl the necessary information to be comfortable with this new life. Perhaps the older woman will share her own story, and stories of women she as known. There is nothing like knowing you are not alone to comfort you, in any situation. Another bit of information which I can share here: When I was seriously burned and had to be hospitalized for seven weeks, my periods stopped. Kidding, I asked my doctor what went on in the OR when I was under sedation! He explained that a physical trauma will temporarily halt the menses process.

So, here's to noting the exact date, and celebrating it annually. It is the first rite of passage for any girl. For many years she will have to be aware of her body's monthly expression. She may find great joy in predicting the birth date of her children - or at least her first one, as I did!

# Parenting

There is no way that I would claim to be an authority on parenting, just because I had four healthy babies. Today they are in their late fifties and early sixties. I would, however, like to share some lessons I learned from Archangel Gabriel, who often visited a small group of spiritual seekers in the Albany, NY area from 1987 to 1999. These are the lessons:

1. We plan our lives before we come to Earth - every situation and every person we meet, whether they are in our lives for many years or only a few minutes. We choose the situations and the relationships in order for us to learn the lessons we have chosen to learn.

2. We are always and *only* responsible for ourselves. We can be responsible *to* another, such as taking care of little children lest they hurt themselves or others. We do, after all, want to raise them to maturity so they can then take care of themselves.

With these lessons in mind, I contemplated parenting in general, as well as my experience of parenting. I am joyous that I chose these children of mine, and that they chose me. They are all healthy, working, caring people who make friends and keep them. Thanks, kids, for choosing me as your parent. We know there are reasons why you may not still love me, yet you do, and for that I am grateful. I can see, too, that as the next two generations come forth they all are healthy, also. My gratitude continues.

I write this to reflect on what I learned in psychology classes about offspring. It is claimed that people are the result of nature or nurturing. It means that what we are is a result of our genetic inheritance or our environment in growing up. This commonly accepted choice is now shattered with Gabriel's statement. This new wisdom provides us with explanations for many questions we have all asked. Where did this red-headed kid come from when both parents are blond or brunette? At the other end of a long spectrum of questions - how did this person grow up to become a serial killer?

13

It matters little why hair color differs from that of the parents. But a whole new era of conjecture opens now regarding the effect of pre-birth choices. To further explain these decisions, we must ask ourselves 'how do we choose our lessons?' We cannot deny any longer that we have lived many lifetimes on Earth, and this lifetime is just another experience. Yes, reincarnation is a fact, as clarified by Gabriel, not a fancy. We choose lessons based on what we learned or failed to learn our last time around. In effect, we get another chance to learn. God gave us all free choice, and with it we decide our lives.

Parents always want to do what is best for their children. This is a given. What is not always understood is what is best? Because they come with their own 'baggage', so to speak, how can we possibly know what it is that babies need to deal with their pre-arranged burden? We can keep in mind this wisdom, and be mindful of early expressions of needs. All babies need nurturing. It has been proven that newborns that are not shown love and affection tend to die very young. The warmth of a mother's love is essential.

One all-encompassing rule is to love the new arrivals unconditionally. This does not seem so difficult, but when a crying infant will not be comforted, when they are feverish or colicky, we have to call on infinite patience and know that all is well and this is a temporary condition. Later, when 'the terrible twos' are raging, we need to know that it is this age when personality is being formed. These growing offspring now seem to be testing us at every turn. They no longer respond to our every command.

Throughout their young lives children present problems and questions to their loving parents. These boys and girls present constant challenges to us. As they come into the teens they present a whole new set of challenges. There is no way that we could offer here all the possible problems and questions that the kids bring into our lives. It would take volumes. What is sufficient is to know these new teachings of Gabriel and constantly keep them in mind throughout the parenting years.

When an infant seems obstreperous from the beginning, it could be the result of having passed over in the last lifetime in a traumatic way. Gabriel said we will pick up from where we left off, in the last lifetime.

Even the birth event is a predictor. I asked Gabriel once (he always took questions from the audience) why some women bear children rapidly and others have a long, difficult labor. It has nothing to do with the mother! It has everything to do with the soon to be baby. If the entity, in recalling its lifetime to come, is hesitant to arrive into the world, it will think should I, should I not? etc. until it finally decides to commence the life ahead. It is this indecision of the baby, before birth, that causes the mother to endure a long labor!

As for the baby born deformed or with a serious illness, those too are choices of the newborn. Perhaps the lesson is for them, or perhaps it is for the parents. Only God and the higher Self of the baby know the answer to this. The higher Self is the spirit of is; the lower self is our physical form, with its shape and personality. Before birth we decide our body's shape and sex.

Here is wisdom from on high for us to use and apply henceforth. For those who read and discount the truth, some day it will be accepted because it *is the truth*. As Archangel Gabriel used to say, why would I come unless we knew that you are ready to learn these lessons? God's messengers come at the Will of God. With our God-given free choice we can accept or deny the truth, but we can never *change* the truth. Now we are ready to learn; now we can understand so much of parenting that we could not understand before.

What all children need is love and loving guidance. When we pray for our children we ought to pray for their highest good. When we pray for ourselves we should also pray for our own highest good. Only God knows what our highest good is, and it is almost always much better than we think it is; much better than we think we deserve. God blesses us with children and we can always look to Him for guidance, no matter how difficult the task may seem.

What we all need to learn is what Jesus taught so long ago: love self and others, forgive everyone. Micah 6:8 tells us what we all need to learn:

"He hath shewed thee, O man, what is good; and what doth the Lord require of thee, but to do justly, and to love mercy, and to walk humbly with thy God?

# Planet Earth and New York City

It has often been said of New York City, "It's a great place to visit, but I wouldn't want to live there".

Today, as I ate my lunch, I thanked God for the food and then looked out at my empty bird-feeder, wishing I had the mobility and strength to re-fill it. Then I thanked God for my return unto Him. For I am now 83, and realize my time here is running short. I am perfectly OK with that. I prayed then that this time around I will not return to Earth again. It has been a great place to visit, but I would not want to live here - again.

This incarnation has been a spectacular adventure. Many dreams have come true from past lifetimes. Many goals have been attained. I have been truly blessed. I could easily list the greatest, most memorable experiences in the past eight decades of my life this time around.

1. Student of Archangel Gabriel
For twelve wondrous years (1987-1999) I was blessed indeed to hear Archangel Gabriel teach us the wisdom of the ages. And yet he said that he told us nothing new; only reminded us of what we already know but have forgotten! Gabriel gave many weekend retreats and many short talks, but always the lessons were permeated with the basic single lesson he brought to us: "You are children of God. Wake up to it and live from the Lord God of your Being." Thanks be to God that all his messages were recorded for posterity.

Hearing him this time (1987-1999) was a second chance to learn his lessons. One day he told the group, "I told you this 500 years ago." I have often contemplated where and who I was at that distant point in time, but it really does not matter. Gabriel said our past lives are only relevant in relation to our current lifetime; an accumulation of all we have learned in the past. This is the lifetime that is important, and how we live it will fashion our next incarnation.

The lessons Gabriel taught became the inspiration and foundation of my writing career. I became an author to pass on his teachings *as I understood them*, in hopes that the hundreds of meditations I wrote would help inspire, inform and comfort future generations.

2. Student of my elder brother, Jesus the Christ
In 1995 the Master Jesus Christ came for the first time. He and Gabriel then alternated in presenting lessons until they both left in 1999. Jesus noted several quotations of his in scripture and gave corrections as to what he *really* said or what he meant by his words. There were two topics which were purged from the New Testament: all references to reincarnation and all references to the many women who followed him.

Many of my meditations quote his words from those four years.
Let it be known that all my writing was inspired. All of it. I was guided to all quotations from the *Bible, A Course in Miracles* and other books. My own words were inspired. I learned this when, in re-reading my own words I have often thought, 'I don't remember writing this.'

3. Trained medium
I studied for three years at Trinity Temple of the Holy Spirit in Albany, NY. to become a capable medium. Although I gave many messages from the pulpit and a few in private, in later years I stopped because most questions put to a psychic, or medium, relate to worldly issues. If I wanted to grow spiritually I had to 'rise above' these mundane problems.

4. Minister and pastor
Reverend Penny Donovan was my Mentor. When I asked Rev. Penny if she would teach me to be a minister, she quickly said "Yes." Later on I had to remind her of my 'checkered' past. But whether I told her I was a recovering alcoholic, a woman who had left her husband and family, was bi-sexual, it did not matter to her! Only much later in life did I realize that back then she saw something in me that I did not. She saw the potential of a minister, a pastor, a counselor, a compassionate person, and an author. When she left the church she had founded 30 years earlier, she entrusted the pulpit to me! Now, much later, she tells me that I inspire her. No, Penny, not like you have ---- and still do, inspire me.

5. Guided speaker, gifted writer.

When I lived a lifetime in the 17th Century my father was a missionary from England and I was his daughter. He would pace and give me his sermon, because he was channeling the sermon from spirit. I admired him and wanted to be like him, but in those days women were not considered capable of becoming ministers. Also, channeling was a forbidden practice (witches were burned at the stake). In this lifetime I have become both a guided speaker and gifted writer. Thanks be to God for these ancient dreams come true!

6. Wife and mother

For twenty-two years a husband who was dependable, faithful, and hard-working was there for me at *all* times. He was the steadfast anchor in my life during those years. He showed me what patience is; was the most patient man I ever met. Blessed with two sons and two daughters, who still are healthy and active, there are no words to express the joys of parenting. Yes, all days were not joyous - accidents, poor choices, bad relationships - but all in all I am supremely proud of my four offspring. They are independent, smart, and caring. They have also blessed me with 9 grand children and 7 great-grandchildren.

7. Author

One year before Archangel Gabriel finished his visitations I began research on my first book *The Laughing Christ*. I thought it was the only book I would write. Four years later, in 2002, I had it published by a POD (print-on-demand) publisher. I ordered a total of 500 copies and sold them, bartered them, or gave them all away. My second book was my memoirs entitled *El's Rae: a Memoir*. My middle given name is Rae and El is the Hebrew name of God. I have come to know that I am a child of God, as is all of humanity. On October 13, 2004, Rev. Penny Donovan, my mentor, brought to me a message from the Master Jesus. He told me my third book would be one of meditations, drawn from scripture, The Course (*A Course in Miracles*) and my own experience. He told me to keep an open mind and he would guide me. *Homeward Bound: Meditations for Your Journey was* published in 2005.

As I wrote *Homeward Bound* I realized it was the first of a trilogy of meditation books. *Be Still and Know* and *The Peaceful Silence* followed. Although the trilogy contained 1,095 meditations I still desired to write a book of meditations of, by, and about Jesus the Christ. So, with another 130 meditations I wrote *Home to the Light*.

18

Long before I began *The Laughing Christ,* I had started a *Concordance of The Aquarian Gospel of Jesus the Christ,* since I placed a very high value on that book. Off and on for eighteen years I would work on the concordance or hire someone else to assist me. I spent hundreds of dollars on it. Finally I decided to destroy or publish it. A friend, who was also the editor of my first 3 books, advised me to publish. Instead, I had a local printer produce 3 copies and comb-bind them. That was June, 2007. Because of the profound impact that Gabriel's teachings had on me, I decided to write a book describing humankind's devolution and evolution back to God, as explained by Gabriel. We never left God, except in our consciousness. And we are, without fail, going to return to Him. So I penned - guided by spirit, as always - *The Beckoning Light,* and published it in 2010. Following that I wrote *Home to the Light.* Then *Divination Through the Ages.*

This incarnation has been full of blessings, for which I am eternally grateful. I have no idea how many more times I will choose to return to Earth. It's been nice to visit, but in the scheme of eternity, I wouldn't want to live here! Several 'past lives' have been described to me, by a medium. In this regard, Gabriel said at one time, "This is the one [lifetime] you will remember." How could we possibly forget visitations from an archangel?

"All that you need to give this world away in glad exchange for what you did not make is willingness to learn the one you made is false." ACIM T 13: VII: 4:4

# The Prayer

Do you believe that God would give you anything but a blessing?

The story goes like this: A woman was laboriously climbing a steep mountain, praying all the while 'Please, Lord, don't let me fall off the mountain.' She climbed, and struggled and prayed, 'Please, Lord, don't let me fall off the mountain.' Finally, she fell off the mountain.

How quick we are to assume that God does not answer all prayers, but only some of them. When we understand angels and their characteristics, we can understand what the woman's problem was. Angels were created by God to watch over us humans, and God gave them free choice of *only good*. Angels do not understand anything negative. Angels comprehend *only* positive.

One afternoon, at a seminar by Archangel Gabriel, he told us a story. During the lunch break his helper angel, Tinkerbell, went to Gabriel and pointing to a woman at the seminar, said, "What is that darkness in her heart area?" Gabriel told her that it was sadness. Tinkerbell asked what 'sadness' is. Gabriel explained that it is the opposite of love. Tinkerbell did not understand, *for all she knew was love*. And she knows that love is all there is, so love could *have no opposite*.

To us, God gave free choice across the board. (And oh, what not-good choices we have made!). Because angels only hear what they understand (like humans), the angel in the story of the mountain failed to hear 'don't' and only heard 'fall off the mountain', and so they helped the woman in the way they understood her prayer. From this true perspective we see that angels actually did help her by answering her prayer.

This story can provide us with a key to valid prayer and know that in using this process of praying all our prayers will be answered by those wondrous angels who watch over us. When we have a near death experience or a near-fatal accident, it is because angels watch over us until we have accomplished what we came to do. They know our life's plan. Our Higher Self also knows our plan, but we have forgotten it. We plan all our experiences and all the people we encounter - whether it is for a moment or for years. Sure, we each have a guardian angel, but Archangel Gabriel told us that *each* of us has 144,000 angels to assist us in our lives. Angels can protect us, but they can never interfere with our choices, no matter how poor. For we have God-given free choice. Our angels help us to find a parking spot; select clothes to wear; choose a career; choose a life partner. Are they not grand? As God's messengers could they be any less?

In the Bible, Matthew tells us "And all things, whatsoever ye shall ask in prayer, believing, ye shall receive". (21:22). Of course, the climbing woman did believe that her prayer would be answered and yet there are the immutable laws of God which pertain. Angels did their best, within their assigned ability. They could not answer a prayer which they did not comprehend. They heard 'fall off the mountain', but not 'don't let me'. How often we pray for something and it seems our prayer is not answered! We then assume that either 1) God did not hear it, 2) God does not care about us or 3) God thinks we do not deserve it. In all cases it seems that God has turned His back on us. (God has no 'back'). In spite of this 'seeming' we must come to know that God loves us, His beloved children, for He created us from Himself. Therefore we are His forever and He would no sooner *not love* us than we would not love our own human offspring. So, what does it mean when God seems to ignore us by not answering our prayer?

When we pray for something and we do not receive it, later we realize that what we had prayed for was not a GOOD thing for us, in the long run. Sometimes we find ourselves thanking God that He did not give us what we had asked for. This all seems like a great puzzlement, and yet with the vision of understanding we know that God wants for us only what is for our highest good. That is what we should pray for, and only that. Asking God for what is for our highest good will result in ALL our prayers being answered. And when we ask for something we think we want, we should add at the end of the prayer, "Or something better", because God always knows what is for our best good. Our prayers are usually within the limits of our thinking, but God knows us better than we know ourselves. That is why we must not limit our prayers. We must leave them open-ended, for God can bring us more than heart could wish. How often he does, if we do not turn away what He sends us.

Oftentimes we pray and the prayer does not manifest, and some time later we experience a response that is far superior to what we originally prayed for. This is probably why we have been told to ask for what we *think we want*, or 'something better'. For God knows what it is we are asking for, but from His objectivity (knowing all things and all thoughts) He knows what is for our highest good; He knows our life's plan.

All our prayers of asking for something we do not have imply lack or need. In the long run, in the truth of our being, what could we possibly lack or need as children of God? What we are is what we have, for all God's creation has a spark of divinity in it. So we are imbued with anything that we could possibly 'need' or 'want'. We view a flower or a flower's bud, and rejoice in its beauty. We behold a new-born kitten - or new-born beast of any kind, and we glory in its birthing. And, Oh, what joy we feel when we see our own new-born baby! What joy! What glory! As Wordsworth said (*Odes on Immortality*), it is 'trailing clouds of glory from Heaven . . ."

This new-born infant, this child of promise, this long-awaited baby, makes us feel special for having viewed it. Here, in our arms, we can hold its glory and become one with it. There is no greater joy than this moment in time. Yet we soon forget the glory when we pace at midnight with a fevered child. We forget the wonder of birth when we become frustrated with potty-training. And through the years of maturation we somehow lose that moment of magic and wonder as infants become growing children and - finally, a new individual with its own unique dreams and abilities. Now they are a person who seeks to learn on its own instead of asking questions of parents and taking the word of teachers. This wondrous individual, now our adult child, is meeting all challenges and seeking new adventures.

Our prayers become requests for our kids' safety, health, and accomplishments. Yet we know they have free choice, just as we did. We also know that they have angels watching over them, as angels have watched over us. So many angels attend us even though we cannot see them. What on earth could 144,000 angels DO for us? Some attend our immediate requests; some are out clearing the path for our plans of the future. Some are arranging to have a parking place for us at our destination when driving. Some help us with our makeup, our hairdo, our wardrobe, and help us decide on what we would like to wear each day. It seems like several would join together to accomplish some long-term goals. But whatever their task, they always do it with joy, because of their very nature of positive ness. Angels love to hear us humans laugh. They also appreciate our words of our gratitude for them.

We must be mindful of the prayer that is ineffectual. It is the rote prayer without feeling. Gabriel explained that when we recite, without feeling, any prayer that we have memorized, that prayer goes up just so far and bounces back. It does not have the feeling behind it that is absolutely required for effectiveness. So, no matter how well we know the words, we need to say the prayer *always* with feeling so that it can rise up to the Source of Life, our Higher Power, the God of our understanding. Gabriel said that in a church service, as people pray, the angels see the rote prayers - repeated without feeling - go up just so far and no farther. But here and there a spark of light rises with the prayer that is said with feeling behind it, and it goes up much higher, and is heard by God.

# These Angels of Mine

Please note I do not say 'those' angels of mine because they are constantly with me. How could I express the surprise and joy that we felt when Archangel Gabriel told us that we *each* have 144,000 angels!

At one of Gabriel's lessons in truth he described the angel world. He told us about the seven archangels, including himself. He described the layer upon layer of angels in Heaven. There are so many angels that our minds could not comprehend the total number. He described the tasks of each layer of angel, including the principalities, powers, and virtues mentioned in scripture.

I believe it was at this seminar, titled *Angels, Earthlings, and Aliens*, that he told us the number of our personal angels. At a later seminar someone went to the microphone and asked Gabriel why we had more than one angel. I never heard Gabriel respond so quickly or laugh as loudly as he did then. He said that we would drive one angel crazy!

When asked about what all those angels do for us, he replied that they help us in many ways, from finding a parking space to helping us decide on a career. I have asked angels many times to help me find a parking space at a busy restaurant. One particular time comes to mind. A friend of mine wanted to go to the Olive Garden in the Albany area (where I lived at the time) on a Friday night. That being America's 'night out' I wanted to refuse, but I did not want to disappoint her, so I prayed for a spot near the door, as she walked with some difficulty, on a cane. When we arrived we found the parking space closest to the front door vacant. I thanked God aloud.

There are several times I can recall when not only did an angel assist me, but I would call them miracles. I guess 'angel' and 'miracle' fit nicely together anyhow. One time I had a blind date with someone who wanted to go bowling. I did not own my own bowling ball, and hesitated to admit it to this bowler. So I went to the local Salvation Army store and thought it would be fine if I could find a green ball. There were only two or three bowling balls there, but one was green. I tried the grip and could not believe it -- it fit perfectly!

Some years later I decided to acquire a dog. I moved to a small house in Saratoga County and saw a dog house in the back yard, so I asked the landlady if I could have a dog. When she said okay, I thought about what kind of dog I would like to have. My daughter had been given a toy poodle when she was young, by her paternal grandmother. We all loved Melody. So I thought if I could have any dog in the world, what would I want? (Gabriel had told us to ask for whatever we desired). I prayed for a black, female, adult toy poodle.

About 3 weeks later when I arrived at work someone said to me that if I wanted a dog, a co-worker had one to give away. When I asked the woman what kind of dog she had, her reply was 'a ten year old black female toy poodle.'! So 'Baby' and I had six wonderful years together before I put her down. No, I would not say that, for I sent her up to Heaven and will see her again when I myself arrive.

Sometimes Gabriel suggested to Reverend Penny Donovan (who channeled his lessons) that we go on a weekend retreat. We would gather on a Friday evening to sign in and hear Gabriel for a time. Then Saturday he gave us a lesson in truth through out the day. Sunday, after breakfast, he would give a closing talk, ending about noon. Those were such wonderful weekends!

One weekend I checked in to my motel room and went to pay for the retreat. But I could not find my checkbook. It was a rainy night and I thought if I lost it outdoors it would be illegible and probably unusable. But even using a flashlight I could not locate it. So I retired for the night. In the morning, on my way to breakfast, a woman at the retreat approached me with my checkbook. I asked her where she found it, and she said 'in the grass, over there'. I shuddered as I opened it. I could not believe my eyes. A few pages were damp on the edges, but that is all! I still can imagine an angel holding a tiny umbrella over it to keep it dry.

But the angelic help which many other people became aware of was at a psychic fair in Albany one day.

I had a lovely amethyst necklace which I wore often. One day it broke and the gemstones scattered. I picked up all I could find and put them in an envelope. I put the envelope in a dresser drawer and forgot about it. Then, when I went to the psychic fair I took it to the women who sold it to me, hoping they could repair it for me. When I went to their table I handed the envelope to them and asked them if they could fix it. One of them pulled out the necklace in one piece, saying 'what's wrong with it?' I was stunned! I told some friends and the word spread quickly about Ellen's miracle! Only in my imagination can I picture tiny little angels in that envelope re-stringing it! Or maybe they just uttered a magic word!

When my car was getting old and need constant repairs, I began looking for a new one. I saw one I liked advertised and went to the dealer with a deposit in hand. On the way home I thought the deal would not go through since my credit was not that good. The next day I got the call - no, the deal did not go through. This scenario repeated itself three times. It was during the twelve years that Gabriel was visiting the Earth. I did not ask Gabriel what was going on with this situation because he made it clear that we should not ask him personal questions, since we had psychics and mediums for that.

However, one day at a seminar I went to the microphone to ask Gabriel a question (he always took questions). I forget what my question was, but before I could ask it, he told me that my very thoughts, expecting *not* to buy a car, made it impossible for me to do so. He said angels chose a vehicle for me each time, and then my negative expectations prevented the sale. He advised me to picture the car I wanted, and imagine washing it, caring for it, putting gas in it etc. and not to add any other thoughts. So I did that, and the next time I went to a dealer I got the car I wanted! That is not the end of the story, for two months later the car was stolen. At his next seminar Gabriel explained that my thoughts after buying the car ('maybe I don't deserve a new car') resulted in its theft! I did get the car back after a police chase. The lesson learned was powerful - our thoughts indeed create our experiences.

Now, at 84 years of age and using a walker to ambulate, I frequently ask my angels to help me do things around the apartment. They never fail. There are times when I plan to do certain things and then forget. But my angels always remember, and remind me! They keep better track of me than I do of myself. And I always, always, thank them. Gabriel said they enjoy helping. When we ask for angelic help, the angels do not say to each other, 'I don't feel like going; you go.' They instantly respond to our every request. Gabriel told us to always thank them, for they love to hear it. Angels also love to hear us laugh. They laugh along with us.

When we walk in the woods, Gabriel said, it is nice to toss a few marbles around. Angles love to play on them! The angel world does not comprehend sadness. It is beyond their abilities. At a seminar one day, after a lunch break, Gabriel told us that Tinkerbell (his primary angel helper) asked him what that dark spot was in the chest of a woman participant. Gabriel told her it was sadness. And Tinkerbell said, what is sadness? Gabriel told her it was the opposite of love. Tinkerbell could not understand because she knew that love is all encompassing in the angel realm and so love has no opposite. Angels are given free choice, like us, except angels have free choice only in the realm of *good*. Humans have free choice across the board. And oh, what terrible choices we have made in the realm of not-good.

# When Truth is Painful

It has often been said that truth hurts. John 8:32 tells us 'the truth shall make you free'. Can the truth be painful *and* make us free? Some people think that there is truth in the adage 'no pain, no gain'. But Archangel Gabriel told us that it is not true. It is an attractive saying because we learn so much through painful experiences. We can learn also from good experiences. One thing we can learn from good experiences is gratitude. We often turn to God in our dilemmas and ask why? But we seldom turn to God when we have joyful experiences and say 'thank you'.

Jesus the Christ said himself, "I am the way, the truth and the life". (John 14: 6) Would he deceive us? We learn early in life that 'a little white lie' never hurt anyone. But when we accept small deceits it is very easy to accept lies a little large than 'little white'. It is interesting to note that little lies are white. Does this suggest they are pure? Clean of any guilt? Small lies can easily lead to 'medium size' lies, and then major issues are lied about. And all of these we readily justify.

As we journey through life and interact with others we draw conclusions about people and our experiences. These conclusions are the basis of our belief system; our reality; our personal truth. We thus lay the groundwork for our faith or lack of it. Then we read or hear something that conflicts with our personal 'reality' and we immediately become defensive. We justify our own truth. We are like the person who says, 'don't confuse me with facts; my mind is made up'. *Our* mind is made up *by us*, it is true. "But in vain do they worship me, teaching for doctrines the commandments of men." Matt. 15:7-9 The 'doctrines of men' and the 'commandments of men' are the basis for our lives. How often do we say; 'that's the way it is', or 'everybody is doing it', or 'it has always been done that way'. And worst of all, 'who will know?' These are the doctrines of men, and their justification.

But when the thoughts in our mind conflict with truth itself, it proves we have a split mind. *A Course in Miracles* speaks of the split mind and presents a series of lessons from which we can learn that we are part of the Divine Mind of God, where only truth abides. Jesus knew that the people he was talking to were hypocrites, and referring to Isaiah 29:13, says "This people draweth nigh unto me with their mouth, and honoureth me with their lips; but their heart is far from me.

As children of the most high God, we are part of Him and we are therefore part of the Mind of God. When we turn away from the truth, things that are not good happen to us. It is not a punishment of God; it is the immutable law of God. What we put out, we get back. Today we say 'what goes around comes around'. But do we *live* based on that concept? Do we realize that every judgment, every condemning word and thought bring back to us the same negativity in our experiences? In II Cor. 11:10, Paul says, "As the truth of Christ is in me, no man shall stop me of this boasting in the regions of Achaia." When we speak truth we can boast about the truth in us, not boast about our accomplishments as though they were done by ourselves. We always have truth in us and when we choose to distort it we do hurt; it is painful indeed. It is painful, but we cannot always identify the source of the pain. We are so accustomed to living our own established doctrine.

We can embrace the truth in our lives, and come into the fullness of the Christ in us, with a unity of faith, as instructed by Paul in Ephesians 4:14:

"That we henceforth be no more children, tossed to and fro, and carried about with every wind of doctrine, by the sleight of men, and cunning craftiness, whereby they lie in wait to deceive;
"But speaking the truth in love, may grow up into him in all things, which is the head, even Christ."

Another time that truth is painful is when we are 'found out' in our lies. The adulterer, the thief, the con artist, the prostitute and others live lives of deceit and make excuses for themselves. They justify their actions and explain their reasons, but still we must remember that the truth is in them. They simply are denying it; they are turning away from it for reasons of their own. "And they shall turn away their ears from the truth, and shall be turned unto fables." (II Tim. 4:4) and "Not giving heed to Jewish fables, and commandments of men, that turn from the truth". Titus 1:14

Those who seek an honest path, a path of goodness and love, are often ridiculed for their attitude. If they remind us of the good they are pursuing or expressing, it is as if they are wearing a badge of goodness. They have their reward. This does not mean that they are worthy of the ridicule, it only demonstrates that they want us to know their faith. Why do we need to know? Others merely go about doing good without saying it aloud to others. God knows their works. Is it necessary for their neighbor to know? Helping others need not be announced. "By their fruits we shall know them." (Matt. 7:20). Now there is a saying, 'pay it forward', and in doing so every good deed is multiplied a thousand fold. One good deed passed on ripples across the Earth for all to benefit from.

Becoming truthful requires simply a change of mind about ourselves and our God. We must ask ourselves if we want to be honest and think honest thoughts for a reason other than it is recommended in the Bible? Accepting the Kingdom of God within us, we demonstrate to ourselves that honesty brings us peace of mind. And by our own fruits we will know ourselves. "For honest thoughts, untainted by the dream of worldly things outside yourself, become the holy messengers of God Himself." (ACIM W pt I: 188: 6:6)

# Section Two: Scripture's Lessons

# The Chosen Few

"So the last shall be first, and the first last: for many be called, but few chosen." Matt. 20:16

". . . By uniting my will with that of my Creator, I naturally remembered spirit and its real purpose. I cannot unite your will with God's for you, but I can erase all misperceptions from your mind if you will bring it under my guidance. Only your misperceptions stand in your way. Without them your choice is certain. Sane perception induces sane choosing. I cannot choose for you but I can help you make your own right choice. 'Many are called but few are chosen; should be, 'All are called, but few choose to listen.' Therefore, they do not choose right. The 'chosen ones' are merely those who choose right sooner. Right minds can do this now, and they will find rest unto their souls. God knows you only in peace, and this *is* your reality."
ACIM T 3: IV: 7: 6-15

This scriptural statement seems to imply that most people will not be chosen. Chosen for what? Chosen to follow the Christ? To be seen by God? To be blessed by God? It is not made clear in this verse what the object of the 'chosen' ones is. Any particular group of individuals may say that *their* group consists of the chosen ones. The Jews, the fundamentalists, and other groups claim that they fit within this select group. It has been so for centuries. Until now many interpretations have been put forth.

Now, in this Age of Truth, Jesus comes to clarify the statement. He comes, in *The Course*, to tell us that he did in fact unite his will with the Will of God. And in the uniting he *remembered* spirit and its real purpose. God breathed us forth in spirit. Spirit means breath. God is a spirit. We are His spiritual children. We can and *will* remember spirit and then will know our real, spirit selves. In that remembering we will be united with God, for we will unite our will with His. That is what it was like in the beginning and with our remembering that is how it will be: at one with God once more!

32

As he said, Jesus cannot unite our will with God's Will, for we must each make that inner journey ourselves. What we must do is turn our will over to the Holy Spirit and His guidance. When we do that He will help us erase all the misperceptions in our mind. Jesus assures us that the only thing standing in our way of uniting our will with God's Will is our misperceptions. What are the misperceptions in our mind? They are legion, for they are all based on our five senses.

First, we believe that what our senses tell us is truth. That is a fundamental misperception, for our eyes can only see the horizon at any moment. Is that all there is? No, beyond every horizon there is more. Our ears hear only a short distance and only sounds which travel in a straight line. Is that all there is to hear? Our other senses deceive us, also. They all have their limitations. Some odors overwhelm us; some kill us. Our emotions carry us to thoughts we do not value. When our emotions are out of control they can lead us to negative behavior which we must later pay for - in guilt feelings or incarceration.

Sickness and death are major misperceptions of the mind. Archangel Gabriel told us that Earth is the only planet that still 'practices disease and death'. We have 'practiced' these misperceptions for many centuries. That is why we need a strong, dependable helper to overcome them. The Christ is the energy that can provide that needed power. Jesus basically says that without our misperceptions our choice is certain. It is certain because without them we will *see clearly* that we can unite our will with God's. It is inevitable, because sane perception brings on sane choosing.

The Master gave us the correct phrasing of the Bible quotation, saying that it should read, "All are called, but few choose to listen". God calls *all of us* to join our will with His, and come home again. But only a few of us choose to listen to the Call. The only way to hear the Call is to make a decision to listen to it. Our frantic, busy lives keep us occupied constantly with our error perceptions. We base our lives on all that we see, hear, smell, taste, and feel. Some have chosen to acknowledge the existence of a *sixth sense*. It is a 'touching into' what is beyond our five senses. It is a knowingness that comes from our intuition. It is as dependable as the sunrise. It will never lead us astray. It is the Voice of God.

The 'chosen ones', then, are those who choose correctly. And we all will choose correctly, sooner or later. Choosing correctly, and thus freeing ourselves of all our misperceptions, uniting our will with God's Will, we will find peace of mind and peace of soul. That is the place of reality and God knows us always and only in *that place*. In that choosing, we will also recall and know the truth of the Bible:

"The Spirit itself beareth witness with our spirit, that we are the children of God:
"And if children, then heirs; heirs of God, and joint-heirs with Christ; if so be that we suffer with him, that we may be also glorified together." (Romans 8:16-17)

# Editing Scripture

When Archangel Gabriel came (1987-1999) to bring the wisdom of the ages, he told us that we were ready for it or he would not have come. He came because it was the beginning of a new age, and Gabriel is the Announcer of the Ages. Whatever he said we knew was truth, for we knew that God would not lie to us. Some of his lessons were painful to hear, such as when he said that we plan our lives and everyone in it, before we come to Earth. Some of his lessons were joyous to hear, such as we are eternal spirit and therefore there is no death, only a transition in which we shed our physical envelope.

Gabriel also taught, among other things, that love is eternal, even when we divorce. And a healing that we send to another is eternal and will stay in the patient's aura until s/he is ready to use it. In sending healing to a person who is terminally ill, they may use it to transition or improve their health. They may choose to use it in another lifetime. He told us that concurrently with his visitations, from 1987 to 1999 eleven master teachers also came to Earth, to give the same lesson in truth that he did: Wake up, children of God, and live from the Lord God of Your Being. Gabriel reminded us of Adam asleep in the Garden of Eden, and said that nowhere in scripture does it say he woke up! Now we must waken to our own divinity and live from that Higher Self of us.

We also learned from Gabriel or Jesus the Christ, who also visited us from 1995 to 1999, that much was purged from the Bible in the early days. All references to reincarnation were deleted as well as all references to the many women who followed Jesus. Omitted from the Bible is the fact that Jesus married Mary Magdalene, who never was a prostitute. He married secretly because he knew what his future would be and did not want Mary endangered. Jesus also opted to not have children, for the same reason.

There are two phrases in the Bible that were most unfortunately mistranslated, which alter the meaning of Jesus' basic teachings. When Jesus was on the cross he is quoted as saying "Oh, God, my God, why hast thou forsaken me?" (Matt 27:46). Because of a tiny difference in the diacritical marks, the translator carelessly presented it incorrectly.

What Jesus actually said was "Oh, Sun, my Sun, why hast thou forsaken me?" What a tragic error of translation! Many people have wondered why Jesus would doubt his own heavenly Father. He did not. In scripture we find that it was very dark at the time of the crucifixion. "Now from the sixth hour there was darkness over all the land unto the ninth hour." (Matt 27:45 Mark 15:33, Luke 23:44). Jesus was calling to the sun, not his God.

The other tragic mistranslation is found in John 1:14: "And the Word was made flesh, and dwelt among us, (and we beheld his glory, the glory as of the only begotten of the Father,) full of grace and truth." John repeats that Jesus is the 'only begotten son' in verse 1:18 and in verses 3:16 and 3:18. Gabriel clarified this serious mistranslation. What the words originally written were, "Jesus, begotten son of the only God". There is a stunning difference in meaning. In knowing the true words, we can more readily understand Jesus' words when he said, "Verily, verily, I say unto you, He that believeth on me, the works that I do shall he do also; and greater works than these shall he do; because I go unto my Father." (John 14:12).

If we keep Jesus on a pedestal as the only son of God, how could we possibly expect to emulate him? That exclusive divinity would prevent us from ever becoming like him, or doing the things he did. Seeing him as the begotten son of the only God, now we can see that it is possible to follow him, which he told us to do many times in the Bible. As we turn to *A Course in Miracles*, we find: "Do not make the pathetic error of "clinging to the old rugged cross". (ACIM T 4: in. 3:7)

There are those who discount out of hand *A Course in Miracles*. This is a most unfortunate situation. Jesus the Christ came to bring to humanity the truth of his life and his teachings. Many people disbelieve in communication between the spirit world and Earth. The spirit world is the domain of God. God is a spirit, (John 4:24), and God is love. "If a mind perceives without love, it perceives an empty shell and is unaware of the spirit within". (ACIM T I: IV: 9)

For what reason would someone believe that God would not want to communicate with us, unless they feared Him? Or feared what He would say to us? God speaks to us constantly. He gives us intuitive thoughts. He gives words to other people so they can speak truth to us;

help us to learn. When we turn to God for guidance, He always instructs us. How could He do these things unless He was communicating to us?

Two thousand years ago Jesus came to bring the Light of Truth to all humanity for all time to come. It was the beginning of the Age of Pisces. Now we are entering the Age of Aquarius. Humanity is capable of comprehending the deeper meaning of the glorious Bible. It is all symbolic, but that was not understood in Jesus' time. He knew that only a few people really understood his teachings. Even his apostles did not fully get the message. Only John understood what Jesus' teachings meant. Gabriel reminded us of this.

Now, at this time, we have the benefit of Jesus' teachings in the New Age; the age of truth. We are blessed indeed to be on Earth at this time to learn from *The Course* the spiritual path we all must take in order to return to the Father in Heaven, our Creator. Heaven is our natural habitat.

# Love as Creator

"Only love creates, and only like itself. There was no time when all it created was not there." ACIM W pt II; 11:1:2-3

God is creator of all life; God is love. Given this premise, we can readily understand that only love creates.

Humans build things; make things, out of basic physical materials; using spec lists and blueprints. But where do the lists and blueprints come from? They all come from creative thought. Creative thoughts do not come from a human brain. The brain does not think; it processes thought. Mind thinks. And the mind of all humans is part of the Divine Mind of God.

God created all life and humans are part of that created life. When God created us, a part of God remained in each of us, hence the phrase given to us by Jesus: "The kingdom of God is within". Humans 'make' things; mind creates things. Creative thought 'sees'; a chair style - human hands 'make' the chair. All creative thoughts come from the Mind of God.

Composers, writers, painters, sculptures, inventors all bring divine ideas from the Mind of God to the printed page, the easel, the hand-shaped clay, the building. Hearing or seeing in their 'mind's eye', they then attempt to express it in physical form so that others may share in the joy of their 'vision'. Artists in metal and other materials first see the image in their minds, and then attempt to produce it in physical form. For example, the first manifestations of all created paintings hang on the walls of heaven's art gallery. Only the true reproductions are seen on Earth.

There was no 'time' when all creation did not exist. There is no 'time' in the spirit World of God. Humans came up with the idea of time to keep track of our days, and each other. 'Space', too, was an idea of humankind. It verified our erroneous belief that we were separate from each other. Worship of a Creator God evolved into divisions in which

God had many different names and all perceived that God is 'out there, somewhere', and needed to be praised and pleaded to for favors.

We persist in believing that we have left God and He will never take us back. Sounds like the Prodigal Son. It *is* the Prodigal Son. The prodigal's father took the lad back - even planned a huge celebration with a 'fatted calf'. Are we less than the prodigal? We think we are, for after all, the Prodigal Son is in scripture. Therefore he must be a more holy person than we. The Bible speaks of real people, with real problems. They were no different from us. The Prodigal's father took him back and so, too, will our Father take us back. And how will those who went before greet us? Along with all the angel world, joyous greetings await us.

Before time began -- before humans invented the idea of time --- Creation existed. All Creation. Perhaps it all came about in one gigantic explosion, like the 'Big Bang' theory. Imagine, if you can, a moment when God created all that is in one supreme instant. In that instant all spirit life was begun, from molecules to quasars. Of course this spectrum of life included all humanity. Every choice that every human would ever make would be included and every option of every decision and its outcome. Who can encompass such a plethora of decisions and options? Where did they all exist before we chose them? That is the mystery of Creation.

Creation is too vast for our human brain to comprehend. That is where faith comes in. We trust in a holy Creator, or we deny His existence. That is our choice, as humans. God gave us all free choice and told us to 'multiply'. We thought he meant we should bear many children. As a result of this misinterpretation we have overpopulated the Earth and put unnecessary burdens on the married female, who was expected to bear as many children as possible, often at the peril of her health. At some point in time, staying on this course, the planet will not sustain all human life. At some point in time a few women dared to suggest that a woman could and should somehow *regulate* her reproductivity.

'Multiply' meant that we should multiply our thoughts - creative thoughts, loving thoughts, caring thoughts. Multiply means to increase by extending. We extend ourselves by helping others. We extend ourselves by loving all our brothers and sisters on planet Earth. We extend ourselves by loving all God's creatures. We extend ourselves by living from the *Lord God of our Being*. It is the kingdom of God within us.

"God is love, and he who abides in love abides in God, and God abides in him." *Oneness*, 104

The one Creator God has been given various names by humankind: God, Allah, Yahweh, Creator, Maker, Source, First Cause, Supreme Being, Great Spirit, etc.

All great religions share this supreme law of love. Buddhism says, "He that loveth not, knoweth not God. For God is love." *Oneness* 104 In reading *Oneness*, we see that all major religions share the basic moral concepts.

There are many small groups world-wide who read, study, and accept the teachings put forth in *A Course in Miracles*. One day they will all join in joyous togetherness and share the love of God in a human symphony of oneness.

"Love is the beginning and end of the Torah." Judaism. Oneness, 104 Instead of Jew and Gentile arguing whether Jesus was the Messiah, they can and they must, comprehend the truth of the matter. Jesus came not to start a new religion but rather to teach *all* humanity to wake up to its own divinity. ("The kingdom of God is within you." Luke 17:21) and live a life of love and forgiveness. Jesus' entire life was a manifestation of that kind of awareness and that expression of love.

The discomfort of life on Earth is the result of our forgetting our one Source. We have dwelt on this aching planet so long that we forgot our Origin. We all are seeking something to satisfy an inner longing, but we think we shall find it outside ourselves. That is the greatest illusion of humankind.

"Sane and insane, all are searching lovelorn
For Him, in mosque, temple, church, alike.
For only God is the One God of Love.
And Love calls from all these, each one
        His home." *Oneness*, 105

We think the constant busy life of the human family is the result of the complexity of life on Earth. Perhaps the rushing to and fro is all an attempt to escape the truth of us. As children of God we can find respite in prayer and meditation, both of which bring us gently into a quiet presence, and sometimes a conscious awareness of God.

Confucianism tells us, "Love belongs to the high nobility of Heaven, and is the quiet home where man should dwell".

# Mirror of Judgment

"Judge not, that ye be not judged." Matt. 7: 1

"When the Bible says, 'Judge not that ye be not judged,' it means that if you judge the reality of others you will be unable to avoid judging your own.

"The choice to judge rather than to know is the cause of the loss of peace. Judgment is the process on which perception but not knowledge rests. . . Judgment always involves rejection. . . . ACIM T 3: VI: 1:4-2:4

It is essential to understand the difference between discernment and judgment. To discern means to see without judgment. We can discern that someone is wearing a green sweater and another is wearing a blue sweater. There is no evaluation assigned to the colors or the wearer. On the other hand, judgment evaluates. Of two actions perceived, one is rejected over the other. A 'judgment call' is a common fault we all share. Our lesson is to learn that no one is better or lesser than another.

I suppose it begins when we are young, and learn erroneously from our parents, that some individuals are 'better' than others. This is not intended to put down anyone's parents; human nature seems prone to making judgments constantly, and we usually pass down to our children the prejudices we learned from our own parents. My own parents held prejudices. My mother hated Catholics and my father hated Jews. I do not know where these judgments came from; perhaps their own parents. Fortunately, by the time I reached the age of twenty-one, I came to realize how groundless, how stupid and how meaningless prejudice is. I did not pass these judgments down to my kids.

The spiritual path I chose brought to me a wondrous experience from 1987 to 1999, when it was my honor and privilege to sit at the feet of Archangel Gabriel. He explained not only that we are all equal in the eyes of God, but we are in fact *all* his beloved children. God, and the angels, see us humans as beams of light. God created us from Himself. "Every good gift and every perfect gift is from above, and cometh down from the Father of lights, with whom is no variableness nor shadow of turning". (James 1:17). And Jesus told us "While ye have light, believe in the light, that ye may be the children of light". (John 12:36). We had the Light then, in Christ himself. He told us, in effect, to awaken to the same Light within us.

The entire human race is the only begotten Son of God. With this truth in mind, how could we honestly judge anyone to be more than, or less than, anyone else? There is a choice we all have. It is to know or to judge. Judgment comes so easily. We see the news (information from the north, east, west, and south) and judge all perpetrators. We do not understand what Gabriel taught us: we all plan our lives, including everyone we meet, every circumstance, and every relationship. This is not easy to accept. Yet, in reviewing our lives honestly, we can always identify the lessons we learned from every situation and every relationship. The lesson was our choice and the situation to teach us the lesson was our choice.

God gave us free choice, unlike all other species. He also gave us imagination and the ability to create beyond ourselves. Beasts and plants create only their own kind; we have designer horses and dogs by manipulating the genes of our favorite breeds. It takes imagination to picture in our mind's eye the concept that all humans are beloved of God, equally. God is no 'respecter of persons' because he sees us all as His Own, without any regard for differences in color, language, religion, lifestyle. We can and must, eventually, choose to accept the oneness of us all with each other, and our oneness with God. Only in this way can we find peace on Earth.

In God, there is no choice. God is love; there is no other option. God is all there is. We are His forever. He loves us unconditionally. But humans have a choice. We can choose to judge or we can choose to know truth. The Holy Spirit, when called on, will bring us only truth, without fail. It is an immutable law. We must ask the Holy Spirit for truth, because He does not come unbidden to anyone. When we know the truth we do not see the difference that judges. Truth will set us free because we will know, and the knowingness sets us free from judgment.

The Bible instructs us not to judge because we judge the reality of others based on the judgment of our own reality. Neither reality is true, because both are based on perception; what our five senses 'teach' us. And our five senses are the foundation for all our judgment calls. If we believe our senses tell us the truth and judgment is okay, how do we teach the blind to hate those of another color, if the blind cannot see the color? And how do we define color itself?

When we consciously choose truth, and seek to know it from the Holy Spirit, there is one and only one outcome: We will know peace. It is guaranteed. And having peace, we will more readily accept all truth, as we continue to see it from the Holy Spirit. Peace is what we all really want, in spite of the busy world of activity. W constantly seek outside ourselves for happiness and joy. And sometimes we find it; mostly it is a brief and unfulfilling experience. The joy that comes with the peace of God, from the Holy Spirit, is deeply comforting and assuring. It is eternal as God Himself. We are entitled to this peace, for it is our birthright and God's Will for us.

# Multiply a Thought

"Be fruitful and multiply . . ." Gen. 1:22

This phrase is found six times in the book of Genesis, in the Old Testament. And in the New Testament, . In 2 Cor. 9:10: "and multiply your seeds sown, and increase the fruits of your righteousness" Paul could have meant planting of crop seeds, or he could have meant human seed, which is what semen was then called. But then Paul speaks of "fruits of righteousness" suggesting that even then symbolism was understood. From this we might assume that the sowed seed intended by Paul was good ideas, good thoughts, good actions, and good behavior.

Thousands of years ago, when this was first written, the people of the Earth valued their possessions, as they still do. Then the possessions included sheep, goats, bulls, and chickens. The larger the herds, the more prosperous the owner. Larger flocks required more people to care for them and so a large family was also a mark of wealth. In the absence of prenatal care and other medical advances, birthing was probably an unpredictable event. Female problems that women have today were probably experienced then, but there was little or no recourse. Premature birth would result in death without incubators, which would not be invented for hundreds of years.

The idea of humans multiplying became a valued concept. Not very long ago, families consisted of eight to twelve children. The author was one of nine. Contraception was not known, or not used, or a woman's religions forbade the use of it. Women must have suffered greatly without the kind of care that modern medicine provides. When contraceptives were finally devised they answered  the prayers of many women. Although some women remain married for many years without a pregnancy, some women are more fertile and easily become pregnant. They are the ones who welcomed contraceptives.

Conceiving and bearing many children was once seen as a fine accomplishment. Rearing children also used to be seen as the natural task of the mother. The father's role was to work, 'bring home the bacon', and be a role model for his sons. If he had his own business, sons could carry on as proprietors. Repairs of the homestead fell to his expertise. For farmers, farm machinery had to be maintained and repaired. Later, with any mechanical talent, care of the family car would also be his task. Today it is not unusual to see a young father with one or two little children walking in the park or shopping in the mall. It always warms my heart when I see it. This is how, in my opinion, it should be. Recently I saw a sign that said, after the business name, "[John Doe] and daughters"!

To expect a woman to bear as many children as she physically is able is to assign her a life of constant pregnancy, birth, and rearing of offspring. Would a God of Love expect such a life for her? Would it bring good health to her? Or does it tire her to the point of exhaustion? Even with both parents taking on the role of rearing the kids, little time is left for the parents' sharing time with each other. There are still rare examples of huge families. They are so rare now that they make the evening news.

In multiplying our good thoughts, expression of our talents and abilities we can find the satisfaction and fulfillment of life which is our inheritance. Construction, mail delivery, management are now things that women can do. Almost every kind of employment is now open to women. The traditional roles have dissolved. No longer are women relegated to teaching, nursing, and secretarial work. In my own lifetime, when I desired greatly to become a CPA, all doors were closed to me. Women did not wear hardhats, climb telephone poles, become CEOs, and never would be sports reporters which took them into the clubhouse!

We are now going forth and multiplying in ways we never thought possible. We can share our time with others by volunteering. We can help others in need by finding them and helping them. We can 'pay it forward' when someone helps us, by helping the next person we meet.

It should bring us great joy, but we still want more stuff than we own, still need to 'get away' from it all on an expensive vacation trip. Our home is what we make of it. Being happy with what we have is one of the challenges for us now. The only things we need to multiply are our positive thoughts and ideas, our opportunities to share and become. Our time is precious to us and we ought to assign our tasks carefully that we can afford to multiply our good deeds and expressions of good will. Some people choose to multiply their wealth. Many of them share their wealth with the benefit of Foundations dedicated to a cause with which they are familiar. Health, education, the Arts, and research are some of the ways in which Foundations help others. Also, many individuals choose to personally become involved in helping others, by volunteering. Many organizations recruit people to serve others without payment.

"You can share only the thoughts that are of God and that He keeps for you." ACIM T 5: IV: 8

# One Hundred Gallons of Wine

"Jesus saith unto her, Woman, what have I to do with thee? mine hour is not yet come." John 2:4

Jesus said this to his mother when they ran out of wine at the wedding feast. She asked him to provide more wine. None of the synoptic gospels mention this first miracle of Jesus. John did. It is a mystery why the other apostles did not report it. In John 2:6 it states that Jesus had just chosen his twelve apostles to follow him. It seems to this writer that Jesus' first miracle would have made a huge impression on these new disciples of his. Not only did Jesus turn water to wine, but it was the best wine of the feast: In John 2:10 the 'governor of the feast tells Jesus that whereas the 'good wine' is usually offered first, Jesus had chosen to offer it last at this feast.

Why did Jesus ask his mother 'what have I to do with thee? We may consider it in light of his later statement (Matt 19:29) "And everyone who hath forsaken houses, or brethren, or sisters, or father, or mother, or wife, or children, or lands, for my names' sake, shall inherit everlasting life". In effect he was saying to his beloved mother that what he came to do on Earth was not merely to be a good son to her, but rather to bring to all humanity the Light of Truth, for all time.

When he said, "mine hour has not yet come." he probably was referring to the fact that he had not as yet 'gone public' with his miracles. He knew what his mission was and his mother was asking him to perform a miracle before he had planned to do so. But, like a good Jewish son, he did her bidding and turned all the water into wine. He did not turn a small amount of water into wine, but a large amount; approximately 100 gallons! We can make the calculations.

"six waterpots . . . containing two or three firkins apiece . . . and Jesus saith unto them, Fill the waterpots with water. And they filled them up to the brim." (John 2:6-7). In the very next verse of John, Jesus tells the servants to take them to the governor of the feast. Jesus is not reported to have had any length of time to perform this miracle. Of course, there is no time in spirit, and it was the spirit of him (the Christ light) that performed the miracle, not the man Jesus.

When we make the calculations based on given measurements, we find that a firkin is one fourth of a barrel, and a barrel is 31 liquid gallons. These calculations result in either 93 gallons (2 firkins in 6 waterpots) or 139.5 gallons (3 firkins in 6 waterpots). This is a very large amount of wine, but we can safely assume that there were a very large number of people there to celebrate.

When Jesus performed miracles, he was not expressing anything of Jesus the man. He was expressing the Christ Love that was in him. Likewise, of ourselves we can do nothing, but listening to the Voice of God within, our intuition, there is nothing we cannot do. "You can do nothing apart from Him, and you *do* do nothing apart from Him." ACIM T 7: VII: 5:6

We like to think that finding a parking spot at a busy restaurant is not as miraculous as walking on water. There is no order of miracles, according to *A Course in Miracles*. "There is no order of miracles because all of God's Sons are of equal value, and their equality is their oneness. The whole power of God is in every part of Him, and nothing contradictory to His Will is either great or small. What does not exist has no size and no measure." ACIM T 11: VI: 10: 5-7

Therefore we can understand the statement "Miracles are expressions of love . . ." ACIM 1:1:35:1. Using this as a basis, we turn then to ACIM 1: I 4:1, which tells us "All expressions of love are maximal." Thus it follows that whatever we do from the Christ in us is maximal. We are all children of God. Jesus came to show us the way. He told us that everything he did we can do, also. "He that believeth in me, the works that I do shall he do also; and greater works than these shall he do; because I go unto my Father." (John 14:12). To learn how to raise the dead, heal the sick, and turn water into wine we need only to believe in the Christ in us, the Kingdom of God in us.

It is essential to take Jesus down from the cross, stop worshipping him, and see him as he was meant to be seen - our elder brother, setting the pattern, in his life, for us to follow. "Howbeit for this cause I obtained mercy, that in me first Jesus Christ might shew forth all longsuffering, for a pattern to them which should hereafter believe on him, to life everlasting." I Tim 1:16

If we persist in seeing Jesus as the suffering son of man on the cross, and idolize him, we shall forever be frustrated in our efforts to live the good life of love and forgiveness which he demonstrated. We could never emulate the god we accepted; he would be perfect and his life beyond duplication. In this generation Jesus has chosen to come to Earth again, to give us a new guidebook for living. It is *A Course in Miracles* and Jesus tells us specifically to wake up to the Christ Light that is in us, and live a life of love and forgiveness. Many times in scripture Jesus says 'follow me'. He repeats it now. When will we choose to listen?

In a close reading of I Cor. chapter 15 we find: "But now is Christ risen from the dead, and become the firstfruits of them that slept". Archangel Gabriel pointed out to us that whereas Adam slept in the Garden of Eden, nowhere in scripture does it say that he woke up. Also, in I Cor. 15:23, Paul says, "But every man in his own order: Christ the firstfruits; afterwards they that are Christ's at his coming." "At his coming" -- and his coming was in this commencement of the Age of Aquarius, or, as Gabriel called it, the Age of Truth.

The New Testament and the *Course* then become our guide books, our reference points. In them we learn to give up all anger, all resentments, all fears, and listen to our intuitive higher Self. By them we learn to forgive, and then to live without judgment so there is nothing to forgive again. From these great books of instructions we can learn to see all humanity as our believed spiritual siblings, and treat them accordingly. Instead of condemnation we can teach them to awaken, also, and by so doing, lift them up into an awareness of their own Christ light. Then, and only then, can we awaken to the Christ within us. Living with that wisdom, we can reach down and help others to be so guided. All of this leads to the awakening of all humanity, and a return unto our Creator.

# Our First Prayer

"But seek ye first the Kingdom of God, and his righteousness; and all these things shall be added unto you". Matt. 6:33

"Instead of 'seek ye first the Kingdom of Heaven' say, '*Will* ye first the Kingdom of Heaven,' and you have said, 'I know what I am and I accept my own inheritance'." ACIM T 3: VI: 11:8

We are always asking for something; seeking something we do not have. If we had it we would not be seeking it. Our seeking may be for health, abundance, resolution of a problem, answer to a question, or answers to a multitude of questions. Sometimes we pray to God to provide what we are seeking. Sometimes we work and struggle, and fight for what we want, and when we do not get it, we turn to God to supply it.

The idea of *first* asking God is still a different concept, as it was in Jesus' time. People then were very busy with their daily tasks of surviving as farmers, shepherds, parents, housewives, and housekeepers. Then along came Jesus telling them to first turn to God in their seeking. Then, as now, I suppose there were varying degrees of faith in God. Most probably believed in an anthropomorphic God, even though they could not *see* him. And those who believed in an all-pervasive God probably expected God did not hear the prayer.

Even today we are so busy with our daily routines that we pray *when we can find the time*. But it must fit into our schedule of activity, and we must have faith in something greater - much greater - than ourselves to pray to. It is even more challenging for us to find the time to meditate. Many people discount meditation for one reason or another. Many of the prophets meditated, the Bible tells us. Jesus went off by himself to pray and meditate. What is meditation, anyhow?

Prayer is talking to God; meditation is listening to God. First, we must believe that God is able to hear to us. Then we must consider ourselves to be worthy of God's attention, then we need to accept the idea that we are able to hear Him. God talks to us all the time. It is that 'gut hunch' or intuitive thought that pops into our head and directs us to a proper path of living - a positive, constructive path of life.

The Sermon on the Mount included the following advice from Jesus: "But seek ye first the kingdom of God, and his righteousness; and all these things shall be added unto you." Matt. 6:33

'All these things' referred to clothing, food, and drink. We ponder about how prayer can put food on the table; clothing to wear. But the point is that God knows what we have need of and will guide us to our every need if we accept His ability to do so. I wonder how many readers have gone hungry, naked, or without a roof under which to sleep.

Why is everything added to us when we put God first? Because when we look to God *first*, we are in effect saying that we are turning our lives over to God for His guidance. Our faith assures us that as long as we accept God as our Guide, our Leader in all life, He will unfailingly point us in the right direction. Also, when we are tempted to stray off in a negative pursuit, He will remind us strongly of our original intent. That is when we hear Him most powerfully, as He whispers in our ear, Is this what you really want to do? Or, is this who you really are?

Now, Jesus comes to us through the words of *The Course* to interpret his original words. When we *will* first the Kingdom of Heaven, we are saying that we know what we are and we accept our own inheritance. Jesus does not say *who*, but *what* we are. The I AM is the same I AM that Jesus spoke of in the synagogue, when he said, 'Before Abraham was, I AM.' John 8:58

We *all* are part of the I AM of God, for He breathed us forth all at once, all as equals in His eyes. Jesus knew this, and comes now to remind us. He still tells us to follow him. He knows we are his spiritual siblings and he desires to show us the way he took so that we might also return to our Source, the Father of all.

Our inheritance is the same as Jesus' was. His inheritance consisted of all the spiritual gifts he had, and used, on Earth. Of the spiritual gifts listed by Paul in his first letter to the Corinthians, all were possessed by the Master Jesus. These all were his inheritance; they all are ours, when we accept them and use them as he did. The other part of his inheritance was the ability to ascend. That, too, is our inheritance. We all will ascend to the Father. Heaven is our *natural habitat,* and when we return Home to the Father we will be at Home, and feel at Home - at last!

Two thousand years ago, when Jesus said, Follow me, all his apostles did so. Few others did of all the people who heard him. Once again Jesus comes to say it: Follow me; will to do first the will of God; accept your inheritance which is the same as mine. How many are listening? How many want to believe he means *them?* How many even read the words in the Bible which are directed to us all?

# The Overcoming

"These things I have spoken unto you, that in me ye might have peace. In the world ye shall have tribulation: but be of good cheer; I have overcome the world." John 16:33

When Jesus said 'I have overcome the world' what did he mean? In this same scriptural verse he said 'in me ye might have peace'. Is it peace, then, that will overcome the world? Where, in this world of form, of duality, of three dimensions, do we *find* peace?

Do we find it in our homes, in our own families, when daily we impose judgments on each other, on our neighbors, on the people of the 'news'? Do judgments bring peace? When we go to our places of employment do we find peace there? Supervisors, co-workers and others also are engaged in judgment and criticism. Where, then, can we find peace? But first we must ask ourselves if peace is even *wanted* by us. Is peace boring, uninteresting, unchallenging? In this busy world of ours peace has no place. We are so busy being busy. Housecleaning, washing clothes, cooking meals -- or running machines at wok, calculating construction, pouring cement, hammering nails etc., etc. The tasks are endless and it would take hours just to list the various employment tasks we do, as a people, every day. Which ones are done in peace? As a result of all this busy-ness, we take vacations to find something 'different' to do and enjoy. Even then, we set ourselves the task of finding things to 'do'--- skiing, boating, swimming, mountain climbing, etc. Are any of these peaceful?

Yet we all seem to enjoy a peaceful evening under a summer sky, perhaps on our deck or at the seashore, or near any piece of water we are fond of; or on a mountain top. Then, the next day, or week, we are off and running again. The first thing we need to ask self is, 'do I want peace?' and 'if so, why?' Master Jesus said 'in me ye might have peace'; he was saying that in him we could know peace. Let us understand the truth of the man. Jesus was his name. He was a man who ate, drank, slept, prayed, and meditated. In him was the Light of Christ, expressed by his very presence. That Light was attended by a peaceful presence - the peace that passes all understanding. So, when he said 'in me', he meant the Christ Light in him. In that Christ Light we too may have peace. But do we want it? Do we consider peace boring? Without joy? Unproductive? Most people do so consider it, and that is why, as a people, we do not consciously seek peace.

In Jesus' time the Romans were hard, unyielding rulers. The Hebrews had no peace. Their homes could be entered at any time by Roman soldiers; the wives and daughters taken at their whim. Property was vulnerable to any soldier who wanted ownership. Peace was an unknown. Peace was unattainable *anywhere*. Is it these circumstances in our memory that makes us long for moments of peace? Humanity, in the not too distant past, had some peace at work and at home. Cottage industries were common. Prior to the Industrial Revolution we were an agricultural society. Without machines we found some peace (after a busy days' work) in the pastures, in the cornfields, in the cow barns. When machinery came into our lives a lot of noise came with them. Jackhammers, electric saws, and automatic screw machines require earplugs. The machinery of warfare - guns, tanks, shells, bombs etc. deafen us with their loudness.

But can we say that decades ago people appreciated peace more than we do now? People seem to think that peace is for 'wimps' or lazy people, or unproductive people. Or senior citizens -- is there a group so 'unproductive' as they? And why, when people are sick and unable to ambulate, we call them invalids (in-valids)? Some seniors long to be busy again. I think it is a phase we go through. Then we accept the idea that being idle is not a sin or something to be ashamed of. We come to realize that on a conscious spiritual path we can find peace if we seek it. There is only one place to find it, and that is through prayer and meditation.

We all pray; some more than others. It may be a daily habit, it may occur only when we are unable to help ourselves, at the moment of an accident, when we or a loved one is nearing their transition ('death'), or has just passed on into spirit. Prayer is talking to God. Meditation is *listening* to God. How do we 'listen' to God? Only in peaceful silence. This may sound redundant. Yet there is a silence which is not peaceful. It is the momentary silence between two people who disagree but have not begun arguing as yet. It is the brief silence just prior to a thunderstorm. It is the temporary silence between gun firing or bombing, in war. Those are moments of stagnant, threatening peace.

The peaceful silence is one that is not threatening, does not precede an argument, and does not portend an immanent danger. I am not speaking only of quiet surroundings, like a starry night in the country (who can enjoy the stars in a bright and roaring city?). I am speaking of the inner peace of each human being. It is there; we simply do not know it or we know it and do not acknowledge our ability to find it. It eludes us if we worry, think, or talk. Peaceful silence is found in prayer and in meditation. To find the peaceful silence takes practice. Meditation takes practice. Some folks fear being silent and 'going within' in meditation because they fear what they will find there. They fear their darkest secrets will surface and have to be dealt with. They fear that all the worst thoughts of self well prove to be true; that God will suddenly know them for what they are. All this fear comes about because we believe that our innermost being is *not good*. This is where we make our greatest mistake. For our innermost being is the Son of God of us. Luke writes "the kingdom of God is within you." Luke 17:21

We can accept Luke's words or believe we are sinners from birth. We usually opt for the latter. Sometimes we are told that we are born in sin. What an onus to put on a pure infant at birth! Let us say we choose Luke's words. Then we need to know what the 'kingdom of God' is. Is not Heaven God's home? Is not Heaven His kingdom? If God is omnipresent, how can all this *fit* in us? It can't. But an individualized portion can! And that is what we are - an individualized portion of the *all that is,* or God, or Creator of us all. *God is a spirit,* (John 4:24) and we are individualized portions of spirit. That kingdom of God within is not noisy; is not busy; is not industrious. It is not only peaceful; it is peace itself.

This unseen, unfelt, inner self of us is peace. 'Going within' is a phrase often used to describe the commencement of the meditative process. It means finding that 'space' within where peace abides.
But there is no space within. To go within, surrounded by quiet and uninterrupted peace, means to still the mind. Impossible! The mind cannot be stilled; will not be stilled. It is constantly thinking. So all we can do is tell the mind, 'let this thought continue on out, so only

peaceful thoughts can reign. With practice we find that there is nothing to fear by going within. A calmness comes over us. In the stillness we listen to the still, small Voice of God. Sometimes it is a whisper, sometimes an idea, sometimes a thought, sometimes a revelation. A revelation is, according to Webster, "an act of revealing or communicating divine truth", or "something that is revealed by God to humans". Only in a meditative state can such revelation take place. It is truth. It never lies to us.

Many individuals travel to distant places to learn how to meditate. We need not go to the Himalayas and sit in a cave with a guru to learn. We all have the capacity to learn how to meditate. This is so because we are children of the One God, and since He created us, inside of us is the individualized portion of Him. It is this individualized portion which is *part of* God. Thus it is that many of us are drawn to communicate with Him in this fashion: meditate and listen and learn how to live a righteous life. Not a life of egotistic belief that we are a chosen few, but that what we learn through listening to God in meditation we can teach to others, as well as teach them how to meditate themselves. Touching into this inner peaceful place is what will provide the salvation of humankind. It is a singular path. It is a personal choice.

In *A Course in Miracles* we find Jesus telling us, in Text 8: IV: 2:8, "My purpose, then, is still to overcome the world. I do not attack it, but my light must dispel it because of what it is." Now, in this century, the Master Teacher tells us that it is '*my light*' that must dispel the darkness of the Earth, and the Earth is a place of darkness because it is a place where we believe that we have left God, and God will never take us back. "The light has come," is found in *Miracles,* also. (WB pt 1, ch 75,88) Jesus comes to us through *Miracles* to bring us to the light of understanding, the light of truth, the light that saves us and teaches us of our at-one-ment with God. This is the goal of all meditation: To know that we are in fact one with God and one with each other. This brings the salvation of the world. Then the world will no longer be needed. We will rise to Heaven, our natural habitat and once more be back where we began, offspring of our Creator, living joyfully with Him and each other, without status, without duality, without separation.

# The Symbolic Lamb

" . . . . Behold the Lamb of God, which taketh away the sins of the world." John 1: 29

"Blessed are the pure in heart: for they shall see God". Matt. 5:8

"I have been correctly referred to as 'the lamb of God, who taketh away the sins of the world,' but those who represent the lamb as blood-stained do not understand the meaning of the symbol. Correctly understood, it is a very simple symbol that speaks of my innocence. The lion and the lamb lying down together symbolize that strength and innocence are not in conflict, but naturally live in peace. 'Blessed are the pure in heart for they shall see God' is another way of saying the same thing. A pure mind knows the truth and this is its strength. It does not confuse destruction with innocence because it associates innocence with strength, not with weakness." ACIM T 3: I: 5:1-6

Thousands of years ago the sacrifice of animals was a common religious practice. The blood of beasts was sprinkled on the altar as a sign of worshipping God. When the Master Jesus was baptized by John at the Jordan River, John said, 'Behold the lamb of God, which taketh away the sin of the world.' (john 1:29). This seems to conflict with the essay on vengeance, but it does not. Although Jesus could not, did not wash away all the sins or the world (we must each be our own savior), his teachings did provide humanity with the means by which we could walk the spiritual path to salvation.

Jesus, as the 'lamb of God' is not the manifestation of a blood-stained, dead body. Like every thing else in scripture the lamb is symbolic It is the promise of a new life on Earth. Jesus taught the lessons we all must learn and put into practice if we want to be saved from our earthly prison. We live in a place of illusion. We live in a three-dimensional world. We live believing in dualism. God is One. Seeking salvation we will find it. Living an honest, accepting, forgiving life we will find salvation and return at last to God, our Creator.

When we picture in our mind the man Jesus, commanding the waves of the sea to be calm, healing the leprous woman, raising Lazarus from the dead, we find it very difficult to understand him as 'innocent'. We look at a new-born baby and we see innocence. And with the innocence we see helplessness, dependence, weakness, vulnerability. When Jesus told us to be as little children he did not see these weaknesses. To him innocence meant accepting, sharing, curious, and wondering. In *Miracles,* Jesus explains innocence and strength as co-features of man. Jesus demonstrated both in his lifetime on Earth. The lion (strength) and the lamb (innocence) lying down together symbolize this combination. We have both within us. We can and ought to express both from within us.

The 'pure in heart shall see God' (Matt 5:8) because they know truth. They know truth because they desired to know truth. Truth comes to those who seek it from God, in prayer and meditations. Truth needs no defense. Truth is strength. Humans tend to confuse strength with destruction. And who can be destroyed but the weak ones; the innocent ones? Destroying with strength is a terrible misuse of the strength from God. Knowing it is from God, man can just as easily use it, in conjunction with innocence, to express the love of God, and to have compassion for others. Considering the extent to which humanity has chosen to express strength by means of weaponry and war, it seems a far-off time when it will learn something else. But eventually we must associate innocence with strength, not weakness, and begin to live from the Lord God of his Being.

The pure in heart shall 'see God' as surely as the sun will rise tomorrow, not only because Jesus said so, but because it means we shall know ourselves as God created us. We shall *feel* at one with our Father. Seeing God is accepted by many as beholding any aspect of nature. Because God is omnipresent, He is in every blade of grass, every domestic pet, every wild animal, every cloud and raindrop. Others 'see God' in meditation as a lovely color, a tender feeling, a decision to 'rise above' a situation that once rankled. The overcoming of an addiction is, for some, a conversion of faith and an awakening to the God within as told to us by Jesus:

"Neither shall they say, Lo, here! or, lo there! for, behold, the kingdom of God is within you". Luke 17::21.

# There is no Death

"And there shall be no more death". Rev. 21:4

"The emptiness engendered by fear must be replaced by forgiveness.
That is what the Bible means by "There is no death."
ACIM T 1: IV: 4:1-2

Prior to Jesus' birth, fear permeated the masses. The Roman Empire
consisted of an extensive land mass, and a huge, powerful, army. The
members of this army had no restrictions of any kind. Any soldier
could enter a house and take anything, or anyone he pleased. Of course
they were feared. Citizens of Rome had no freedoms as we know them
now. Strangers feared each other and it was common in those days for
anyone traveling to hire an assassin to protect them. Death itself was
greatly feared. Archangel Gabriel told us that originally 'hell' meant a
shallow grave. To have one's bones dug up and chewed on by a beast
was anathema.

Into this trembling society came a man of peace, a man of love. A
teacher of God, who saw his spiritual siblings in everyone, when they
saw only separate strangers in each other. Jesus knew he was part of
the Sonship of God, which consisted of all humanity on earth. He did
not understand why all God's children did not perceive themselves as
God's beloved offspring. So he came to show us the way of salvation
The love of God was made manifest on Earth in this fearless, loving,
accepting, man. He would have stood out in a crowd just because of
his quiet composure. He stood out in a crowd because he was so
*different* from anyone else. But he stood out mostly because his aura was
so large that, though unseen by the masses, attracted them like a
magnet to hear him.

He preached love and forgiveness. He *lived* love and forgiveness.
Even on the cross, he did not condemn his torturers or crucifiers. Nor
did he ask God to forgive them their trespasses against him. He only

prayed for their understanding of how futile it was to kill a physical form, when the essence of a man is his eternal spirit.

*The Aquarian Gospel of Jesus the Christ* (177:1-19) provides us with an interesting story about Jesus, disguising himself as a fisherman, appearing at the Sanhedrin and quizzing the priests about the details of the resurrection. They tell him lies about the incident and then he tells them the truth of it, and suddenly reveals himself as Jesus, the man from Galilee whom they *thought* they had killed. As the priests tried to seize him, he disappeared. I love this story. Jesus could have said 'nyah, nyah, nyah, you didn't kill me after all', but he simply appeared to them to prove to them that indeed there is no death.

Jesus could only abolish death by overcoming it, which he did at the resurrection. No one had *ever* demonstrated eternal man before. In the resurrection, Jesus brought life and immorality - the truth of our existence - to light. What light? The light of understanding. The light of awakening. In this demonstration of bringing back to life a physical form, he showed that we, too, could do the same. He even promised that he came as a way-shower, when he said,
"He that believeth on me, the works that I do shall he do also . . ."
(John 14:12)

Paul explained the manifestation of the resurrection well in his first letter to the citizens of Corinth:

"So when this corruptible shall have put on incorruption, and this mortal shall have put on immortality, then shall be brought to pass the saying that is written, Death is swallowed up in victory. (I Cor. 15:54)

"O death, where is thy sting? O grave, where is thy victory?"
(I Cor. 15:55)

'when this corruptible' means when we *each* put on the incorruptible - when each of us is ready to accept the resurrection for self, - we shall have put on the immortality of Self.

Later in the Bible, we find in The *Revelation of Saint John the Divine*: 'there shall be no more death.' Here is the *promise*, given to John by spirit that the day would come when death would no longer exist. This means

61

that *we will all ascend*, as Jesus did. But our ascension will not follow the death of our body; we will by-pass that illusion and ascend with our physical form. Fortunately we will be able to ascend without suffering on the cross, as Jesus did. He told us, during is visitations to Earth (1995-1999) that the crucifixion was his one regret, because it was unnecessary. He came to save the world - that was his intent - but only on the cross did he realize he only saved himself.

In *Miracles*, Jesus tells us that what fear engenders is emptiness. And only forgiveness can replace the emptiness. Anyone who has forgiven another will testify that forgiveness brings a kind of relief, a burden lifted from the mind, a feeling of comfort and well-being. God's children are not worthy of feeling 'empty' because we are part of God. God created us and what is created carries within it a portion of the creator. The human experience of birthing children confirms the genetic component of the offspring; now we can even prove it with DNA testing! And so God, which is a spirit, breathed us forth and we have within us this same spirit vibration. When we become aware of that spirit Self of us, that is when we will 'put on the incorruptible.'

"But is now made manifest by the appearing of our Saviour Jesus Christ, who hath abolished death, and hath brought life and immortality to light through the gospel" II Tim. 1:10

# Twelve Legions of Angels

It was in the Gethsemane Garden, and the chief priests and elders of the people came to seize Jesus. Peter grabbed a sword from one them and 'struck a servant of the high priest, and smote off his ear.'

In Matthew 26:53 Jesus says 'put up again thy sword unto his place, for all they that take the sword shall perish with the sword'.

'Thinkest thou that I cannot now pray to my Father, and he shall presently give me more than twelve legions of angels?'

In Roman times a legion consisted of 3,000 to 6,000 foot soldiers and cavalry. Twelve times that would be 36,000 to 72,000. This is quite a large number and surely enough to overwhelm the people who were about to grab Jesus and arrest him. This moment was meant to be, for Jesus came *to be a savior of his fellow men*. He was certain that if he came and preached love, came to Earth and lived a life of forgiveness and love, and sacrificed himself on the cross, that he would save humankind from their sinful ways. This was his intention.

Prior to his appearance on Earth Jesus went to Archangel Gabriel and told Gabriel what he planned to do. And Gabriel, in effect, said, 'Go for it.' Now in his infinite wisdom as the Announcer of the Ages for God, Gabriel knew that one man could not actually save another. But Gabriel also knew that God gave all humans free choice and he sensed that Jesus had made up his mind about his mission on Earth. The beloved Archangel Gabriel explained this to his several listeners, in the last decade of the 20th century. Gabriel said that only on the cross did Jesus realize he could only save himself. And he ascended unto our Father, as the Bible explains.

Before his experience in Gethsemane, Jesus had been pursued often by Roman soldiers, but he always 'escaped' their arrest. Because he had 'all power in Heaven and Earth', he had the ability to disappear and re-appear at another place in the flesh. It is what today is known as an 'out of body' experience.

As our elder brother, who chose and lived out his lifetime as Jesus the Christ, he told us that all that he did we also could do. But Gabriel told us we do not all have to die on the cross. That was the common 'punishment' for those who went against the rule of the Roman Empire.

As Jesus could call forth legions of angels, so could we. The problem is that *we don't know that*, and thus we become victims - of others, of the opinion of others, of our own self-deprecating thoughts, and of our belief system that we are not worthy of angelic help.

When we take Jesus down off 'the old rugged cross,' and see him as our elder brother, we will begin to accept our own divinity. That will be the first step. Then we will need to practice using the power Jesus had, and we have now. For like the Master Teacher, Jesus, we too possess all power in Heaven and Earth. Is this blasphemy? Or is it blasphemous to deny our sonship of a Creator God who breathed us forth eons ago?

Will we continue to hold on to the old belief system which was held by the humans 2,000 years ago - a belief system which denies women the right to participate in religious rituals and services? A belief system which designates how long a person's hair should be? A belief system which holds Jesus up as our personal savior? A belief system that insists God has only one son, and sent him to Earth to be physically abused, and condemned to death on the cross. If God did that to his only son we should indeed be very fearful of such a creator. We should fear that God at all times and pray He will not so condemn us to suffer. But there are those who believe that if this God who can condemn and punish his son, how easy for Him to condemn us all. And if he did that, why are we still here on Earth?

Of course there are those who will tell us that God is a loving God, and the only one we need fear is the devil. But Archangel Gabriel said that he has been around since time began and said that he has never seen an entity called the devil or a place known as hell. Both were devised by humans. Now we can accept the fact that God is in us. What would God have us do, but awaken to our Christ light within (the Kingdom of God)?

In worshipping Jesus we deny ourselves the opportunity to seek and find the God within, which was promised by Jesus himself. If the Kingdom of God is within, then we are all God's beloved children, and as such we all have the power of Heaven and Earth within us. What else could it mean?

If we persist in accepting Jesus as the only son of God, there is no way that we could possibly emulate him. Worship is for God, the one God of us all. (Malachi) If this were so, why would Jesus have said it? "He that believeth on me, the works that I do shall he do also; and greater works than these shall he do; because I go unto my Father." (John 14:12). He would have known that we could never do what he did, because he would have known that he was the only son of God. As we cling to the old rugged cross, and see Jesus as the sacrificial Lamb of God on the cross, we preclude our growth as God's children. We cannot have it both ways, nor can we compromise them.

Now is the time we must take Jesus down from the cross, embrace him as our elder brother, thank him for coming 2,000 years ago to show us the way to live and begin our own personal journey back home to God as his offspring. What a journey it will be! What a grand and wondrous journey it will be! Some have begun the journey - not the clergy, not those in high political places, not the rulers of the world governments - but ordinary individuals who have acknowledged and accepted their place as children of God. Having taken the first step, they now are practicing their God-given power in various ways, such as forgiving all, loving all, worshipping our Creator God, staying on that loving path. Such as volunteering to help those in need, praying for the down-trodden and the criminals, healing those who come to them by teaching, and demonstrating love. We all have the choice of living a loving and forgiving life, by focusing on only the good, only the holiness of all our spiritual siblings on Earth.

# The Ultimate Forgiveness

"Then said Jesus, Father, forgive them; for they know not what they do." Luke 23:34

"Miracle-minded forgiveness is *only correction*. It has no element of judgment at all. The statement "Father forgive them for they know not what they do" in no way evaluates *what* they do, It is an appeal to God to heal their minds. There is no reference to the outcome of the error. That does not matter." ACIM T 2: V: A: 16 (6): 1-6

When Jesus was crucified everyone there thought that Jesus was dead, and that was the end of him. After all, while still alive on the cross, had he not asked John, the apostle, to care for his mother in his absence? They may have thought, also, that his teachings left with him. They grieved for the man they had come to love and worship. They comforted each other. But, in accordance with the Old Testament prophecy,
". . . weeping may endure for a night, but Joy cometh in the morning." Ps. 30:5

And, oh, what joy did come that first Easter morning! The whole earth rang out with joy at the rising up, the resurrection of Jesus the Christ. It probably was many days before the apostles realized how often Jesus intimated that he would overcome death with life and  so prove that life, real life, the life of spirit, is everlasting.

On the cross, Jesus did not complain. He did not curse his persecutors. He did not blame them for crucifying an innocent man, a man of God, a man of peace, a man of love. He knew them for what they were: all children of God, Roman soldiers and citizens alike. He knew them for what they were, even though they did not see themselves that way. He saw his spiritual brothers and sisters, whom he had come to save. He knew they did not understand his teachings. But he also knew that he did what he came to do: save the world.

It was only on the cross that he realized he could only save himself. He hung there, nailed to the tree, a Light in the darkness of the times. He overlooked the crowd and saw the bleakness of the scene: the fear, the anger, the hatred that permeated the very air below him. How could we know this? Because Gabriel told us Jesus' awareness of the truth, as he hung on the cross of judgment by the Romans and the Hebrew priests, who resented a man who could perform miracles that they could not. When he prayed to the Father to forgive those who crucified him, he never mentioned their transgressions. He only asked God to forgive them for their lack of understanding.

Jesus also knew that his body was a temporary form to house his holy spirit while on earth. He was fully aware that he was going to give up his body only for a time, until he resurrected it. Then he would ascend in body and spirit unto the Father in Heaven. From before birth, when he asked God if he could come and save the world, God did not deny him his choice. God gave us all free choice at creation. In his infinite wisdom, God knew that Jesus could not save everyone, because we each are our own savior. We each must make that singular choice to seek and find salvation.

What the people of Jesus' time failed to understand was that the Light which Jesus grounded to Earth for all time was for *all people* on Earth -- not a chosen few, not a separate and separated religious sect. Jesus was a good Jew, with faithful Jewish parents. Why would he come to establish another church? His teachings are universal. His basic doctrines are shared with other major religions. When we accept them as such we will accept each other as our true spiritual siblings. We are all children of the most high God. Praise God for his variety, for his imagination, for his all-encompassing Light of Love and Peace.

In three short years Jesus taught all humanity what we need to know about life and salvation. Everyone on the face of the Earth has heard the name Jesus Christ, whether they worship him, love him or discount him.

"And all flesh shall see the salvation of God." Luke 3:6

# Section 3: Human Frailties

# End of Vengeance

In the Old Testament the word 'vengeance is found over thirty times, from Gen 4:15 to Micah 5:15. It fits with the dictum found in Ex. 21:23-25: "Eye for eye, tooth for a tooth, hand for hand, foot for foot, Burning for burning, wound for wound, stripe for stripe."

". . . Vengeance is mine; I will repay, saith the Lord." Rom 12:19

". . . is a misperception by which one assigns his own 'evil' past to God. The 'evil' past has nothing to do with God. He did not create it and He does not maintain it. God does not believe in retribution. His mind does not create that way. He does not hold your 'evil' deeds against you. Is it likely that He would hold them against me? Be very sure that you recognize how utterly impossible this assumption is, and how entirely it arises from projection." ACIM T 3: I: 3: 1-8

We can continue to look at these words and ask ourselves, if this holds, where does vengeance *end*? Even Paul wrote it to the Romans. How could anyone who really understood Jesus and his teachings of love believe this old adage was still true? Now there persists the urge to never accept something new. Perhaps that is why we still have not accepted Jesus' lessons in love and forgiveness. Tradition holds with an iron grip the mind of modern man, especially modern religious man.

In *Miracles,* Jesus comes to make clear to us our erroneous concept of vengeance. We see our past actions as 'evil', and then assign them to God. In so doing, we expect God will take vengeance on us for our 'evil' doings. And whenever we are in tribulation we believe that it is an effort of God to get back at us for our 'evil' actions. This does not make sense when we believe in a God of love. In *Miracles* The Master states clearly that vengeance is not a creation of God; that God does not make nor maintain it. God does not hold against us what we perceive as our 'evil' actions. As a matter of fact, God does not believe in retribution at all.

It is our projection - assigning our desire for vengeance on God - that is our distorted thinking. We seem to want to believe in a god of vengeance *and* a God of love. But those two concepts do not fit together. We must choose one or the other. The Old Testament is replete with vengeance, judgment, malice and other negative characteristics of the men of that time. Then Jesus came to teach love and forgiveness. It was a strange and new concept at the time. Today it is still a strange and new concept. It explains why God rejected Adam and forced him out of the Garden of Eden. It also explains to many current believers that Jesus could not possibly come today to teach us, through any book, person, or experience. If Jesus once said 'I am with you always', why could he not come again at this time? And who would determine *how* he would come to us? And who would deny him?

We cling to the idea of vengeance because it seems to balance the scales for those who wound us in any way - physically, mentally, or emotionally. Another pattern of erroneous thinking is that others do things *to us*. But in this age of truth, when Jesus comes to teach us anew (in *A Course in Miracles* and other writings), we must accept the truth of the matter:, no one ever, ever harmed us without our permission, and we never harmed anyone without theirs. Nor do we experience any pain or illness unless we choose it - for a lesson to be learned. This is indeed a strange and new concept, and yet it is the truth of our lives. We need to take responsibility for all that happens to us. We must ask ourselves what the lesson is.

Archangel Gabriel, in describing the crucifixion, asked the audience how we would feel if someone down the street asked us to be hung on the cross to pay for his sins. It did not seem logical or fair. Nor was the concept logical or fair then. Humans all have free choice - we are the only species that does - and Jesus had the choice to sacrifice himself for humanity. He did so with the intent of changing us all. But, as Gabriel so clearly explained that only on the cross, as he beheld the fear and darkness of the masses, did he realize he could only save himself.

What must we do to give up the idea of vengeance? Since vengeance is the result of judgment, we must relinquish judgment. And judgment is the result of believing others can harm us. Taking responsibility for everyone and everything in our lives frees us from judgment and the idea of vengeance. We have the power to change our minds. We have the power to seek God's Will for us. What we need is a willingness to do so. Faith in a God of love, peace, and forgiveness brings to our own minds all positive options. When we choose those options we find a new kind of peace in our lives, in our minds, in our outlook.

# Power of the Ego

"God is love" (I John 4:16) God is a Spirit (John 4:24). Everything God created contains a spark of divinity; a particle of love. A very long time ago God created humans; a spirit family. God loved us, and we knew it. We all loved God and each other. It was a Perfect Place; some call it Heaven. Then, one day, we decided to 'play' with the vibration which, as we know, is the attribute of everything. We devolved downward, away from God in our consciousness; until we reached the nadir point of the vibrational scale which is physical form. It is called Earth. We co-created with God all the animals and plants. We even co-created a physical form called a body, for ourselves.

Then the animals we had created began to chase and eat us; we fell off cliffs, and sunk into quicksand. Each time we had to create a new physical body. This was possible because we still co-created with God. We still knew that we were God's Own. But then one day we forgot our connection to God. We thought that we had left God (an impossibility), and He would never take us back. Fear set in. Now we were 'on our own' and in a lonely place. We saw each other now as separate from each other and separate from God. Fear is a most uncomfortable feeling. So, we made an ego to protect us from the fearsome beasts and the sudden cliffs. We felt 'safer' and a little surer of ourselves.

We became so enthralled with the voice of the ego that after awhile we gave it power, then more power. Finally it not only was activated into the world of form, but it went into the emotional body, and there warned us not to love. Then it went into the mental body, and it warned us to be careful of our mind. [it said] "Don't let your mind get great power". Our minds are wondrous instruments of power. Finally after a bit, the ego became our master, and all we listened to was the ego. Our listening became deaf to the 'still, small Voice of God' within. (I Kings 19:12)

Our connection to God, our Creator, had been completely forgotten. We relied solely on our ego, and our problems escalated. God did not create the ego; we made it from our fear. Fear is therefore the ego's favorite weapon. Ego uses that weapon at every possible turn. Distrust of others became a pattern for us. There is a multitude of problems with living from the ego.

One of the problems is that the ego's voice is so loud. It attracts our attention much quicker than the 'still, small Voice of God', which is ever available to us. But it eludes us because with 'leaving God', we also left behind the belief in God's Voice in us. When fear shouts at us it is impossible to hear God's quiet whisper. We give all the power of the ego to it. The Kingdom of God is One, perfectly united and the ego will never prevail against it. But we do not believe that in our daily activities. And so the power we give it is magical.

Because we made it, the ego has no being. All of God's creations are real; nothing else is. Therefore the ego is not real. The fear that rules us is ego-based. The belief system of the ego is chaos. It denies us of our free will. The ego cannot love, which is proof it does not exist, for God is love. But it tries to convince us that it is real. From the ego comes belief in poverty, limitation, illness, guilt, anger, failure, arrogance. Without guilt, the ego has no life. Conflict is the ego's favorite condition.

The ego makes its home in the body, and uses the body for attack, for pleasure and for pride. The ego tells us that heaven is here, as it drives us to hell with its negativity. 'Giving to get' is an inescapable law of the ego. It always compares itself to other egos, which it also makes. In essence, the ego has no purpose. It shouts at us not to look inward. Of course, that is where the Kingdom of God is. The Kingdom of God is placed in us by God, and the ego has no faith except in itself. That is idolatry. The body is the symbol of the ego, and the body is finite, and so the ego is *not* us.

The ego is not the Self, which is spirit, which is eternal. The ego does battle with the Holy Spirit, constantly. But the Holy Spirit does not fight back. It waits patiently for us to realize the truth of the matter: that the ego does not really exist. The ego believes it can attack God. That is its insanity. Nothing can attack God. The ego believes *it* is God, and its only need is guilt. Strangely, the ego believes that anger makes friends. This is an example of its insane thinking.

The ego does not understand humility. It does not understand love. It does not believe in God but knows there is something higher than itself and continues to fight it. When we listen to the ego constantly, it takes us in endless circles that lead nowhere.

Because the ego lacks reasoning, to introduce reason into its thought system is the beginning of its undoing. When we realize what the ego is (it is nothing; it has no reality, having been made by us, out of fear), then we can open its erroneous thought system to reason. Since we made the ego it must obey our command. We can tell the ego that we love it but we must work from the spirit self of us and will call upon it later. Unaware that we are going to call it back, it clings to us and fights for its life and gets in our way. We need to assure it that we will invite it back later.

We need to consciously decide to listen to the still, small Voice of God within us. When we accept the truth that we are still as God created us - love; spirit - it will be the end of the ego. This truth, in itself, renders the ego silent and entirely undone. When we learn to tap into our spiritual beingness again, the ego will become smaller, back down to where it was meant to be in the first place. It is a very useful instrument, but not when we give it free reign over us.

The truth of us frees us from guilt and opens us to eternal joy. The ego is afraid of the spirit's joy, because once we have experienced it we will withdraw all protection from the ego ("Love casts out fear" ACIM T 1: VI: 5:4) and become totally without investment in fear.

And "Where fear has gone there love must come."
(ACIM T 28: V: 2: 4)

# Temptation Resisted

"And lead us not into temptation". Luke 11: 4

One unfortunate characteristic shared by humankind is the willingness to be tempted and follow that temptation. Because of its universality, it is included in The Lord's Prayer. God knows how easily we are tempted, and how quickly we reach for what tempts us. Many will proclaim that it is 'the devil's work'; that all temptation stems from the devil himself. We must forego that belief because we know now - from Archangel Gabriel - that there is no entity called 'the devil'. Nor is there a place where such an entity would reside, called hell.

Humans came up with the idea of hell and the devil for several reasons. We had to blame someone for our faults and mistakes. So we decided to have a 'scapegoat', so to speak. The idea for a scapegoat is found in Lev. 16:8-22. And so the goat was chosen to take upon himself all the sins of Israel. Through this ritual all can be 'cleansed' of their sins, or shortcomings. Also, when we judge another to be lesser than us, we tell him to 'go to hell', the final condemnation that one person can wish upon another. As for the early church, the idea of hell and the devil was very popular, for when individuals feel guilty, they want someone (like a priest) to forgive them their 'sins'. And so the priest, who *represents* God to them, forgives the 'sinner' and in return accepts a donation to the church. It is this 'fear of God' (found seventeen times in the first five books of the Bible) that set the stage for the teachings of the Old Testament. It would be many centuries before a new teaching came to us; a teaching of love instead of judgment.

A man named Jesus came to teach us to love God (Matt 22:37, Mark 12:30, Luke 10:27), to love our neighbor, and to love ourselves. 'Love thy neighbor as thyself' is found in Matthew, Mark, Luke, Romans, and Galatians. How could we love ourselves when we have succumbed so often to temptation? The answer is a simple one: forgiveness. When we read, accept, and choose to live by the New Testament, we learn that forgiveness is essential to a spiritual path. We begin a program of forgiving others, by reviewing our lives and honestly admitting whom we still resent. Another option is to enter into a counseling relationship. Another choice is joining a self-help group.

When we have forgiven all others whom we can identify, we must then look at the issue of forgiving self. It does not matter who we have 'harmed' in our lives, because we understand now (thanks to Archangel Gabriel) that we *never* harmed another without their permission. Two people make an agreement, before coming into this world, to participate in the activities they choose. They agree to it in order that both may learn a lesson from it. Often the lesson is forgiveness. But what keeps us from forgiving self is the deep, rutted guilt that we have dug over time. It is often said 'I will forgive but I will never forget'. That is *not* forgiveness, because it is the pain of the memory that comes to mind, not the event *without* pain. Without the pain, the memory will go.

The importance of forgiveness cannot be over-emphasized. Perhaps that is why Jesus told Peter, who asked the Master if we should forgive seven times. Jesus replied, 'seventy times seven' (Matt 18:22). I hardly think Jesus meant that we should keep track of 490 forgiving times, but rather we should forgive endlessly. When we have forgiven others and self, it is possible to decide not to be tempted again to lash out at others in judgment. We can decide this by a diligent application of Jesus' teachings. We can decide this by accepting others *as they are*, instead of comparing them to some imaginary bar of behavior.

"Jesus said unto him, Thou shalt love the Lord thy God with all thy heart, and with all thy soul and with all thy mind. " This is the first and great commandment." (Matt 22:37-38)

Also, in Mark 12:30 we find:
"And thou shalt love the Lord thy God with all thy heart, and with all thy soul, and with all thy mind, and with all thy strength: this is the first commandment." It is interesting to note that Mark includes the word 'strength'. Perhaps he himself requiredstrength to maintain a love of God.

Keeping this first commandment is not an easy task for the ordinary citizen. That is why Jesus, in his Sermon on the Mount, said,

"Enter ye in at the straight gate; for wide is the gate, and broad is the way, that leadeth to destruction (temptation), and many there be which go in thereat:
"Because strait is the gate, and narrow is the way, which leadeth unto life, and few there be that find it." (Matt. 7:13-14)

Some people have interpreted 'narrow' as restricting and difficult. Yet for those on a spiritual path, the choice of directing our attention to the love of God results in a glorious freedom. Those people interpret 'narrow' to mean well-defined, explicit, and clearly marked.

All our heart, mind, and soul constitute the totality of us. But there are so many distractions in our lives to keep us from that focus of loving God completely: the media, neighbors, family, and co-workers. As *they* focus on the past and the future we are tempted to join them in that focus. Looking at the past was not recommended in scripture. In Genesis we find the story of Sodom and Gomorrah: when Lot's wife, disobeying the angel's - and Lot's - warning, turned to see the destruction, she turned to salt. Focusing on the past is not conducive to focusing on God. The past is gone, never to be re-written or re-lived. Focusing on the future is likewise distracting from loving God *now*. As we base our decisions on the past we are likely to repeat all the errors of it. The only time in eternity is *now*.

Diligence is necessary to love God *all the time*. How does one do this in our busy world? One can do this through prayer and meditation. Prayer is talking to God; meditation is listening to God. All through the day we can talk to God. In one tiny instant we can put out a prayer. We can pray for patience with another or with a situation. We can talk to God all day long about what we are doing and thinking. God easily reads our minds; he knows our every thought. But when we consciously talk to him, it takes our attention to him, if only for an instant. All the moments add up! God is omniscient (all -knowing). God is omnipresent (everywhere at once). There is no place where God is not. God is omnipotent (all-powerful) (Rev. 19:6).

When our thoughts are on God we feel comforted and loved, because God is love. (I John 4:16) God created us from Himself, and therefore

we are love. This relationship is undeniable and strong, as so well explained by Paul in his letter to the Romans: (8:38-39):
"For I am persuaded, that neither death, nor life, nor angels, nor principalities, nor powers, nor things present, nor things to come,
"Nor height, nor depth, nor any other creature, shall be able to separate us from the love of God, which is in Christ Jesus, our Lord."

When we are living from the Lord God of our being, remembering that we are rooted and grounded in love, focusing on positive, guided by the Holy Spirit, then others and things do not tempt us.

"And lead us not into temptation". means "Recognize your errors and choose to abandon them by following my guidance".
ACIM T 1: III: 4: 7

# The Separation

The idea of separation - humans from God and from each other - began so long ago we have no conscious recollection of it and yet it was our own doing. Our Origin and Source is God, the magnificent Creator of all life on Earth. When we, as a group of humans, decided to play around with the vibrational rate which is the essence of all life, we reduced its velocity time and again until we reached its nadir point. And that nadir point is physical form. Here we got 'stuck' on the idea that form is all there is and we are it.

In our soul's memory is the recollection of our Beginning, and the soul longs to return home to God and Paradise. Paradise is our natural habitat. Yet we cannot consciously recollect life in paradise and its perfection. We have taken the idea of separation into our religions, the various races and even to our next door neighbors. We can 'prove' the differences in religions because of the ideas brought forth from the founders thereof. We can 'prove' the differences in the races because of skin color, language, and social mores. Our neighbors are different and separate because they do not think the way we do.

All these differences fortify our concept of separation. It is gratifying to see, in recent years, an effort on the part of many religions to join in ecumenical services and rites. Also, since WWII the world has shrunk considerably due to military troops' extensive travel around the world. This has resulted in 'mixed' marriages across lines of language, religion, and race. Perhaps this is the beginning of seeing all humankind as one.

As world commerce increases, there are many individuals who travel extensively and in their travels they often find a 'soul mate'. The governments of the world are establishing or continuing embassies in other countries, leading to increasing exchange of language and customs, and inter-marriages. At this rate it will take several generations to see a world of one race. And even then, it will be a race of bodies. Yet we are not just bodies. As children of God we are much more than that. We are souls and spirits and all are one with God, who created us. Names of God vary, but God is One and we are all part of Him.

Some individuals and groups are beginning to accept this oneness. This oneness is addressed in *A Course in Miracles,* and *Oneness.* In order for oneness to take hold in our thinking, we need to become willing to learn outside our belief system. Many belief systems are based on ancient criteria, old thought systems that must change. Tradition is used as an excuse to not change. How valuable has it proven to be? If all our decisions are based on the past, how can we ever hope to learn anything new? It is time to ask ourselves if the old ways have really 'worked'. Is life any better for our having obeyed old laws, old rules, and old ideas?

For some of us, the idea of separation from God sounds so logical, because we all pray *up* to God. We all lift our gaze upward in prayer, even if our eyes are closed. Surely he is 'up there, somewhere', since Earth is so full of negative thinking, negative attitudes, negative behavior. Even our so-called 'entertainment' is full of violence, rage, and destruction. We ask ourselves why God would allow such not-good stuff. It is far easier to blame God for all this, instead of seeing it as of our own doing. All humans have *free choice*. By free choice many have chosen negativity to rule their lives. By free choice many others stand by and allow it. We rage against it, but do nothing. We blame others for not acting instead of asking self 'what can I do?'

Seekers who want something more in their lives, a 'better way' to live, or a new way to express their love of God to love of their fellow-man, *will* find the way, the truth, and the life that they desire. It is the soul, longing to return home to God, which inclines us to inquire about 'something better'. And when we find it, we will pursue it. Perhaps some of the time, most of the time or all of the time. But we will pursue it. A missionary will devote himself full-time to such a calling. Others may teach, heal, pray for, or spend time with those in need of companionship. When we feel the love of God in prayer and meditation, we become seekers. And God will always show us the way to express our love for Him to others.

When we do this we overcome the idea of separation. We begin to feel united with all other humans. When a child in Burma is starving we can relate. Why? We don't even know this kid, but now we know that what happens to one happens to all. Of course we can anonymously donate money to charities that will pass on our money, or a portion of it. Or we can find a way to *personally* assist another. Recently a movie portrayed a person 'paying forward' a favor or a gift. Now it is becoming a habit for some. One fast-food restaurant in Canada saw a 'pay forward' experience over 200 times consecutively! It's a beginning. Money is power and with our free choice we can decide to share our funds with others. What is much more powerful in giving is our time. We use time for work and play and entertainment, but we could also plan some part of our time to do for others what they cannot do for themselves. One idea would be to tithe our time; at least our waking time. What a different world would result if we all did this!

The Christmas season is replete with people helping people. Ringing bells for Salvation Army, working in soup kitchens, delivering dinners, etc. are examples of assisting others. Carrying that idea into the New Year immediately after Christmas could be a New Year's Resolution, or just a personal choice to help our fellow-citizens make it through their day, their task, their life. In doing so the idea of separation finally disappears. We will feel closer to our Creator, and prayer and meditation will become habitual. Then we are on our way to *knowing* our oneness with God.

# Worldly Thoughts and God

One of the most repeated phrases in the Bible is, "The kingdom of God is within." With our thought system this seems totally impossible. Impossible because we feel like we have all 'sinned' or done things we feel ashamed of. Impossible because we believe that God is 'up there somewhere' and we are 'down here' on Earth. Impossible because no surgeon ever left the operating room declaring, "Yes, I saw the kingdom of God inside that body." Impossible because we see ourselves as tempted, judgmental, and unforgiving. These are not attributes of God.

The kingdom of God is within because, as we have finally come to accept, we are holy children of God. Not adopted by God; not a piece of flotsam and jetsam thrown from a big explosion or bang in the universe. If God's kingdom is within, we had the kingdom of God within at birth - or did we somehow bring it within by our own will? If we live according to the laws of the world, it would be impossible for us to bring it by ourselves. Therefore, it must have been there since we were born - or even before we were born. We simply have not been *aware* of its existence inside of us. Psalm 46:10 tells us "Be still and know that I am God". Wow! All we have to do in order to become aware of the kingdom of God within is to be still. But that is not an easy task in this world that is driven by activity; driven by constant movement. Society implies; no, insists, that we keep moving. When we keep moving we cannot become aware of the kingdom. The ego loves this because it, too, wants us to keep moving, lest we become still and know God and do not need the ego anymore. The thinking of the world is upside-down, compared to the truth of God's holy Will. Some examples are:

Sharing and Losing
Worldly thought:
If I have eight apples and give three away, I have only 5 left. Sharing then tells me that to be generous means to lose something myself.

Will of God:

If I have eight apples and give three away, I have been generous, gained a friend, acknowledged a brother. Therefore I have gained.

## Abundance and security

Worldly thought:

The only way I can have everything is to work hard, save money, and climb the corporate ladder. Then I shall be comfortable, secure and maybe even wealthy and famous.

Will of God:

"Therefore take no thought, saying, What shall we eat? or, what shall we drink? or, Wherewith shall we be clothed?

"(For after all these things do the Gentiles seek:) for your heavenly Father knoweth that ye have need of these things.

"But seek ye first the kingdom of God, and his righteousness; and all these things shall be added unto you." Matt 6:31-33; Luke 29-31

We see that we need to work hard in order to gain things for ourselves what we all need. God knows what we need. We want more than basics, because *others* have them. And when they have more, it means that they are better. The world's thinking tells us that newer is better, bigger is better, richer is better.

It is necessary, if we truly seek the kingdom of God within, why more is better. Do we really sleep better on a mattress that costs more than our entire bed, or on a bed that costs more than our refrigerator? Does our breakfast taste better seated at a marble table than a pine table? Do we enjoy a movie more on a large screen? Are we healthier wearing an expensive jacket than a warm, less expensive jacket? Do we value ourselves less because we *have* less? Who told us we should? Who set the baseline for ownership?

## Belief in God

Worldly thought:

We must convince others of our own religion. With all due respect to the numerous missionaries of Christianity (I do not know if other religions have missionaries), do they truly believe that another belief in God is wrong, inadequate, contrary to God's Will? Does not God have many names? Is Allah, Yahweh, or Great Spirit any less a Creator God than the God in Christian scripture?

Will of God:
"Throughout the ages, the scriptures of all religions have proclaimed that humanity is one great family. This is a simple truth, and it is simply and directly stated in every religion. In fact, almost all the principles that are associated with religious thought are shared by every religion. The Golden Rule, Love Thy Neighbor, Honor Thy Father and Mother, Speak Truth, It Is More Blessed to Give than to Receive - these principles and others are common to all religions and are very similarly expressed in each." *Oneness*, Foreword,1.

Does is really matter if we pray once a week or five times a day? Can God know us any better than he already does? Will we get to Heaven any sooner with more praying? It is the sincere prayer, however often, that reaches to Heaven. It does not even matter what Heaven is called by others. The Decalogue and the teachings of Jesus the Christ incorporate all teachings of God, by whatever name we call Him.

Want, need, and desire
Worldly thought:
We constantly feel that we need something that we do not have. We may not truly need it, but then another person tells us that we do. Or we see something on TV and suddenly decide we need it. Often we do not distinguish between needs and wants. When we want something, we somehow begin to believe that we need it. If we truly need it, or think we do, we find a way to obtain it, by ourselves. If we cannot get it by ourselves, we may find it necessary to ask another to provide it. This asking is a humbling thing. It suggests that somehow we are inadequate and not self-supporting. Society tells us that we should be able to take care of ourselves and get, ourselves, anything that we may need - or want. All this 'wanting' and 'needing' keep us very busy. And busy is what the world is and wants from us.

Will of God:
Gabriel explained that want and need are both and always based on a sense of lack. As children of God we lack nothing, for we have, and are, everything. However, he told us that we ought to use the word

'desire,' for it means 'de-sire', or 'from the Father'. So, if we need something - and God knows it before we ask, we should pray to God for it; desire it.

There is a story about a woman who was praying for money. Since she was both clairvoyant and clairaudient, she saw Archangel Gabriel appear to her.
He said, "Why are you praying for money?"
She said, "Because I want a computer."
He said, "Why not pray for a computer?" And so she did.
A few weeks later a friend of the woman said, "I just won a computer, complete with a printer. I have no need of it now; do you want it?"

This story tells us that we need to be specific in our prayers. Asking for money is not a good idea. There was a man who ardently prayed for $5,000. One day he was in an auto accident and hospitalized. He became healed and then he received a check from the insurance company, for $5,000. It covered his hospital expenses, which he *needed,* but he still did not have the money which he wanted. God does not deal in money. God deals in the needs of all His children.


<u>Having and Being</u>
Worldly Thoughts
In this world, what we have is what defines us. If we have wealth we see ourselves as 'wealthy'. If we are poor we see ourselves as 'needy'. If we are working we are 'productive', and if we cannot work then we are 'disabled' - from working. If we are not mobile then we are house-bound or in a wheelchair. If we cannot move about in any way then we are invalids (in-valid?).
As humans we readily label ourselves and others. And this labeling defines us. We judge others based on where they live. At one time the poor lived 'on the other side of the tracks'. We know where the 'haves' live and where the 'have-nots' live. We can tell on the street, by the cars they drive, or the clothes they wear. Most of us fall between these two extremes. We are called 'the middle class,' which is interesting because we supposedly live in a classless society - that is what a democracy is, or should be. In the thinking of the world we have no definition for, or even an understanding of, what 'being' is.

Will of God

How can God see us all the *same*? "Of a truth, I perceive that God is no respecter of persons." Acts 10:31

This does not mean, of course, that God does not respect his children. It means that He sees us all in the same way; in the same light. "If thy whole body therefore be full of light, having no part dark, the whole shall be full of light, as when the bright shining of a candle doth give thee light." Luke 11:36

This light is known to us only when we focus on God through our single eye, the sixth chakra, between the eyebrows. See Luke 11:34

God sees us as the light that we are; the light that is within us, whether *we* see it or not.

# Section 4: Our True Selves

# The Christ in Us

When Archangel Gabriel told us that he would come often for twelve years there was excitement in the air. We all felt so blessed to be at his feet to listen and learn the wisdom of the ages. We did not realize at the time that some of his lessons in truth would be painful to hear. For me, the following lessons were difficult for me to take in. I think part of me was silently saying, I don't care if you are an archangel, I don't believe what you are telling me. And yet, when I looked more closely at his teachings, I had to acknowledge that they all made sense.

1. *Before birth here, you plan all your life and everyone in it.*

My first reaction to this was 'no way'. I was born into an upper middle class family, the youngest of nine and spoiled. But in the midst of the Great Depression my father passed away and after that my mother became addicted to alcohol. Why would I plan this? But then I asked myself what lessons I had learned. (This is the first question we should ask ourselves when anything befalls us). I learned to be a survivor. I learned to be independent. I learned to keep out of the way when another is out of control. I learned to be resourceful.

When my children were in their teens I left them, my husband, and my home. It was the source of a great deal of guilt for many years. I left because I listened to my ego self. I listened to the voice of addiction. I had hit what is known as an alcoholic 'bottom'. I was so in love with alcohol that it was the only thing that mattered. It would be a long time before I saw this event as a necessary part of my life. After moving far from home I found remission for my alcoholism. And three years later I heard Archangel Gabriel the first time he visited. In retrospect I can see that I had planned (before birth) to be a student of Gabriel and therefore I had to be in the Albany, NY area to attend his seminars.

In another essay I wrote about 'all my mothers', and it is with great joy that I realized, in later years, that I had planned their presence in my life. Eventually, after I stopped drinking alcohol, I became an alcoholism counselor. Also, I earned a master's degree in counseling. Then I became an ordained Christian Metaphysical minister, followed by years of serving two different churches as pastor. I gave guest sermons at a Unity church in Endicott, NY, and wrote several articles for the Albany Times-Union. All these accomplishments were possible only because I stopped abusing alcohol, and gained a degree of sobriety.

That opened the door of spirituality to me. Without it, none of these things would have been done, and I never would have found Archangel Gabriel!

2. *You plan when, where, how and with whom you will die.*

When I first heard this my immediate question was, Why can't I know it now? The first time I received a message from a medium I was fifty. I was not seeking to know anything about my demise or how it would happen, or when. (this was before Gabriel's visitations). An entity in spirit told Millie, the medium, that I had lived half of my adult life. Through the years I contemplated this information and tried to identify what spirit meant by 'adult'. 'At first I thought my adulthood began at eighteen or twenty-one. Then I realized that spirit would not care anything about man-made legislation. These ages identified who was eligible for a military draft, the right to obtain a driver's license or the right to drink alcohol. Spirit would more likely, I decided, consider adulthood beginning at puberty. Since I was thirteen then, I subtracted thirteen from 50 and deduced that my demise would come when I am eighty seven. Now I am 84 and I have *no problem* in having only three more years on Earth. In addition to the accomplishments listed above, I have written eleven books. I told my daughter, who is a nurse,that I would like to die in my sleep. She said, 'Everyone does, mom'.

3. *Nobody ever hurt you without your permission, and you never hurt anyone without theirs.*

In reviewing the experiences of my early years this seemed quite unrealistic. Later it became clear that it did not make sense because I had built up a 'justified' resentment against those who had 'hurt' me. Now I know that no anger is justified, that it hurts no one but myself, and it takes a lot of negative energy to carry the heavy load of resentments. That is why forgiveness is such a freeing decision. Forgiving others came first for me. Now I continue to work on forgiving myself.

4. *You all have been saints, murderers, and, homosexuals.*

With this statement, Archangel Gabriel made it clear to us that reincarnation is not a theory, but a fact. He told us that we keep on the karmic ride and we must decide to get off of it. The karmic cycle means coming to Earth, returning to the astral plane, coming to Earth and returning to the astral plane - over and over again. Gabriel said that we have lived so many lives here, that we have met *every person now living on Earth!*

To get off the karmic ride we must begin with forgiveness of everyone, including ourselves. We must forego listening to the ego, with its weapon of fear. Following Jesus' example of love, and listening to the still, small Voice of God, we can and must live a life of love because everyone is part of the Sonship of God. We are all prodigals and eventually we will all return to our Father in Heaven, because Heaven is our natural habitat. It is the place of our origin.

5. *This is the only planet that still practices disease and death.*

God created us perfect. How could He do otherwise? The physical body is a unique machine with an unbelievable capacity to run itself as long as we give it fuel and occasional rest. There are monks who have lived to be 900 years old *on Earth*. When we experience illness or any disease (dis-ease) it is because we have created the problem in order to learn from it. In healing we do not add to anything, we remove the negative thoughts and negative expectations of ill-health.

We think that because of our advancements in technology and space travel we are so talented, so wise. We can't explain UFOs because they travel at speeds the scientists cannot explain. The truth is that our technological expertise has far our-stripped our spiritual growth. This is what we need to work on now. Technology of warheads will not bring about peace on Earth (isn't that what we all want?). Only our change of mind will bring peace on Earth. Only by *following* in the footsteps of the Master Jesus the Christ, as he asked us to do, will we finally bring about a world without war. Some day children will read history books and ask 'what is war?'

Gabriel told us that entities from other planets come to Earth and watch us bury the dead, and wonder why we are so wasteful. They wonder why we don't just ascend, as they do. They do not realize we haven't learned how, as yet. Ascension will be learned by all. It is a matter of time only. Our task is to truly apply the teachings of Jesus the Christ: love self and neighbor, forgive everyone, live a life of positive application as he did. The most painful message we hear is that we are all Sons of God, because we have invested so much time in believing it is not so. And we still believe that we left God, and He will never take us back. As the Prodigal Son, we must all decide to return Home. The choice is ours; the time is now.

# God's Image

And God said; Let us make man in our image, after our likeness . . .
Gen. 1: 26

"The statement 'God created man in his own image and likeness' needs
reinterpretation. ' Image' can be understood as 'thought,' and 'likeness'
as 'of a like quality.' God did create spirit in His Own Thought and of a
quality like to His Own. There *is* nothing else. ACIM T 3: V: 7: 1-4

In *Miracles* Jesus corrects the biblical text to help us understand more
clearly just what the original words mean. In this Age of Truth we can
now accept and understand the symbolism of the Bible. If the Bible
were not symbolic, why would Jesus come at this time to open our
minds to the truth of this holy book? Gabriel, in slightly different
words, told us that we are not made in God's *image*; we are actually part
of God.

When Jesus said 'There is nothing else', what could he mean except
that all reality is what God created, and that nothing else has reality?
God is all there is; God is spirit. Spirit is the totality of all life, and all
that God created constitutes all life. All life includes humans, animals,
and plants. Even inanimate objects, such as stones, have a livingness in
them. Proof of this inter-penetrating life is the fact that all life
communicates. There are a number of books which explain the ability
of this diversity of communication. All forms of life can and do
communicate.

True communication is a two-way dialogue. Animals, plants, stones can
and do speak out, in their own language. As yet, only a few humans can
or will accept this possibility. Most do not participate in a dialogue with
other species because they either never heard of it, discount the
possibility out of hand, or have never attempted it. What makes such
communication possible is our willingness to *listen*.

Humans do not even understand each other unless they speak the same language. Even then, communication is fuzzy at best because firstly, many of us do not have the ability to express our feelings and thoughts. Secondly, we are often unwilling or fearful to express our thoughts and feelings lest we be judged. Finally, we often perceive that what we think and feel are not worth describing. Members of the human family cannot communicate unless both parties speak the same language. If we speak different languages, we cannot communicate without an interpreter. In addition, most people have a problem with listening. While someone speaks to us we have the habit of judging what is said, planning our response, or thinking of something else. A good listener is a good communicator.

If life is all there is and life takes many forms, it seems logical that all life forms ought to communicate with each other. One might well ask what inter-species communication has to do with God making man in His own Image. In the scheme of creation, as described by Archangel Gabriel, God made humans from Himself, spirit. Therefore in each of us is a spark of divinity. Then, as co-creators with God, we brought forth creatures and plant life. From us these other species also contain a spark of that spirit; that same divinity. That is why there is nothing else. Life is all there is. Life is the only reality.

The advantages of listening to other life forms are:
1. We need not express ourselves, but only have a willingness to listen to what the frog, the stream, the tree have to say *to us*.

2. Other life forms do not judge us. Even when the plant devas tell us what humanity needs to learn, it is a teaching experience, not one of judgment.

3. Listening is part of communication. When we listen to other life forms, we can learn. We can learn about all life and the perspective of each species on life.

This all-encompassing reality is not what we experience in our daily lives. The reason for this is that what we experience in our daily lives is based on all the error perceptions that entail our daily life. What are these error perceptions? *All that our senses perceive.* Our five senses deceive us because we believe they bring us truth. In fact, they bring us only perception. And perception is deception. We are deceived by all our perceptions as they support us in what we want to believe. If we are prejudiced against a certain group of people, our senses will be interpreted to support that prejudice. In essence, then, our senses provide for us with a world which *we desire to know.*

In searching for truth, instead of error perceptions, it is essential that we do certain things. We must use our sixth sense to receive the truth of any situation, event, or person. We must discount as false all that our senses tell us. We must come to understand that the world we live in is a world of illusion *because it is fed by our senses.* Truth is ours for the asking. All we need to do is knock and seek. It will come to us through our sixth sense; through our intuition; through the Voice of God speaking to us. It is that simple to understand. It is not simple to accomplish. True prayer and devout meditation will open the door to truth. Constantly turning our will and our lives over to the Holy Spirit will bring to mind at any given moment what we need to say, do or think. It is an immutable law. It is the Will of God.

# God's Peace

"And the peace of God, which passeth all understanding, shall keep your hearts and minds through Christ Jesus.

"Finally, brethren, whatsoever things are true, whatsoever things are honest, whatsoever things are just, whatsoever things are pure, whatsoever things are lovely, whatsoever things are of good report: if there be any virtue, and if there be any praise, think on these things". Philip 4:7-8

Two thousand years later, the Master Jesus came to explain the reason why peace eludes us: "Pursuit of specialness is always at the cost of peace . . . Specialness is the idea of sin made real." ACIM T 24: II: 2: 1; 3:1

Archangel Gabriel, on occasion, would ask his audience what our greatest desire was. Most of us, if not all, chose 'peace on Earth.'
Is the Christmas season so popular among Christians because we love fir trees? Or mistletoe? Or gifts? I submit that there is a deep and inner desire for peace on Earth. It is as though we believed that God would somehow suddenly shower the planet with peace. Like so many prayers, we expect God to shower us with blessings without doing the leg work ourselves. When unemployed we pray for a good job, but we spend only one or two hours a day in our effort to make it happen. Peace on Earth begins with the individual. Working at having peace with a mate, children, parents, extended family members *all takes time and effort on our part.*

This peace of God is not understood by humankind because we think peace is something we can have only in a fleeting moment of time, as we stand on a mountain top, or by a quiet stream, or on the ocean's shore. We think it eludes us because we see it as illusive. In Phil. 4:7, Paul reminds us that the peace of God must come *through* Jesus. It is our task to accept the fact that this can occur, by turning to the Christ in us and seeing Jesus as our elder brother. In Phil. 4:8 Paul spells out the positive characteristics we ought to see, value, and incorporate into our lives. 'Pure' conjures up a goody two-shoes idea - and who likes *them?* They often act 'holier than thou.' But no one is holier than we, for God created us holy - in His Image.

Honesty is abrogated every day. In the workplace we see no problem in purloining a few pencils or a few reams of paper. After all, who will miss them? Who will know? God will know, and those who come to believe in God will soon realize that redemption is an option. It is a cleansing, releasing option, which will provide us with a new start in life. It is never too late to make a new, fresh beginning. We can choose to do so, but others may not be forgiving. *It does not matter.* When God knows our intent of living a good life, what matters it if our neighbor disagrees with God?

Reviewing the personality traits listed by Paul, we see the very traits we seek in a mate. Honest, pure, lovely, just (fair). We see the perfect person for us in that other. And yet, that is not why we 'fall in love'. Gabriel explained that when we 'fall in love'; the other person awakens *in us* the love that *we are.* Perhaps that explains why we 'fall out of love' after awhile - those old feelings of unworthiness and low self-esteem return to us, and the inner light we felt before dims, and the 'other' is not so desirable anymore. The peace of God we seek is ours for the asking. We need to rise above every judgment call, every negative thought, and every prejudicial attitude. When we feel that peace, we will not be able to describe it, for it is not understandable to us, much less describable. We can only feel it and know it and embrace it.

Loving virtue, praising God, living honestly and fairly, and accepting all others as they are, will bring to us that peace of God we claim to cherish. It is so strong and powerful that nothing can reduce or destroy it. The peace we seek will surely elude us if we see self, or any other human being (all our spiritual siblings), as special in any way. Society reeks with the idea that a person of wealth, title, talent, or unique ability is special. They are not. In the eyes of God we are all His children of light. He loves us all equally. He loves the famous pianist and the serial killer alike. Why would He do this? Because He sees His children as part of Him and knows that we all are coming home to Him someday. The serial killer is a child of God who has chosen many wrong roads to travel; has made many poor decisions, has seen self as 'special' in a negative way. The famous pianist has chosen and followed a path of many positive options. He has heard the Voice of God in applying his ability for his joy and the pleasure of others. When we honestly choose peace for ourselves, we will find that it denies anything to affect us which is not of God. This denial is not a 'hiding' but a correction of error automatically when we bring it into the light of God; the light of understanding.

"This peace is totally incapable of being shaken by errors of any kind. It denies the ability of anything not of God to affect you. This is the proper use of denial. It is not used to hide anything, but to correct error. It brings all error into the light, and since error and darkness are the same, it corrects error automatically." ACIM T 2: II: 1: 10-14

# Light

"In the beginning . . . God said, Let there be light . . ." Gen.1:1-1:3

"There is a light in you which cannot die; whose presence is so holy that the world is sanctified because of you." ACIM W pt I: 156: 4:1

Is it possible that in our limited thinking we fail to fully understand the true meaning of these statements? All that we have learned is derived from our past experiences on this planet in our earthly 'evolution'. Humans usually interpret this to mean light in contrast to the darkness we have ourselves created – a light which affects the material world; the world of physical form. All physical form casts a shadow *from the light*. Without light impacting on physical form, there is no shadow. Without our awareness of the light within, there is no awakening from the shadows of form to the light of God.

From our essence, spirit, in which God breathed us forth, we decided to create something other than the perfect state in which we lived – in Heaven. As we created we manipulated vibration and slowed it down, and we came with it, creating forms compatible with our surroundings. Finally we slowed it to its nadir point, which is physical form – material, solid form. We created physical forms for ourselves. And so it is, that over the centuries, through many mortal lifetimes on planet Earth, we have forgotten our Source, our Origin, which is spirit, which is God Himself. "God is a spirit." John 4:24

"But the natural man receiveth not the things of the Spirit of God: for they are foolishness unto him: neither can he know them, because they are spiritually discerned." I Cor. 2:14

Mortal eyes behold physical matter, spiritual vision beholds truth. Spirit cannot be seen with physical eyes. There are those who say they do not believe in God because they cannot *see* God. We may ask if they believe in love, in wind. Neither love nor wind can be held in place, nor pictured, nor captured. Both love and wind can be identified only by their *effect*. From a gentle affectionate touch to the act of making love, we do believe in love *by its expression*. From a gentle breeze to a hurricane force, we believe in wind *only as we behold its effect* – from a field of waving wheat or a roof blowing off a house. Is it then so untenable that God Himself cannot be seen with mortal eyes? If God cannot be seen with mortal eyes, then it follows that we cannot see His Kingdom, either; although it resides in us, as told by Jesus: "The kingdom of God is within you." Luke 17:21

Did the people of Jesus' time understand this? Do *we,* today, understand this? Perhaps the phrase 'spirit casts no shadow' applies to *us*, too. Our physical forms cast a shadow, but the true essence of us, spirit, casts no shadow. The Kingdom of God, being within, must then be reached by our consciousness. It can *only* be reached by our consciousness. This is the goal of meditation. "Cause me this day to be aware of the bread of life; thy presence in my consciousness." (The Lord's Prayer, Female version, from Archangel Gabriel)

Jesus said . . . "behold, the kingdom of God is within you". Luke 17:21 With all our modern medical equipment we have never been able to *see* that inner kingdom the master spoke of. No x-ray or MRI has ever revealed to the medical community the inner light in all of us. "Ye are the light of the world" Matt. 5:14

One of the many phrases I recall which Archangel Gabriel gave us is, "Walk you in the light – you *are* the light". If the kingdom of God, then, is in us and we cannot see it, then we must accept the fact that we can only identify its existence by its *effect*. One of the effects is our desire for peace; peace in the world and in our lives.

"Blessed are the peacemakers: for they shall be called the children of God." Matt. 5:9. When we accept peace as the Will of God, and align our will with His, we awaken to the God-self within. We become aware of our Source, spirit.

Archangel Gabriel said, "Peace is the highest form of love, is it not?" No wonder, then, that we do not have peace on earth. Love, by definition of humans, is divided into kinds of love. We love our children in one way, our neighbor in another, our significant other in yet another way. Love is not to be sorted out, dissected, and applied here but not there. The love which the Master Jesus spoke of, and lived by, was love unconditional. He loved every person he met. He saw beyond the weeping sores of the lepers, the misshapen legs of the crippled, the fear in the eyes of the people. He saw the light within them all; the true spirit, higher self of each. And he wondered why we were unaware of our own light; our own kingdom of God.

How does one find and live unconditional love? By first accepting everyone we meet – just the way they are. Not because they agree with us, or accept us, or have something we want. Accepting them just as they are is possible when we realize the truth of them - that all are our spiritual siblings. In truth, we are all children of the one God.

Then it is required that we forgive all those whom we perceive have wounded us – physically, emotionally, or mentally. If we think 'I forgive, but I will never forget' – we have not forgiven - for every time we *remember* an event, we recall the situation *and the pain of it*. True forgiveness stems from the truth that no one ever wounded us without our permission, and we never wounded another without theirs. Therefore, in the final analysis, there is *nothing to forgive*.

It is unconditional love which will lead to peace within every human soul. In that day when we all love each other unconditionally, seeing with spiritual vision, then we all, every child of God, will find peace of soul; peace of mind. Only then will there be peace on Earth. Only then.

"Ye are the light of the world." Matt. 5:14

# The Real World

"Yet you can learn the truth about yourself from the Holy Spirit, Who will teach you that, as part of God, deceit in you is impossible. When you perceive yourself without deceit, you will accept the real world in place of the false one you have made. And then your Father will lean down to you and take the last step for you, by raising you unto Himself." (ACIM T 11: VIII: 15: 3-5)

This finite world we live in will end some day and everything in it will be no more, including all physical bodies. The real world is the world of God; the spirit world; the world that is infinite and eternal. It is that world from which we came, and to that world we will return. It is a journey we each must take, for our soul longs for that return.

There are clear guidelines in scripture for us on this required journey. "But seek ye first the kingdom of God, and his righteousness; and all these things shall he added unto you." (Matt 6:33). This is the roadmap for our return. What does it mean? God would not send his messenger, Matthew, to tell us to seek something we cannot find. God does not play tricks on us. If we seek the kingdom of God, we *will* find it. Putting our search for God foremost in our thinking, in our actions, every hour, we will find it. Finding it, we will rejoice and the angels will rejoice with us. 'All these things' will be added to us, also.
All the things we used to pray for - health, shelter, clothing, jobs, etc. They will be added to us because we will be following guidelines from the Holy Spirit, the transforming energy of God. God did not create us to suffer, to lack in anything. We must all ask ourselves, do you really believe that God would give you anything but a blessing?

There is only one way in which we can turn our lives around, from asking out of need to knowing there is no need. The Holy Spirit awaits our request for help. He only comes to those who ask. But once we ask for help, His help is guaranteed. It is an immutable law of God. The way to turn our lives around and keep them so is to dedicate ourselves to God, and to be ever vigilant in our devotion to Him. As was said by

Jesus "Thou shalt love the Lord thy God with all thy heart, and with all thy soul, and with all thy mind. This is the first and great commandment." (Matt 22:37, Mark 12:30, Luke 10:27). This sounds like a pretty tall order for us, who live in a 3-dimensional world. The Bible informs us of four dimensions. In Ephesians 3:17-19 we find:

"That Christ may dwell in your hearts by faith; that ye, being rooted and grounded in love,
"May be able to comprehend with all saints what is the breadth, and length, and depth, and height;
"And to know the love of Christ, which passeth knowledge, that ye might be filled with all the fulness of God."

Could the fourth dimension be anything but spirit? What a visual concept of our connection to God 'being rooted and grounded in love'! And to know that 'with all saints' we too can know God! Yes, we are filled with the fullness of God; we simply deny it is true. The belief in duality reminds us constantly that every good has an opposite. When we focus only on good, we will realize that only good is real. God is love, and God is everywhere at all times. What is in all can have no opposite. When we look at only love it becomes clear to us that hate is merely the perceived opposite of love, but on a scale from love to hate, we find that love *is the scale* and we have made it up.

It is our God-given free choice to make a change in our lives. If we are completely content with life as it is, then we will not want to change it. And we will continue on the karmic ride, back and forth from the Astral Plane to Earth and back, like a rat in a cage that goes nowhere. The 'somewhere' we can go is the real world.

"The real world can actually be perceived. All that is necessary is a willingness to perceive nothing else . . . Perceiving only the real world will lead you to the real Heaven, because it will make you capable of understanding it." ACIM T 11: VII: 2:6-3:9

# Sparks of Divinity

"The power of one mind can shine into another, because all the lamps of God were lit by the same spark. It is everywhere and it is eternal."
ACIM T 10: IV: 7: 5

When we first hear the idea that we are children of God, we pull back mentally and recall all the reasons why it could not be true. We bring to mind some of the hurtful things we have said to others. We remember our actions of the past which affected others in negative ways. We hold resentments toward others who have hurt us. We believe that we are 'less than' many other people - if not everyone else. This self-denigration is all too common in the human population. It is our ego, which loves its weapon of fear, and reminds us constantly that we are small, unimportant, and insignificant.

To God, who loves us *just the way we are*, we are still His beloved children. When we see ourselves as parents we can relate to this. We love our offspring *just the way they are*. We may not agree with their religion, their politics, their philosophy of life, but still we love them. We may not like what they do, but we love them for what they are - flesh of our flesh, bone of our bones. Mothers can relate to the joy of knowing they are carrying a precious offspring, the product of making love with another. And when the new-born infant is placed in our arms, there is no way to describe the joy of it.

We watch the kids grow up, from total dependency on us to independent individuals, running their own lives as they choose.
I have often said that the most difficult part of being a parent is letting them go. They go out into the world, so unaware of the ruts in the road, the options good and bad that will be offered them, the difficult choices they will have to make, and the variety of people who will cross their paths. But we must let them go physically, although they will forever be in our hearts and minds, with love and acceptance. Even the offspring who commit crimes are not denied parental love.

We are thus an analogy ourselves to the parental love that God has for us, his offspring. God loves us no matter what we have done, who we have hurt, or what negative behavior and attitudes we have chosen. He loves us eternally *because we are His own.* Humans bring forth children in flesh; God brings forth children in spirit. Our offspring are ours for a lifetime; we are God's offspring forever. God is a spirit and we are made in His image. In us, hidden from our consciousness, by our own choice, is that tiny spark which was placed by God. When we think about it, we realize it must be so. Otherwise, what is in us that matures eventually into a caring person? What in us responds with compassion when we hear of a tragedy in which many are maimed or killed hundreds of miles away? Why do we care about them, unless we are somehow connected to them?

A friend meets a personal trauma, and we are there for them. A stranger on the street is hit by a car; we run to help; we call for help. The news reports of a flood, or fire, or murder, and our hearts respond automatically with compassionate understanding. Perhaps we have been so affected. But even if we never were, we care about the individuals who have been wounded or killed and we pray for their passing. We pray for their survivors. Sometimes we even pray - as we should - for the perpetrators. Where does all this compassion and caring emanate, unless our very being contains a spark of divinity that makes us care?

One of the outcomes after a tragedy affecting many people is the response of others. Of course we have what we now call 'first responders'; those who are paid or volunteer to rush to the aid of those in need after an accident. But many who are nearby also run to help in any way they can. Pleas go out for aid in the form of clothing, food or money for long-term assistance. Money pours in to help. Everyone can relate or just respond because they care.

We are family, this human race we are part of. We all have a spark of divinity within us. God knows it is there; we sometimes suspect it is there. Now we must wake up to the truth of it; the truth of our being. We must acknowledge our sonship of God and our brotherhood with all of humankind. Races, religion, language, social mores all are included. God must have a broad imagination to encompass it all, but we know He does. With all our differences we all bleed red blood, have feelings, procreate, eat, sleep, drink and cohabitate. Yet we are all connected by a strong thread of love and compassion. We are all sparks of divinity, the world over.

What does this mean? Accepting our oneness with each other and with God, what does it indicate for our behavior, thoughts, and attitudes? It means that first we need to acknowledge the oneness. Forgiving those who 'hurt us' will free our mind of the burden of resentments. Forgiving ourselves will further free us. The past is past; it is prologue to our future. If the past looks ugly, we can choose to make a beautiful future. Looking back is not a productive option. One might recall Lot's wife, in the Bible (Gen.19:26), who looked back at Sodom and Gomorrah. She turned to salt. We don't turn to salt when we focus on the 'old days', but to base all our choices today on the past will guarantee that nothing will change in the future.

New ideas come to us all, especially the artists. All the arts are full of new idea people. That is what makes them artists. Others of us get a new idea and quickly discount it with ego thoughts that shoot down the idea quickly. Thoughts like 'I haven't got time now', 'I can't afford it', 'someone else is more qualified', etc., etc. Now is the time to realize the new idea comes to us because of that spark within. It is not gone; it is merely out of our mind. Ignoring it constantly means that we are out of our minds to doubt our ability, our strength, and our power. We must acknowledge and then listen to the spark within. It will never lead us astray; never take us on a dangerous journey, never lie to us. It is, in fact, the Voice of God in us.

The spark does not speak to us but we can *feel* it when we get a new idea, a revelatory thought. We also can feel it warning us, when we put our foot upon a negative path. But we don't always listen and respond with thoughtfulness. Sometimes we go down that negative road in spite of the feeling and then our self-will runs riot in our lives, and we wonder what went wrong. Listening to that inner spark persistently brings great rewards of loving relationships, accomplishments, self-confidence, and self-actualization. When we listen to the spark one might say we are running on all cylinders. Listening and responding to the spark means we will have a well-oiled machine; one that runs smoothly. Our lives will not suddenly be perfect, but we will know that whatever comes is a lesson for us, and to know the lesson we must listen to that inner spark.

Man has not made a machine that works as well as the human body. It is made to last a very long time. Some people live for a hundred years without 'repairs'. Archangel Gabriel told us there are some individuals who live 800 or 900 years on the Earth! God's spark is in us all, whether we live ten hours, ten days, ten years, or hundreds of years. Now we must stop ignoring that spark, pretending it is not there. Let us wake up to our divine spark, express it freely and confidently. When all humanity does this, then we can know peace without borders; love without animosity; caring without hindrance.

# Section 5: Promises of The Father

# Alpha and Omega

"I am Alpha and Omega, the beginning and the ending, saith the Lord, which is, which was, and which is to come, the Almighty". Rev. 1:8

"Jesus saith unto them, Verily, verily, I say unto you, Before Abraham was, I am". John 8: 58

Two thousand years later Jesus wrote:

"Right perception is necessary before God can communicate directly to His altars, which He established in His Sons. There He can communicate His certainty, and His knowledge will bring peace without question. God is not a stranger to His Sons, and His Sons are not strangers to each other. Knowledge preceded both perception and time, and will ultimately replace them. That is the real meaning of 'Alpha and Omega, the beginning and the end,' and 'Before Adam was I am.' Perception can and must be stabilized, but knowledge *is* stable. 'Fear God and keep His commandments' becomes 'Know God and accept His certainty." ACIM T 3: V: 6: 1-7

*The Revelation of Saint John the Divine* is symbolic, as is the entire Bible. Archangel Gabriel told us this. Gabriel spent two entire days explaining the symbolism of the Book of Revelations. How could I begin to share all this information in a short essay, or even four, which are found in this book? Suffice it to say that early in his explanation, Gabriel said of the book "This is you." For starters, Gabriel explained that the seven churches are states of mind:

Smyrna = intellect
Pergamum = emotional state
Nicolaitans = undecided
Thiatira = understanding
Sardis = intuition
Philadelphia = love
Laodicea = knowingness

From there, Gabriel expounded on all these definitions and proceeded to explain the balance of the book and how it applies to us. Before the first day, Gabriel requested that we use the *Good News Bible,* and that someone read from it until Gabriel stopped them to explain each portion. This process was repeated until the entire Book of Revelations had been explained. I know this to be true, because I was the one chosen by Rev. Penny (channeler of Gabriel) to be the reader. I was ecstatic when she chose me!

Would anyone argue that God is the Beginning and the End? God made all of us in His Divine Image. All humanity is the only begotten Son of God. We all constitute the Sonship. Jesus, the man, had experienced many lifetimes, just as we have. His penultimate earthly experience was a man who came to be known as Buddha. Buddha believed that the most important thing to know in the world was wisdom. As Jesus he came to show us that the most important thing to know in the world is love.

Jesus knew, throughout all his lifetimes that he was a Son of God. He could not understand why the rest of us did not. And so he came as Jesus to bring the light of truth from God to Earth, to awaken all his siblings to their own divinity. So far, as a society, we have not awakened. That is why Jesus came again at the end of the twentieth century to bring us *A Course in Miracles.*

Before Jesus came, John the Baptist was sent to announce Jesus' coming, and to baptize him in the Jordan. John said "Prepare ye the way of the Lord . . ." (Matt 3:3).
Then Jesus came to show us the way. He said, "I am the way, the truth, and the life . . ." (John 14:6).

He came as an example "For I have given you an example, that ye should do as I have done to you". (John 13:15).

He came as a way-shower. "Verily, verily, I say unto you, He that believeth on me, the works that I do shall he do also; and greater works than these shall he do; because I go unto my Father." (John 14:12)

When we turn to the Bible for serious study, how do we understand the phrase 'the kingdom of God is within?' (Luke 17:21) What else could it mean than that in each of us is an altar to God? When we desire to pray, do we immediately think we must find a physical church, with a formal altar? No, we silently offer up a prayer, with eyes turned upward, closed or open. Is that because in our memory lies a knowingness that we indeed *are* divine children of God? Is it because we know, in our innermost hearts, that God *always* hears us?

Some people still believe that God is 'up there, somewhere' and we are down here, victims of fate, of life, of family or 'friends'. Friends do not victimize us. We have no problem seeing the kingdom of God in someone we love. We have no problem seeing the kingdom of God in someone who befriends us. Why is it so difficult for us to see it in *ourselves?* Too many of us have been taught that we were born sinners. How do we overcome such a negative concept? Is this idea the foundation for all those who are depressed? Are we walking through life with low self-esteem because we were told this? And, can we overcome it with diligent effort and a firm decision to do so?

In *A Course in Miracles*, Jesus quotes scripture and assures us of the correct understanding of it: "Know God and accept His certainty." must replace the phrase ". . . Fear God, and keep his commandments. . ." (Ecc. 12:13). Time is an illusion of earthlings. Perception - erroneous view of life - also is illusory. Before both time and perception there was knowledge. Knowledge is stable, unchangeable, and reliable. We all have the key to knowledge. It is called intuition. We have heard it, but not paid attention to it. It is the Voice of God, whispering in our ear every time we start off on a negative path. The more we ignore it, the dimmer it becomes. This Age of Truth is our time to listen, listen, listen; and then become aware of the Christ in us.

# Ascension for All

There are approximately seven billion humans now residing on the planet Earth. Some day we are all going to ascend unto the Creator God. I do not speak from the standpoint of merely a Christian. I speak from the standpoint of the truth imparted to us by Archangel Gabriel. He is the Announcer of the Ages and came several times to impart to us the wisdom of the ages, from October 1987 to December 1999. I was blessed to be in that group of seekers; students of Gabriel, and later Jesus himself. "God is Light." (I John 1:5). Jesus said, "I am the light of the world." (John 9:5) and "While ye have light, believe in the light, that ye may be the children of light." John 12:36

Light exemplifies awakening. Our task is to awaken to the Christ Light within ourselves. Gabriel explained that Jesus the man contained within him the Light of the Christ. We all do, but Jesus *knew it*. Jesus came to awaken us all - all humanity - to our own Christ Light. The Bible tells us that Jesus often said 'follow me'. When Jesus said "He that believeth on me, the works that I do shall he do also; and greater works than these shall he do; because I go unto my Father" (John 14:12), he meant *all his works*. By 'believe on me' he meant not Jesus the man, but the Christ Light in him. One of the 'works' that he did was to ascend. And as we follow that Light in him, use him as an example, awaken to the Christ Light in us, we will ascend also unto the Father.

Lest the reader think that the day of our ascension is far off, please make note of the fact that at one of Archangel Gabriel's seminars there was a pregnant woman in the audience. Gabriel said to her, "The child you are carrying will ascend." We each have our own experiences on Earth as we come back again and again to this aching world in order to learn lessons. We choose the experiences and we learn - or not - the lessons contained therein. Our spiritual journey is not horizontal, but vertical. Today we have the parents, the children, the mates, that we have chosen. And they have chosen us. One hundred years from now we will have other parents, other children, other mates, as we choose them on our singular spiritual path Home. We have come here to learn, as we came here to learn six hundred years ago, or six thousand years ago. Gabriel said that we have visited this planet Earth so many times that we have *met* every person now living on Earth. That is a tremendous number of lifetimes! What is it that we have not as yet learned, so that we can ascend, never to return to this darkling planet? We have not as yet truly learned love and forgiveness. We have not yet learned to live peacefully, without war.

We see life as a complicated journey. We see ourselves as complex individuals. Are we more complex beings than those that walked in Jesus' time? Yes, we have more technology and agriculture but most of the population has been replaced by the many advances of machinery and electronics. Our thinking, too, is more advanced than 2,000 years ago. We are able to absorb and use knowledge of science, mathematics, and esoteric principles. But as then, we still love and laugh and work and play. We still bleed and hurt and heal. We still dream and plan and build. Now we have freedoms that the Romans did not. We have freedoms as individuals and as groups. What Jesus taught then is still the lesson we must learn before we are ready to ascend. He taught love and forgiveness. The love he taught was unconditional love -- agape love; love that seeks no reward, does not keep score, is not full of boasting. In reading the first letter of Paul to the Corinthians, chapter thirteen, we have a thorough definition of what love is. He describes it well and completely. Can anyone reading this claim to *live* this love?

Forgiveness means many things to many people. True forgiveness means to forgive self, for any seeming injury done to us is done actually *by* us. We invited the experience to learn from it. The unwillingness to forgive self lies in the presupposing guilt of our many actions. Shame and guilt are bedfellows. We have all done something to feel guilty about or ashamed of. The guilt and shame are the feelings of our emotional body. The Spirit Self of us is created by God and is perfect eternally. But the guilt and shame prevent us from feeling the Atonement or the 'at-one-ment' with God. This guilt and shame seem like an impenetrable brick wall, but it is simply a thin veil. In prayer we ask God to forgive us, but we never did anything that needs forgiving. God loves us just the way we are. He knows we are trying to learn and from His truly objective view he knows that we are sound asleep to our oneness with Him.

In the book of Genesis we are told that Adam fell asleep. Gabriel reminded us that nowhere in the Bible does it say that Adam woke up! As Adam, we fell asleep to our own God-self, our own divinity, as children of God. We think we left God, in coming to Earth, and He will never forgive us for leaving. But Jesus told us the story of the Prodigal Son to show us that regardless of our wanderings, our extravagances, and our base choices; our Father will always take us back. Not only will He take us back, but He will celebrate our return. We must always remember, however, that in truth we never left God, and so the 'return' manifests only in our conscious awareness of same.

The Prodigal Son was full of guilt and shame before he returned to his father's home. We can surely relate to that. There are many ways to overcome guilt and shame. Writing about them, talking about them, or seeking counseling, are ways to bring them to the forefront and then let them go, forever. Some people say that they have forgiven but will never forget. That is not forgiveness, because as a moment or event is remembered, the guilt, shame, or judgment is also remembered -- because that is the reason for remembering, the trigger for the recalling.

Jesus recommended that we forgive 'seven times seventy' times. He knew that we would be judgmental and require a forgiving attitude. He demonstrated love in his everyday life. Because he did not judge others, he had no need to forgive them. Even on the Cross he did not judge or condemn his perpetrators. He did not list for God all the abusive treatment he had received. He prayed instead to God, "Father, forgive them; for they know not what they do." (Luke 23:34)

Jesus saw the ones who sought to kill him and the ones who inflicted the wounds as his brothers in spirit. He knew they acted out of ignorance. He knew their actions would bring on guilt and shame later on and then they would have to learn to forgive themselves. He knew that, like Adam, they all were asleep to their own divinity. And if they were awake to it, they would not, could not, sentence him or inflict the wounds.

The ascension will occur on an individual basis, as each human becomes fully aware of their own divinity. The kingdom of God within is the Christ Light that was in Jesus; is in Jesus today. He said he would not leave us comfortless. He said, "I am with you always". And always is forever. He meant it literally. Do you not feel him near you in meditation; do you not have a knowingness that he is guiding you when you are incapable of recognizing the path which is for your highest good? Our only task is to awaken to our own divinity and then live by it. We all have that holy, inner Light. We simply have become totally unaware of it. Our unawareness does not diminish nor extinguish it.

"How long is an instant? As long as it takes to re-establish perfect sanity, perfect peace, and perfect love for everyone, for God and for yourself. As long as it takes to remember immortality, and your immortal creations who share it with you. As long as it takes to exchange hell for Heaven. Long enough to transcend all of the ego's making, and ascend unto your Father." ACIM T 15: I: 14:1-5

# The Awakening

" . . . . a deep sleep fell upon Adam . . ." Gen. 2:21

From *A Course in Miracles:*
". . . and nowhere is there reference to his waking up. The world has not yet experienced any comprehensive reawakening or rebirth. Such a rebirth is impossible as long as you continue to project or miscreate. It still remains within you, to extend as God extended His Spirit to you. In reality this is your only choice, because your free will was given you for your joy in creating the perfect." ACIM T 2: I: 3:6-9

We read the Bible and accept the story of the Garden of Eden. Archangel Gabriel came, at the end of the last century (1987-1999) to inform us that it is an allegory; there never was an Adam and Eve. There never was a reptile of temptation. There never was a God who would create a beautiful garden and then forbid His children from it. This ancient story was written by those who feared God, feared death and succumbed to temptation. But they resolved all this by using a reptile as a tempter, a lovely garden as a place prohibited by God, and a luscious, healthy fruit as a forbidden food.

The story stems from the belief that we had left God, and He would *never* take us back. It must have been in the back of their minds that at some long distant past they lived with God in Heaven and now, on Earth, they were 'locked in' to physical form, never to return again to their place of origin; their natural habitat. It stems from the belief in 'original sin'. Was our 'original sin' our birth, or our decision to 'leave God' and create something other than perfection?

If we were 'born in sin', who birthed us? Are we the 'devil's children?' No, we can no longer say that, because Archangel Gabriel told us that there is no devil. Nor is there any 'hell', anywhere in creation. Gabriel said he has been around forever and never saw such place as hell or such an entity as the devil. The very presence of Gabriel was a loving, calming comfort, and provided a blessed assurance that we are, as he said, children of God and beloved by Him.

We are asleep to our own divinity. What keeps us in this dream world, this place of illusion, is our bad habit of projecting. Projecting means we find another to blame for our 'lot in life', a negative experience; a fearful event. We project blame onto another instead of owning responsibility ourselves. Yet we are the source of all our discontent. Carefully, Gabriel explained how we, before birth on Earth, gather with others and lay out our lives in every detail. All agree to the role they will play in our lives, based on lessons we believe we need to learn. This is *not* predestination. At any point in our lives we can re-write the script.

I found this so interesting that I asked Gabriel what the others would do if we did re-write the script. And he said they would all have to find another with whom to interact. These decisions occur when we sleep. Another person in that same seminar by Gabriel asked a question as to why a woman would choose to participate in a battering situation. Gabriel explained that if the woman, in a previous life, beat another person, she would decide to return to experience herself what that behavior felt like. That would be her chosen lesson. I had met a person who was married to her *second* battering husband. So I inquired of Gabriel how long such a relationship would last. He said that about twice a week the two would meet, in sleep, on the astral plane and she would decide if she felt she *deserved* to continue to be beaten. Only when she decided she had learned the lesson would she tell him to stop. One could easily ask, 'Why would someone agree to hurt another?', because before birth, on the astral plane, we love each other. But if someone said, 'Please do this if you love me,' then would a person agree to that kind of relationship.

This sole responsibility for our entire life means that we cannot, in all fairness, blame another for our problems. In thus projecting, we not only put the blame on one who is not responsible, but we dodge the issue of responsibility. So what do we do when a problem confronts us? The first question we should ask is what is the lesson in this for me? When we identify the lesson, *and learn it*, the problem will go. If we do not ask, or ask but do not learn, the problem will persist or re-appear in another form. For example, if we have a co-worker who rankles us to the point where we leave our job, without asking what the lesson is, the next job will have for us another co-worker with whom we cannot get along.

We miscreate when we manifest for ourselves or others a negative situation. We misuse the power of God in us. This is done with thoughts as well as deeds, for thoughts are things. The New Thought poet, Emma Wilcox, understood this when she wrote:

"You never can tell what your thoughts will do
    In bringing you hate and love,
For thoughts are things, and their airy wings
    Are swift as a carrier dove.

"They follow the law of the universe -
    Each thing must create its kind,
And they spread o'er the track to bring you back
    Whatever went forth from your mind."

*The Heart of New Thought,* 25

It was once believed that thoughts did not matter, as long as we did not put them into action. We know better now. Not because Mrs. Wilcox said it, but because *it is the law of the universe.* And these laws are immutable.

God created us to create perfection. We have fallen far short of that. The time is now to wake up to that which is already within us - the power of God Himself. Our awakening begins with valuing ourselves as His offspring. We not only *can* do it; we *must* do it. It is our only real choice.

# The Fatherhood of God

My father, Robert Bruce Wallace, and my mother, Ida Mae Armstrong gave birth to me. My body is a product of their love for each other and their physical union. This occurred in 1928.

My spirit is the product of my Father in Heaven. This occurred eons ago, when God first breathed us forth. He is the God of Creation and He created the human family *from Himself.* God is love. God is forever. God is changeless. I am part of the divine creation; therefore I am love. I am forever. I am changeless. This is my *spirit Self.*

My ego, my personality, my attitudes and beliefs are *my own* and are products of my imagination and thoughts, gathered through the centuries, as I lived out several incarnations on Earth. All my lifetimes I was human, for reincarnation is always species-specific. Archangel Gabriel told us that we all have been saints and murderers and homosexuals. In all these experiences through time we have been guided by our five senses. We have come to believe that *we are our bodies.* We are not. Our bodies are temporary shells to provide our real selves with physical form, as a means of communication on Earth. Our only real selves are our spirit selves - perfect, eternal, and changeless. It is this real Self that we must come to accept in our knowingness. Only then will we know that we are truly children of God; Lights of the world; one with our Father God.

Sometime after God created us perfect spirit, we (as a group-- all humans) decided to manipulate the energy which is the power of Creation. To make a very long story short, we continued to manipulate that energy to the mental plane, then the astral plane, then the material plane. The material plane is here, Earth, and we know it as physical form. We created all these planes with our creative ability; received from God in His Creation. We think that in all this creation we moved further and further away from God, and we have come to believe that He will *never* take us back.

Yet if we turn to the Bible we will find the story of the Prodigal Son. It is a perfect analogy. The son of the 'certain main' spent all his inheritance until he found himself eating swill with the pigs. Then he decided that although his father would probably not take him back, it was his only choice left. When he returned to his father he was welcomed with open arms and a feast ensued to celebrate the prodigal's return.

As children of God we 'spent all our inheritance' by turning to our body (made by our parents) and our ego (made by us) and believing they are our true selves. We have now reached the nadir point in our 'running away' - in our creation of physical form - and believe that our Creator God will never take us back; never restore us to our original Self, spirit. We have our God-given free choice to continue wallowing on this plane of sorrow and grief, this aching world called Earth, by staying on the karmic wheel of Earth and astral plane, back and forth as we have done for centuries. Or we can *consciously* opt to go back Home. We have nowhere else to go now.

We have created planes that are not real. Now we can choose to return. To do so, we must redeem all those planes of existence. Only then will we complete our journey back Home to God and Heaven. Gabriel made clear to us that Heaven is our natural habitat! And so, like the Prodigal Son, we have come to Earth - this 'far country' - and we can *and must* eventually return home to our natural habitat and God. Then we will know that we are His own, and part of the All-that-is. The journey must be made by our own free choice. The Guide is the Holy Spirit. The Holy Spirit comes to all who call on Him - but we *have to* call on him in order to receive His help.

It was startling to hear Gabriel say 'God is not complete without you.' It suddenly gave me an urgent desire to begin my journey back Home, so that I can do my part in making God complete! This is such a powerful concept; that we all are that important to God. But when we fully accept our Sonship with God -- and all humanity is the Sonship -- we *know* that we are that important to our Father God.

This journey is not about any one religion. Jesus came to bring the Light of truth to all humanity for all time. Only the early church fathers interpreted Jesus' teachings as a basis for an elaborate and narrow path called Christianity. How have we put into our lives the teachings of Jesus? Love for self and all others; unending forgiveness; peace on Earth which must begin with peace in each heart. Can anyone say we are employing these tenets in our daily lives? Many have taken Paul's teachings in place of Jesus'. For Saint Paul narrowed the clergy to men only; said that wives must be submissive to their husbands; that some humans were 'saints', as noted in the Old Testament. Paul also spoke of predestination.

Predestination is a human concept. In order to accept it we must believe in a god of punishment. A god of punishment is a judgmental god; a vengeful god; a god to be feared. How can we fear a god whom is in essence Love? God is love and all-forgiving. To love God instead of fearing God is the greater of powers. It is this power that we must not fear, but rather connect with. When we go against a god of fear, we have a lot of company, for we all have erred; all have transgressed. But to go against a god of love brings to our consciousness a seemingly impossible situation - unless we know that God is also all-forgiving. And so we must forgive ourselves, also. In that forgiveness of others and self we find our way to the all-encompassing love of our Father God.

# Oneness

Five major religions proclaim that man is made in God's image. (*Oneness*, 108, 109)

This makes human kind one divine family, belonging to God and, in truth, *part* of God --- whatever the five major religions choose to call Him. The question then becomes 'why don't I feel that I am part of God; divine by nature?'

We are not the first to ask the question. Paul remonstrates:
"For we know that the law is spiritual: but I am carnal.
For that which I do I allow not: for what I would, that do I not; but what I hate, that do I." (Romans 7:14-15)

When first upon this planet Earth, we made for ourselves an ego, to protect us. But it has become our master. It tells us we don't need a god, for we are the power unto ourselves, and must fend for ourselves. In essence, our ego tells us that we are separate from God because once upon a time - very long ago - we left Him and He will never take us back. We listen constantly to the voice of the ego, which is very loud and raucous. It wants us to believe and even to know, that it is in charge of us.

This belief in separation from God convinces us that the only real power in our lives is self. Thus we feel attacked by anyone who does not agree with us. If they do not attack us physically, they attack our beliefs and confirm for us that they are separate from us. In this constant dissension, we each become the standard of behavior and principle, opening the terrible door of judgment. As we each and all listen to the erroneous message of the ego, the judgments grow and become common. Judgment leads to resentments. At worst, judgments lead to violence and eventually to war.

As we review history, and in retrospect view all its violence and all its wars, we ask 'Why does God allow it?' The answer, of course, is God does not. God, upon Creation, gave us all free choice. Would anyone deny that? As each and all make our choices, the negative choices include judgment, anger, hatred, fear, doubt, etc. These negative options that we freely choose - all made from our ego selves - lead to violence and wars.

Thinkers and writers in this current century (21ˢᵗ) are bringing forth the ideas that we have an ego, it is contrary to the Voice of God, and now is the time when we must begin listening to God instead of our ego. How much longer must it take humanity to *remember* our Source and know that because we are God's own, we have the power in us that Jesus the Christ had, that Paul the apostle had. Jesus said "He that believeth on me, the works that I do shall he do also; and greater works than these shall he do; because I go unto my Father". (Romans 14:12)

What could be more clearly stated? The only requirement to enable us to do these things is *believe in him and his works.* It means that we too can heal the sick, raise the dead, walk on water. A few people have done these things. They have done them because they *know they can.* Our belief in Jesus the Christ must be strong, unwavering, and constant.

Mentally stepping onto a spiritual path in which we come to know Jesus the Christ and his works means reading scripture. Learning about this Master Teacher we come to know that we can follow in his footsteps, and do all that he did; and *more.* This knowingness can only be realized when we do two things: learn about Jesus and his life *and* stop listening to the ego and all its thoughts of limitations. Only in quietness can we hear the still small Voice of God. Only in that quietness do we overcome the loud shouting of the ego. There is a holiness in that quietness. There is a knowingness in that quietness. There is the assurance that we are, indeed, children of God and one with Him. Many artists will attest to the fact that what they drew, painted, wrote, sculpted, or designed, came from an unseen Source. Entering the quietness takes courage, for society is against quietness. It is against it because all of us have an ego.

Society has become a huge listening box to the ego. Society, which is the sum total of us all, keeps busy, keeps noisy, and keeps listening to the ego. And because it is such a common occupation, it is accepted by all others. Spiritually speaking, there are no 'others'. We are one family of God; in God. When we take the time to enter the quietness and listen to the Voice of God, we have knowingness. "Be still, and know that I am God." (Psalm 46:10). When we know that God *is*, and we know Him in us, then we shall begin to awaken. Adam fell asleep in the Garden. Nowhere in the Bible does it say that he woke up. Humanity still sleeps. We shall all awaken to the God Self of us, and then we will be Home once again, in God.

In the 21$^{st}$ century we must be willing and courageous enough to seek the peaceful silence in which we can hear the Voice of God whispering to us. In the peaceful silence we will come to know that we are in fact all part of the Sonship of God. This is the message of the century upon us: the century of a New Age. It is the Age of ius. It is the awakening time of humanity. When Jesus came to Earth it was at the turning of the ages. Jesus' birth was the onset of a new age. It was the Age of Pisces. That is why the fish became the early symbol of Jesus. It continues to this day.

Archangel Gabriel, who visited the Earth for twelve years, told us that it takes humanity 2,000 years to learn a new idea. Now, 2,000 years after Jesus' life on Earth, we are ready for a new idea. The idea is that we are all children of God and we all are therefore divine by nature. We all have within us the powers that Jesus had. The Christ Light in him is the same Christ Light in us. We deny that truth because we listen to the ego tell us we do not. We have the innate ability to choose to listen to the still, small Voice of God as written of in I Kings 19:12

# Section 6: Our Journey Home

# Breaking the Illusion

*A Course in Miracles,* in the early lessons of the Workbook, guides us to understand that the world we perceive is actually an illusion, and we have given it all the meaning that it has to us. How could this be? How could these houses of wood and brick be an illusion? How could those cars of steel and glass be illusions? How could this solid earth upon which we stand not be real? What our eyes see, we believe. What our ears hear, we trust. What our other senses reveal to us, we take for granted and defend. That's the way we were raised. That's the world we have inhabited for so long. Generations come and go, but we still believe in what we see, and we still deny the reality of any other world. How long can we continue to inhabit this world of illusion and not awaken to its unreality? If this world, then, is illusion, what and where is the real world? It is God's world of spirit. Spirit is eternal.

The Bible mentions 'spirit' hundreds of times. God Himself is a spirit! (John 4: 24) There are so many references in the Bible to spirit, and so many references to the spirit within us, that quoting them all would be a waste of paper and print. Of course there are those who truly believe that what occurred in the ancient days, when the Bible was written, could never occur again. Spirit would no longer be a part of humanity; spirit would not be available to guide us on our journey through life. Never again would humanity be able to interpret dreams or, like Paul, have an 'out of body' experience: (whether in the body, I can not tell; or whether out of the body. I cannot tell: God knoweth)" II Cor. 12:2 Some believe it could not happen again, not in future generations. I wonder why not? And if not, why would Paul write it - just to give us another mystery about ourselves? God is a mystery to us. An ever-present, all loving, all powerful God is beyond our imagination.

Also in scripture we find numerous references to the light within. Luke 1:78-79 reminds us:
"Through the tender mercy of our God; whereby the dayspring from on high hath visited us,
"To give light to them that sit in darkness and in the shadow of death to guide our feet into the way of peace."

Here, in this brief phrase, we find ourselves described, for we still sit in the darkness (ignorance)of our light within; unaware of it or denying that it is there, or denying that it is accessible to us. And by that light we will have our feet guided along the way of peace. How clearly stated! How precious to know! We are all - still - children of light! Archangel Gabriel told us that Earth is the only planet in the universe which still practices disease and death. We must, someday, awaken to the truth of us. It is in scripture. It is in other holy writings. It is in the words of Jesus the Christ, as he brought to us *A Course in Miracles*. This book should not be taken lightly. It is a serious book. It requires our full attention. By its own definition it is a required course - not for any worldly education degree - for our awakening to the truth of us; to the light within of us; to the spark of God that *is* us. Gabriel told us that *The Course* will stand beside the Bible in its importance for future generations.

It is surely not beyond our ability to comprehend that tiny spark in us. We can comprehend it in meditation. Only in meditation. Only by going within to our innermost center, in the peaceful silence. This practice, over time, brings us to that split second when we feel at one with God. But in that split second we do realize our divine connection to God. Then we realize that if we can feel it for one split second, we can feel it for two moments, and more. When we become comfortable with a daily, or hourly, meditation we come to know that indeed we are part of the God of all Creation.

Then, ever so slowly, we begin to look at the world of physical form and accept the idea that it is all illusion. It is all illusion because it is not part of the spirit world of God. Spirit has no form. It simply *is*. We have access to all wisdom because we are all children of God. The Master Jesus came to awaken us to the light that he knew was in him and he knew was/is in us. He was manifestly aware that we were in the darkness and he ardently prayed for our awakening to the light within. He said, several times, to follow him. He assured us that believing in him and his works, we could do the same things he did.

How many of us want to walk on water? Heal the sick? Raise the dead? The power to do so is available to us, because the power to do it is in us all. To become aware of that power we must see Jesus the Christ in the proper light. The proper light is that Jesus was a man - an eating, sleeping, laughing, crying man. In him was the Light of Christ, which he brought to earth and grounded to earth for all time, for all humanity. We ought to emulate the Light, not the man. Up on that old wooden cross is a man who was *thought to be killed*. But in his resurrection he proved that Christ never dies; the Light of Christ is never snuffed out. And we have that eternal Light. in us.

Now is the time to read the Bible for the truth in it, and read *A Course in Miracles* for the truth in it. It is time to meditate and feel the God within. Those of us who meditate on a regular basis have not yet learned to walk on water, but I have known people who have walked on fire. I have read of others who, in other times and places, have walked on water. Is this beneficial? Maybe, if we want to cross a stream on foot. But walking on water is a phenomenon. Jesus worked many phenomena - miracles. And that, unfortunately, is the way we remember him. We ought to remember him, instead, as a man of love and forgiveness - and then emulate him.

Accepting this planet as a world of illusion does not mean that we must preach that truth to others. Accepting the real world of spirit we can live our lives as Jesus lived his; full of light and love and peace. How else can we ever hope to have peace on Earth unless we each, in our own way, seek and know and live peace in our individual lives? It all begins with the individual. It is good to join with others at times who share that belief, but we must always remember that we are not separate from each other. No group, including religious groups, is better than others. Love is in us all. Love is what we are, as God's beloved offspring. The unity of all humanity, with its infinite variety, is what we ought to strive for. That is our task. With God's help; with all His wondrous angels, we cannot fail.

"The world has no purpose as it blends into the purpose of God. For the real world has slipped quietly into Heaven, where everything eternal in it has always been. There the Redeemer and the redeemed join in perfect love of God and of each other. Heaven is your home, and being in God it must also be in you." ACIM T 12: VI: 7:4-7

# None So Blind

"The only really blind are those who will not see the truth - those who shut their eyes to spiritual vision. For them alone darkness is irrevocable". Helen Keller

Archangel Gabriel came to a small church in Albany. One might ask why he did not come to a cathedral in New York City. The answer is simple: Gabriel could only come to where communication with the spirit world is accepted. Trinity Temple of the Holy Spirit was founded by a woman who was born with the ability of mediumship. She also prayed *always* that only truth come through her from the spirit realm.

Those who disbelieve in spirit communication have closed the door of opportunity to learn *any* information from the spirit world of God. The same people ardently accept the idea that in the Old Testament times the prophets frequently heard God's voice speak to them. There are numerous examples of spirit communication in the Old Testament, such as prophecy, guidance, and warnings:

Psalm 95 exhorts us to 'hear His voice'. This is an example of clairaudience; the ability to *hear* spirit. Also when the New Testament was written there were other examples of spirit communication:

Matthew (17:2) and Mark (ninth chapter) describe the transfiguration. This is an example of clairvoyance; the ability to *see* spirit. In Luke 3:2 "the word of God came unto John".

Peter dreamed (Acts Chapter 10 and 11) and heard a voice from Heaven instructing him. Acts 10:44 also refers to a heavenly voice heard. Here is an example of receiving spirit guidance in dreams.

We can easily justify all of these instances as natural *to the apostles*, but not applicable to us. Did not Jesus instruct us to 'follow me' many times? He came as an example (John 13:15). Jesus even told us that all that he could do, believing in him; we could do the same things! (John 14:12), which would include listening to God's Voice, which he implied in, John 18:4, that God informed him of his future on Earth.

Gifts of the spirit include 'discerning of spirits' (I Cor 12:10). To suggest that we should fear spirits is to substantiate a fear of God. Surely Jesus taught us to love God; for God is love. God gave us free choice to test spirit information. By free choice we can opt to listen to spirit and discern whether it is truth or not, by using our God-given intuitive ability. Many people freely choose to continue to see Jesus the Christ as the only Son of God. They find great comfort in scripture and study it ardently; sometimes memorizing passages. It is blind faith, but it is faith. Why question it? These same people will point out certain verses of scripture to support their beliefs. Archangel Gabriel told us that to believe something affirms that one can have *unbelief.*

Some will argue that there are mediums and psychics who misuse their God-given ability and seek their own gain instead of providing a pure channel of productive guidance to the seeker. Fundamentalists will tell you they all are. All professions have individuals who misuse their power. We have the ability to discern and the magnificent choice to seek wisdom from God's messengers, angels, and guides.

To take the so-called 'mystery' of communication with God, one needs to understand the power of intuition, which is the Voice of God speaking to us. It is a soft, gentle whisper of suggestion. We might call it a 'gut hunch', or a 'gut feeling', or a 'revelatory thought'. But in fact it is listening to God, when it is positive, productive, and peaceful. Any shouting that we hear is of the ego, which is why we are so inclined to listen to it, instead of God's Voice.

Gabriel told us about prayer and meditation, and how important they are to our spiritual path. He told us that Jesus was a man who came to ground the Christ energy to Earth for all time; for all humanity. If we didn't believe in spirit communication, we could not hear, at this time, the definitions of the symbols in the Bible. After two thousand years, now we have the wisdom of God's world, when we are ready to accept it.

Besides Gabriel, eleven master teachers also came to Earth, to centers of light where seeking listeners were, (believers in spirit communication), to give the same lesson that Gabriel gave us: Wake up to the truth of what you are; children of God. Live from the Lord God of your Being. You are so much more than what you think you are. You are much more than a body. You are free, as God created you. During the twelve years which Gabriel channeled wisdom to us, the Master Jesus came for four years also, to clarify the story of his life and tell us of some errors in translation of the Bible. As he told us 2,000 years ago, ("I will not leave you comfortless") he still comforts us, when we listen to him.

When I was in the seventh grade, we put on a mime play of *The Courtship of Miles Standish*, and I was chosen to stand in the wings and read the story as it was acted out. One sentence has remained with me all these years: "There are none so blind as those who *will not see*."

The awakening of humanity will occur. It is only a matter of time. We have been in this 'far country', Earth, many times and the karmic wheel has gone on for centuries. God wants us to get off it and stay off it. He desires our return unto Him. For the few who listen to Gabriel and others in the spirit realm, we are the first ones to know the truth of us. And we must, therefore, pass on this wisdom of the ages to anyone who will listen. And upon listening, to live it.

"If you choose flesh, you never will escape the body as your own reality, for you have chosen that you want it so. But choose the spirit, and all Heaven bends to touch your eyes and bless your holy sight, that you may see the world of flesh no more except to heal and comfort and to bless." ACIM T 31: VI: 7-8

# Omega and Alpha

"But many that are first shall be last; and the last shall be first."
Matt. 19:30; 20:16; Mark 10:31; Luke 13:-30

Several times Jesus said these words. The first and third time he said them in response to an apostle asking Jesus what the apostles would receive *in return for* following him. The second time he said them in explaining why the last laborer in the vineyard received the same wages as the first, who had worked all day. And the fourth Jesus was responding to one of his followers who asked who would be saved.

In all cases the issue seemed to be an expectation of payment, or benefit of some kind because of an action; because of a dedication to a spiritual path. But Jesus' answer was not specific. As in so many other cases, his words cause us to pause and reflect on their meaning. He said, in effect, if you are asking for recompense it has no bearing on the benefit you will receive. Asking for payment may put you at the end of the line for being 'saved'.

The last of the vineyard workers did not complain; he felt that he had received a fair wage: a penny for a short period of time. *Only in comparing with the last worker did the first feel underpaid.* Do we receive God's mercy based on what others receive? Do we spend a lifetime comparing what we get with what others get? Does this make sense in the scheme of eternity, when we know that God bestows blessings on all of us, *as we expect; as we plan?*

God's mercy is our birthright and when God created us He made us in His image. On Earth, in this sad world of experiences, we have chosen many roads that continue to lead away from God. We will have to forgive others and ourselves for all these negative options. Forgiveness is essential to our spiritual awakening. Our awakening will lead us back home to God.

We may well ask who decides will be first, and who last, in returning to our Source, God. God is the decider, but we must make the initial decision to forgive - not seven times, but seventy times seven. (Matt 18:22) Our forgiveness must be unlimited, all inclusive, and complete.

To say we will forgive but never forget is *not* forgiving, because the negative experience that makes us remember will come to mind again when we remember. Total forgiveness means total forgetting.

The 'last' as mentioned by Jesus would be, for us, the people who we put at the bottom of our 'judgment' list. Maybe it is a thief, a murderer, an arsonist, a serial rapist. How in God's name could a rapist be saved *first*? The greater the perceived 'sin' that is forgiven, the more likely the person will be saved ahead of the one who forgives an unpaid ten dollar debt. What precedes forgiveness is repentance. Jesus forgave the prostitute ( it was *not* Mary Magdalene) for her perceived 'sins' because he knew that her customers were as 'guilty' as she, and no one was bringing them forth to be stoned.

In Mat 18:35 we find "So likewise shall my heavenly Father do also unto you, if ye from your hearts forgive not every one his brother their trespasses." Jesus said this in response to the lord who forgave his servant, but when the servant was owed money he did not forgive. It sounds as though God is keeping track of all our trespasses against others. He very well may be, but we know our past behaviors, and we are the ones who must repent and forgive.

This is the time on Earth when we take the 'required' course presented in *A Course in Miracles*. It explains that whatever infraction we perceive that we have done; whoever we have wounded; whoever has wounded us - all of it was planned by us in order that we might learn a lesson. Love and forgiveness are the lessons before us. It is past time to learn what the Master Jesus taught so long ago. He taught, *and lived* love and forgiveness, from birth to the crucifixion. Can we honestly say that we have learned to love and forgive everyone, including self?

The Sonship of God is the totality of the human race. Jesus came to save the people of the world; to show us the way back home. Jesus never forgot his Oneness with God, but he knew that we did. So he came to save us; to show us the way to salvation; to save us from our wayward path which leads only to destruction. Is not this world in a state of destruction? Where is the unconditional love? Where is the total forgiveness? Why are we still here, struggling in this three dimensional world, locked in by time and space? Because we have made so many poor choices, walked down so many roads of judgment, anger, fear, and resentment.

Heaven, our natural habitat, awaits us. All our loved ones who have already transitioned await us. God awaits us to wake up and live from the Lord God of our Being, as he created us. God's patience is infinite. He knows all our thoughts, our faults, our ambitions, and dreams. He knows that when we wake up to our own divinity, our own oneness with Him, we will joyfully return home to Him.

"There will be great joy in Heaven on your homecoming, and the joy will be yours. For the redeemed son of man is the guiltless Son of God, and to recognize him *is* your redemption." ACIM T 13: II: 9:6-7

# Rising Up With Christ

"No man cometh unto the Father but by me". John 14:6

". . . Does not mean that I am in any way separate or different from you except in time, and time does not really exist. The statement is more meaningful in terms of a vertical rather than a horizontal axis. You stand below me and I stand below God. In the process of "rising up", I am higher because without me the distance between God and man would be too great for you to encompass. I bridge the distance as an elder brother to you on the one hand, and as a Son of God on the other.

My devotion to my brothers has placed me in charge of the Sonship, which I render complete because I share it. This may appear to contradict the statement "I and my Father are one", but there are two parts to the statement in recognition that the Father is greater. ACIM T 1: II: 4:1-7

The apostle John correctly quoted Jesus here. But it must be remembered and accepted that many words of Jesus now require clarification for the following reasons:

A) Two thousand years ago the man Jesus and the Christ Light in him were seen as one. They are not. Jesus was a man and lived like a man. He embodied the Christ Light. Because today the average person is capable of understanding symbolism - in art, literature, and music - they can also comprehend it in scripture. For those who see symbolism as anathema there is an unwillingness to accept and understand the deeper meaning of the Bible. But for the seeking person the symbolism is a welcome invitation to the deeper meaning of the Bible. In effect, scripture 'comes alive'. The symbolism can be found in *The Metaphysical Bible Dictionary*.

B) The mental capacity - the thinking ability - then was much duller than now; any symbolic application of Jesus' words was not understandable to the common man. In Jesus' time the primary concerns of ordinary people were family, animal stock, planting and harvesting, the seasons, and the weather. Except for merchants, who had to be cognizant of money, products, and their values. But it was not the merchants to whom Jesus spoke. It was the farmer, the shepherd, and the carpenter. Jesus also seemed to be speaking only to *men*. The reason being that in those days women were considered chattels. They had no say in the daily tasks, no rights of ownership or inheritance, were not seen as having anything of value to say. Archangel Gabriel told us that many women followed Jesus, but such stories were purged from the Bible.

At this time, knowing of the acceptance of symbolism by some seekers, Jesus the Christ comes to explain the symbolism to us, in *A Course in Miracles*. It was published in 1975, published by Foundation for Inner Peace. Many times does Jesus use the word 'peace' in the Bible. He came to bring peace to the world (Matt. 10:34) because he was/is the Prince of Peace (Is. 9:6). He stilled the ocean storm with the very word 'peace' (Mark 4:39). He said, 'Peace I leave with you' (John 16:33). In this last instance Jesus even expounded on *what peace is:* "Peace I leave with you, my peace I give unto you: not as the world giveth, give I unto you. Let not your heart be troubled, neither let it be afraid." Jesus states clearly here that he *is peace*. Also, he has the power to give it to others. And his peace is not as the world offers, but a deeper and more lasting peace. Then he tells us that if we are not afraid or troubled about anything, we can know the peace that he knew. In *A Course in Miracles* the word 'peace' appears 999 times!

At this time - when the ages are turning from Pisces to Aquarius - Jesus came to tell us the symbolism of scripture so that we could understand fully what he meant by 'the kingdom of God is within', 'there is no death', and 'I am with you always'. Also, Gabriel came to give us the symbolism of *The Revelation of Saint John the Divine*. It is not about an apocalypse. That interpretation is based on the ego. It is the story of us and our journey back home to God, told in the genre of symbolism.

In *Miracles* Jesus says that he is no different from us, nor separate from us - except in time, which only exists on the earth plane. He - the Christ - is the bridge we all must cross, from Earth to our natural habitat, Heaven. Christ is the bridge because the distance from here to God is so great - not in reality, but in our erroneous thinking - that we need a bridge to help us across in our understanding. Jesus is the Son of God. We are all sons (and daughters) of God. Jesus the Christ is in charge of the Sonship because he shares it with us. Jesus is also our elder brother. Like an elder brother he reaches down to us, takes our hand (when we are willing), and helps us across the bridge to Heaven, where we belong. Therefore, it is a vertical axis. The horizontal axis we erroneously perceive is that of genealogy. Heaven is our home, and has been our home since God breathed us forth.

This journey without distance is our journey, when we are ready to ascend *with our bodies*, and not return again to stay on the endless karmic cycle of reincarnation. We have lived many lives, as Jesus did, and the journey he took is the journey we must take. With his help we can. With his help we *will*. Jesus tells us in *Miracles* that the book is a *required course*. When we understand it, we will be ready to ascend with his help. Everyone is not ready for *The Course* at this time. Many people have never heard of it. Some have opened it only to decide it is not for them, for whatever reason. Others feel that the workbook is too demanding of time, the text too complicated, the manual for teachers could not mean them because they do not believe they qualify.

One of Gabriel's statements rings in my ears: "Walk you in the light; you *are* the light!" God is the Father of lights (James 1:17), and as His children we are children of light (Luke 16:8). But we have spent so many lifetimes on this planet Earth that we have come to believe that it is our home and everything in it is real. No! Nothing in it is real. Everything in it is transitory. When the time comes for us to accept this truth, then we will understand Jesus' words from Miracles:

Nothing real can be threatened.
Nothing unreal exists.
Herein lies the peace of God. ( ACIM, Preface, x)

It is confirmation that the only thing that is real is spirit. God is a spirit (John 4:24) and created us from Himself, and in no way can spirit be neither threatened nor changed. All matter - physical form - is unreal (temporary), and therefore does not exist. Only God and His Kingdom of spirit are eternal and unchangeable. By our own choice, we can access in us the Spirit of God, as Jesus did (Luke 4:18). It takes diligence to think and do good; only good. It takes a passion for knowledge; a hunger for truth.

# The Vertical Journey

"No man cometh unto the Father but by me" does not mean that I am in any way separate or different from you except in time, and time does not really exist. The statement is more meaningful in terms of a vertical rather than a horizontal axis". ACIM T 1: II: 4:1-2

The Master Jesus makes it crystal clear here that he and the rest of us are no different, except in time. He reached the full awareness of his Christhood two thousand years ago, after many incarnations on Earth. Throughout all of his lifetimes on this planet he *knew* that he was a Son of God. From His penultimate incarnation as Buddha he also knew that the rest of us were unaware of our own God-given divinity. For God breathed us all forth from Himself in the beginning. As His Own, we had/have within us a spark of divinity.

Jesus wondered why his many brothers and sisters here did not know of our own divinity. We know now that we lost awareness of our higher self when we came down - devolved - through the many levels of vibration - to this planet of form, and became so enamored of form that we came to believe it was *all there is*. How wrong we were! How wrong we remain; how in the darkness we continue!

And so Jesus came to lead us; be an example. He was the firstfruits (ICor. 1:23) and thus came as a way-shower. His mission was to awaken us to our own divine spark and come to know ourselves as God's beloved children. All humanity is the Sonship of God. When we each will awaken is up to each of us, for God gave us all free will. This means that every minute of every day we can make choices that lead us back to our awareness or keep us in the dark about our divine spark. We choose the dark path out of ignorance, out of fear, out of a desire to stay in the comfort of what we know, even though it is not the truth of us.

The ignorance is from a self-concept that tells us we are not worthy to be God's Own. The fear comes from the belief that we left God and He will never take us back. This is an erroneous belief. We need only to look at the Bible story of the Prodigal Son to know this. When we find ourselves wallowing in the garbage of despair, of pain, of self-deprecation, we can then choose to begin a *conscious* journey back home.

We choose our own time to begin the conscious journey, for in fact we began our journey back home to God when we decided to 'leave' Him. It is *impossible* to leave God. He is in our mind and soul. He is in every cell of our physical form. Spirit - God - is the nucleus of every physical cell. This wisdom came from Archangel Gabriel, and what a thought to contemplate! It is extremely helpful to know when we meditate.

On Earth there is no time, for space and time are concepts 'made up' by humans, so we could keep track of our days and years, and each other. "Father, I wake today with miracles correcting my perception of all things. . . What I seek today transcends all laws of time, and things perceived in time. I would forget all things except Your Love." ACIM W pt II 346: 1:1-5

Because we believe in the concept of time, we put value on our ancestry. We believe that those who came before us, in our family tree, set the stage for our journey this time around. Thus we see our lifetimes as part of a horizontal continuum. We construct charts to show who our forefathers were and what they did. It is a form of entertainment. In the absence of time we can more readily accept the idea that our journey back home is vertical instead. Our physical bodies are so temporary, so transient. The spirit self of us is on a journey of awakening. That journey is vertical because we are rising up, back to our Source, which is God. As we devolved, so must we evolve back through the stages of our devolution. Each level of awareness must be redeemed until we have the full conscious awareness of our Oneness with God, as Jesus the Christ found in his last incarnation.

For the serious seeker of truth, Jesus' journeys will be found in *The Aquarian Gospel of Jesus the Christ*. This book describes the many countries Jesus visited. He also went to the Himalayas and visited temples there (scrolls there mention his visit, as Issa). Finally, Jesus went to the temple at Heliopolis, in Egypt, and became a student. There he passed six degrees of study, the last being that of Love. Upon successful completion of the last degree, he was told:

". . . in the Great Lodge of the heavens and earth you are THE CHRIST. This is your great Passover rite. . .

". . .and while the hierophant yet spoke the temple bells rang out; a pure white dove descended from above and sat on Jesus' head.

"And then a voice that shook the very temple said, THIS IS THE CHRIST; and every living creature said, AMEN.

"The great doors of the temple swung ajar; the Logos journeyed on his way a conqueror."

Referring back to the original quotation, "No man cometh unto the Father but by me", it has been interpreted by many to mean that we must take Jesus as our personal savior in order to be 'saved.' If the statement 'by me' meant Jesus the man, how could we do that when Jesus the man died on the cross? If 'by me' means the Christ Light, the eternal, Living Christ - we all are part and parcel of that same Light. We will be saved form our ignorance as we awaken to our own Christ light. Early in his lessons of *A Course in Miracles* we find Jesus the Christ informing us, "The light has come. You are healed and you can heal. The light has come. You are saved and you can save. . . "
ACIM W pt. I: 75:1-4

When we read, practice, repeat and learn all the lessons the Master gives in this fine book we will begin to *see the light*. And we will finally know that we are part of the Light. We must learn to see it in ourselves and everyone else. This can only occur when we see beyond appearances and accept all our brothers and sisters on earth. Acceptance thus leads to forgiveness. And the freedom that forgiveness affords will enable us to hear the Voice of God, and see His Light in others and ourselves. Yes, the Light has come! God provides us with Guides to see it in ourselves.

"You cannot behave effectively while you function on different levels. However, while you do, correction must be introduced vertically from the bottom up. This is because you think you live in space, where concepts such as "up" and "down" are meaningful. Ultimately, space is as meaningless as time. Both are merely beliefs." ACIM T 1: VI: 3: 2-6

# Section 7: Revelation Revisited

# Door to Revelation

"Be perfect, be of good comfort, be of one mind, live in peace; and the God of love and peace shall be with you". 2 Cor. 13:11

"And he took bread, and gave thanks, and brake it, and gave unto them, saying, This is my body which is given for you: this do in remembrance of me". Luke 22: 19

"The injunction 'Be of one mind' is the statement for revelation-readiness. My request 'Do this in remembrance of me' is the appeal for cooperation from miracle workers. The two statements are not in the same order of reality. Only the latter involves an awareness of time, since to remember is to recall the past in the present. Time is under my direction, but timelessness belongs to God. In time we exist for and with each other. In timelessness we coexist with God."
ACIM T 2: V: 17: 1-7

When some religionists claim that we are 'born in sin', the idea of being perfect seems to be diametrically opposed. How could one born in sin ever overcome it? Also, the same people worship Jesus the Christ; keep him high on a pedestal and bow down to him as though he were the only son of God. They quote John 3:16 to support their belief.

Archangel Gabriel told us there are corrections that need to be made in scripture, since it contains some erroneous translations. Gabriel said this not in a tone of condemnation but merely to note the correct words as *originally* given. John 3:16 ". . . needs only one slight correction to be meaningful in this context; 'He gave it *to* His only begotten son." ACIM T 2: D VII: 5: 14

God's only begotten son, as explained by Gabriel, is all of humanity. God, eons ago, created us all perfect - perfect spirit. The idea of a human form was ours, but that is another story entirely. When Paul told the Corinthians to be perfect, he meant that they should be aware of their perfection as spirit entities. In that very awareness they would find good comfort. Paul then exhorted the people to 'be of one mind' meaning they should listen only to the Voice of God for guidance. And then Paul said the people should 'live in peace' - not live with anger, fear, judgment and all the other negative attitudes that then beset the people of Corinth and their neighbors. Paul told them that in living that way the God of love and peace would 'be with' them. It is doubtful that any who heard Paul actually changed their thinking or behavior, but they loved the words and probably wished 'wouldn't it be wonderful if it were so.'

Two thousand years later, Jesus came to give *A Course in Miracles* to a Jewish woman who was impelled to hear the words of wisdom and find a scribe to write them. Humanity is blessed indeed to have this book of wisdom. Gabriel said the day would come when it will stand beside the Christian Bible in importance. 'Be of one mind', *Miracles* tells us, is 'the statement for revelation-readiness.' Revelation: 'unites you directly with God . . . is intensely personal . . . and is literally unspeakable.' ACIM T 1: II: 1:1-2:7

When we willingly become of one mind we are ready for a revelation. We are in direct communication with God and His spirit world. How could we ever explain that experience?

The communion words of Jesus 'do this in remembrance of me'; Jesus tells us at this time, is 'the appeal for cooperation from miracle-workers.' To explain a miracle-worker we turn to ACIM 2: V: 5:1:

*"The sole responsibility of the miracle worker is to accept the Atonement for himself."* Another way to read atonement is at-one-ment (given to us by Archangel Gabriel). It is the at-one-ment with God, which means to become aware that one *actually is one with the Father,* as we were created in the beginning, exist now and are eternally so.

The word 'remembrance' involves time, and time on Earth (the only place it is recognized) is under the direction of the Christ. He will guide us as long as we need him on Earth. In Heaven we co-exist with God in a world where there is no time.

The sacrament of Communion is symbolic. It was then and it is now. Jesus presented the bread as the bread of life, because people would understand bread as a basic necessity of life. Also, they could travel with unleavened bread for a long time and it would not spoil. Taking it into the body meant incorporating it with life in man. Back then the population could not see the symbolism of the communion offering. Now we understand it means the incorporation; the combining of the mind of man with the mind of God. Wine, which everyone drank in those days, was easily acquired. It represents the flow of eternal life. For centuries worshippers took, and still take, communion. Eventually all will come to understand the symbolism of it and then be ready to seek and know our at-one-ment with God.

# From Magnitude to Littleness

"You who have sought and found littleness, remember this: Every decision you make stems from what you think you are and represents the value that you put upon yourself. Believe the little can content you, and by limiting yourself you will not be satisfied. For your function is not little, and it is only by finding your function and fulfilling it that you can escape from littleness." ACIM T 15: III: 3: 3-5

Following is Archangel Gabriel's explanation of our devolvement from Heaven to Earth; from magnitude to littleness. Second person plural is used because he speaks to all of us.

Since we are made in God's Image, we have within us the spirit of God. It is love. It is the unconditional love which Jesus the Christ demonstrated throughout his life. He told us that the kingdom of God is within us. We have forgotten our origin. Originally, when we were first breathed forth by our Creator, we knew and loved each other. We knew and loved God; we knew He loved us, His children. Some of us decided to create something other than perfection and we began manipulating the vibration of creation. Everything vibrates. We learn this in school. Spirit is the highest rate of vibration. As we engaged in manipulating energy we slowed down the high vibratory rate of spirit. We devolved down into a mental realm, then an emotional realm, then a physical realm. The physical realm is the planet Earth. We think we left God and He will *never* take us back. All our fears in life go back to that first fear.

So, from the magnitude of the spirit word down, down, to Earth we came. We came to believe in a separateness from God and each other. We came into a belief in littleness. We substantiate that belief when we look at the night stars. We confirm that belief when we view Earth from space. We accept that littleness in our lives when we see others with more money, bigger homes, or fame. God sees us all as His beloved offspring, regardless of what we do, what we own, what we choose. He knows that someday, like the Prodigal Son, we will return unto Him. We have been on a very long journey; have lived many

147

lifetimes, have chosen all our experiences through time. Now we are beginning the age of truth; the Aquarian Age. Archangel Gabriel came for twelve years to teach us. All were welcome to hear him; some chose not to stay and listen. They either disbelieved that Gabriel would channel through a medium, or they were not ready for the lessons he taught. Gabriel said it was okay, because they simply were not ready for the truth.

The last book of the New Testament is Revelation. It was given by the angelic realm to John the apostle. Its words suggest an Armageddon of huge proportions. For centuries it has been read as an apocalyptic book. Gabriel came to interpret the symbolism of it, for in truth it is the story of humankind and its journey away from and back to God. There is no way that we could 'leave God', for He is All in All. But in our consciousness we think we did leave God and He is angry with us. God does not know anger. The 'wrath of God' is a terrible phrase of untruth. It is based on the idea that we have made God in our image, instead of the reverse.

Here are some of the interpretations that Gabriel provided us. the Island of Patmos means separated entirely from anything of the Earth. That is where John received the Book of Revelation. Angels represent creative thoughts. The seven churches represent states of consciousness. A king is an attitude form. Coming in clouds means your blurred vision of who you are. Coming through clouds is the awareness of the Christ in you. Snow-white hair is the purist pure; the seventh chakra is the throne in Heaven. Eyes that burn mean clear vision; the fullness of knowing. Face means what you present to the world. Face that shone like the sun - Christ within.

A two-edged sword is the word of truth. Whatever you say is true for you. When you say "I am sick", your body will give you sick. When you say "I am blessed", you will experience blessings. So be careful what you say after the words "I am", for you are owning it and confirming it for self. "I was dead" means we are *all* dead to the Christ within us. "They are liars" means the Christ within cannot bear that which is not perfect. Love and hate cannot co-exist. All wounds are self-inflicted. Jesus "suffered" and died on the cross to show how unnecessary it is; for he resurrected and proved eternal life. He did not suffer because he had the ability to be 'out of' his body, as many people today can demonstrate.

Thunders and lightnings are perceived as such by the ego of humans. To the angel realm they are heard as harmony. The sea stands for emotions; always changing. When perfectly still it is a 'sea of glass'. A lion is fearless; has very few enemies. 'Calf' should read 'bull', which is strength. To fly like an eagle means limitless; boundless. 'Eyes before and aft' mean all-knowingness. 'Holy, holy, holy' is humankind; it is your divine nature. Crowns are accomplishments. The seals are the chakras. 'No one who could open the seals' means no one else has your memory, your experiences, but yourselves. The east is the direction from which comes illumination. Your minds have the 'power to destroy' anything. Winds signify change. Do not damage the Earth; it represents the nurturing aspect of your nature. "Mark of the Lord upon their heads" is the third chakra; limitless vision to understand all things. "People too numerous to count" equals all the creative ideas manifested by you and through evolution, brought before the throne of God.

"Who are these people?" is asked by the ego which cannot recognize the totality of God. Prayer defines the 'gold incense container'. When you have a burning desire to *be*, it is the all-consuming flame of Christ; "the fire from the altar". All references to blood should be understood to mean 'new blood', or a new way of thinking/doing. Geneticists improve various species by mixing the (new) blood of different creatures. Bitter stars are divine ideas brought down to earth and used for malice; unforgiving people. Scorpions mean regret. Nothing stings more than remorse. Like a locust, it "eats us up". Horses represent emotions. "Hair like a woman" means growth and intuition. A woman's hair is her crowning glory. That is why, in ancient times, it was a sin for a woman to cut her hair. Samson believed his strength was in his hair, therefore he perceived himself to be weak without it.

The flight of thought - which has power to destroy - is "chariots racing through the air". "Release the four angels" means release creative thought; set it free again. Sulfur (an overcoming odor) affects the nose and the taste buds. It means you have no taste for life. "Stop worship of the demons" means you are slow learners. Each generation is a little bit higher; you don't burn people at the stake anymore, but you drop bombs on them instead. "Take and eat the scroll" means ingest what nourishes you. God-based ideas do not turn sour. You have done some terrible deeds in the name of God.

The "two witnesses" are wisdom and love. To "shut up the sky" means you do not allow rain to wash from man's consciousness the truth of his being. Once you know the truth of you, [that you are a child of God] nothing can wash it away. "Rainbow about his head" means covenant of God; the promise of God that is *life*. A "woman clothed like the sun" is the Mary aspect of you. It is the pure center of the innocence of love; capable of bringing forth the Christ. "The woman gave birth to a son" means, of course, Son of God. "Woman" means sustaining abilities. You take in 'new blood' and uplift the human race with Christ consciousness.

"War broke out in Heaven": This is your Armageddon that you are told about. Heaven is a state of evolvement in which all things are of a spiritual nature, when you are at one with the Father. Your ego will try to pull you out of it. But Michael says, "Who is like unto God?" Your Michael aspect (power) recognizes your own divinity and the surliness, emptiness of the ego. The "accuser of our brothers" is your ego self. The "blood of the lamb": Lambs are defenseless creatures; totally dependent on shepherds. The "lamb of God" is totally dependent on the Father. In its pureness it is safe in the Father's care. "Those who be glad they died" is death of ego ideas.

The devil is a non-existent entity. Gabriel made it abundantly clear that *there is no devil in the physical world or in the spirit world.* "Pursuit of the woman" is the ego pursuing that which will nurture the Christ, for with the life of the Christ, *it is dead.* The "two beasts" are fear and greed; greed is a form of fear. "Those who are living on the Earth" are those in a state of realization (not consciously) that they are more than a body. A book is a record and "Being written in a book" is an ancient memory of their selves. "Meant to be captured" means allowing selves to be entrapped by ideas of limitation (illness, failure, death, poverty etc.).

"Sexual relations with women" does not refer to literal sexual encounters. Joining with another in a sexual act is much more than physical. It is an exchanging of energies. Once joined in copulation you are joined with that person for a very long time. It is one of the most binding things you can do. When a person engages in the sexual act with several partners, instead of a binding there is a depletion of energy. That is why scripture condemns harlots and a man should not waste his seed.

For centuries humankind has been traversing from Heaven to Earth and back again, in a never-ending cycle. This cycle is called karma. And karma is a device of the ego, which made up the idea of karma to keep us from returning to our home, our Source, which is God. The good news is that God is still in us all. And from that spark of divinity in us we can take a conscious step upon our spiritual journey home, when we tell the ego to take its rightful place in our lives - as protector, not ruler.

"In returning the little light must be acknowledged first, for the separation was a descent from magnitude to littleness. But the spark is still as pure as the Great Light, because it is the remaining call of creation. Put all your faith in it, and God Himself will answer you." ACIM T 10: IV: 8:5-8

# From Littleness to Magnitude

"In many only the spark remains, Yet God has kept the spark alive . . . If you but see the little spark you will learn of the greater light." ACIM T 10: IV: 8:1-3

We have become content with littleness because we believe everything the senses have taught us. And they are all liars because we are not a body; we are spirit in essence. As God's beloved children we have a spark of that divine Source in us - all of us. Some have seemingly devolved lower than others; all of us have been saints, murderers, and homosexuals. We have lived so many lives on Earth we think it is our home. Yet we are all prodigals, believing that we left our Father and He will never take us back. We must - and we will - wake up to that untruth, and begin our spiritual journey back home. Earth, Gabriel told us, is known in the angel realm as 'the darkling planet', for it is the only planet in the universe that still practices disease and death. He came to awaken us to our truth, to our spirit selves, so that we might consciously walk a spiritual path back to Heaven, our natural habitat.

The path back home is delineated in the Book of Revelation in the Bible. Symbolic through and through, it describes the erroneous beliefs and terrible choices we have made. It explains how to journey upward to our original magnitude. Babylon (tower of Babel) symbolizes our confusion of earthly and spiritual thoughts. When 'Babylon has fallen' all these errors will be ended. We have forgotten that we are children of God and in that forgetting we have given the ego more and more power to rule us. We allow corporate minds to tell us what to eat, wear, play with, listen to, engage in. They insist that we need a lot of 'stuff' that we do not need at all.

Martyrdom has been worshipped; it is in truth a total waste. We have accepted for 2,000 years Jesus' 'suffering' on the cross. He did not die for our sins; for if he had, why are we still living as though we are 'sinners'? The glory of Jesus' life is not the crucifixion, but the resurrection. He proved that killing the body is not the end of life; life is eternal. He came for all humanity to awaken to its essence of spirit; its eternalness "faith in Jesus" ought to read "faith in Christ". We have the ability (sickle) to separate truth from error. From our true inner, spiritual selves (the city) we have ventured forth into all our experiences, many of them painful and all of them limiting.

God does not know wrath in any form. God is love and love does not know wrath. In the 13th chapter of Paul's letter to the people of Corinth, he gives an excellent description of love. When we see clearly, we have pure vision (sea of glass) and we become like a consuming flame (Christ) to burn away (fire) the error perceptions and see our path correctly. We have taken the law of Cause and Effect (Moses' law) and brought it down into the baser idea of karma. The law we must abide by is the Law of Love (Law of the Lamb). The totality of us (all the nations) is unaware of the seven states of consciousness (churches).

The sanctuary of our knowingness (temple of God) is where we know we are one with God. It is where we go in meditation. The Ten Commandments (Tabernacle of God) represent the law; Moses lived by these 'thou shalt not' commands. Turning from these limiting rules, we focus on the love of Christ that Jesus grounded to Earth for all time; for all humanity, not just Christians. As we focus on love and forgiveness, which he taught throughout his life, we find great joy in living (clean linen). Continuing on this spiritual path we awaken automatically our energy centers (chakras). The plagues in Revelation are the human traits we have developed and must transform into positive thoughts and actions.

The first plague is lust. Lust for anything of an earthly nature must be seen as natural desire (from the Father) turned upside down. Lust seeks for instant gratification, and then moves on to something else. Greed, another plague, seeks to have and keep for a long time; such as hoarding. Fear, the ego's only weapon, is a plague instilled by us, long ago, to protect us. We have, over time, given it our power. Now we fear God, each other, and our own negativity. Ever since time began on Earth God has sent prophets to bring us truth and we have proceeded to slaughter them all; the last being Jesus the Christ. He lived a life of unconditional love, to teach us, but we have not chosen to live a life of unconditional love. We remembered the miracles, but forgot the inherent love message he brought. We participate in negative behaviors and then live to regret them. And remorse, the most burning emotion we can have, is another plague to overcome.

With our ability to understand (the sun) we can turn away from another plague: materialism. We garner more stuff than we can ever use; we store it; we value it. It is a false god. The ability to express our spiritual selves (bit their tongues) has been diluted by corporate minds (the Bible speaks of business men) which try to convince us that we always need something more; something new. Want and need are both based on the belief in lack. We lack nothing, as God's own. The belief in lack leads to a belief in limitation, another plague that haunts us. The coming together of all the plagues (the beast) is so overwhelming that we find it difficult to accept that there is another way of thinking and of living (turn from their evil ways). This is the Armageddon we have come to accept (River Euphrates), for our conscious connection with the spiritual has dried up. Our fears have brought us to the terrible race consciousness of a belief in separation. Unification can and must come to all people on Earth.

The Creator has imbued us with imagination and free choice. With our free choice we have opted for some extremely negative attitudes and behaviors. Stripped of our ideas and ideals (walk around naked) we can also opt to know the truth of our being, which is love (happy is he who stays awake). The final plague ("Praise God", Gabriel said), is the destruction (greatest earthquake) of the ego (dragon). With that destruction, all ideas of separation from God will disappear (islands disappeared). And the sacred ideals which we embrace will bring down (plague of hail) the ego, and enable us once again to know our at-one-ment with the Father. We must never fight the ego; for when we do we give it power. Ignoring it will disturb it greatly, for who wants to be ignored? The egos (dragons) of nations, cities, corporations all are expressed on Earth and therefore it is not an easy task to overcome them.

Our intuition (Voice of God) must supersede the idea of limitation (the woman). It will prevail (in one hour she has lost everything). The Earth, as well as humans, has cycles (waters that you saw). We have been through five, including the Ice Age. We are in the sixth and the seventh is yet to come. There is an unfolding of time on Earth and our grandchildren will live in a very different world. The sea always represents emotions; it is ever moving and changing. The emotions have great power when out of control. They prevent us from thinking clearly; we must rise above them (all the ships' captains) and accept our intuition as our only guide. It never fails. It is the Voice of God.

The Bible notes "And fear not them which kill the body" (Matt. 10:28; Luke 12:4). Gabriel said "never fear those who cause physical death . . . but when your ego, or another's, tell you there is no hope; there is nothing to live for, they are bringing about the desolation of your minds and of the very spirit of you, and cause you not to seek life. This is whom to get away from."

The life force that we are is forever (blood upon the garment), and as we grow spiritually we will learn how to live from that divine center of us, where the intuition is (coming forth out of Heaven). Then is when we totally overcome (armies of Heaven) the collective consciousness of humankind. With pure inspiration (birds of the air) we shall not bring divine ideas down into physical form. We will be our own person, guided by the Father. All the lesser things of the earth shall be devoured into the higher (eat the flesh of kings). The ego (beast) and the false prophet (tells you untruths) are purged in the consuming flame (fire) of Christ to burn away untruths and allow Christ to reign in our lives.

We have begun a thousand years of peace (tied him up for a thousand years) during which the mass consciousness will be raised up. This will occur because most of the souls born upon earth will be of a nature that will not know war; will not know hatred. Some of them have never entered the earth plane and thus will have no memory of a past (mark of the beast on their forehead); nothing to lock them into old ways. They will rule with Christ consciousness, with an awareness of truth. And in that awareness, they will help others to be raised also. We who have lived on Earth and those new-comers (the great and small) will bring about a world far different from the one we have known. Today, we cannot even imagine what that new world will be like.

When we decided to come to the earth plane we reached a certain dimension at which point we divided our asexual, spirit selves, into male and female. Hence 'soul mate'. In our return home to God, we will merge the male and female entities (wedding of lamb and bride) and be one again in Heaven. Involution down into matter and evolution back up out of it is the alpha and omega; the completed circle (number 12: gates, angels, stones).

The 'homecoming' of humanity back home to God is our crowning glory (jewels) and the circle completed is total perfection (measure the city). That is the destiny of humankind. That is the story of Revelation. That is our blessed state, as children of the Mother/Father God. We are forever (crystal river); our supply is continuous forever (tree of life bears every 12 months of the year). We will be all the power we have; we will have complete dominion over ourselves (will rule as kings forever). When we awaken our own Christ consciousness ("I am coming soon") we will see others who choose to remain on a negative path (who must go on doing evil) but in our awareness we can help them awaken to their own Christ selves.

When we let go of all the memories of our past (soul) and command the ego to take its rightful place in our lives (as a protector on Earth), we will know the second death. It will be the death of our soul, which, as residents of Heaven forever hereafter, we will have no need of.

The old Heaven and the old Earth of binding, limiting religions and ways of thinking will yield to a new Heaven and a new Earth. God awareness will be a constant conscious thing. We have so much to look forward to, as a race of humans. We are, in fact, the holy city noted in Revelations.

"For He will heal every little thought you have kept to hurt you and cleanse it of its littleness, restoring it to the magnitude of God."
ACIM T 13: III: 7:6

# John's Joyous Revelation

The book of Revelation, in the New Testament, has been read for centuries as an apocalyptic book from God.

In 1992 Archangel Gabriel told us that nothing could be further from the truth. In fact, Revelation is all about humankind's journey back home to our Source, God the Father of us all. In its written words the ego perceives it as horrific. But when we understand the explanation of John's joyous revelation we find that God has laid out therein a path which we can, and must, walk to return home to Him.

From the angelic realm, when we see the truth of the images, we are given all the data we need to set the sail of our lives toward the horizon of salvation. Prior to his interpretation of Revelation, Gabriel requested that the Good News Bible be used, and that someone should read from it, paragraph by paragraph, for him to interpret. Reverend Penny, devoted channeler of Gabriel, asked me to be the reader. I was ecstatic!

How blessed was I to read the words on those two days. How blessed was that small, seeking group of us who heard Gabriel's words. And how blessed am I to be writing this for all who are ready to accept and understand. These essays on Revelation are written in second person plural, because Archangel Gabriel was addressing all of us - not just the attendees at the two seminars, but all humankind.

Clergy of all Christian denominations have struggled with this last book of the New Testament. It has even been called the book of the apocalypse. The reason is that all the words have been taken literally, and like all the rest of scripture, it is symbolic from first to last. Gabriel made this clear. In order to understand the essays on Revelation, one must be:

1. Willing to accept the truth of communication from spirit entities to earthlings. For Gabriel channeled all his wisdom of the ages through a spiritually dedicated woman named Rev. Penny Donovan. She had been prepared for this task by the angels of God.

2. Familiar with the metaphysical interpretations of the Bible. One source is *The Metaphysical Bible Dictionary*, by Charles Filmore.

3. Able to accept that Jesus was a man, and as such he ate, drank, slept, walked, and laughed. Christ is the Light of God which Jesus brought to Earth, and grounded to the Earth for all humanity, for all time. And he said he would not leave us comfortless, for he said, "I am with you always". He has come to me and several of my friends - and I am sure, some readers - and we happily confirm that.

Jesus' apostles represent the several powers (aspects; virtues) inherent in all humans. John represents love. Love unconditional is the perfect balance of the action (male) and the sustaining (female). Gabriel told us, during his 12 years of visitations, that John was the only apostle who truly understood Jesus' message. Probably for this reason, he was the one chosen to receive the Book of Revelation. As Gabriel put it: "only he [John] had the vibrational rate necessary" to receive it.

Peter represents faith. James stands for discrimination, or judgment. The reader may recall that when Jesus went up the mountain where the transfiguration took place (Matt 17:1-8), he took with him John, Peter, and James: Love, faith, and judgment. Love would appreciate the transfiguration, faith would accept it, and spiritual judgment would truly perceive it as holy.

Andrew represents strength; Philip, power; Bartholomew, imagination. Surely we can see that all these attributes are necessary for a good life on Earth; for a meaningful journey through life. We know now that Thomas means understanding; Matthew is will, and James the lesser is said to be order. Luke stands for luminous, or light-giving. We are given to know that Simon the Zealot is that in us that responds with zeal to our chosen passion. Judas (who did not commit suicide but rather was slain by one of his enemies), represents life, the generative function. And Thaddeus, who took Judas' place, stands for renunciation or elimination. In the light of wisdom received from Gabriel, this elimination refers to the required elimination of all negativity in our thoughts, words, and deeds. For only in this wise can we hope for redemption of our past, and salvation.

There is a plethora of numbers in scripture, and Gabriel explains their importance in his lessons on Revelation. Three, of course, represents the Trinity; in humans it is mind, body, and spirit. Thirty pieces of silver, given to Judas for his betrayal of Jesus, reduces to three.

Five, once thought to represent evil, is actually the number of balance, between 1 and 10. The number 7 represents the number of states of consciousness through which we all must pass. To pass through each state we must be willing to fast and pray. Not fast from food, but from negation on *any* level.

The number seven is found in many places in Revelation: Seven seals, lamps, candlesticks, churches, spirits, stars, angels. In the human body there are seven chakras; energy centers which must be awakened as we travel our spiritual path. Each chakra is consonant with an endocrine gland.

Nine stands for the evolution of humankind. Refer to three and a half years, as found in James 5:17 and Rev 11:11. Forty-two months times 30 days would equal 1,260, which reduce to nine. When we find 144,000 we add that to find nine. And the 666, anathema to some Christians, we find 18, or nine, again. Here it means the mass consciousness of need. Do we not spend much of our time needing and wanting? At another seminar Gabriel told us that both need and want imply lack. But when we desire something we ask for it from the Father ('de' is from, and 'sire' is Father).

The number ten consists of a pillar and a circle. The pillar is the masculine, action, positive which moves upon. The circle is the feminine, nurturing, which is moved upon. It is this combination that is the completion; the alpha and omega. Jesus healed ten lepers. Also in scripture we find ten pounds, ten cities, ten virgins, ten talents.

The twelve powers of God are described in a book entitled *The Twelve Powers of Man,* by Charles Filmore. Twelve was the number of apostles, the number of twelve is the number of years the woman had an 'issue of blood' (Mark 5:25), the number of baskets with remaining scraps when Jesus fed the 5,000 (Mark 6:43). The girl Jesus raised from the dead was twelve years of age (Mark 5:42). On earth we have twelve hours in the day and night; and twelve months in the year. Twelve also adds up to three; the Trinity. In Gethsemane, Jesus said he could have twelve legions of angels if he desired. (Matt 26:53). Twenty-four represent the two sides of the twelve powers of God.

As children of God, we have within us the love and power of God. We simply have forgotten that. Gabriel told us, more than once, that he came not to teach us anything new, but only to remind us of that which we *already know* and have forgotten. He also told us that when he came to Earth another eleven heavenly entities came - master teachers - to other parts of planet Earth, to bring truth to all mankind. It must be understood that angels can only come to teach in places where it is believed they can; where people have come to accept spirit communication as a reality; where people go to seek truth.

Since 1992 (21 years ago) I have thought that someday an individual would put, in their own words, the imagery in Revelation which was explained by Gabriel. Then, only a few weeks ago, I thought to myself - I should say my angels brought to mind - 'why not me; I was there!' And so, with constant angelic guidance I put forth this wisdom of the ages from that beloved Archangel, Gabriel. These are the angel's lessons. I am blessed and honored to be the one to put Gabriel's interpretation into words for the seeking reader. God bless humanity as it seeks to know and become what it always has been; to know *and live* the truth of its being, as it consciously steps upon the path of evolvement back home to God.

"Your chosen home is on the other side, beyond the veil. It has been carefully prepared for you, and it is ready to receive you now. You will not see it with the body's eyes. Yet all you need you have. Your home has called to you since time began, nor have you ever failed entirely to hear." ACIM T 20: II: 8:1-5

Printed in the United States
By Bookmasters